Vending Machines

ALSO BY KERRY SEGRAVE
AND FROM MCFARLAND

Jukeboxes: An American Social History (2002)

Shoplifting: A Social History (2001)

Age Discrimination by Employers (2001)

Movies at Home: How Hollywood Came to Television (1999)

*American Television Abroad: Hollywood's
Attempt to Dominate World Television* (1998)

Tipping: An American Social History of Gratuities (1998)

*American Films Abroad: Hollywood's Domination of the
World's Movie Screens from the 1890s to the Present* (1997)

Baldness: A Social History (1996)

Policewomen: A History (1995)

Payola in the Music Industry: A History, 1880–1991 (1994)

*The Sexual Harassment of Women
in the Workplace, 1600 to 1993* (1994)

*Drive-in Theaters: A History from
Their Inception in 1933* (1992)

*Women Serial and Mass Murderers:
A Worldwide Reference, 1580 through 1990* (1992)

*The Post Feminist Hollywood Actress: Biographies and
Filmographies of Stars Born After 1939* (1990)

*The Continental Actress: European Film Stars of the
Postwar Era, Biographies, Criticism,
Filmographies, Bibliographies* (1990)

Vending Machines

An American Social History

by KERRY SEGRAVE

McFarland & Company, Inc., Publishers
Jefferson, North Carolina, and London

LIBRARY OF CONGRESS CATALOGUING-IN-PUBLICATION DATA

Segrave, Kerry, 1944–
    Vending machines : an American social history / by Kerry Segrave.
      p.   cm.
    Includes bibliographical references and index.

    ISBN-13: 978-0-7864-1369-0
    softcover : 50# alkaline paper ∞

    1. Vending machines—United States—Social aspects.
2. Vending machines—United States—History.
HF5483 .S44   2002
381'.1—dc21   2002514062

British Library cataloguing data are available

©2002 Kerry Segrave. All rights reserved

No part of this book may be reproduced or transmitted in any form or by any means, electronic or mechanical, including photocopying or recording, or by any information storage and retrieval system, without permission in writing from the publisher.

Cover illustration from photographs by Marty McGee and PhotoSpin

Manufactured in the United States of America

McFarland & Company, Inc., Publishers
  Box 611, Jefferson, North Carolina 28640
  www.mcfarlandpub.com

Contents

Preface	1
1. From Hero of Alexandria to Tutti-Frutti of New York: The Years to 1918	3
2. Robots Can Sell Anything; Robots Will Sell Everything, 1918–1931	21
3. Cigarettes Blaze the Way, 1932–1939	47
4. The War on Slugs Goes Federal, 1940–1944	108
5. Optimism Returns, 1945–1949	119
6. The Four C's Dominate: 1950s	141
7. Dreams Placed on Hold, Cigarettes, Coffee, Cola, Candy, 1960–1985	169
8. VMs Cut Down on Smoking, Adopt a Healthier Lifestyle, 1986–2001	191
Appendix A: Vended Dollar Volume	233
Appendix B: Vending Sales by Location Type	234
Appendix C: Vending Sales by Type of Product	235
Notes	239
Bibliography	261
Index	277

Preface

This book looks at the history of vending machines in America, from their arrival in the late 1880s up to the year 2001. Vending machines are defined as self-contained automatic machines that dispense goods (such as candy and soft drinks) or provide services (such as weighing scales) when coins are inserted. Excluded from consideration in this book are amusement games and jukeboxes.

For some 30 years in the United States the machines lived a fairly obscure existence as they gave out penny candy and gum. With the arrival of the cigarette machine in the late 1920s, plus other technological advances around the same time, a new future was envisioned for the vending machine: It was to become a dominant method of retailing a vast array of different products. Automatic stores and restaurants were seen in the immediate future. Those dreams were featured in the mass media at the end of the 1920s, for the first time, as the pubic was swept along with the idea. Obviously such grandiose plans never came to pass, but the vending industry would never give them up completely, not even to this day.

For a time the industry kept its hopes alive in a series of innovations. After the cigarette machine of the 1920s came the soft drink unit of the 1930s and the coffee machine of the 1940s. However, little that was revolutionary in the industry took place after that. Products which came to be known in the trade as the four C's—candy, cola, cigarettes, and coffee—became the items most frequently sold by the industry, accounting for 80 percent or more of total sales volume. As cigarettes declined in importance, soft drinks became more dominant.

Over the decades a host of other ideas for new machines were tried in the trade, from shoe shining machines to lighter fluid dispensers to popcorn vendors to French fry units. Many within the industry refused to accept what seemed to be the natural limitations inherent in the business:

that customers on impulse bought relatively inexpensive products that could be easily consumed on the spot. Well over half of all vending machines on location today are sited at spots where the customer base is captive, such as at factories, offices, and warehouses. Often the machines are there only because the employer felt some kind of food service was required and the use of vending machines proved the most cost efficient way of providing that service.

Research for this book was conducted at the Vancouver Public Library, the University of British Columbia, Simon Fraser University in Burnaby, and the University of Victoria. The most helpful source was the back files of *Billboard* magazine.

1

From Hero of Alexandria to Tutti-Frutti of New York: The Years to 1918

"... articles such as paper, orange-peel, and other rubbish have been maliciously placed in the slit provided for the admission of the coin...."
                                    Percival Everitt, 1886

"[The perfume vending machine] will dole out a drop or two of liquid which passes for perfumery, and which, in many cases serves as a thin mask for bodily uncleanliness."
                                    Scientific American, 1891

"The Midget [vending machine] turns the available waste space on the back of the [theater] chair into a gold mine."
                                    Variety, 1914

While the start of the vending machine era in America is generally dated to the 1880s, references to earlier devices go back far in time. The earliest reference involved Hero (or Heron), a Greek mathematician, physicist, and engineer who probably lived in Alexandria during the first century A.D. He may have been Egyptian by birth but little is known of his life. His years of greatest renown centered around the year 62 A.D. In one of his books, *Pneumatika*, Hero described and illustrated a coin-operated device to be used for vending sacrificial water in Egyptian temples. Completely automatic, the device was set in operation by the insertion of a five-drachma coin, said to be equivalent, in 1961, to 75 cents. Intrigued by inventions and mechanical gadgets, Hero presented some of his own ideas as well as those of others in his writings. The most likely candidate, besides Hero himself, to have devised the water dispenser may have been Ctesibius (or Tesibius) of Alexandria, who flourished around 270 B.C. Ctesibius focused his work in hydraulics and was most famous for an improvement he made in the water clock.[1]

In addition to the lack of knowledge as to who devised the machine, it was also unclear if any were actually manufactured and used. Possibly the device never went beyond the point of a design drawing. None of this stopped some accounts from adding "detail" to the story. *Scientific American* said, in 1891, that when a worshiper was about to enter the temple, he sprinkled himself with lustral water, taken from a vase near the entrance. "The priests made the distribution of holy water a source of revenue by the employment of the automatic vending machine." Writing in the *New York Times Magazine* in 1941, Sidney Shalett reported that around the first century B.C. there was a minor economic crisis in some of the old Egyptian temples with collections being low. Thus, the water vendor was devised to increase the flow of money to the temples. Shalett went on to state that even earlier priests in some of the ancient Eastern temples thought up something that worked in the following fashion: The worshiper came in and laid a coin on a prescribed spot before an image of one of the gods. The weight of the coin depressed a lever that, in turn, worked a valve in the cellar which was connected with a hot-water apparatus. Immediately, that sent steam up through the bamboo tubes to the eyes of the image, where it condensed into "tears." Impressed by the spectacle, the awed worshiper reportedly made a large financial contribution to the temple.[2]

Andrew Hecht declared, in 1956, that Hero invented the first vending machine in 219 B.C. A small unsigned piece in the *New York Times* in 1960 stated that Hero Ctesibius invented the device in 219 B.C. and added the thought that Greek customers did not use slugs in the machine for fear of incurring the wrath of the gods. A year after that, *Advertising Age* reported that Hero Cstebus invented the machine in 219 B.C. and that he was a "Grecian high priest." Also reported in this account was that China had a coin-operated pencil seller in the year 1076. Ancestors of today's pencil date only to around 1400.[3]

From the time of Hero's description, next to nothing happened in the vending industry until the 17th century when snuff and tobacco boxes activated by the insertion of coins appeared in taverns and inns in England, around 1615. These devices were less sophisticated than Hero's unit and left considerably more to the honesty of the customer. When the coin was inserted in the top of the device, it flipped a trigger that caused the lid of the contraption to fly open. A patron could then reach inside to retrieve a pinch of snuff or to fill the bowl of his pipe. These machines were very much like today's newspaper "honor box" vendors in that the insertion of a coin gave the customer access to the entire contents of the machine, not just the single item his coin entitled him to. After each purchase, the barmaid or innkeeper pushed the lid shut and moved the device to the next customer. Taking up little space (9.9" long, 4.5" wide, 4" deep) the unit had a handle for carrying and held about one pound of tobacco. If patrons did not help themselves to the entire contents of the box, or to more than their coin entitled them, it was likely due to the fact that these boxes were never out of sight of the bar owner or employees.[4]

The first attempt to vend something other than snuff or tobacco also took place in England. In 1822 an English bookseller and freethinker named Richard Carlile designed a vending machine (VM) he hoped would keep the censors and the police at bay. At the time Carlile and a handful of other booksellers and publishers were struggling to establish freedom for the English press. Carlile and some of his employees had been jailed for selling items such as Thomas Paine's *The Age of Reason*. To prevent any more such arrests, Carlile decided to sell books by machine, believing that by doing so the bookseller could not be legally identified. Describing his device, Carlile wrote: "In the shop is the dial on which is written every publication for sale. The purchaser enters and turns the hand of the dial to the publication he wants, when, on depositing his money, the publication drops down before him." However, the court still held him responsible and convicted one of his employees of selling blasphemous literature through the device. It remains unclear whether the unit was truly automatic.[5]

By the 1830s in Britain more sophisticated versions of the tobacco honor boxes were to be found. These units vended a predetermined amount of tobacco for a given coin. The tobacco was wrapped in paper and stacked in a column. Since the insertion of a coin still gave customers access to the entire contents of the devices, they remained honor boxes. Such devices were manufactured and operated in New York in the 1840s, and were based on earlier British machines.[6]

The first patent issued for a fully automatic selling device apparently went to Simeon Denham of Wakefield in Yorkshire, England, in 1857. In that year he applied for a patent for "A Self-Acting Machine for the Delivery of Postage and Receipt Stamps," designed to sell a stamp for a penny from a strip of postage stamps contained within it. Denham was given provisional protection for his invention. However, it was a crude device which seems not to have moved beyond the idea stage. It would be 30 more years before inventors began an all-out assault on the problem of selling postage stamps automatically. Attesting to the idea that Denham's machine was not a commercial success was the fact that the inventor never bothered taking out a full patent for his invention.[7]

In 1867 two more patents were granted. One went to the German inventor and engineer Carlade, who built models of machines to sell handkerchiefs, cigarettes, and confections. The second was granted in Britain for a fortune-telling device designed to answer questions by the coins inserted into it. Percival Everitt received a UK patent in 1883 for a postcard vendor. Two years later he got a patent for an improved version of the machine. Noted a contemporary account: "In England all places are closed on Sunday, and the only way to get a postal card or stamped envelope is to have recourse to the supply box [VM]. We should not be surprised to see this ingenious vendor before long supplying small objects of regular prices and dimensions such as boxes of matches, cigars, omnibus tickets, etc.!"[8]

A late 19th century machine from London, England. These units delivered postcards, stamped envelopes, and notepaper, and could be found in railway stations.

The first US patent for a VM went in 1884 to W. H. Fruen (#309,219) for an "Automatic Drawing [of liquids] Device." His invention bore a resemblance to Hero's machine, but was never produced in quantity. One year later, in 1885, a group of New York promoters introduced the penny weighing scale to America. Imported from Germany, the scale was 600 pounds, its works enclosed in a mahogany cabinet ornately decorated with carvings. In 1886, a group of patents, some for new devices and some for improvements of earlier inventions, were applied for at the U.S. Patent Office. All the inventors involved, Percival Everitt, Charles H. Russell, and Frederick C. Lynde, were Englishmen. Everitt, in his American patent application (#374,297), noted it was an invention improving on an earlier UK patent dated July 28, 1885. In his application, he wrote: "It has been found in practice that although the apparatus is perfectly successful when not designedly misused, articles such as paper, orange-peel, and other rubbish have been maliciously placed in the slit provided for the admission of the coin, and that in consequence the channel provided for the passage of the coins from the slit became blocked."

1.—From Hero of Alexandria to Tutti-Frutti of New York

Even at that early a point in vending machine history, the public had come to see the silent salesmen as fair game to "beat." On November 25, 1887, the Sweetmeat Automatic Delivery Company, Ltd., was registered in England—reportedly the first company organized to install and maintain VMs as its principal business.[9]

The real beginnings of practical vending in America came in 1888 when Thomas Adams, founder of the Adams Gum Company (later the American Chicle Company), had VMs designed to sell his Tutti-Frutti gum, which he placed on the platforms of New York City's elevated rail stations. In 1930, *Business Week* magazine reported that the concept "was promptly dis-

An envelope and paper dispenser, New York, circa 1896.

missed as an amusing novelty with scant practical value." Charles Stein, writing in the 1960s, said the venture was "immediately successful," while G. R. Schreiber, writing around the same time, declared, "From the outset they were successful."[10]

In 1934, trade reporter J. H. Hirsch commented that in 1888 a few crude penny gum machines were placed on location. Later that same year, the Adams Gum concern put out a number of machines vending a five-cent package consisting of five slabs of gum. Those machines were said to be "very poorly constructed, easily slugged, and could be emptied by using a wire or bent hairpin." They did not last long and were replaced by improved mechanisms. The success of the Adams gum machine sparked interest in VMs and soon other VMs were fighting for space, almost all of them being dispensers of penny gum, candy, or peanuts. It remains unclear what prompted Adams to have a VM made to vend his product, why he chose the locations he picked, and so forth.[11]

Arch Andrews bought into the penny scale business in 1924. He understood that several thousand of the German machines were imported

This early unit (date uncertain) delivered a piece of gum from between the clown's teeth.

before American firms began to manufacture and distribute rival machines. Those US models were initially cast-iron, although some had wooden cabinets. Steel and porcelain soon became the main materials used in weigh scale manufacture.[12]

The sudden interest in VMs in America in the 1890s was matched by a similar interest in Europe. In both places many devices were invented to vend items beyond the usual gum, candy, and nuts. While they drew a good deal of interest and media coverage, all failed to catch on with the public. Commercial vending was introduced in France in 1889 to raise money for philanthropy. The Society of the Stores for the Blind, a charitable organization, installed 10-centime chocolate and bon-bon machines in the railroad stations along the Paris to Marseille line and their success led to the rise of the French vending industry.[13]

The last decade of the 19th century witnessed a rash of new vending inventions, the formation of dozens of early vending companies, and those developments caught the attention of the American press. In its June 28, 1890 edition, *Scientific American* took note of the invention in England of an automatic picture-taking machine. It was proposed, said the publication, "to erect automatic photographing machines, corresponding in a general way to the other machines of this class for weighing, selling candy, etc., with which the public is now familiar."[14]

In Paris streets that same year appeared kiosks containing machines which projected a faucet and a place to set a pail. Near the faucet was a coin slot and beside the slot was a button. To use the apparatus, a pail was set in place, a five-centime piece was dropped in the slot, and the button was pushed. Whereupon, observed a contemporary account, a jet of "steaming hot water issues from the faucet and runs until nine quarts have been delivered, when it stops." *Scientific American* believed that, in an area densely populated with poor families, the cost of hot water obtained from a VM would be much less than if a fire were kept in the cooking stove to heat it. Another use in Paris was in hacks, where it was the custom of the hackmen to keep "bouillottes," or cans of hot water, in their carriages in cold weather to warm their customers' feet, "and it is often troublesome and expensive for them to get the water renewed as it cools." With the hot water vendors, the bouillottes could be replenished "with the smallest trouble and expense, to the great benefit of the drivers." In granting the concession to the vending firm (which drew from city water pipes), Paris officials stipulated that the company should rapidly supply the carriage stations with vendors in order that the coachmen could easily renew the water for their foot warmers. "It will be possible then to forbid the use of charcoal heaters, which have several times occasioned accidents."[15]

Also in 1890, in Birmingham, England, a new penny-in-the-slot device was adapted by the gas department of that city, for the benefit of small consumers who did not want to be bound by regular contracts. Gas was priced in Birmingham, as everywhere else in England, at 30 cents per 1,000 cubic feet of gas. A type of meter was constructed which, on dropping a penny in the slot, would deliver 25 cubic feet of gas, a rate of 40 cents per thousand feet. Up to nine pennies at once could be dropped into the slot to deliver 225 cubic feet. Accumulated pennies were collected once a week by an official of the gas company. Burners on house fixtures were set to burn five cubic feet of gas per hour but could be adjusted to burn more slowly. No direct charge was made for the vendor; the extra price of the gas delivered through it covered the expense.[16]

Silent salesmen became vocal for the first time in New York in 1890. It was an idea that would keep recurring over time. The first "talking" VM was a penny scale which incorporated a crude phonograph, using a cylinder, not a disk. When a patron inserted a coin and read his weight on the dial, the phonograph played a brief passage from some well-known opera or popular tune. Supposedly it would increase business by attracting the attention of passers-by. This fad was short-lived.[17]

Reporting on the presence of VMs in America in 1891, *Scientific American* observed that at the railway stations, ferry houses, and even on the street corners, "there may be found in almost every city and village in the United States automatic vending machines, which, for a nickel, or more or less, will deliver the various goods for which they are adapted to sell. The purchaser may procure a newspaper and a cigar to smoke, or, if averse to the use of the weed, he may secure a tablet of chewing gum or a package of sweets." Also mentioned were the weigh scales and the latest crazes. One was the automatic photograph device which took a customer's photo while he waited. A second craze was the perfume VMs which, for a penny, "will dole out a drop or two of liquid which passes for perfumery, and which, in many cases, serves as a thin mask for bodily uncleanliness." That perfume device was patented by Lewis C. Noble of Boston, Massachusetts, on November 19, 1889.[18]

Around the end of 1893 in Paris, France, it was observed that for a few weeks there had been seen at the doors of stores and in theaters, concert halls, and so forth, small metal bottles of various colors provided with an enameled plate. They were "automatic distributors," which were distinguished as much by "their pleasing form and the simplicity of their mechanism as by their practical utility as retail vendors of expensive perfumes." Resembling bottles, these units, at 18 centimeters wide and 40 centimeters high, took up little space and were fixed to a wall by means of a bracket. When a 10-centime piece was inserted and a button was pressed, "a few drops of liquid fell at the bottom." Inventor P. Leoni hoped to see his device put to other uses, specifically to dispense antiseptics, "either gratuitously or in exchange for a small coin." The question of whether to use VMs to vend antiseptics had reportedly been submitted for study to the municipal council of Paris. Meanwhile, those perfume vendors had already been installed "in large numbers" in Paris. "A great number of persons are always to be seen congregated around the distributor. Some examine it and seem to wish to divine the internal mechanism, while others cause it to operate and receive the odiferous liquids on their handkerchiefs."[19]

Another fad that struck Paris, and other large cities of France and other foreign countries in the 1890 to 1891 period, was that of the automatic fountain. When a patron placed a coin in the slot he received a small glass of wine, a large glass of beer, and so on. The customer first placed a glass under the spigot. Reportedly, the quantity of liquid was "always accurately measured, its volume varying with its nature." For example, a five-cent piece would produce two ounces of wine or eight ounces of beer. Some of these units were said to serve hot liquids (such as coffee) or iced ones. Installation of these units occurred mostly in Paris bars. One in operation at 32 Montmartre Street had a battery of about two dozen of these machines, each one dispensing a different liquid. This was probably the first instance of VMs being placed together, in a bank or a battery. A contemporary account speculated that such devices could also be used with the charitable object in mind of providing the poor with "wholesome and strengthening beverages (such as milk, bouillon, etc.) at a low price." A counter on the machine enabled the attendant to know when to refill the vendor without opening the machine. The VMs were also said to reject coins that were too small.[20]

Among other VMs invented in the 1890s was a "slot machine"

designed to vend a wide variety of articles, especially those commonly supplied in elongated-sized packages. Patented by Charles W. Goldsmith of New York, the unit delivered stamped envelopes and notepaper of different kinds. Samples were visible in the vertical glass-covered case at the rear, while the top of the machine was shaped so that it could be used as a writing surface. When the merchandise was sold out, a stop lever automatically came into operation to close the end of the coin way and prevent the insertion of additional coins.[21]

John Milo, of New York City, added amusement value to the vendor when he patented a "slot machine" that was enclosed in a case shaped like an animal, such as a cow or pig. It was arranged so that after inserting a coin, the customer had to apply force by means of pulling on a lever (the animal's tail). That applied force automatically registered on a dial and the purchased item was delivered. Milo's device was a combination VM and strength tester.[22]

Commenting on the situation in Europe, in 1895 a Dutch publication said: "One cannot enter a public place nowadays without seeing a weighing-machine, a chocolate machine and frequently, a penny-in-the-slot machine rendering some popular waltz at the cost of a copper or two." Many VMs were then on display at the World Exhibition being held in Amsterdam.[23]

Back in the US, the postage stamp VM was coming into its own. Early attempts had been made to launch it, but the first successful large scale operation of stamp vendors was undertaken in 1891 by the Automatic Machine Company of Buffalo, New York. It used a penny stamp vendor invented by William Dutton. Newspapers of the day hailed the machine as an "honest slot machine" because it sold a penny stamp for a penny.[24]

In 1892 John Williams of Manchester, England, invented and patented a ticket VM. Once a coin was inserted, a bell rang and a ticket was issued. A register on the device indicated how many tickets had been dispensed. Cigar VMs were being manufactured in Chicago by M. B. Mills Manufacturing Company; book vending was done in Belgium; and a law firm in the American West came up with the idea of a divorce papers VM. For a while, at least, legal divorce papers were items that could be bought from a vending machine in Corinne, Utah. A purchaser could insert $2.50 in coins, pull a lever on the side of the machine, and pick up his papers from a delivery drawer that popped open like a cash register drawer. Those papers were then taken to the local law firm — whose name was printed on the form — where the names of the divorcing couple were written in and witnessed. The Pulver Company introduced a fully automatic gum machine in 1897. A customer needed only to insert his coin into the machine and a stick of gum dropped automatically into the delivery tray; no lever needed to be manipulated. By 1900 Pulver added mirrors to the face of their vendors, starting a trend that would last for half a century. In 1898 M. B. Mills sold his three-year-old cigar vending company to his son, H. S. Mills, who changed the name to Mills Novelty Company. Mills went to work on a penny machine that would deliver a pre-determined amount of peanuts in bulk. This machine was introduced in 1901 at the Pan American Exposition in Buffalo, New York.[25]

James E. Martin of Braddock, North Dakota, received a patent around 1899 for a VM that dispensed cigars and other items. The machine was so constructed that articles of various prices could be sold from the same unit, although it had a single coin chute. This was an unusual feature in that most early vendors which sold merchandise at different prices from the same unit had a separate coin chute for each item. One observer commended Martin's device for the precautions taken to prevent the operation of the mechanism by anything except good coins: "Washers, pieces of metal and steel disks which cannot pass down the chute likewise complete the circuit and sound the alarm."[26]

Around 1900 the first non-alcoholic drinks, in the form of chilled water, were being sold for a penny-a-glass from machines with coin-controlled spouts on location at Coney Island in New York. A problem here was that a common drinking cup was used. Doctors, public health officials, and some members of the general public were concerned with the sanitation aspects of the common drinking cup, and in 1908 a company was formed to remedy the situation. That year the Public Cup Vendor Company of New York introduced a VM that dispensed an individual drink of water in a paper cup for the price of one penny. Later the company became the Individual Drink Cup Company, and still later the Dixie Cup Company. After a few years, the combination water and cup vendor was replaced with a penny vendor which sold only cups. That penny Dixie Cup machine remained a ubiquitous part of the American vending scene

A combination cigar and gum vendor, circa 1900.

for many decades. Water to fill the cup was usually freely available from a nearby fountain or tap.²⁷

In June, 1902, Joseph Horn and Paul Hardart (the Horn & Hardart Baking Company) opened their first Automat at 818 Chestnut Street in Philadelphia. For almost a decade prior to this, automatic restaurants had been in operation in Europe, mainly in Germany. That opening created a sensation and, by 1903, H & H had opened a New York outlet. For a brief time H & H operated an Automat in Chicago, but this was closed as the company concentrated its attention on New York and Philadelphia. These automats

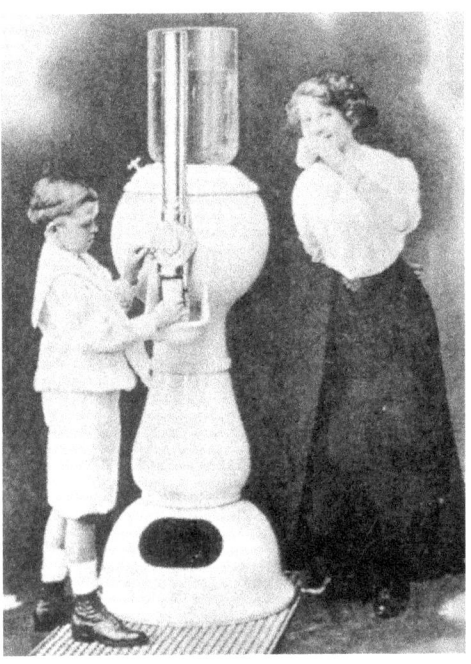

This 1908 machine delivered both cup and water for a penny.

were the forerunners of the automatic cafeterias now found in plants, offices, colleges, hospitals, and so on. Despite the initial sensation, the Automat concept never really spread beyond its two base cities. At their peak in the 1940s and 1950s, automats served 350,000 patrons per day. However, fast-food chains eventually eroded their business—the last Horn & Hardart outlet closed in 1991 in New York City. These Automats were also never fully automatic. Most food was served by employees of the Automat. Supplementary items such as cake, sandwiches, drinks, and so on were served through machines. Even in those cases, only one item was available. Once the single sandwich behind a particular window had been purchased it remained empty until a behind-the-scenes employee refilled it. Full main meals were never served in Automats through machines.²⁸

Harassed by manufacturers and inventors who wanted the Post Office to grant them exclusive royalty contracts, in 1905 the U.S. Post Office appointed a committee to investigate the merits of the devices. In his report for the fiscal year ending June 30, 1907, Postmaster General George Von L. Myer (who had just issued a directive to produce stamps in rolls that could be used in VMs) wrote: "This method of selling stamps is in use in other countries and the proposition to consider its adoption in the United States has excited no little interest." So universal and popular had VMs become in other fields that there seemed every reason, thought Myer, "why they should be adapted to the sale of stamps, stamped envelopes, and postal cards, provided machines can be built which combine the necessary features of moderate expense and absolute accuracy in operation." Accordingly, the department examined a dozen postage stamp vendors. Although the Post Office later reported that nine of the machines had "unquestionable merit," it concluded that all failed to measure up to its precise standards. A year later, in 1908, the department examined 25 different stamp dispensers. This time it thought enough of six of them to conduct tests in New York, Washington, Baltimore, Indianapolis, and Minneapolis. Mainly because none of the machines were slug-proof, the project was abandoned. However, publicity surrounding the tests at the post offices was great enough to allow the main manufacturers to begin to develop public locations for their machines. Also in 1908, the Post Office finally began to manufacture coils of 500 stamps suitable for use in VMs.[29]

Incorporated in New Jersey in April, 1906, was the Franco-Swiss Chocolate Company, a holding company with five subsidiaries whose principal business was the installation and maintenance of candy VMs. Thus, it was one of the earlier operating companies. Packaging posed a problem then for operators — as it would for a long time to come — and Franco-Swiss had to set up its own packaging department to box the candies for sale in the vendors.[30]

In Chicago in 1906, 14-year-old Bert Mills, the youngest of M. B. Mills's 13 children, quit school to go to work at his brother's Mills Novelty company. Bert would go on to found a firm which bore his name, and decades later help pioneer the hot coffee vendor. Recalling his start in the business, Bert said that one of his brother's machines was a 10-selection soda pop dispenser. The pop was vended from 10 five-gallon bottles which were mounted behind a cabinet built in the shape of a barrel. In those days, said Mills, "they didn't use paper cups. There was a long trough running along the front of the machine and they had glasses sitting on the trough. At either end of the machine were tanks of water. If you felt like it, you picked up a cup and rinsed it off in water before you used it. But most people didn't bother." No refrigeration was used, but the man who operated the machine put cracked ice on top of the bottles in the morning. "In a couple of hours, the ice melted and the drinks got warm. Believe it or not, they sold a lot of drinks."[31]

One of the most popular public locations for VMs in this era was at the subway, elevated rail, and urban rail stations in the larger cities. In 1906

1.—From Hero of Alexandria to Tutti-Frutti of New York   15

the Supreme Court of New York granted the application of New York's Interborough Rapid Transit company, heard a year or so earlier, for an injunction restricting the city of New York from removing from the subway stations the advertising signs and "nickel-in-the-slot machines." It was ruled that the subway was not a street in the legal sense, and therefore city authorities had no power of supervision over it. The contract made with the transit company, both directly and by inference, "grants the right of subletting advertising, slot machine and newsstand privileges."[32]

The largest chocolate and cocoa maker in Europe was the German chocolate manufacturer Stollwerck Brothers. They had a large manufacturing plant at Stamford, Connecticut. Around 1908, Stollwerck obtained the exclusive right to place their chewing gum and chocolate machines in the stations of the subway and elevated railroads in New York. During court proceedings over bank loans, it was revealed that those machines "bring in a daily income of $1,000 from the Subway stations and a similar sum from the elevated railway stations."[33]

Made in 1916, this VM dispensed a handful of peanuts for one cent.

In 1911 the Northwestern Corporation (founded in 1909) brought out a penny match box VM, the first in a long line of vendors to bear the company's trademark. Doctor Emil Luden arrived home in the US, after traveling abroad, with a coin-operated lock he had discovered in Germany. He took out American patents on the device and, in 1909, formed the Nik-O-Lok Company. After he failed to sell his device in any quantity, a discouraged Luden sold his mechanism to C. C. Van Cleave, who became the first president of Nik-O-Lok. When the firm decided to place its toilet locks on a service and commission basis (whereby the company installed and maintained its machines and retained ownership while splitting income with the location's owner), it went on to become a large vendor service company; and the pay toilet industry was born. In the years before World War I, the Doehler Die Casting company of New York developed machines for Wrigley penny gum and for Life Savers candy; a small counter VM, designed to look like a gasoline pump, was developed which dispensed lighter fluid; Sani-Serv paper towel machines and a sanitary napkin vendor were developed and distributed nationally by West Disinfectant Company.[34]

A Michigan company, "Taking its cue from the fortunes that have resulted from the harvest of pennies dropped into chewing gum slot machines..," said a contemporary account, placed on the market in 1913 a gasoline "vending slot machine." A customer simply dropped a 50-cent piece in the slot, put the end of the hose in his gas tank, and turned the crank. A visible gauge showed if the tank of the VM was empty. If a patron accidentally put money in the slot when the tank was empty, "it is promptly returned at the first turn of the crank, just as your penny is returned when the chewing gum slot machine is empty." While the unit accepted only 50-cent pieces, a customer could put in as many as he wanted. The amount of gas delivered was determined by the price per gallon, with the unit being adjustable by the service station. One of these machines installed by a garage owner in Lansing, Michigan, was said to dispense some 200 gallons of fuel per week.[35]

In 1934, when reporter J. H. Hirsch analyzed the beginnings of the American vending industry, he commented: "The industry practically stood still until about 25 years ago [1910], when automatic merchandising began a slow upward movement." In mentioning vending developments of the 1910s, he noted that the Stollwerck Chocolate company constructed a two-sectioned chocolate machine to be fastened to the back of theater seats, with a five-cent coin acceptor on each section, which contained one piece of chocolate. It was necessary to fill these machines after each performance. Around the same time, a 10-cent coin-operated opera glass machine was attached to the back of every fourth seat in theaters. Glasses were secured to the seat by a heavy linked steel chain to prevent them from being carried away. Hirsch argued that the opera glasses were quite popular until the building of smaller theaters, when they rapidly disappeared. Although the Stollwerck machine never caught on, candy remained in the cinemas but was vended differently. The back-of-the-seat machine was replaced by an upright standing cabinet, inside of which were combined as many as eight single units, each of those units having its own coin device. These VMs offered an assortment of eight kinds of candy at five and 10 cents, and were the beginning, said Hirsch in 1919, of candy vending machines in the theater. Clumsy and awkward to refill — the unit had to be pulled from the wall and opened from the back — these machines also were short-lived. Handkerchief VMs were also in use at this time, located in railroad stations, hotels, and so on. Of all the machines described by Hirsch, he observed that few remained on location for any length of time owing to "easy 'slugging' and breakage."[36]

Another effort to sell back-of-the-seat cinema VMs was made in 1914 by the Inter-State Vending Company of New York. Offered for sale directly

1.—From Hero of Alexandria to Tutti-Frutti of New York   17

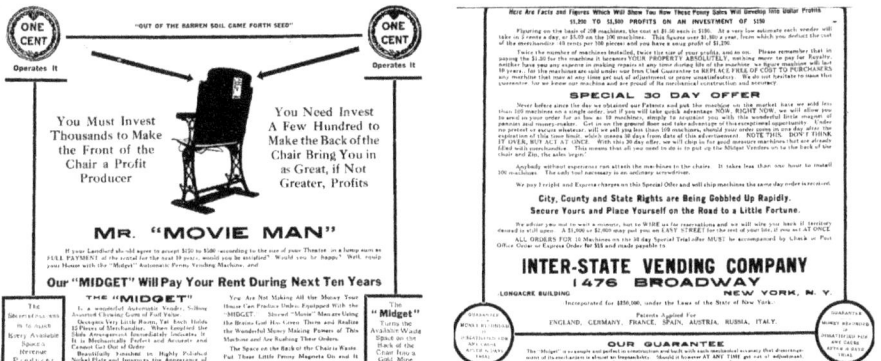

An ad touting the profit possibilities which awaited the people who would install the Midget VM on the backs of theater seats.

to theater owners was a penny gum machine called the Midget. Each had a capacity of 15 pieces of chewing gum. Sold in lots of 10 units, the cost for each Midget was $1.50. Inter-State claimed that 100 machines would take in $5 per day (five cents per machine). That came to over $1,800 a year from which was deducted the cost of the merchandise (40 cents per 100 pieces) "and you have a snug profit of $1,200," on an investment of just $150. Even allowing for some shaky math from Inter-State, the numbers seemed too good to be true. Anyone could easily attach the small VMs to the seats, the reader was told. An ordinary screwdriver was the only tool necessary, and "It takes less than one hour to install 100 machines." As added inducements, the seller was paying the cost of freight to ship an order and promised, for a limited time, to ship the units already filled with merchandise. The Midget was another VM idea which quickly and quietly vanished.[37]

Even though the American vending industry was still in its infancy, the first wave of mergers and consolidations swept through it in 1911. Many operating companies were then in existence. For example, some firms operated scales and VMs in railroad stations while others placed their units on street corners, in drug stores, and other places with heavy foot traffic. The *New York Times* stated that, by early 1911, plans had been completed for the "consolidation of practically all of the important automatic vending machine manufacturers in this country and a large number of manufacturers of chewing gum and other specialties distributed in this way into a single organization." This new organization was said to be going to use "the slot machine devices largely as an advertising medium through which to create a market for the large packages of the same goods which will be sold over the counter." Called the Autosales Gum and Chocolate Company, the main organizer was Charles R. Flint & Company. Flint was principal in the formation of the American Chicle Company and the Sen-Sen Chiclet Company, then the dominant firms in the chewing gum trade. Autosales consisted of 18 firms, plus the two already mentioned gum concerns. American Chicle was formed in 1899 through a consolidation of practically all of the large manufacturers of chewing gum then in existence. Sen-Sen was organized that same year to consolidate American and Canadian makers of "breath perfumes." Those firms in the consolidation then controlled some 250 trade names and brands, while the VM makers in Autosales controlled a host of patents and distributed all over the country. A major goal of Autosales, said a Flint representative, was the building up of an over-the-counter business in larger packages: "All of the goods sold in the slot machines will be facsimiles in miniature of the larger packages which the company will manufacture."[38]

According to the *New York Times*, Autosales started off with about 200,000 VMs on location. Historian G. R. Schreiber put the number at 100,000 while Arch Andrews, writing in 1930, declared that Autosales had some 70,000 VMs and weigh scales in 11,000 stations of more than 160 US railroads.[39]

The problem of machines being slugged and vandalized continued to plague the industry. In Britain, the earliest recorded case related to theft from a coin machine dated back to 1887, when three young men were convicted of larceny for using brass disks to obtain cigars. In St. Louis in 1891, a policeman on his beat was attracted by shouts of delight from a crowd of spectators in a public street. He found the center of attention to be a man who was manipulating a "slot machine" that dispensed cigars. He had punched a hole through a nickel and was dropping it into the slot and then pulling it out again. Each time he did so a cigar was dispensed. By the time the policeman arrested him he had acquired 25 cigars, some of which he had distributed to the crowd. Taken before a magistrate, the complex question arose as to whether the offense was larceny. Unable to decide, the magistrate compromised by fining the man $5 for disorderly conduct on the streets.[40]

During a 1914 court case in the UK, it was disclosed that 200 metal discs issued to householders as an advertisement of a boot polish, had been found in the "automatic penny-in-the-slot machines" at Kingston railway station. In 1915 Sidney Belmont, a 31-year-old London steelworker, pled guilty in court to stealing two chocolate bars valued at one pence each from machines at Liverpool Street station by inserting metal discs in the slots. He was fined five pounds Sterling and a guinea costs, with the alternative of a month's imprisonment. Later that year, during the hearing of a charge of stealing chocolate from a VM which was brought against two boys at Grimsby, UK, the manager of the company owning the machines said that over 2,000 packets of sweetmeats had been stolen that summer season from machines on Cleethorpes Promenade. The boys were fined five shillings each.[41]

America's vending industry settled into a quiet period that began in the middle 1910s and would last for a decade or more. The period of intense development of VMs, especially in the 1890s, slowed down considerably as virtually all of the unusual VM ideas failed to find a spot. Vending in America was limited almost entirely to penny machines which weighed the customer, or doled out chewing gum, candy, chocolate, or peanuts. Next to nothing was known about the industry at this time, in terms of its profitability, the number of machines on location in America, and so on. If occasional mention was made of VMs being vandalized or beaten by slugs, nothing was said about it. How often did these machines fail to deliver merchandise when a coin was inserted? How often was a coin not returned? One example came from the UK, where the question of the working of penny-in-the-slot machines was raised in the Court of Appeal in London in 1914 in regard to a specific case (details not specified). VMs were said to vary. One person placed a penny in the chute and obtained nine shillings worth of chocolate. When he tried again he got the same results. Another machine would not respond to the insertion of a coin; in yet another case, the chocolate was all broken. The insides of some machines were handed to the Bench where the three judges tested them with pennies.[42]

Grandiose plans on the part of the American vending industry would soon become a common feature of the trade, but at this early stage no such grand designs had formed. Most of its ideas to automatically vend unique items had died quick deaths. Dreams of fully automatic stores and "robot" vendors for everything under the sun would not surface until the 1920s.

The highly successful ideas in this period were weighing scales and gum vendors. The former were, of course, a service vendor as opposed to a merchandise vendor. Gum was successful because it was the lowest-priced item that could be vended. It could be easily consumed at the point of purchase. Chewing gum was a socially acceptable practice on the subways and in public in general. The product was packaged so that the purchaser could easily dispose of the nonedible parts. No health hazard was present in the gum sold through the VMs. That is, there was no worry about food poisoning. Gum had a long shelf life, and the product held up well in temperature extremes. This was important since the VMs quickly took on the ambient temperature. Gum did not melt or degrade the way chocolate would during a heat wave. In other words, there was no real need or desire on the part of customers to see the gum before purchasing it.[43]

Back in 1899, reporter R. I. Clegg singled out two factors destined to have long-range consequences for the vending industry: One was a growing tendency on the part of some early vending inventors to combine an element of chance with their merchandise machines. The second was the growing menace of slugs and other forms of cheating. Said Clegg: "A nickel with a hole in it for a string was occasionally employed, not only to work the machine without recompense ... but sometimes, too, the ingenious fisherman baited the coin with a coating of adhesive gum, or some other sticky substance, and thus armed, fished for the contents of the till." Clegg also related the story of a man who weighed his entire family for the price of one. It would be the 1930s before the industry came up with a slug rejecter efficient enough to make the VM a less attractive target for larceny.[44]

Gambling machines would also plague the vending industry for many years to come. Today, the term "slot machine" clearly refers to only a gambling device. However, at this point in the vending industry's history, and for some time to come, "slot machine" was regularly used to refer to VMs and any machine with a slot for a coin. As gambling slot machines came under increasing public opposition, the entire coin-operated trade felt the wrath. The public often failed to distinguish one type of slot machine from another. As Clegg observed: "But for many years the feeling persisted that vending machines were somehow slot machines and the men who built and operated them were suspect." Generally firms which made VMs did not make gambling machines. The main exception being Mills Novelty.[45]

During this period, the problem of unreliable and inefficient coin entry mechanisms inevitably consigned most of the more elaborate schemes to a quick oblivion. As early as the first half of the 1890s, when a coin machine boom was underway, conservative business publications were warning prospective investors away from sinking their capital into automatic firms. As a consequence, wrote Nic Costa, "vending machines tended to develop in the following decades primarily as purveyors of cheap everyday items such as matches, cigarettes, or chewing gum, whilst their more ambitious counterparts, such as gold sovereign changers, and fully automatic restaurants and public houses faded from the scene."[46]

2

Robots Can Sell Anything; Robots Will Sell Everything, 1918-1931

"He told me that he was going to sell cigarettes through his machines for 15 cents.... I thought he was crazy.... I was sure he was wrong and we refused to sell him cigarettes."

Hymen Goldman, 1927

"That was what was needed, a machine which could not only sell, but talk...."

A. Granat, 1928

"Of the salesman's work, 60% is the work of an automaton. Why not give most of this sort of work to an automaton?"

A Granat, 1928

"I weighed myself on a penny machine and found I weighed 205. Another machine said 98. A chocolate machine gave me nothing, not even my penny back. Out of a peanut machine I got six moldy objects I wouldn't feed to a goat."

Nathaniel Leverone, 1928

"Jobs galore for robot salesmen."

Business Week, 1930

It was in this period that the vending industry saw its greatest innovation — the cigarette VM. Soon it would become the single largest source of revenue for the trade; a position it would hold for decades. During this time, the industry and the general media would focus on the idea that "robots" could sell just about everything and were the future. Fully automatic stores were envisioned. These dreams would resurface from time to time after 1931, but never would they be articulated so passionately or examined so uncritically as they were in 1929-1930.

By the end of World War I and the start of the 1920s, the concept of operating firms was well established—they owned and serviced the vending machines and paid a commission to locations. From 1918 until around 1926, almost nothing new or newsworthy happened in the American vending industry. One exception was in Dallas, Texas, where trolley cars were fitted with gum and candy vendors. Apparently they operated with success until a tax placed on each machine drove them out of business.[1]

An omen of things to come could be found in a 1919 article which commented on some VMs that had been exhibited at a recent electrical show. That itself was a comment on the industry which then had neither a national organization nor its own national convention, relying on displaying machines at conventions of other industries. According to the account, the increased cost of hiring clerks and the scarcity of such help had caused merchants to look for ways to increase their self-service area. A large drug store chain (unnamed) was reported to be looking to obtain a machine that could sell 10 or 12 different toilet articles. Through the operation of such a machine, the chain hoped it would be possible to sell standard articles at well-known fixed prices to customers who appreciated "the time-saving advantages of the machine." Once that type of machine was installed by the drug store chain, it was believed that many other retailers would follow suit.[2]

At the electrical show, the displayed VMs were capable of handling articles such as postal cards, cigarettes, toothpaste, shaving sticks, face powder, and small grocery items such as soap, starch, and tea and coffee packaged in tins. In other words, each single VM could vend a variety of different products, at different prices, with a single coin slot—a first for the industry. One feature which captured much interest was the coin acceptor, which received but rejected "all spurious coins." These machines, designed for retail stores, were equipped to sell cans and packages for 25 cents each, or for any sum below that figure. Articles for sale were placed into adjustable tube carriers—adjustable in price and in physical size to handle the dimensions of the package. For example, one carrier tube might sell soap, the next one a pound of sugar, and others might vend cans of corn, peas, soup, and so on. For retail stores in which there was a constant demand for staple articles supplied in cans, packages, or small boxes, it was felt, said the account, that "the time and labor saving advantages of the machine will prove very appealing. No clerk is needed to take the package from the shelf and wrap it, no sales ticket need be written, and no cashier is required." Interest in this retail VM was reported to be not limited to America. Inquiries had been received from many other countries. In some of those nations, "it might be thought the low wages paid would be a bar to the purchase of such machines." However, nothing more was heard abut this idea for almost a decade.³

Inventors of VMs began to consider selling cigarettes. In 1925-1926, three machines were developed specifically to sell cigarettes. These VMs were the first serious attempt to sell quantities of products at prices greater than a nickel. At the start, few people took the cigarette vendor seriously. Many otherwise shrewd merchandisers were sure it would fail. William H. Rowe was a minor police court official in Los Angeles. According to one account, he was escorting a bootlegger through downtown Los Angeles one day. He stopped to buy cigarettes at a crowded counter and, in the jostling which followed, the prisoner got away. Rowe reasoned that if a cigarette VM had been handy the escape would not have happened. In 1926, he developed a machine which vended a pack for a dime and a nickel. However, the first ones responded just as well to the insertion of two bone buttons. A quickly improved model became popular. Rowe, who would soon found the Rowe Corporation, quit his job to devote himself full-time to VMs.⁴

In 1927, Robert Zemon Greene was looking for both a job and cigarettes in Los Angeles. He found the latter when he used a Rowe machine in an apartment building lobby. Intrigued by the machine and its possibilities, he went to see Rowe and landed a job. On the road with a cigarette VM in the back seat of his car, Greene embarked on a sales trip which lasted a year and took him to virtually every important American city. When he arrived in New York early in 1928, he had already sold 2,500 machines for $187,500. Rowe soon moved his firm east to be near the bigger markets. At the time Greene called on Rowe, the latter had 50 handmade units on Los Angeles locations. He built his first VM from an empty whiskey barrel and some odd pieces of metal.⁵

Gordon Macke wanted to set up his own cigarette VM operation in 1926 in Philadelphia. He had met William Rowe on the West Coast, and became enthusiastic about Rowe's vendor. However, police in Philadelphia blocked his efforts by telling him the VMs were too much like slot machines. Undeterred, Macke moved to Washington, D.C., to set up shop. Looking for a supplier of the cigarettes he proposed to vend, Macke went to Hymen Goldman's tobacco and candy wholesale firm in Washington. Recalling that meeting, Goldman explained: "He told me that he was going to sell cigarettes through his machines for 15 cents. At that time our retail customers were selling cigarettes for 11 and 12 cents, and I thought he was crazy. No one would pay that much more. But he said they would because the machines were more convenient. I was sure he was wrong and we refused to sell him cigarettes." In 1969, the Macke Company had annual sales of over $100 million.⁶

Cigarette VMs proved enormously popular and spread all over the country—even a talking version was briefly available. In April, 1928, a new machine was installed in the United Cigar Store at Broadway and 33rd Street, New York. It took three or four nickels, depending on the cigarette brand desired. After a twist of the crank, a pack of cigarettes and matches was delivered to the customer. "Then a gruff voice comes out of the depths of the metal, saying 'Thank You' and repeating the slogan of the cigarette just bought." Installation on a nation-wide scale of cigarette VMs (the more usual silent ones) in department stores was by then underway by operating companies. Among such locations where machines had been placed were the Kresge department store in Newark, Abraham & Strauss in Brooklyn, and the Adams Flanigan store in the Bronx.[7]

One of the first articles to set off a frenzy that riches could be amassed from pennies appeared in the *New York Times* in November, 1927. It concentrated mainly on the penny weigh scale. "Catchpenny devices have developed earning powers that command the attention of Wall Street...." opened the article which pointed out that New York City alone did a daily business running into the millions of dollars. "It is in the penny field that the vending machine flourishes at its best," declared the account. When a customer walked into a five-and-ten store, "he all but walks upon a weighing machine craftily in his path." Mentioned also were the many gum machines and, between acts, at the theater, the line formed for the water fountains, "whose inverted drinking cups drop down accurately upon a hook when pennies are put in a slot. Pennies similarly bestowed open the gates elsewhere to nuts, sweets, matches, perfume and what-not." At one New York chain store which had six scales, some 60,000 people, mostly women, were said to weigh themselves in less than a month's time. A scale located on Broadway near 51st Street had been averaging 200 customers per day for some time. With 40,000 weighing machines distributed across America, the manufacturer said they took in 450 million pennies, or $4.5 million dollars, in a year. That averaged out to $112 a year per machine, $9 to $10 a month, 31 cents a day. The concessionaire who operated the gum and weight machines at the 978 city subway and elevated stations was reported to use about $2 million worth of "box gum" annually.[8]

Five-and-ten-cent stores installed the penny scales liberally, with one chain store having over 3,000 such devices in its outlets. One manufacturer with a scale "which showed weights conspicuously" on a dial found that women who had failed to stay thin were avoiding the machine because passers-by could easily see the weight. The maker began to convert his dial scale into the more secretive ticket machine which did not display weights, but printed that information confidentially on a ticket which popped out to the patron. Sales of ticket scales were said to outdo those of dial scales by a ratio of eight to one. A second lesson was learned from female patrons by this manufacturer. On the back of each ticket he had printed a bit of fortune-telling. In order not to have prophecies too much alike, nor too "monotonously optimistic," he inserted an occasional doubt or misgiving, implying that the recipient might not find everything completely rosy. "The women were instantly up in arms. They demanded that news of the future be exclusively good news," said the report. "Various merchants who had leased the machines advised him anxiously that the women were beginning to threaten violence." So the maker ordered an entire new printing of tickets with no negative sentiment. Since then, he observed that his fortune-telling scales had never forecast anything but "sweetness and light." On subway and elevated platforms, these VMs were placed some distance from the entrance where people had come to a stop and were waiting — never at the front where people passed by in a hurry.[9]

About this time there was another wave of consolidations and mergers in the industry and a new holding company, Consolidated Automatic Merchandising Corporation (CAMCO), was born. CAMCO marked the first attempt to establish a truly diversified national operating organization. At the center of this development was Joseph J. Schermack, who is generally credited with building the first practical postage stamp VM. In 1910 he introduced his first "profit-sharing" stamp vendor, a device that sold either four one-cent stamps or two two-cent stamps for a nickel. Until then postage stamps had been vended at face value, with the idea being that the retailers who owned the machines were providing a service for their patrons. Schermack formed the Sanitary Postage Service Corporation in September, 1926, to install and operate stamp vendors, Financier A. J. Sack, another important figure in CAMCO, first met Schermack in 1924, at which point Schermack had placed about 8,000 of his stamp VMs on the market. The pair found themselves in "full accord as to the understanding that this country is entering the automatic age." It took two years to do preliminary work until Sanitary was organized and bringing in substantial capital. This capital allowed them to eliminate the outright sale of the stamp VMs and to adopt a policy of placing them free with the merchants on a profit-sharing basis. The machines were placed in such well known outlets as United Cigar Stores, Liggett's Drug stores, and other chains. When the stamp VM was installed on a profit-sharing basis, the location kept the machine stocked, collected the money, and sent Sanitary its share of the profits. According to Sack it had taken eight years (up until 1926), to sell 12,000 machines outright then "it took us less than two years to place an additional 20,000 machines on a profit-sharing basis." Schermack, Sack, and other partners

CAMCO's talking VMs, 1928.

such as the Automatic Merchandising Corporation of America, Sanitary, the United Cigar Stores, and the Remington Arms Company took the step of forming CAMCO. Overseeing the $25 million capitalization was Wall Street banker F. J. Lishman.[10]

In 1928, with considerable fanfare in the general press, CAMCO announced it was in business, operating 36,000 penny scales, 30,000 postage stamp VMs, and 25,000 nut vendors, and that it was moving quickly into candy and cigarette vending. Its goal was to be fully integrated vertically by manufacturing, distributing, and operating its machines. The more usual method was, and is, for a concern to engage or specialize in just one of those three aspects. CAMCO boldly predicted it would have 1.5 million VMs on location and would be making "fantastic profits" within five years. The previously mentioned talking cigarette VM in the United Cigar Store at 33rd and Broadway was best known of its installations. Eventually that vending bank would hold 15 cigarette machines along with three separate change making machines.[11]

Schermack remarked that the first machine CAMCO was bringing out was "the slot machine which delivers a pack of cigarettes, a coupon, and a paper of matches and says 'Thank you' to the customer who had dropped his money in the proper slot." Using such machines, said reporter Milton Wright, was a "logical development" for the cigar store business because "heretofore, only one side has been doing any business; that is to say, a counter runs down only one side of the store."[12]

Independently, and around the same time, United Cigar Stores vice president A. Granat explained: "Why could we not have a battery of vending machines instead of a lot of mirrors on the side of the store opposite the counter, was the question I kept asking myself." He felt the biggest problem was in getting the right kind of machine. For two-and-a-half years, he talked to various kinds of inventors and was pitched many conceivable ideas, except the kind he wanted. All of the inventors also wanted to be financed, while Granat was looking for someone who would finance his own invention. Finally, he got in touch with Sanitary who agreed to place a VM in a cigar store at its own expense. As the product to vend, Granat chose cigarettes. "Because cigarettes are necessarily unprofitable ... there is not much opportunity for profit. Therefore, they were considered the logical thing to vend through the machines." A machine was developed and placed in the Broadway store. Soon thereafter, Granat happened to be in that store when he overheard a VM patron saying he missed the "Thank you" the clerk always said. Explained Granat: "That was what was needed, a machine which could not only sell, but talk. We set to work on the machine and, with the aid of the best-known manufacturers in the country, we developed an apparatus which would say 'Thank you' and repeat the slogan of the particular brand of cigarettes every time a sale was made." Thus, if a patron selected a pack of Lucky Strikes, a voice would say: "Thank you, they're toasted;" if Chesterfields was picked the customer heard: "Thank you, they satisfy." United Cigar Stores was enthusiastic enough that it became one of the partners in the CAMCO venture.[13]

Another photo of a CAMCO battery of talking vendors, 1929.

CAMCO's plans were far more ambitious. Until the goal of developing an "automaton" that could sell a wide variety of articles was reached, the currently existing machines would be used. Eventually the company planned to establish the equivalent of automatic department stores. Those new automatic VMs would be placed in the chain stores of retailers such as the Woolworth company, Liggett Drugs, Walgreen Drug company, J. C. Penney, Owl Drug company, United Cigar Stores, and so on. Additionally, CAMCO planned to rent space for the units in office buildings as well as railroad, steamship, and bus stations.[14]

Those yet-to-be-invented VMs would also talk. CAMCO was even reported to be considering having their speeches recorded by stage and film stars, "to humanize the robots." Talking VMs were envisioned as giving directions for the products they sold and/or repeating advertising slogans.

Among articles expected to be vended by these multi-purpose machines were shaving cream, razor blades, cough drops, sanitary products, cigarettes, cigars, magazines, and stamps. The robots would be able to make change in any form devised from coins of denominations up to 50 cents.[15]

Waxing even more eloquently on the future was CAMCO executive A. J. Sack who in 1928 said that a department store containing nothing but VMs would be opened in New York City within a month (it was not). Set up to vend 150 different items of merchandise through automatic machines, Sack explained that this proposed store "is contemplated as an educational laboratory for the inspection of prospective machine purchasers." Items vended were proposed to be groceries, confections, cigarettes, some articles of wearing apparel, "and other staples of nationally advertised standing, which are available in compact form for machine vending." Sack boosted that this entire automatic store would be under the control of just one employee.[16]

Publicity from CAMCO's pronouncements soon caused a more general comment and debate in the media about retailing, VMs, and the future of automatic selling. It was not a debate about vending machines expanding in areas where they already existed, but rather about VMs moving into, and succeeding in, areas from which they were then absent. The era was a technical, machine age in which radio had become pervasive in households, the automobile was moving in that same direction, and movies had gone from silent flickers to almost the "talkies." Reporter Milton Wright articulated the general 1920s enthusiasm in science and the machine age when he wrote: "If something can be done by machinery, let a machine do it, has been our motto for some years past. That this is the keynote of our industrial progress is self-evident. It now becomes the principle for commercial progress. Why have a high-priced human salesman perform the mere mechanical task of handing out a package of cigarettes, receiving a quarter, dropping your money in a cash drawer and passing back to the customer ten cents in change...." It seemed logical to Wright that automatic work such as that should be left to automatic equipment, allowing the man behind the counter to persuade the customer to buy a $2.50 pipe, "then being a salesman in fact as well as in name."[17]

Leon Wieder, vice president of New York department store Arnold, Constable & Company, felt the introduction of robot department stores and the arrival of mechanical salesmen in existing stores would do at least two significant things for the "better class" of stores, such as his own: It would permit more careful selection of selling employees at such stores, with a resultant lowering of the current high cost of labor turnover, and it would stimulate employees of only average ability to do better work. A further effect could be forcing incompetent employees out of selling positions and "into work for which they are better fitted." Wieder believed it was not difficult to replace clerks who regarded their work as merely filling customers' requests with mechanical salesmen. "This is the unimaginative type, which fails to fall in line with the idea of suggestive selling. It is obvious that very little salesmanship is required to give a customer what is asked for, and stores can no longer afford to be hampered by employees of that variety." Replacement sales alone, argued the executive, were not enough for merchants, who needed the extra business that came from clever suggestive selling. "The clerk who makes no attempt to have his or her store share in that business is not better than a machine as far as the store is concerned."[18]

Another unnamed executive, said to be in close touch with developments in the vending field, believed the industry was due for big gains in the following 12 months and, while some of that increase would be in areas already having VMs, "the brightest future for machine vending undoubtedly lies in the use by department stores, and retailers generally, of machines to handle many types of popular, standardized merchandise, the sale of which has required that the clerk be merely an order taker." He cautioned that this development might take some time due to the investment required in these machines and since they had not yet been invented.

Commenting on the vending industry to that date, the executive said: "Until quite recently the vending business was more or less a piker affair. It was haphazard, grossly unstandardized and maintained by small business men who carried their offices in their hats and were content with a comparatively low net return. But ambitions have changed because of economic reasons akin to those which have brought the chain store to the fore. Distribution costs have increased notably and the machine aims to reduce them by eliminating inefficient and costly selling and by affording greater convenience to the customer."[19]

According to this executive, the vended items having the highest turnover were chocolate bars, paper drinking cups, candy mints, fruit drops, chewing gum, and other confectionery, followed by handkerchiefs, drug products, and cigarettes. For a profitable business in such items, he estimated that each VM should average at least $1 in gross sales per week. However, he did note that some companies operated thousands of machines averaging less than 75 cents gross a week and still made "much money" while some VMs grossing $2 a day or more lost money. The difference was that in the former case servicing was simple, products were not perishable, and the units were of sufficient capacity to need refilling only once a month. Noting there was then a move afoot to vend magazines from machines, the executive thought that such a plan would not work with newspapers "because they must be serviced with new editions several times a day. In the case of magazines this is required but once a week." Vending machines were said to then cost from $20 to $100 or more each.[20]

A long 1928 article by business journalist Peter O'Shea, assessing the role and dynamic future the vending industry could look forward to, also spoke of the scientific side, focusing on things like efficiency, division of labor, wasted motions, and time and motion studies. Many of these were the result of the still lingering effects of "scientific management," a method of controlling labor that took the country by storm in the 1910s. Chief proponent and popularizer of that method was Frederick Winslow Taylor. Belief in science was strong enough in the 1920s to believe that if humans could not be transformed into robots, then at least they could be trained and conditioned to work more like them. Another area covered by O'Shea was the development of both national media and advertising as well as a trend toward more standardized packaging through the 1920s. While those things made it easier for VMs to be successful, VMs could only vend products people knew about and were familiar with. Vending machines were not the place to first introduce a new product.[21]

O'Shea opened his piece by commenting that the retailer's "dream" of a machine to sell in place of salespeople had to await two conditions: small standardized packages and volume demand. Both conditions were then present in American business, at least in some lines. Argued O'Shea: "A large number of standard package goods are now on the market. And a billion dollars of advertising every year builds a ready-made demand for them. Hence the recent rapid development of automatic sales machines." On many sales persuasion and selection were unnecessary, he said, and those could be done by machine. When a customer went into a store for widely advertised goods, he knew what he wanted. All that remained for him was to state his desire, accept it, pay for it, and make his exit. "The sooner he can do this, the better he is satisfied.... Theoretically, the quickest way to service him is by machine." A customer for cigarettes, stated O'Shea, did not come to the store to buy. He had already done his buying, in the sense of selecting, before he came to the retailer. "As a nation we do much of our buying in the pages of magazines and newspapers and from billboards and other media. Such a purchaser goes into a store to obtain, not to buy." Thus that retail clerk did not have to sell, he had only to deliver. "Any additional motions or words waste time both for the salesman and the customer. Many customers resent superfluous motions or words ... and to add injury the proprietor has to pay the salesman for his wasted moments." O'Shea thought retailers should follow the example of factory management, where time and motion study men did not hesitate to tackle problems just as complex in a straightforward and routine manner. "Retail selling has not been sufficiently subjected to division of labor," he wrote. "When this is done, the knotty problems will be given to a sales executive, the persuasive sales to a persuader, and the mechanical, repetitive motions of selling will be given over to a machine."[22]

O'Shea then interviewed Granat of the United Cigar Stores, both men enthusiastically accepting the idea that retailers should embrace scientific management. The idea that a method used in the industrial sector of the economy might not easily or successfully transfer to the commercial sector did not appear to occur to them. After an analysis, Granat determined that "Of the salesman's work, 60% is the work of an automaton. Why not give most of this sort of work to an automaton? That is why we are giving more and more cigarette sales over to machines. They occupy space against the outer wall which is otherwise useless, though we have to pay rent for it." Those machines, he said, were built on the skyscraper principle—tall and narrow, making the most economical use of a square foot of floor space within the store just as a skyscraper used a square foot of land. He was also thinking of the automatic loading of the machines from bins, which would be positioned high up in space then unused. Granat felt machines released human energy for creative, original, and variable work that required intelligence and real selling. If machines took care of the five-cent sales, then the salesman was free to make the $5 sales. Trying to allay fears that VMs such as he envisioned would lead to increased unemployment, Granat argued that machines promoted the salesman to an executive: "They do not degrade or replace him. He has a battery of mechanical aids working for him all the time." Eventually, the wages of such salesmen would increase, he added. "Repetition, even of the best, tends to turn men into automatons. Flesh and blood make poor automatons. Men are glad to turn such sales over to real automatons made of steel and glass." Again Granat stressed that the intention was not to replace salesmen by automatic machines, but to supplement men with machines which were at their service as a fast selling tool. "Men will simply improve. Burden-carriers who had formerly used their heads welcomed rickshaws as a promotive tool. When rickshaws became automobiles, coolies improved to become taxi-drivers.... It is possible that retail salesmen are as yet not far advanced from the coolie stage."[23]

Forcing the final step of adopting machines, he declared, was the high value of human labor and time. And VMs could sell after hours. For example, in England the law required tobacco shops to close at 8 PM, but store proprietors attached VMs outside the shop where they continued to sell. According to O'Shea, another important factor in the rise of VMs was that

"Uniform packages are now widespread in this country.... A uniform package allows design of uniform machine parts and uniform repetitive motions of selling. Uniformity is inseparable from the idea of a vending machine." When an item was sold through a machine there was no need to wrap it or to sell by persuasion since advertising had already done that. Therefore, declared the journalist, "Let a machine receive the price and deliver the goods." With multi-purpose machines on the horizon, retail prices of the different items dispensed by a single VM could range from five cents to $1. Even if an item was priced at an odd level, say 18 cents, it was "only necessary," noted O'Shea, "to put two cents change with the merchandise in each compartment." In fact, this method must have been cumbersome and labor intensive despite that it was a method regularly used, especially for cigarettes, which were often oddly priced due to taxes imposed on them. It meant someone at the operator's warehouse had to tape two pennies to each pack of cigarettes heading for a VM.[24]

According to O'Shea, over 30,000 VMs were then selling postage stamps in America and performing five million transactions monthly. Yet each of those mechanical salesmen "take up only 7 inches of space." One cigar store chain had 1,113 machines, a drug store chain had 508, and a grocery chain had 416. Change-making machines were beginning to appear, at least where there were banks of machines, such as the United Cigar Store battery of cigarette VMs. They were separate stand-alone machines that could change half-dollars, quarters, or dimes into dimes and nickels. Over the first seven or eight months of that operation, O'Shea argued, the battery had done enough business to represent the work of at least two salesmen. Since the annual rental of the entire VM battery was $1,000, the salary of at least one clerk had been saved. A general lack of VMs had blocked the full results of the effects of widespread national advertising, concluded O'Shea. "Machines are the fastest possible spout to the consumers at the end of the commercial pipe-line, so machines may enable advertising to take on a new effectiveness. Advertising as a tool may grow into a steam shovel, considering it as a spade now."[25]

Less than six months after the above article, reporter William McGarry wrote a similar piece enthusiastically touting the vending industry in the *Saturday Evening Post*. With America in a mechanized age, an age of the "(true) robot," that may have been a reason, he thought, why a "humble cousin of the mechanical man" had been able to move close to one million in number without attracting national attention until recently. His list of vended products included apples; gasoline; ice cream; candy, wrapped or in boxes; soft drinks, loose and bottled; handkerchiefs; soft collars; men's garters; toothbrushes and toothpaste, separately and in combination; a wash cloth and a bit of soap; postage stamps, at cost in some instances and with a 20 percent mark-up in others; change for larger coins; cigars and cigarettes; notions; lead pencils; and the use of a washing machine. Coin-operated telephones and gas meters were considered "old familiars" in the trade. McGarry observed that in recent months bankers had helped draw national attention by engineering a series of mergers and consolidations in the industry, all of which had been widely publicized. More were said to be underway. All of those new combinations were reported to have launched well-capitalized programs for expanding the field of present equipment and for the development of machines to operate in other areas. They all wanted "the vending of higher-priced and more essential commodities."[26]

According to McGarry, some 250 manufacturers had produced and put into operation automatic vending equipment. Acknowledging that many of the machines were experimental, he said an analysis of that list of makers "shows that only a negligible percentage of these manufacturers and pioneers are interested in equipment of the catchpenny type, and then only as a byproduct." Most were devoting themselves to units to vend products of universal and daily use for which "the market already has been established." None of those companies new to the vending industry were refusing pennies, but what they wanted then was the "important money in nickels, dimes, quarters and half dollars...."[27]

Analyzing the history of American vending, McGarry argued that until about five years earlier VM owners and operators, as a whole, put in very little and got back less. But starting around 1924, the great American passion for improvement got around to the catchpenny. New entrants to the field discovered, among other things, "that one of the chief reasons why coin machines didn't pay was because they didn't work. Sometimes this was due to slugs and sometimes to poor servicing, but more often it was attributable to the deadly malady of public suspicion and distrust." A program of reorganization and modernization was launched. Gum, candy, and other penny VMs were dressed up — with new, more attractive cabinets — and made more colorful in general. Coin acceptors were improved. These advances reportedly led to an increase in the number of penny VMs and a trend toward industry stabilization.[28]

McGarry also dealt at length with the cult of mechanization then sweeping the nation. He cited business analyst Roger Babson who said "you cannot produce by machine and distribute by hand." That conviction among businessmen proved the real explanation for the growth of automatic merchandising. From that perspective, "it has become instantly apparent that while every other function of business has been mechanized — management, production, transportation, and even sales, through the medium of advertising — distribution of the goods is still being performed by the methods in use a hundred or a thousand years ago." While all sorts of improvements had been made in getting the goods to the clerk, especially in chain stores, when it came to passing the merchandise to the consumer "a man with bare hands is still performing this simple operation over and over again." As an example of the efficiencies of the VM, McGarry cited the example of a machine to vend handkerchiefs installed in a railway station washroom. Previously the product had been sold by the attendant. Although the coin machine took up no more room than the cabinet previously used to display the merchandise, sales from the VM averaged 60 a day, compared to 11 by the attendant. Addressing the idea that increased use of VMs would lead to more unemployment, the reporter dismissed the notion as not possible, stating that "the machine may be expected to create more jobs." This was an extreme statement that few made. Most contented themselves with saying simply that unemployment would not rise. McGarry based his statement on the idea that the manufacture and servicing of VMs would produce jobs. He also believed robot stores were the "wave" of the future and would soon arrive.[29]

Fueling all the hype was the fact that, starting in late 1928 and continuing through 1929, some department and chain stores were installing VMs. Among the establishments in which VMs were said to be in use were the J. L. Hudson company in Detroit, Bamberger's of Newark, and the Boston Store of Chicago. Installations were said to range from 30 to 100 machines, with three to 10 in a battery. Products sold included drug sundries, notions, candies, packaged groceries, and cigarettes. Those machines, said the *New York Times*, have now passed from the novelty to the utility stage. Because the merchandise vended was of the "pre-sold" or convenience type, "no consumer antipathy to their use is said to exist."[30]

In September, 1929, *Literary Digest* noted that the 250 manufacturers produced about 400 different machines, and that "those in the business prophesy huge arcades where customers are waited on by vending and change-making automatons." One unit at an amusement beach near New York sold 58 different commodities. Also mentioned by this publication were a number of developments which would be short-lived novelties. Joseph Schermack had developed an improved coin acceptor in which a rejected coin formed an electric contact which started a disk phonograph in the top of the cabinet. As the slug was returned, a voice from within the VM said, "Please use good coins only!" Someone came up with a talking scale which announced the patron's weight. It did poorly because "No woman living will submit to a public announcement of the fact she weighs a hundred and ninety-five." Another invention was the automatic wheat cake vendor—electrically operated—that had a compartment which held enough dough for a hundred servings. A quarter deposited in the slot entitled the customer to four wheat cakes and started a "fascinating series of operations." One by one the portions of batter dropped on the hot plate. When one side was brown an automatic flipper turned the cake over. Syrup was applied by the machine but butter had to be served by hand. New York had a Sodamat in which 11 machines sold loganberry juice, root beer, orangeade, and so on.[31]

In 1926, the first Sodamats, forerunners of the more recent soft drink cup machines, appeared in New York and New Jersey amusement parks. Those machines were not self-contained devices because they did not contain in a single unit the coin mechanism, refrigeration system, cup dispenser, carbonator, and syrup tank. Rather, the Sodamats were installed in batteries built into a wall. Units in the battery were fed by one compressor, one pump, and one carbonator located at the rear and out of sight. Attendants working behind the scenes kept everything functioning. Installed in Coney Island, Asbury Park, Atlantic City, and New York, Sodamats continued to supply soft drinks long after World War II.[32]

Over a 10-month period in 1930-1931, *Business Week* produced three separate articles, each a glowing tribute to the technological advances said to be underway in vending. One true sign of growth and maturity in the industry was that the manufacturers and operators of all types of coin-operated machines held their first annual convention in early 1930. The business publication noted that many in the industry were predicting that, within a short time, apartment buildings would devote "considerable space to batteries of machines for supplying their tenants with toothpaste, proprietary medicines, and other small articles of which a household is in constant need." Large chain grocery stores were said to utilize VMs to dispense canned goods, eggs, tea, and coffee, thereby giving a 24-hour service. Cunningham Drug Store in Detroit, one of the largest single-unit drug stores in America, operated a battery of approximately 50 VMs selling many varieties of creams, pastes, powders, soaps, tobacco, and other packaged products. A change machine was located at one end of the battery, which stretched some 60 feet along the wall of the Griswold Street drug store. After only a few months, this experiment at Cunningham was abandoned for various reasons. One difficulty was the use of slugs in the changer. Also, the machines took up a large amount of floor space and the sales per square foot were unimpressive.[33]

Major hurdles in the path of automatic selling—change-making and slug rejection—had been successfully cleared, said *Business Week*, in the line of automatic "stores" just placed into production by Snax Automatic

Stores of Detroit. They were actually multi-purpose VMs which could vend different items from a single machine. A small circular model displayed 24 separate compartments and sold five, ten and 25 cent items. A larger model offered separate display compartments for 28 items such as canned goods, spices, and packaged food of all kinds. Each compartment had a change-making unit set to handle change according to the price of the article. Snax units were said to be then operating in Albany, New York, Lansing, Michigan, and Milwaukee, Wisconsin.[34]

The unlikely event of multi-purpose VMs coming to apartment buildings happened by early in 1931. A company called the Robert Harvey System, Inc., was then producing a VM called the Delamat (delivers automatically). The equipment was furnished in sections with each one providing five separate units for displaying and delivering merchandise. The actual package or can that the purchaser received furnished the display. A separate coin acceptor was provided for each selling unit. If the price of the item was an odd amount, "the package you receive has attached to it a small envelope containing your change." Slugs and bad coins were rejected at the rate of "at least 85%," a number thought good enough to boast about. The number of items in a unit varied, depending on size. Coin insertion started an electric motor which turned the sprocket wheel to move the merchandise from the display position to the delivery window immediately below, while the next tray moved into the display position. The fact that some of these early VMs operated on this mini-conveyor belt principle was viewed positively because it made them seem closer to the prevailing model in the industrial sector. Estimates were that an average apartment building installation would require 35 non-refrigerated sections, five units each, providing for 175 items of merchandise, plus five electrical refrigerated sections with space for 30 items of meat, butter, eggs, and so forth. Such "stores" were said to require only one attendant—to make change and to restock the machines—while the sales capacity was said to be equal to that of an ordinary food store employing two clerks and a manager or cashier. Delamat stores were then being installed in

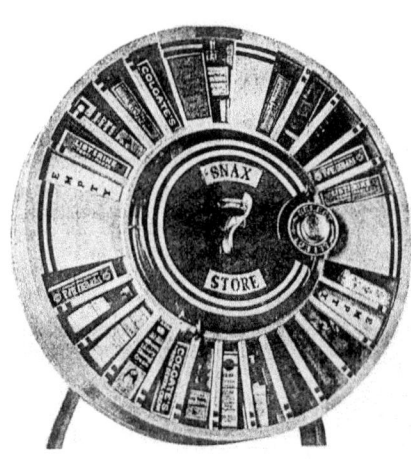

The circular Snax machine, 1930.

selected apartment buildings where 24-hour service was in demand and where a building had "enough potential customers to insure profitable operation."[35]

One of the first Delamats installed was on the ground floor of a large apartment building on West 44th Street, New York. When a reporter visited, he found that in the daytime a girl made change and restocked the machines. At the end of her shift, she emptied all the coin boxes and the VMs

An "Automatic Grocer" designed for apartment buildings, 1931.

operated without human aid for the following 14 hours. The unit to handle cold items was simply built into a large General Electric refrigerator. The non-refrigerated units held 30 different items in cans, glass jars, cartons, and paper bags and included such staples as coffee, sugar, canned vegetables, fruit, and ginger ale. This was the first attempt to refrigerate and vend foodstuffs.[36]

The last article to appear in this unrelated group of pieces appeared in November, 1930, in the *Saturday Evening Post*, and became the best-known and most influential of the articles. Decades later this article, "Profits from Pennies," was usually the one cited when reference was made to the VM hype of this era. What set this article apart from the others was that it devoted almost no space to "nickel and up" machines. Nor did it devote any space to the next generation of machines which were supposedly just around the corner. Instead, author Arch Andrews—an operator in the industry—discussed at length mainly the existing penny machines, and the good profits that could be made from them.[37]

Andrews noted that a chain of five-and-ten-cent stores that installed penny scales some 10 years earlier was making a net annual profit of about $600,000 from them in 1930. When the head of a cinema chain visited Andrews to make a test of weigh scales in New York's largest theater chain, Andrews sent two scales that were placed in the men's lavatory in the basement of the cinema. Each scale took in about $3.50 in its first day. Soon thereafter, 10 scales were placed in that theater while other houses in the chain were being equipped with units as rapidly as possible. In addition, Andrews installed penny VMs in the theater that vended paper toilet seat covers as well as machines that sold candy and peanuts in five and 10 cent packages. For the first years of its existence, said Andrews, "this chain of theaters would not tolerate any scheme for the sale of candy, on the theory that the costly carpets and other fabrics in the houses would be injured to an extent that would devour a good share of any profits."[38]

Andrews also stated that, in New York City's subway system, about $5,500 was gathered from VMs every weekday by two operating companies. Just past the subway turnstiles leading into the Times Square station of the Interborough line, a patron was immediately exposed to about 200 scales, chewing-gum, chocolate, and peanut slot machines. In the same station, inside the turnstile barrier of the Brooklyn-Manhattan Transit Company, there were another 100 VMs. The paper drinking cup business was said to be thriving as practically every railroad car in America became equipped with such machines. These machines were also found in thousands of theaters and in other public places. Surprisingly, Andrews found a phenomenon which was the reverse of slugs. In a check of a group of scales, it was discovered that coins of higher denomination than a penny equaled about eight percent of the total value.[39]

A peanut VM operator's route covered 12 stations and contained 80 machines. In warm weather, said Andrews, those machines went through 100 pounds a day, with consumption reaching as high as 200 pounds per day in colder weather. The salted peanuts cost him eight to 16 cents per pound and were vended at a rate of 20 to 26 peanut pieces per penny—a rate of 40 cents a pound. Yet the volume of business done by peanut and chocolate VMs was "insignificant" compared to chewing gum units. One gum manufacturer annually sold three million boxes of his product to VM owners—each box contained 100 sticks and wholesaled for 40 cents. Another chewing gum maker sold one million boxes yearly to VM operators. Andrews claimed the penny gum machines grossed $5 million a year while penny scales took in two to three times that much from the 100,000 scales in the country—one for every 1,200 people.[40]

Andrews believed scales still possessed lots of potential. For instance, an old model scale in a five-and-ten-cent store had been collecting about $8 a month. When a new model was installed, the take increased to $60 a month. If a second scale was placed beside one that had been doing a satisfactory business, the total would still increase because patron after patron would weigh themselves on both machines. They did that to see if the first scale was correct, thought Andrews. "It is amusing and decidedly profitable for the scale owners." When coat hooks were first placed on scales the business done by those units promptly increased. "I have seen men strip off their coats and then transfer everything from their trouser pockets—keys, money, papers and pencils." Over the course of a three-day test, Andrews found, to his surprise, that more men than women weighed themselves, taking into account the proportion of their store patronage. Formerly scale owners paid their collectors a commission but, since there was no check or control, the method left the way open for skimming off the money. Locations containing Andrews's scales collected the money from the scales and kept it all. Andrews calculated the operator's share by selling the tickets—which gave the customer his weight—that were placed in the scales. If a location had only a few scales, it might pay as much as $7.50 for 1,000 tickets; if it had many units it might pay only $6 per 1,000. On that latter basis, the owner/operator of the scale received 60 out of every 100 cents.[41]

Another major development of this period was the coin-operated washing machine. Makers of such equipment had been looking with growing concern at the increasing popularity of apartment buildings. There were no washing machines in these apartment units. Finally, a coin-device "expert" equipped a number of washing machines with quarter slots and a time clock—permitting the use of the machine for 35 minutes—and succeeded in finding a ready market on a commission basis in the basements of apartment houses. More than 1,000 of these coin-operated washing machines were said to be in use in 1929, and the yield was said to reach $200 a year per machine.[42]

Hershey chocolate bars were among the first to be offered for sale in VMs, and some of the most popular types of candy machines in 1929 and 1930 were designed specifically to sell these bars.[43]

M. T. Ziegler, general manager of the Central Ice and Cold Storage Company in Los Angeles, hit upon the idea of vending ice in 1931. His Serv-Ice VM held 25-pound cakes of ice sealed in wax-coated manila paper. The ice was trucked to large outdoor vending stations (12 feet high by eight feet square) where it retailed at 15 cents per block. The first station was installed in Los Angeles in July, 1931. By the end of 1932, Ziegler had 24 Serv-Ice machines in operation in Los Angeles and San Diego.[44]

In 1931, the Automatic Sales Company of New York installed periodical VMs in some 75 Eastern cities. Curtis Publishing used these to vend the *Saturday Evening Post* and the *Ladies Home Journal*. At the same time, a VM found on German ocean liners allowed a customer to put four ten-pfennig pieces into the slot, set the two dials to select a book, pull a lever, and receive the book. A glass front on the unit allowed the customer to see the covers of all 12 titles held in the machine. An Englishman named Noel Pemberton-Billings invented a book VM and at this time he was touring the US by car—with a machine—trying to place them.

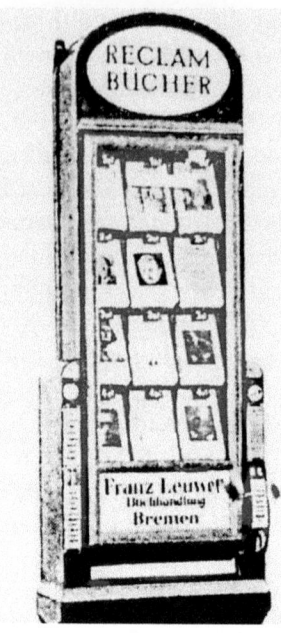

A book VM on the deck of a German ocean liner, 1931.

Standing three feet wide, three feet high and one foot deep, the unit could either sell or rent its 100 books.[45]

The sale of drugs from VMs was often viewed as an area of growth. While some such vending did take place, it faced considerable opposition. An example of that pressure could be seen in a 1930 case from the UK. L. Moreton Parry, president of the Pharmaceutical Society of Great Britain, observed that the use of VMs for the sale of drugs had increased in recent months, both in the UK and abroad, and it seemed desirable that members of the Society who might be approached with proposals for the installation of VMs in conjunction with their pharmacies should have guidance upon what this attitude should be. In stating the views of the Society, Parry listed the reasons against allowing such sales—lack of professional advice, exposure of children to poisons and dangerous drugs, possible mistakes in stocking machines, and so forth—before concluding, "the sale of drugs from automatic machines is to be deplored ... [we] sincerely trust that members will refuse to install automatic machines for the supply of drugs."[46]

Later that year, the Council of the Pharmaceutical Society brought an action against druggist and Society member Harry Watkinson of Tottenham. On January 14 and 28, 1930, bottles of Lysol bearing the label "poison" were bought by an inspector in the employ of the Society from an automatic machine outside Watkinson's shop. This was a friendly prosecution in that Watkinson cooperated in the operation. The pharmacists wanted a ruling under the Poisons and Pharmacy Act of 1908, which required that the business of a chemist be conducted only by a bona fide druggist. Acting for the Society, Glyn Jones said, "The use of these machines is enormously extensive." The defense called no witnesses and presented no evidence. Judge Crawford found in favor of the Pharmaceutical Society and declared the sale of drugs and poisons from automatic machines to be illegal. Noting than any child tall enough to reach the coin slot could purchase a poison like Lysol, Crawford stated, "Beyond all question this ought not to be allowed to continue."[47]

Yet another major development in this period was the entrance, in

1928, of Nathaniel Leverone into the vending industry. One day that year in Chicago, the 44-year-old automotive parts manufacturer was waiting for the elevated train at the Wilson Street station. As he waited, he idly started feeding coins into the VMs—and got madder by the minute. He recalled: "I weighed myself on a penny machine and found I weighed 205. Another machine said 98. A chocolate machine gave me nothing, not even my penny back. Out of a peanut machine I got six moldy objects I wouldn't feed to a goat." Many years later, Leverone said that experience prompted him to get into the vending business. "Why in the devil, I thought, haven't some honest men seen the opportunity in these things?" A year later in 1929, Leverone and 11 associates put up $5,000 each to start Chicago's Automatic Canteen company. It became the unchallenged leader of the industry. Today, after some name and ownership changes, Canteen remains one of the major vending companies. Initially Leverone found the business controlled "by sharpers and racketeers; chewing gum sticks were cut in half, sold for a penny apiece ... peanuts costing 8 cents per pound dribbled out at the rate of six per penny. And when the machines ran out of merchandise, they returned nothing but a hollow, insulting clank." Canteen hired an engineer to design an "honest" machine—one that returned coins when it was empty—as well as an improved slug rejecter.[48]

The company went into candy vending with a non-selective machine —that is, a machine with no choice, just one specific item vended—after contracting with well known candy bar makers to supply full-sized bars for a nickel. For a time, Canteen sold only the 12 candy bars then produced by Curtiss Candy company. However, as Leverone recalled, "people just got tired of eating candy made by the same manufacturer. So we went to Hershey, but Hershey refused to sell to us at first because he said he didn't want to get us into financial trouble." Hershey had briefly attempted its own vending operation in the 1920s, but regarded that venture as a failure. Instead, William Murrie, then Hershey president, suggested that Leverone build a candy VM that would offer patrons a choice of bars. Canteen went to International Register Company who designed a five-column machine with a total capacity of 60 bars. The selective candy vendor convinced Hershey, setting a pattern in the vending industry.[49]

Despite the occasional mention of improved slug rejection mechanisms, slugs continued to bedevil the vending industry in this period. In the UK in 1924, Frederick Haines, a painter's laborer, was charged at Croydon Police Court with stealing a shilling pack of cigarettes. He had admittedly inserted into the VM a halfpenny that he had filed and weighted with lead. When arrested Haines, it was alleged, had three more of the doctored coins in his possession.[50]

Also in the UK in 1926, was the case of 19-year-old clerk Denis Philip Wienel. He was charged with attempting to steal a pack of cigarettes, the property of Mrs. A. R. Mills, by means of a "trick" from a VM outside her shop. A sympathetic Magistrate Oulton said this was a case in which automatic machines acted as a sort of trap for the innocent, adding, "This young man would probably never have stolen but for the machine being there." Mills had the machine for only one week during which cigarettes to the value of 30 shillings had been sold, but the equivalent of 16 shillings of the takings had been represented by foreign coins and slugs. Oulton placed Wienel on probation, and said it would be interesting to find out the number of thefts committed in the UK since VMs were introduced.[51]

Automatic machines for selling cigarettes and chocolates were installed in Moscow in 1925 by the municipal authorities. Yet so many ways were discovered to "beat" the VMs that their use was abandoned in 1927. Chiefly instrumental in putting the devices out of business were said to be the "besprizorny," or homeless children. Despite the best efforts of a special corps of watchers, the children "managed to limit the daily collections to a harvest of buttons, improvised metal disks and worthless Czarist coins."[52]

In the mid 1920s, just after one of the New York subway lines was completely equipped with coin-operated turnstiles, it received some 3,000 slugs a day. In 1929, experts were called in to design a better mechanism, resulting in the number of accepted slugs decreasing to 600 a day. Given a total of 2.5 million passengers a day, the total was remarkably low. All of the systems using coin turnstiles had trouble for a short period just after World War I, when an enterprising traveler discovered a South European coin the exact size and weight of the American nickel. He was said to have made a good living importing those coins for 1.5 cents each and reselling them for three cents. Subway fares were then a nickel. The unnamed man was finally discovered and made a "guest of Uncle Sam."[53]

Police constable Francis Blandford of Plymouth, UK, was charged with stealing cigarettes by means of a "trick" from a VM. He was fined 25 pounds Sterling or three months imprisonment. He paid the fine.[54]

In his article, Andrews noted the penny VMs "get plenty of worthless objects in their coin boxes." One operating firm, after placing some VMs in the vicinity of a tin-manufacturing plant, finally abandoned all locations near that factory due to the proportion of slugs received in the coin boxes. A second operator abandoned some locations when its investigators discovered that slugs, "which outnumbered pennies in the coin boxes," were coming from a button factory in the neighborhood. Those buttons were made by stamping bits of fabric on to metal disks.[55]

Business Week remarked that slug use was more prevalent in areas where mechanics abounded, as in Chicago and Detroit. Punching out disks to be used as slugs was a simple machine operation. To counter the slug menace, the vending industry encouraged the improvement of anti-slug devices as well as lobbying to make the possession and use of slugs illegal. By 1931, New York State had a law against the fraudulent use of slugs and tokens. Ohio had gone farther with a statute against the possession and use of slugs while Tennessee and West Virginia had laws similar to that of New York. The Federal Trade Commission had ruled that it had no power to stop the interstate sale of slugs.[56]

Reporter Sandford Brown, writing in 1957, recalled that, "By the 1920s the business of cheating the machines had become almost a national sport." Novelty companies advertised dime slugs at a penny each in pulp magazines, pointing out in bold-face type that their product was "not for use in VENDING MACHINES." Brown also raised a subject not much reported in this period: that vandals "went at machines with feet, shears, and crowbars."[57]

Growth in the industry led to its organization, with the Vending Machine Manufacturers' Association of America holding its first annual convention in 1931. At that convention, the National Vending Machine Operators and the Coin Machine Operators joined to form the Automatic Merchandisers Association. This new association strengthened further with the addition of the Vending Machine Manufacturers, which affiliated but remained a separate division. One reason for organizing was to battle the industry's common evils: "Important among them is the slug, the use of which has increased with the [business] slump." The now-combined industry expected to launch a special drive to enact prohibitory slug statutes in Congress and in State legislatures. Other powerful financial groups could be counted on for aid since, for example, the New York subway lines and the Bell Telephone system suffered from the slug evil.[58]

Other negative aspects of the vending industry — some of which would survive permanently — also surfaced during this era. Charges filed in Federal Court in New York in 1927 against the officers of the then defunct Little Ritz Automatic Service Company alleged fraud and the obtaining of money under false pretenses. One of the defendant officers charged was Otto S. Bowling. He denied the charges and pointed out that the federal and city prosecutors' offices had investigated the affairs of the company for fraud and had failed to find any. Little Ritz, claimed Bowling, had "a first-class idea" — that of selling VMs to investors, locating and servicing the machines, and then collecting the money and sending 20 percent of the take to the machine owners, that is, the investors. However, the firm went bankrupt in June, 1926. Among the plaintiffs was G. Creighton Webb of New York City who paid $3,000 for 20 machines and received a bill of sale, but not the machines themselves. Grace Lesser of New Jersey petitioned to recover $150, her payment for one machine, while Henry Beckmann of New Jersey sought $2,400, his payment for 16 machines. Plaintiffs' lawyer T. John McKee said he served as counsel for about 300 buyers of the machines all over the country. This type of fraud would surface again and again over time in the vending industry. Promoters would offer to sell VMs to investors (always at highly inflated prices) while promising to find good locations, service the machines, and return high profits to the investors. After payment was received for the machines, of course, little or nothing happened. These operations would become so commonplace that a generic term was invented for them — "blue sky" promotions.[59]

Retailers often lived in fear of the effects of VMs on their livelihoods, especially in the 1928-1929 period when there was excessive hype about their future potential. Fear among retailers was particularly high in the UK, where stores' opening hours were strictly regulated. During a 1928 National Chamber of Trade meeting at Grimsby, delegate J. S. Young made a resolution in favor of a tax on automatic machines. Those machines, he complained, competed with the established trader, but were not subject to the same restriction of hours. They occupied prominent sites without an adequate contribution to the tax base and "tended to create unemployment." Young suggested a tax on VMs of one guinea per slot per year, and the resolution was carried.[60]

A letter to the editor of the *Times* of London by UK Member of Parliament Walter De Frece observed that, in common with most members of Parliament, he had received suggestions from retailers and other trade groups urging the government to introduce legislation to make it illegal for those who owned automatic machines to utilize them outside their premises or elsewhere for selling purposes after the hours that shops by law were required to close. De Frece was opposed to the idea, believing that sooner or later retailers would have to accept longer opening hours to get "the benefit of the extra trade which ... exists after the normal closing hours, because otherwise you would not have automatic machines doing so well."[61]

Just when vending machines took their first life is unknown. Over the course of time it would happen more often than might be expected. The victim in the UK in 1925 must have been among the first. VMs of the era were mostly small and light in weight. It was hard for them to inflict mortal damage on a human, but not impossible. In July, 1925, Stephen Hammond, 52, of Tilbury received fatal injuries at Camden Town Station. He put a coin in a cigarette vendor at the station and, when it did not deliver any product, he pulled at the machine's drawer. As the device toppled over it pushed Hammond back to the edge of the platform where he was caught by a passing train engine. Spun around, he fell between the platform and the second engine of the train and later was pronounced dead at a London hospital. An inquest recorded a verdict of accidental death.[62]

Walter Hurd, coin machine editor for the trade publication *Billboard*, summarized the industry at the close of this period. First, he noted the rapid rise of coin-operated amusement games, especially pinball and slot (gambling) machines, to national importance in 1931 and 1932. VMs were being pushed into the background. As early as 1928 and 1929, high-grade coin-operated cabinet games had gained considerable attention in the trade. Those cabinet games, mostly focusing on sports, were built for more elite types of locations. Then came a craze for miniature games (small pool games, for example), followed by a skyrocketing rise in the popularity of pin games. However, Hurd agreed that VMs were "decidedly in the limelight during the balmy days of 1928 and 1929." Magazines and publications gave them considerable publicity and it was often predicted, he found, that automatic selling would revolutionize merchandising.[63]

Hurd stressed the promotional hype of the era, especially regarding the CAMCO firm and the *Saturday Evening Post* and other media, which "joined in the grand parade of heralding the new day of automatic selling. Vending machines were getting priceless publicity as a sort of acme of perfection of the new machine age. It was all so much like a dream and the stock promoters were just getting set in this new dream world when the crash of 1929 knocked the bottom from all stock promotions." By then much damage had been done to the industry. Hurd reported that, by 1930, a powerful group of organized labor had become alarmed at the idea of machines displacing clerks in stores and had started a national crusade against VMs. When Nathaniel Leverone conducted a study of the effects of the Depression on automatic machines, he concluded: "We have learned that the vending machine cannot compete with the popular American girl." With the sharp rise in unemployment, Hurd said, clerks could be had at a very low price, "and there was danger of widespread criticism of selling by machine. So it was well for the time that publicity for merchandising machines was left in the background." Hurd later argued that VMs "almost dropped from the coin machine trade press until repeal [of Prohibition in 1933] brought new opportunities for many types of vending machines."[64]

In 1932, when Hurd looked at the future of the vending industry, he concluded: "No doubt the greatest opportunity for merchandising machines in the future will be for their advertising value." He seemed to see them as giant billboards, to be used for product launches. Stating that a few attempts had been made on a national scale to use VMs for the introduction of new products, he admitted those efforts had not met with success and cited bad promotion as the cause.[65]

In the first 10 years of the period between 1918 and 1931, very little happened within the vending industry. That was followed by a period of feverish activity and media hype, centered around the years 1928 and 1929, during which VMs were credited with having a grandiose future they could not live up to. When CAMCO's first five years had elapsed (in 1933, at which point CAMCO had boldly predicted it would be making huge profits), the firm declared bankruptcy. VMs failed to attain great heights for many reasons: the consumer-spending collapse of the Depression; the subsequent cheap and plentiful supply of labor; the multi-purpose machines did not work very well; slugs continued to be a problem; and consumers' shopping needs were not psychologically or socially met by vending machines. Following the massive hype, VMs fell again into a period of quiet. By the end of 1931, nothing was sold in VMs for over a nickel, in any quantity, except for tobacco. The coming of the cigarette VM in the 1920s was the great success of the industry in this period, although it may have been too early to know that then. As the period ended, the VM industry was much the same as at the start of the period — mostly penny machines dispensing gum, candy, and nuts, with the addition of cigarettes. However, the dream that robots could sell anything and would sell everything would never really die.

3

Cigarettes Blaze the Way, 1932-1939

"... the great army of smokers ... would gladly deposit a penny in a machine to obtain one cigaret."

C. A. Roth, 1932

"We started out some time ago with a machine for selling prophylactic goods. Maybe we ought to have been shot for that...."

I. W. Schulman, 1932

"Salesgirls could be had for $5 a week and machines could not compete with that."

Nathaniel Leverone, 1934

"... one day the public would receive a large bag of fresh hot pop corn, scientifically popped by a sanitary method, without the necessity of an attendant."

V. H. Rowlette, 1938

"The Foot Oscillator will reduce foot fatigue and at the same time pile up many dimes in the cashbox for operators."

Billboard, 1939

Despite the incredible economic hardship of the Depression, the 1930s was a very good time for the coin-operated machine industry. It was a time of spectacular growth. For the amusement device sector that growth was most pronounced in the early years of the 1930s, but remained strong through the close of the decade. Slot (gambling) machines and pinball games enjoyed better growth than the rest of the amusement field. At one time, both dispensed cash prices. Community protests soon caused slots to be banned in many areas, and withdrawn from even more in anticipation of a ban. They were banished to the few jurisdictions designated as gambling meccas. Pin games remained viable and popular since an element of skill was involved in their play—a key part of the definition as to whether or not a machine was a gambling device. However, pins did cease giving out cash prizes or tokens redeemable for merchandise. The third division within the coin-operated machine industry—jukeboxes— also flourished intensely after the repeal of Prohibition. Music machines on location in America had numbered 20,000 to 25,000 at the end of 1933; by 1939, they numbered 300,000 or more. While vending machines could not match the growth rate of the amusement or jukebox sectors of the trade, VMs did experience a slower, but steady growth. They were less profitable than the other two divisions, but steadier in that they were subjected to fewer gyrations in their income. They were also the safest division of the industry. Operators of early pins and slots always had to worry about citizen protests, sudden legal bans, and police raids and seizures. In this period, the vending industry concentrated on building up its core segments—the cigarette and candy vendors. The fanciful dreams of selling everything, of entirely robotic stores, were for the most part gone. It was a time when innovation was mostly limited to vending specific items which had until then not been successfully dispensed by machine. Few of these efforts succeeded. The coin machine trade's rate of growth in the 1930s would have been excellent for any decade and, given that it took place in the midst of the Depression, the growth is all the more remarkable.

Remarking on the abating of the frenzy in the vending industry, a *Billboard* editor writing under the name of "Silver Sam" said that, at the beginning of 1932, the standard merchandising machines were being placed in a more consistent way "without any artificial boom. They are not being placed as a revolutionary development now: they are simply being placed as a sensible way to sell goods in suitable locations."[1]

Illustrating the kinds of problems affecting part of the coin machine industry was the experience of Mills Novelty company—one of the few manufacturers to make both VMs and gambling devices. During the first few months of 1933, police in Hartford, Connecticut, seized a number of the company's machines, alleging they were gambling devices. In an unrelated incident one month later, police in Brooklyn seized around 40 Mills's machines, also because they were alleged to be gambling devices.[2]

In a short-lived strategy to prevent their machines from being labeled gambling devices, some manufacturers in the early 1930s tried to disguise them as vending machines. This usually meant adding something like gum dispensing to a gaming device. For example, in 1933 the manufacturer H. C. Evans & Company of Chicago announced plans to produce a new and improved version of its very popular Saratoga Sweepstakes gambling amusement game, stating that "A ball-gum attachment is now part of the equipment of this machine."[3]

3.—Cigarettes Blaze the Way, 1932–1939

Progress in the VM industry was measured, at least in one 1934 account, by the wide variety of products and services being vended through automatic devices. These included drug sundries such as toothpaste, toothbrushes, quills, combs, hair brushes, nail brushes, nail files, hair nets, and hair pins. Medicinal and hygienic goods such as aspirin, corn remedies, headache powers, sanitary napkins, throat discs, and toilet seat covers were also available. Other vended items included fruits, bakery goods, candy and confections, various kinds of nuts, chewing gum, cigars and cigarettes, books and magazines, newspapers, perfumes, cosmetics, and bottled and bulk drinks. Service machines available included weighing scales, shoe-shining machines, razor blade machines, postage stamp units, drinking cup dispensers, paper towel and soap vendors, toilet locks, and so on. As accurate as the list may have been, most listed items were only available in a limited number of machines. The average citizen coming in contact with VMs chose from fewer items and services.[4]

Harry Alexander, president of H. W. Alexander company of Chicago, was nationally known as a merchandising counselor in selling by machine. His firm specialized in research and merchandising counsel on vending and service types of machines. In 1933, he estimated that coin-operated VMs—excluding gambling units—generated above $100 million in annual sales, with cigarette machines doing a business of $25 million a year. Alexander stated that there were VMs dispensing 37 different items of merchandise and services.[5]

When *Billboard* editor Walter Hurd reviewed the year 1932, he declared that there had been a decline in vending machine exhibits at the 1932 trade show when compared to 1931. Hurd also stated that the prolonged business depression had crimped the expansion programs of the VM firms, but at the same time the Depression had helped put the pin game boom in motion. Progress in merchandising machines during 1932

A coin-operated exercise bicycle, 1932.

A very large VM that delivered packaged ice, 1933.

consisted largely of conservative promotion in restricted territory. "That is, not much happened," concluded Hurd. He felt it was generally agreed that VMs proved their conservative earning power during the business depression: "They earn steadily, but not so spectacularly as the amusement machines."[6]

Another 1933 article analyzing the industry included a symposium by industry leaders. Speaking of the recent past, Harry Alexander said that part of the problem was too many vendors had used the VM ill-advisedly, attempting to sell articles by machine which could not be successfully marketed that way. "In 1929 began a perfect barrage of half facts and dream stuff about the vast economic changes that coin robots would bring. The baby giant was to create mountains of profits." W. E. Bolen of the Northwestern Corporation (a VM maker) spoke of the increase in the profit possibilities of the penny machines, an increase due to the development of the all-product merchandise vendor. He added, "For years the only products that the operator of penny bulk vendors could offer were peanuts, ball gum and a few hard candies. The all-product vendor quickly proved that the public's taste was by no means confined to these few items." Relatively new products available for bulk vending included pistachio nuts, chocolate-covered raisins, chocolate-covered peanuts, jelly beans, pecans, almonds, gum drops, and cashews. Bolen argued that penny machines were important to operators in establishing themselves permanently with each location owner. They gave operators "steady and dependable profits" every month and also set up a base from which to site amusement games in the location. In his view, operators who handled only pin machines were making a mistake. He advised such operators to also handle merchandising machines, because "An operator who wishes to safeguard his locations from other operators must install in his pin-game locations all the other types of merchandise vending machines which his location can profitably use."[7]

Within the universe of items sold automatically, the cigarette was dominant. For a brief period of time, VMs which sold single cigarettes were popular. They reflected, of course, the hard economic times of the

3.—Cigarettes Blaze the Way, 1932–1939

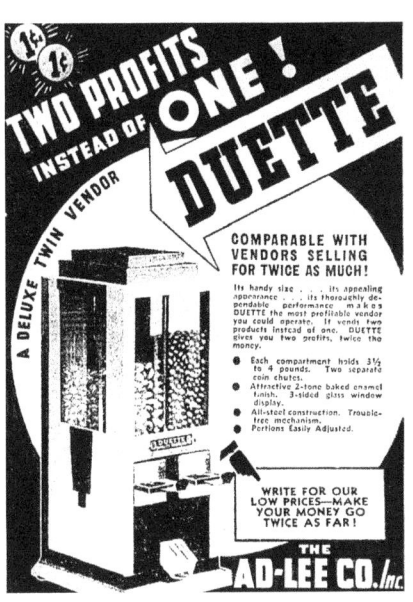

Above: Some of the small penny units available in 1936.
Right: A dual-compartment penny VM, 1936.

1930s wherein people often could not afford 15 cents for a pack of cigarettes. At an industry trade show in 1931, penny machines for cigarettes attracted quite a bit of attention. In the spring of that year, American Tobacco announced it would sell its Lucky Strike brand through a vendor that dispensed a single cigarette for one cent. Rival tobacco firms reportedly studied the issue. These machines held a special appeal since they returned 20 cents for packs of 20 that otherwise were machine-vended for 15 cents.[8]

A year later, a man named C. A. Roth announced he had invented and was marketing a new penny cigarette machine. Designed to hold 120 cigarettes, it could be adjusted to contain

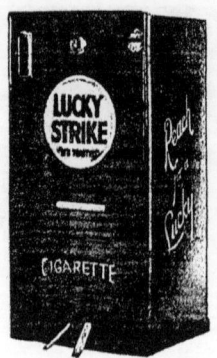

A single cigarette dispenser, 1933.

180. The cigarettes were loaded vertically, one on top of the other, in two columns of 60 each. According to the inventor, vertical dispensing both ensured positive delivery and eliminated jamming. Convinced the loose cigarettes would stay fresh for 36 hours, Roth argued that it would be better to service the machine every day than to "install an expensive arrangement or humidifier in the machine" and service it less frequently. "The penny vendor meets a modern need, considering the great army of smokers and the places where they would gladly deposit a penny in a machine to obtain one cigaret…. It offers a convenience that the smoking public will hail with joy, once the service is well distributed over the country."[9]

Just one month later, Roth returned to announce he had improved his machine. He insisted that his new container would keep the cigarettes fresh for up to 12 days. In the preceding week, approximately 40 of his machines were said to have been placed on location in New York. Gas stations, beauty parlors, confectionery stores, restaurants, and lodging houses were among the types of locations in which machines were sited. According to Roth, the lodging houses, beauty shops, and confectionery stores sold out each day. Although gas stations were not as successful, they also showed a good profit.[10]

When the W. H. Block company of Kenosha, Wisconsin, unveiled its penny cigarette machine, it said the machine would be marketed at first to operators who wished to enter a specialized business—that is, novices to vending. Block felt the operation of the machine was a specialty and would appeal to men who wanted a unique business.[11]

Philadelphia's Helms Vending Machine company unveiled its new penny cigarette vendor and stressed its unique feature—it delivered both a cigarette and a match for a penny. These units also used advertising to a greater extent. The display model had the Lucky Strike name on the front and the "Reach for a Lucky" slogan on the side. However, the unit held a maximum of 20 cigarettes. The best locations, thought the maker, were restaurants, lunch wagons, cigar stores, poolrooms, bowling alleys, hotels,

3.—Cigarettes Blaze the Way, 1932–1939   53

cafes, shooting galleries, waiting rooms, stations, lavatories, dance halls, clubs, factory entrances, ladies' restrooms, bathing beaches, and so forth. Helms recommended a 25 percent commission be paid to locations. A company spokesman acknowledged that the Depression had produced a tremendous increase in the demand for penny cigarettes. While that also should have meant more profits to storekeepers when compared to full pack sales, Helms warned that many factors contradicted this idea, such as 20 handlings for the clerk instead of one, leaks due to the storekeeper smoking himself, and employees helping themselves from broken packages. In short, the message was that VMs were the best choice. Helms argued that "Plenty of money is going to be made by those who get in on the ground floor.... The penny cig business is ideal for the retired man looking for a few hours' occupation per day; those out of employment who have a little money to invest and cannot secure work, or the college student with time on his hands who wishes to earn his way through college...."[12]

Another machine that delivered single cigarettes for a penny, 1933.

General Metal Products of St. Louis introduced its Smok-A-Taire penny vendor in 1936, publicizing it as also serving as an advertising item. The unit held 100 cigarettes and was equipped with four wings on which advertising cards for laundries, tailors, and so on could be placed. By selling the ad space for $6 per wing per year, the machine owner could pay off the cost of the machine — $24 — in one year. Later that year the Midget Vendor was promoted as producing a profit of 35 percent on the sale of penny cigarettes, after paying a commission of 15 percent to the location. If a pack of 20 cigarettes was purchased wholesale for 10 cents, 3 cents went to the location, and 7 cents remained as profit. However, single cigarette VMs would soon disappear entirely as the economy recovered.[13]

Meanwhile, full-pack cigarette VMs kept increasing in number. The

Less than two feet high, this single cigarette model was introduced in 1936, when the fad was just about over.

California Cigaret Vending Operators' Association was the first branch of the West Coast coin machine industry to prepare a code of fair practice under the provisions of the National Recovery Act (NRA), part of a package of economic reforms in the 1930s that were implemented by President Franklin D. Roosevelt in response to the Depression. Among various trade practices proposed by cigarette VM operators was a rule that there "shall be no free matches, coupons, rewards, premiums or moneys of any denomination inserted in packages or attached thereto, to be delivered free with a package of cigarettes sold thru vending machines." Additionally, location owners received no rebates other than the contracted commission rates. That rate was to range from 7.5 percent to 13.33 percent, based on the volume of business. No cigarette VM was to be placed on location unless it was under "constant" supervision. In this trade code, operators were forbidden from selling cigarette VMs to individual locations. Lastly, it was to be trade practice that all standard brands of cigarettes such as Lucky Strikes, Chesterfields, Camels, and Old Golds would be vended for 15 cents a pack.[14]

Commenting on the California cigarette code, "Silver Sam" of *Billboard* remarked that cigarette VMs had been among the most successful vendors and had enjoyed consistent progress for a number of years. However, among the problems facing them were price fluctuations, retailers selling 15 cent packs for lesser amounts, for example, and wide variations in state and city tax laws. In cities like Chicago, where a $50 license was required for each location to sell cigarettes, the use of VMs in non-licensed stores was impossible. Sam also noted objections from reform organizations "on the plea that minors can buy from the machines."[15]

In a separate article, Detroit operator Morris Davis of the Michigan Vending Company said that his company had never cut prices on 15 cent packages and, as a result, reduced prices in many other retail stores had hurt business. A recent stabilization of wholesale prices eliminated a lot of the competition from retail outlets selling packs at 10 cents. With change making capabilities nonexistent in VMs' experimental beginning, changing the price to an odd amount, 14 cents, for example, was a huge undertaking. A penny had to be manually attached to each package.[16]

When it came to locations for cigarette VMs, Abraham Bello, manager of the Detroit-based Vendo Cigaret Company, said beer gardens were not as good a location as were restaurants. For one, the former were less often patronized. In any case, beer gardens were profitable only after 8 o'clock in the evening. During the day they had no patrons, whereas restaurants opened at six or seven o'clock in the morning. The crowd may not have been as large in restaurants at certain specific times, but the patronage remained steady. Bello added, "Patrons are ready for a cigaret after a meal, but they will not always want them with their drinks."[17]

C. A. Shoemaker, of the Detroit operating concern Howes-Shoemaker, agreed that restaurants were, by far, the most successful location for cigarette VMs, "in practically any type of restaurant, aside from the ultra-exclusive places having cigaret girls." Other profitable locations included all-night spots. Shoemaker mentioned in passing that stores sold packs a cent or two cheaper than did vending machines. Rowe Manufacturing (a leading maker) believed the opening of beer gardens and taverns (beginning after repeal) had brought about a general demand for the units.[18]

Based on a 1936 survey of the average sales made through cigarette machines in various parts of the US, the manufacturer Stewart & McGuire estimated that approximately 100 million cigarettes were sold weekly through VMs, amounting to some $37 million in annual sales. Putting that in perspective was the total cigarette output—based on sales of tax stamps—of roughly 10 to 11 billion cigarettes per month. Thus, VMs accounted for approximately four percent of all cigarettes sold in America. Stewart & McGuire argued that most smokers were brand conscious, meaning the manual method of selling this product was "totally superfluous." They felt it was remarkable to observe how many more locations were realizing the desirability of being "relieved" of the task of the over-the-counter method of selling cigarettes. "Obviously they now appreciate that this function can be more efficiently fulfilled by a beautiful, silent, automatic salesman, thus avoiding the distractions and many other inconveniences incidental to manual selling."[19]

Advances continued to be made on cigarette machines. Mills Novelty introduced a new model in 1936 that had 12 columns and a 300 pack capacity. A free or penny match unit was attachable. While each column could have a different price, the unit accepted only nickels and dimes.[20]

A 1936 cigarette machine.

In 1937 St. Louis-based National Vendors became the first manufacturer to place an automatic separating unit on its line of cigarette VMs. According to the company, the unit gave an accurate counting of the machine's sales by automatically paying the location's share, ranging from 0.5 cents to 2.5 cents per pack, into a separate, second coin box within the machine, which had a separate lock and key for the location proprietor. This system was supposed to eliminate any question about the accuracy of commission payments. "Years ago, when the cigaret machine was more of a convenience to the location than a money maker, it was not as necessary that a true accounting take place," explained a National spokesman, "but today with the ever-increasing consumption of cigarets and thereby the greatly increased sale of cigarets thru vending machines the necessity for a perfected mechanical contrivance as a protection to the location has become obvious."[21]

In an article printed in their bulletin, the Cigaret Merchandisers' Association of New Jersey argued that the idea of any territory being completely full of cigarette machines was "usually unfounded." There were always locations to be secured, regardless of how "saturated" an area might be. This group advocated employing solicitors on the basis of so much per location — a system that would "usually produce results."[22]

Enemies of the cigarette VMs were not numerous in the 1930s, but occasionally they did damage. In December, 1936, the city of Chicago completely banned cigarette VMs by way of a city ordinance. Apparently agitation for such a move began early in 1935 when the Chicago Better Business Bureau placed an ad in local newspapers condemning VMs in general. Additionally, a representative of that organization appeared before the city council to argue in favor of the cigarette machine ban. A research group connected to the University of Chicago had assisted by gathering some data about minors buying tobacco from machines. The Juvenile Protective Society also apparently supported the ban. According to one article, the vending trade held a suspicion for some time that the department stores and other interests financing the Better Business Bureau supplied the impetus for the movement. It was a pity, thought the trade, "that such reputable organizations as the University of Chicago and the Juvenile Protective Society should unwittingly become a tool of special commercial interests." The ban proved to be short-lived.[23]

Balancing against this was the fact that another foe had been won over. *Tobacco Road*, a publication for retailers and distributors, had conducted a vigorous drive against cigarette VMs on the ground that such machines competed with the retailer. However, in its issue dated February 9, 1938, the publication announced a complete policy reversal. An editorial in *Tobacco Road* said, in part, "Since the onslaught of cigaret vending machines *Tobacco Road* has staunchly and fearlessly attacked the evils of these robots, which in the name of progress mercilessly vie with the tobacco retailer ... we turned away thousands of dollars in advertising by refusing to publicize or accept vending machine advertising." In arguing why the foe should be turned into a friend the editor observed that a VM in every retail tobacco outlet, to serve those in a hurry, allowed the merchant and the clerks to concentrate on higher priced merchandise requiring "sound salesmanship." Guaranteed uniform prices meant additional profits for the retailer. It all added up to be, said the editor, "a sound thesis for our 1938 campaign FOR vending machines."[24]

The well-known, high-class New York restaurant McGinnis of Sheepshead Bay opened a new location at 48th and Broadway in October, 1938. The sale of cigarettes in the establishment was left entirely to three nine-column cigarette machines. This fact was said to stand as proof of the growing realization among restaurateurs, night club operators, tavern owners, and so forth, that the cigarette VMs were an efficient and economical way to handle such sales. An enthusiastic reporter concluded, "They are a glowing testimonial of the fact that New Yorkers are becoming vending machine-conscious and are beginning to prefer to buy their cigarets from a vending machine where they can serve themselves." This placement was important precisely because it was in an upscale concern. For the most part, vending machine and jukebox operators, had great difficulty in locating their machines in any upscale spots. Such victories were few enough that they were enthusiastically celebrated in print.[25]

Jackson Bloom was the manager of New York-based operator Cigarette Service, Inc. (which handled the McGinnis units). He admitted that those in the industry had looked forward to the day when their machines would be sited in the higher class restaurants and night clubs all over the country. "But for some time the larger and higher

A 1937 cigarette machine.

class spots have been tough nuts to crack." Bloom said it had taken a lot of argument and hard work to break down the barriers, but with units in such spots as McGinnis, Jack Dempsey's, and Billy Rose's Casa Manana, he hoped the industry was on its way to realizing this goal. Reasons for resistance included the fact that many establishments felt they could make more money handling cigarette sales themselves. Also, some of the better spots believed they would be "lowering the standards" of their places by installing any device containing a coin chute. Concluded Bloom: "The ice is broken. Such installations as McGinnis ... are the crowbars we need to pry our way into similar spots throughout the land."[26]

If the penny weigh scales were unglamorous, they nevertheless remained popular and profitable throughout the 1930s. Berkeley, California's Exchange Club reported that the penny scales it purchased from a San Francisco distributor had netted the club 30 percent on its investment in a short period of time. Club management decided to invest its charity surplus fund in scales rather than at three percent interest in the bank. Receipts from the scales were turned over to the charity fund maintained by the club. The merchants in whose premises the devices were located were also club members and sited the machines for no commission.[27]

Silver Sam remarked in 1932 that a couple of years earlier the scale was largely an inconspicuous device: "The profit possibilities in weighing people in every store were entirely unappreciated. But today thousands of stores, in every town and city, are finding that accurate and attractive scales have a surprisingly popular appeal and good earning power."[28]

L. S. Lyday, a Detroit operator specializing in hotels and similar locations for Boston-based Colonial Scale Company, reported conditions were fair in his area. Lyday added that women liked to weigh themselves frequently in the summer and the newer, intimate scale, revealing the weight only to the person standing on the device, appealed especially to females. "Many women do not like their men friends to know their real weight."[29]

A scale kept inside of a store all day could be moved out front at night and, if properly secured, could increase its income from after-hours window shoppers. Main streets in towns and cities throughout America were said to have thousands of these machines so situated at night. Some of the major chain department stores such as Sears, Woolworth, and Kresge were reported in the 1930s to "follow this plan in varying degrees of thoroughness."[30]

Combination weigh scale and horoscope machine, 1937.

Within the penny bulk vending area, the use of pistachio nuts and later cashews enjoyed a certain favor in the early 1930s. However, peanuts still remained the dominant item. Silver Sam noted in 1932 that peanut machines were definitely entrenched in Brooklyn, the Bronx, Long Island, Harlem, and certain other parts of the city, but up to that time none could be found in "the rialto of the city itself." In other words, much of Manhattan. Sam stated that he saw five peanut machines in one small candy store in Brooklyn, and the storekeeper told him they all needed a new filling once a week.[31]

Reporter George Crook wrote that, unlike Chicago, there were few peanut vendors in New York. Bars in New York reportedly furnished free lunches and free saltedpeanuts to their patrons while those in Chicago did not.[32]

At the 1934 Coin Machine Exposition, Chicago's In the Bag Company displayed a new VM said to incorporate the most advanced sanitary practices. In

One of the more popular weigh scales of the 1930s, Rock-Ola's Lo-Boy.

the unit, the peanuts were placed in bulk in a clear glass bowl. When a penny was inserted, the unit automatically put the merchandise in a glassine bag and delivered it to the customer. Said to be a radical departure in the vending of bulk products, the machine was touted as 20 years ahead in the VM field. According to tests made by the company, sales were reportedly increased two to five times in locations where this type of machine was installed. Nothing more was heard of this company.[33]

In 1939, this idea resurfaced when O. D. Jennings & Company began delivery of their new, sanitary "In-a-Bag Bulk Vendor." After depositing a coin, the customer received his peanuts or other bulk product "in a fresh clean sanitary glassine bag." Pointing out the unit's advantages, a company official asserted: "Fastidious people will appreciate not getting salt or grease on their hands. People wearing gloves need not remove them to enjoy a bagful of peanuts."[34]

Candy vendors — both penny vendors of bulk candy and nickel vendors of chocolate bars — remained highly popular and well-used, surpassed perhaps only by cigarette machines. Silver Sam argued the most advanced steps in machine selling had been made in the sale of candy, with those units being "well known" in theater lobbies as well as being "very profitable" in all amusement places. Yet a few weeks later he contradicted himself by stating that, with regard to penny candy vendors, operators often complained of too small a profit margin.[35]

Nathaniel Leverone was president of the Automatic Canteen Company of America, a company described in one 1932 account as "perhaps the most spectacularly successful organization using merchandising machines for the distribution of candy in the world." Leverone declared that, while Canteen had been frequently approached to sell razor blades, toilet articles, and various other products through their VMs, they had developed their system with candy and intended to stick to this one article because of its adaptability for selling by machine. Leverone also felt many schemes and ideas for selling merchandise

A "sanitary" penny VM, 1934.

by machine were a little too far advanced for the time. Meanwhile, machine selling was becoming a significant factor in the distribution of candy. The "canteen" machines or "stores," as Leverone's firm called its VMs, had been improved recently to do a better job advertising the product for sale. Older machines carried decals which could be easily scratched and marred, but the new canteens were equipped to hold a large lithographed card extending about two-thirds the length of the machine. These cards suggested "the taste appeal of candy by illustration and by an appropriate advertising message."[36]

Canteen also utilized incentives that enjoyed a brief popularity in the 1930s. "We are trying the use of premiums to stimulate sales, and it works. Coupons are used with our merchandise, which may be returned to our headquarters for premiums," explained Leverone. He added: "We use only the standard, nationally known candy-bar goods in our machines, which brings the profit margins down. But that is the only way to maintain the reputation of machines for selling good merchandise.... We make use of 'specials' in our machines also."[37]

J. W. Coan, head of a Chicago distributing firm, was handling a new selective candy bar vendor in 1932 that dispensed up to 54 different varieties of chocolate bars. Although his firm still carried non-selective candy units, Coan declared that operators were quickly learning about the many advantages of the selective device for selling candy. Location tests had shown, he said, that a selective machine increased sales from three or four bars a day to as many as 14 bars.[38]

In response to the Depression, the pricing of Hershey chocolate bars was altered. Whereas a one-ounce bar had formerly been vended for a nickel, in the early 1930s two bars, each weighing .75 ounce, were dispensed for five cents. One account stated: "The Hershey chocolate bars have been very poplar sellers for years through vending machines, and the new idea of retailing two bars for a nickel is pepping up sales...."[39]

Coan returned late in 1937 to complain of a practice in the industry whereby vending machine companies had manufactured, specifically for them, well-known, brand name

A 1938 model of a selective candy vendor — customers could choose from a variety of bars, not just a single kind.

chocolate bars that were slightly smaller in size than the same bar found in retail outlets. For example, a bar of X ounces sold for five cents in stores while a VM firm would have the same bar made to their order to contain .9X ounces and to vend for a nickel. "I feel that every manufacturer of candy bars, and particularly those of national reputation," said Coan, "should see to it that his merchandise sold in vending machines reaches the consumer at a par of quality and value that can be purchased in the retail stores." After estimating that $15 million was spent annually on candy through VMs, Coan added: "We all know that no business has suffered the abuses as has the vending machine business. Promoters and schemers of all kinds have played upon the ignorance of people, picturing get-rich-quick schemes in the sale of candy through vending machines." A year later Coan's company was distributing a large capacity candy bar machine — the 108 bar U-Select-It VM.[40]

Candy manufacturer Pan Confections of Chicago said that, according to their sales records, the most popular candies for bulk vendors, with VM operators from coast to coast, were, in 1939: 1. Pee Wee Boston Baked Beans, hard shell; 2. Boston Baked Beans, hard shell; 3. Smooth Burnt Peanuts; 4. Assorted Licorice Pastels, hard shell; 5. Fruit Dibs, hard shell; 6. Pee Wee Smooth Burnt Peanuts; 7. Cinnamon Peanuts, hard shell; 8. Assorted Licorice Lozenges, hard shell; 9. Black and White Licorice Dibs, hard shell; and 10. Toy Jelly Beans.[41]

One new VM introduced in this period would go on to match the outstanding success of the cigarette vendor — the soft drink unit. Actually, two distinct types of units appeared in the 1930s — one vending bottled soft drinks, the other dispensing soft drinks in paper cups. Back in 1928, Coca-Cola first set about developing a low-cost effective cooler. Six months later Coke put the new design out for bids. Glascock Brothers, a sheet metal fabrication company in Muncie, Indiana, submitted the low bid of $25 per unit. Enticed by the potential of selling large numbers of coolers to Coke bottlers, Glascock eventually cut its price in half.[42]

Silver Sam commented in 1932 that drink vendors were going to make a bid for practical usefulness in places

A Hershey one-cent candy unit, 1937.

3.—Cigarettes Blaze the Way, 1932–1939

of amusement. A few attempts had already been made to launch a bottled soda vendor, but with little success. Then new on the market was a unit called the Quenchitere that was said to offer a wide selection of flavors and a large holding capacity as its chief advantages. "But the old problem of what to do to prevent loss of empty bottles is still there. This has been the bugbear of all the bottled drink vendors," wrote Sam. Nevertheless, he thought it was possible for these machines to find a "limited field of usefulness" in places of amusement.[43]

Later that year the use of drink VMs was under way to a large enough extent to give the city of Davenport, Iowa, something to think about. Davenport had no ordinance regarding the selling of soft drinks through VMs, but was looking into establishing one because retailers who sold soft drinks in their stores complained they were being discriminated against.[44]

In 1932, a new VM was displayed at the American Bottlers of Carbonated Beverages convention. Made by the Globe company of Sheboygan, Wisconsin, the machine contained five compartments, holding 12 bottles each. It had an ice compartment at the rear for the pre-cooling of 40 bottles (separate from the 60 bottles available to purchasers). As with most new coin machines of any type introduced in the era, the manufacturer claimed it was "fully slug proof."[45]

Throughout this period, major soft drink makers such as Coca-Cola encouraged their bottlers to enter the bottled soft drink vending field. An ex-real estate man, Elmer F. Pierson, and three associates formed the Vendo Company in Kansas City in 1936 to market a vending top for existing reach-in Coca-Cola coolers. The machine was made by the Mills Novelty Company. When it had been on the market for a little over a year, some 3,000 of the machines had been sold and placed on locations. A contemporary account observed: "The machine is equipped as a complete electric refrigerator, with a vending capacity of 104 bottles and also a reserve of 108 bottles pre-cooled.... The automatic feature of the coin operation is stressed, as there is not cranking or pushing of button necessary to get the merchandise." By the time production of bottled soft drink machines was halted in 1942 (along with other coin-operated machines, and other items, due to the war), tens of thousands of bottled soft drink machines were a familiar sight at grocery stores, service stations, and other locations across America.[46]

Lincoln Park Zoo in Chicago was the test site in 1934 for the first self-contained cup-type soft drink VM. After testing and revising his drink machine during that summer, inventor Leslie Arnett permanently placed it for public use in a W. F. Monroe Cigar Store in Chicago in April, 1935. One year later, the group with which Arnett worked formed the Vendrink Company and the cup (or bulk) soft drink dispensing phase of the industry began.[47]

The J. P. Seeburg Company of Chicago introduced its own machine in 1936, a single-flavor, 200-cup capacity machine similar to the Vendrink. Mixing the exact amount of syrup with the proper amount of sufficiently carbonated water took four seconds from the time a nickel was inserted. The greatest obstacle to overcome was the perfection of a small carbonator that could produce highly carbonated water.[48]

In 1937-1938, Bally Manufacturing Company, also of Chicago, produced the first practical premixed cup drink vendor, which dispensed the drinks from already carbonated tanks. Around the same time, inventor W. W. Bowman of Dallas, Texas, developed the Frostidrink machine, first as a single flavor unit then as a two-drink vendor.[49]

For every success in vending there were many more failures. One of the biggest busts of the 1930s was the attempt to produce a popcorn vendor. *Billboard* observed in 1932 that at least two popcorn VMs had been announced to the trade within the previous 12 months.[50] One of the firms, the Ohio Popcorn company, had manufactured a large line of popcorn machines (not coin-operated). At one point it had developed and promoted an automatic electric popcorn VM which produced a bag of the item after the deposit of 10 cents. According to one report, "The machine had considerable novelty to it due to its automatic mechanism. The customer could see much of the operations of filling and discharging the package after depositing the coin."[51] It went out of business completely later in 1932.

Rising out of the aftermath of that business failure, and taking over the patents of the Ohio Popcorn concern, was the newly organized Cleveland Popcorn Company. At the end of 1932, it was stressing its Electrovend coin-operated corn popper after giving the machine what it described as "very thorough testing," the result of over seven years of practical development. Ten of the units had received extensive tests on the Boardwalk at Atlantic City. Company manager William D. Root explained that, "With this unique device a floor space of only 30 by 30 inches is required.... It is suggested that the operator pay 25 per cent of the gross for the location, including the electricity. He nets 75 percent less cost of material, which amounts to about 15 percent maximum. Thus the operator can count on about 60 cents to the dollar." Root added that the machine was built to take advantage of the enormous sales created through the demonstration of popping corn, which had always "been very fascinating to the public." Customers could watch as the machine measured raw corn into the popping chamber, popped it over electric coils, and then separated the popped kernels. Popped kernels passed into a large (reserve) heating

3.—Cigarettes Blaze the Way, 1932–1939

oven where they were drawn upon after the insertion of a coin. When the nickel or dime was deposited, a shower of popped corn was blown five feet up through a tube where it spiraled into a measuring device. From there the popcorn ran down through 17 streams of warm butter into the dispenser where a measured amount of salt was added. A full popping cycle took three minutes, but service to the patron reportedly took just 20 seconds — provided enough was in the reserve area. Exclaimed Root: "All of this spectacle is exhibited under glass and proves an unusual attraction to the public.... The popping display to the public attracts additional onlookers, who usually wind up with an appetite for popcorn themselves." The machine had a cash box in the bottom with a separate key from the one that opened the machine area for servicing. Root argued the Electrovend eliminated the two usual sources of loss that all manually operated eating stands faced — loss of product eaten by operators and other employees, and the loss of cash through dishonesty.[52]

Top left: Bally's Coca-Cola machine in Montgomery Ward's department store, St. Paul, Minnesota, 1939.
Top right: Bally's unit installed at a Los Angeles service station, 1939.
Above: Bally's Coke VM in the West Coast ticket office of United Airlines, 1939.

Little else happened in the popcorn VM field until late in 1937 when a subsidiary of Daval Manufacturing (Chicago), Ranel, Inc., announced it was in production on U-Pop-It — said to be a sensational new merchandise vendor attracting much attention. Company president A. S. Douglas declared

A 1934 popcorn machine.

that at no time in the history of the coin machine business had there been a greater need for legitimate vending equipment. Alluding to the official and unofficial community pressure on pin and slot (gambling) devices, Douglas explained that "Operators the country over have seen their incomes shrink through the questioning of legality of this or that type of amusement game ... the need was never greater for a really fine piece of equipment in the legitimate merchandise vending field." In a fashion similar to his predecessors, Douglas also stressed the drawing power of having the popping operations clearly visible to onlookers. They received "a bag of delicious hot pop corn, all made and sacked and salted to suit their individual taste in one minute—for five cents—just one lonely nickel."[53]

Another entrant into the field in 1938 was Popmatic Manufacturing Company. Company vice president V. H. Rowlette recalled that the first Popmatic VM, built in 1934, had to be scrapped, as did the next, and the one after that, and so on, totaling 31 failures. "We lived, slept and dreamed automatic pop-corn machines, never losing faith that some day we would have an automatic machine, coin-controlled, that would create a new industry," reminisced Rowlette, stating "that one day the public would receive a large bag of fresh hot pop corn, scientifically popped by a sanitary method, without the necessity of an attendant."[54]

Said to have moved beyond the experimental stage, some of the more optimistic operators were already prophesying that popcorn machines would soon become as important a factor in the VM field as candy, gum, and cigarette machines. Popmatic general sales manager Walter Gummersheimer called the popcorn VM area the fastest growing and most profitable business among the "new industries" of America. He described the devices as time savers and compared them to having extra salesmen in the store without having their names added to the payroll.[55]

Yet another machine was called Airpops-It. In 1938 the company announced that, after six weeks of tests, the Walgreen Drug Company would soon install 300 of its popcorn VMs throughout the company's coast to coast chain. According to company sales manager H. H. Hull, drug store managers everywhere were demanding the machine because it was a bigger sales stimulant than the penny scales found in virtually all drug stores; it created a thirst, thereby stimulating business at the outlet's soda fountain. Airpops-It popped the kernels dry by a fan blowing past a small heating element rather than using hot oil as did some models. A bag of seasoned popcorn was delivered to the customer in a little over a minute's time. All of these models failed because the technology needed to deliver the manufacturers' promises on a reliable and efficient basis was not there. Fires from hot VMs were not just a danger, but an occasional fact. Added to fire hazards was the cost of regular mechanical breakdowns. Also, nothing indicated the product delivered was of an acceptable quality to the consumer.[56]

Top: The Popmatic unit, 1938.
Bottom: The Popmatic on location somewhere in St. Louis, 1938.

Attempts to vend other food items also enjoyed little to no success. Sandwich machines began around 1930. At that time the Food Service Company made a food vendor which sold sandwiches and other food items at 10 cents, and was reported to have been a success in its mostly factory locations. However, the company went out of business in the early 1930s. The National Sales Machine Company was producing a sandwich vendor in 1932. Also mentioned was the Jenkins sandwich VM which was said to have received a lot of publicity a few years prior to 1932. Also reported in 1932, a New York firm had a machine for vending coffee. None of the machines in the 1930s designed to vend sandwiches or coffee were successful.[57]

Vending fruit juices, either fresh or canned, proved impossible in

Another popcorn model, 1938.

this period. One of the largest distributors of fresh orange juice in America became interested in a VM to sell its products. A number of machines were placed out on test sites in 1931 and, while sales were reported to have been excellent, "there were many technical points unsolved, and one of them has always been the necessity of agitating the juice constantly." Apparently several different types of juice vendors were introduced around this time, but, commented Silver Sam, "a machine for dispensing fruit juices and similar drinks has two serious problems, the preservation of the liquid and providing proper refrigeration."[58]

The Florida Citrus Exchange reported in 1939 that six orange juice VMs, the first to be made for commercial testing, would be ready in a matter of weeks. Plans were to deliver a cup of chilled juice fresh from an orange for a nickel.[59]

Around the same time, Wichita, Kansas, operator John S. Stevens handled eight-column vendors manufactured by the Can-O-Juice Company of Cleveland, through which he vended seven flavors of canned juice. Standing over six feet tall, these units had a refrigeration system. Each machine also had a mechanism for punching a hole in the can into which a straw could be inserted. Straws were kept in a recessed container on the device. After finishing his drink, the customer could dispose of the empty can in a bin built into the VM. However, admitted Stevens, "there were a good many bugs in the machine."[60]

Fresh fruit vending, mainly of apples, was also tried in this period with no success. Extensive experiments were conducted in Chicago during the winter of 1930-1931 with apple vendors constructed by a Portland, Oregon-based manufacturer. In 1932 Silver Sam admitted that he did not know what happened to them, but speculated that "The appearance of unemployed men on the city streets selling apples has no doubt been a discouragement to the progress of the fruit-vending machines."

Sam talked to one restaurant owner who had an apple VM in his place of business, and had given it a favorable location near the front entrance,

3. — Cigarettes Blaze the Way, 1932–1939   69

Yet another popcorn "robot," 1938.

but "He did not seem so enthusiastic about it." Among the companies manufacturing fruit vendors in the 1932 period were the Ford Vending Machine Company, the Fruit Vending Machine Company, and the H. N. Knight Company. An apple growers' association in the Pacific Northwest reportedly had plans to make extensive use of vending machines. Some of the machines announced were also made to sell oranges.[61]

In a 1935 discussion over whether or not permission had been granted by New York City (Manhattan) officials to place some VMs in city buildings, it was revealed that a number of apple machines had been so sited by the Fruit Automat, Inc. The company was to give the city 20 percent of the apple machines' gross receipts.[62]

Unsuccessful attempts to vend ice cream were made regularly. *Billboard*'s Silver Sam acknowledged that he took a keen personal interest in refrigerated vendors of all kinds and was hopeful a machine would be developed to successfully dispense frozen confections. He did admit that "Up to the present I have not been able to observe such a machine actually work and stand up under the stress of selling conditions." Acknowledging that the problems involved were great, Sam added that "some leaders in the trade have said it will be impossible to construct a vendor to dispense them [frozen confections] successfully, except when the machine is given almost constant attention."[63]

One of many people working on the problem was the head of a distributing firm J. W. Coan. He had been working on a machine for ice cream and frozen products and, in 1932, Coan said: "I spent several thousand dollars in trying to get a machine that would work successfully with dry ice as refrigeration but found it impossible to control the temperature and keep it within reason." It was an interesting piece of work, he thought, and if there ever was a development for controlling the temperature from dry ice, "then I have my mechanism all ready." Arguing that refrigeration was the sole problem in constructing machines for selling frozen products, Coan said that devices using electric refrigeration were possible, but that dry ice would allow a much wider placing of machines as well as lessen the manufacturing costs and weight of the unit.[64]

The Ice Cream Vending Machine Company of Kansas City, Missouri, first displayed its Ice Cream Bar VM to the trade at a 1931 convention. It received a lot of attention at the time due to the refrigeration by dry ice feature, but it had to be withdrawn after some "bugs" were discovered. In 1933, it was finally reintroduced to the market. Using dry ice, the VM maintained a temperature of zero degrees or lower, and handled ice cream bars of any size up to 3.5 inches long by 1.62 inches wide. Capacity of the Eskimo Pie type was 60 bars. George A. Aylsworth, company president, declared that "The market for ice cream bars is already made, and we feel that we have the machine for the operator to sell them and cash in on the popularity of frozen confections."[65]

Yet another new ice cream vendor was placed on two busy New York subway stations' platforms in 1937. Manufactured by a firm from the Netherlands, the unit had a capacity of 150 bars that were kept frozen by dry ice. Cost to the patron was five cents per bar.[66]

Some success was achieved in vending milk. Louisville-based Kentucky Dairies installed and serviced milk VMs in plants, offices, and shops in 1938. A cold bottle of milk was delivered for a nickel from a vending machine that was serviced daily and electrically refrigerated to dispense the milk at a temperature of less than 40 degrees.[67]

Within the non-food area (cigarettes excluded), vending was tried for a number of items, most of the efforts proving unsuccessful. Compared to food and cigarette vending, the automatic dispensing of non-food items was a very small part of the industry. Books, magazines, and newspapers continued to receive the occasional mention, but the future for them as vended items was not seen as bright. Reporter H. F. Reves commented in 1937 that a few machines could still be found selling magazines, particularly the *Saturday Evening Post*. He added that machines used for vending large objects such as periodicals tended to be rather cheaply constructed, making damage or pilferage easier to accomplish. While acknowledging that some newspapers had been sold by VMs, Reves felt the size of the machine required to handle a newspaper, the variable thickness of the paper and number of sections, difficulties with the large Saturday or Sunday supplements, and the low price of the product made such ventures "poor profit-making" propositions. Further discouraging factors were the competition from newsboys on every important corner, papers in every kind of retail store, and the short life of the merchandise. These early newspaper VMs were not the simplified honor boxes that would later dominate that field.[68]

In 1939, book publisher E. Haldeman-Julius of Girard, Kansas, placed his Blue Books in machines. They were available in the Little Blue Book Vendor manufactured by the Automatic Libraries Division of O. D. Jennings & Company and units were installed in subways, bus stations, drug stores, and so on. Each VM contained 18 different titles at 10 cents apiece. Haldeman-Julius claimed the machines were a "sensational" success. He said that in 20 years he had sold 200 million Little Blue Books by mail. From his list of 1,800 titles, he intended to supply VMs with different books every month, with a professed hope of selling one million books a week.[69]

Top: An ice cream bar vendor from 1933.
Bottom: The Little Blue Book Vendor, 1939.

One non-food item that did enjoy great success in the 1930s was the coin-operated washing machine. If the field was just getting started in 1929, it spread quickly — one 1938 account said the field was getting overcrowded. Most of these machines were located in larger apartment houses on the usual basis, with the operator owning and servicing the units while giving the apartment house a percentage of the gross receipts.[70]

In 1936 in Buffalo, New York, an Easy washing machine dealer named Lars Hedstrom came upon the idea of putting a number of coin-operated washing machines in a single store. He called his outlet the Launder-Ur-Own Station, thus giving birth to a new kind of automatic service business — the Laundromat.[71]

Razor blades could also be found in machines. The Trophy Tower Sales Corporation of Cleveland held a contract with the Trophy Blade company for the exclusive distribution of Trophy razor blades. That machine first became available in 1931 and, around the same time, the Automatic Retailing Corporation was distributing a new vendor designed to retail Duke razor blades at two for 10 cents or five for a quarter.[72]

Aspirin was one of the only medical products to be found in American vendors, and only to a limited extent. Squibb aspirin came on the market in 1931 and engaged in an advertising battle with Bayer aspirin, who until then had a near monopoly. The resulting publicity and a general trend to self-medication were listed as reasons for an increase in aspirin sales through VMs. However, a number of states had legal statutes forbidding the sale of drugs except where a registered pharmacist was in charge. Reporter Reves made similar observations before mentioning that a couple of Detroit firms had manufactured aspirin vendors that failed. Reves felt the requirements of a fresh stock and a careful servicing of machines had not been met — faults of the operator and not the maker.[73]

Less available in VMs were condoms. Detroit city council passed an ordinance in 1934 banning the sale of prophylactic rubber goods or any form of contraception in coin-operated machines. The ordinance was designed to restrict sales of such products to registered pharmacists and druggists and had the support of the Detroit Retail Druggists' Association. Such sales in Detroit had been "negligible," but the law was passed just in case the situation changed.[74]

A new perfume vendor came on the market in 1938 when Mechanical Sales Corporation of New York introduced its new machine after two years of development and six months of location tests. This machine vended perfume in small bottles, not as a mist to be caught on a handkerchief. It dispensed the Ris-Charde perfumes in small cut-glass, purse-sized flasks containing a dram. With five columns the VM could hold 12 boxes of each of the five odors chosen by the company as being the most popular.[75]

Soap had been vended in various ways with the most successful being the industrial soap vendor for hand paste soap. One such unit was made by the National Dispensing Corporation and operated on one cent. The unit held two standard paste soap cans, each weighing eight to 10 pounds. After a coin was deposited, the soap passed over a knife that cut the soap to the appropriate size. Eight years had been spent in developing this vendor, followed by two more years of testing in which 30 machines were placed in industrial plants. Finally, in 1936, the device went into full production. Factories were the locations mainly targeted by the maker although other, general locations were also considered. Apparently at this time factories required their workers to supply their own soap.[76]

Perfume VM, 1938.

Born during this period, parking meters were quickly embraced by city after city. On the occasion of the device's first birthday, Albert Silberman, general sales manager of National Parkograf, observed that revenue was estimated at 40 cents per meter per day. Cost was generally a nickel per hour. Rock-Ola Manufacturing Corporation had recently expanded its plant by an additional 65,000 square feet of space for the exclusive manufacturing of the Parkograf meter. "It is significant that a coin-operated machine is destined to be adopted in the not too distant future to solve one of the nation's most perplexing problems," said Silberman. "The parking meter is the solution to the heretofore hopelessly tangled problem of traffic regulation and control."[77]

Louis A. Colen, a Detroit operator, handled, among other VMs, an automatic typewriter made by the Coin Automatic Company of San Francisco. It gave 30 minutes of use for 10 cents and was said by Colen to have proven to be very valuable to a number of hotels in the city. Colen felt it was an area with sound growth potential as it was a service a modern hotel would have to provide for commercial travelers and other business guests.[78]

There were also the strange—and downright dangerous—oddities of the time. Machines dispensing fluid fuel for cigarette lighters in the form of "gas station" pumps were made from about 1930 by the National Vending Company of Detroit. They proved a popular item and were still on location in some territories in 1937. D. Robbins & Company offered a penny lighter fluid dispenser in 1934 said to earn 90 percent profit on every dollar in revenue. Ordinary cleaner's naphtha was used as the fuel.[79]

A first attempt to clean clothes automatically was launched when a machine called the Val-A-Vac was built in San Francisco in 1932. Nickel-operated, it incorporated an electric vacuum that its inventor claimed would pull the dust and dirt from clothes and hats. Designed for use on Pullman railroad cars and in rest rooms, it failed to displace the old-fashioned whisk broom.[80]

In 1939, Stockton, California-based Viped-Ex Corporation announced the completion of their latest model of the coin-operated Foot Oscillator, a massaging VM for tired feet. Built with the cooperation of the General Electric Company, the machine sat on the floor and was shaped to comfortably accommodate both feet. On an inclined surface were two vibrating discs that, said the firm, stimulated circulation and massaged the feet. Shoes were removed prior to the treatment. Said a company official: "The method of operation is simple, the physiological principles are simple and the effects on the foot-ailing public are profound.... It has won the endorsement of stage and screen stars." Company officials concluded that "The Foot Oscillator will reduce foot fatigue and at the same time pile up many dimes in the cashbox for operators."[81]

Pacific Amusement Manufacturing marketed the Shinette, which gave an automatic shoeshine for two cents. A sample

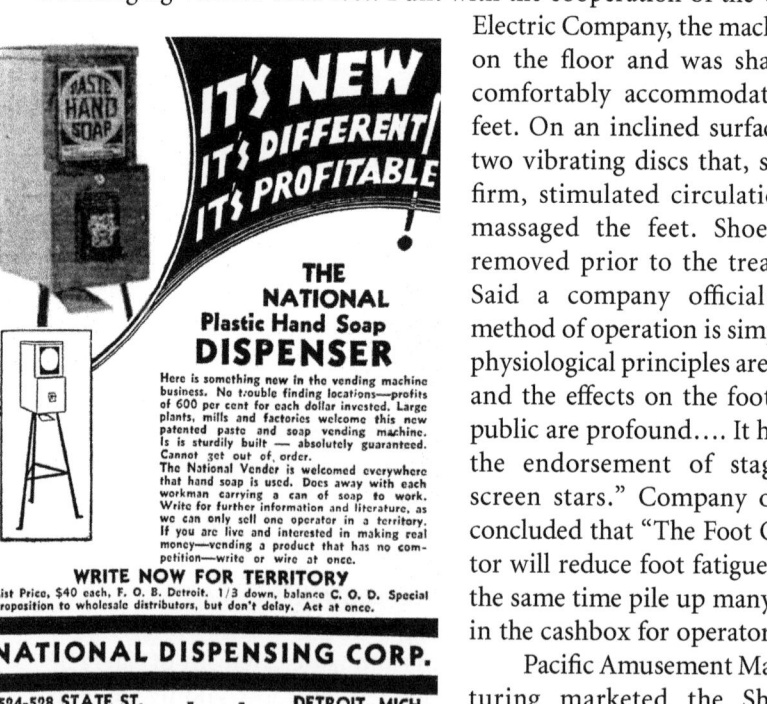

Hand soap dispenser, 1936.

machine in the office of Pinkerton's National Detective Agency was "enthusiastically" received by agents "intent on personal neatness and they stood in line to get at the polish and whirling brushes." Distributing firm Gibb-Lewis representatives said they confidently expected to revolutionize the shoe-shining habits of the nation: "Millions of Americans polish their own shoes with the old brush and rag method. These will never change to the 10-cent-shine class of people, but they will pause to use a machine that does the work for 2 cents without the fuss and time taken by an operator."[82]

Another device that enjoyed a brief and limited popularity was the fortune telling or astrology machine. In Washington, D. C., the first one appeared around 1935 in the lobby of the Keith Theater near the White House. According to reports, after only a few weeks it was grossing up to $300 a week. Also, the forecast machine was said to be "going like a house afire" in Britain.[83]

Louis Colen also handled the Planetellus Astrology machine. He had placed a dozen or more in theaters, many calling attention to the machine in the lobby with the use of a special trailer on the screen to advertise it. Colen had also placed a number of units in downtown Detroit department stores. In 1937 he said: "We are almost alone in this field. It has been tried in New York, Chicago and elsewhere but operators have not seemed to succeed with it. However, we have been getting along well." Discussing limitations, he said the field was limited to just two major types of locations—theaters and department stores. Also, "The Planetellus is strictly a vending machine giving a specialized service, and usually one person will patronize the machine only once but the field is wide as far as potential customers are concerned."[84]

In 1938, manufacturer Rock-Ola introduced its Talkie Horoscope, the machine that "talked" to the future and gave printed horoscopes to people at a dime apiece. James Harvey, the astrologer who compiled the dispensed birthday readings, declared: "These birthday readings from the Talkie Horoscope are a splendid guide for everyday living. One reading is most helpful, but if a person secures the entire set of 10 for his own birth date, then he will have a much more complete and detailed horoscope."[85]

The Foot Ease Vitalizer, 1939.

Planetellus Astrology machine, 1935.

With regard to locations for VMs in the 1930s, nothing received quite as much attention as the drive to "modernize" the public washroom. That vision was defined as filling all of the "empty space" found in washrooms with as many vending machines as possible, thus turning them into profit centers for operators. Things taken for granted today as freely available in those facilities—such as soap and paper towels—were to all be put on a fee paying basis. *Billboard*'s Silver Sam felt that comfort stations, washrooms, lounging rooms, and so on, were just so much necessary overhead for hotels, theaters, and other buildings. "Few have stopped to consider what a fine array of coin-operated vending and amusement machines the automatic trade offers to provide a service and at the same time yield some returns from these public rooms," he said. According to his figures, more than 20 different types of machines were especially recommended for use in washrooms, including a full line of Hy-G-Toi dispensers and the Berghman shoe-brushing and shoe shining (separate machines) units. The latest addition was the Samco Toothbrush Vendor. For five cents a sterilized toothbrush sealed in cellophane and a small amount of tooth powder were dispensed. From a Kansas City manufacturer came a lipstick vendor, including a small capsule of face powder, all for a nickel. At least two or three large organizations operating on a national basis were leasing sanitary napkin VMs to locations. Sam was a big proponent of the idea of modernizing washrooms and had long advocated that there was a place for specialized operators dealing only with restrooms and comfort stations.[86]

A 1932 account observed that penny scales, toilet seat cover vendors, and prophylactic vendors were about the only coin machines then found in modern comfort stations and restrooms. After summarizing some of the other types of VMs available for use in such locations, the article concluded that "Pay-toilet locks are already standard, of course."[87]

3.—Cigarettes Blaze the Way, 1932–1939　　　77

In 1932, Chicago's Medical Products Sales Company offered an extensive line of staple medicinal and sanitary products for sale through VMs. It claimed to be the first firm in the country to offer a complete line of products that would be introduced and sold strictly through vending machines. Their products included such items as aspirin, prophylactics, ladies hygiene powder, perfume, anti-acid tabs, sunburn lotion, a cold remedy, and indigestion tabs, among others. A standard type of machine, an upright metal cabinet with a square base and top, had been developed to handle those products. A removable base meant it could also be placed on a counter or fastened to a wall. While Medical Products recommended these vendors for many locations such as lunchrooms, confectioneries, service stations, and factories, they were offered as "especially suited to the modern movement for equipping restroom and comfort stations with a full line of service and vending machines." Medical Products was reported ready to push "the movement for a better type of restroom for all it is worth." Hotels, restaurants, clubs, theaters, bus stations, airports, and many other types of public buildings had been forced, said one account, to stint on the money put into restrooms, "except where prestige required an expensive outlay, because the restroom has always been an expense with very little if any income." A successful move to modernize restrooms would mean a "fair income" could be derived from comfort stations.[88]

Also in 1932, a Chicago distributor named the Wardell Company, poised to undertake a program of national advertising, explained it had a plan to place VMs for selling specialized products with operators all over the country. Wardell Company president I. W. Schulman explained: "We started out some time ago with a machine for selling prophylactic goods. Maybe we ought to have been shot for that...." Although they still handled those machines, Wardell's main merchandising machine was then a vendor for dispensing Midol tablets in ladies' restrooms. "This is proving to be a new and very profitable field." Wardell had an exclusive arrangement with the makers of Midol tablets, whereby they dispensed a small glass tube containing two Midol tablets from their units for 10 cents. Schulman said, "I understand that the *Billboard* has become an advocate of the modernized restroom. Well, you can put our service down as catering directly to that field. We offer a neat, attractive machine for installing in ladies' restrooms to vend a product which meets a real need." He added that *Billboard*'s idea of publicizing the need to modernize restrooms by installing the latest vending and service machines "is certainly a great work, and the movement should become national." Midol vendors recently installed in the Sears Roebuck stores in Milwaukee and Chicago had indicated, said Schulman, "how important concerns are coming to recognize the movement for modernized restrooms."[89]

E. H. Faber, president of the Famill Corporation, also discussed the movement to modernize washrooms. He explained that machines for selling penny or nickel cakes of well-advertised brands of toilet soap were also available for use in restrooms. The long list of potential locations for Faber's soap machines included day coaches of trains, hotels, schools, public lavatories, beaches, resorts, swimming pools, clubs, YMCAs, community centers, steamships, theater dressing rooms, carnivals, fairs, circuses, and many others. According to Faber, the principle underlying the demand for soap sold by machine "is that the average person doesn't want soap that has been used by someone else." Worried that soap vended for a penny might not entice operators, he felt the vend price might have to be a nickel. Famill was then trying to develop a machine that would dispense a towel "and a thin piece of soap sufficient for one washing." Faber felt that with a well-advertised brand of soap, such as Lux, there was no question about the soap being sold in quantity. One of the stranger ideas was uncovered when Faber, discussing the paper toilet seat cover VM, remarked: "The possibilities of having advertising printed on the sanicover paper is being investigated by more than one firm making products known nationally." Twenty percent was said to be the standard commission that operators of toilet seat cover VMs paid to locations.[90]

Toilet seat cover VM, 1933.

Silver Sam happily announced in 1933 that the Railway Express Agency had started to install 50,000 cosmetic VMs in its restrooms and was training many of its agents in the servicing of those machines. He thought that products for sale in restrooms should be items that came under the classification of emergency demand, everything from aspirin to hair pins. Railway Express's move coupled with the VM installation at the Chicago World's Fair of 1933 were felt to be big advertising and publicity boosts that would dramatically advance the cause of the modern restroom.[91]

As part of the move to modernize restrooms, Los Angeles-based Utility Coin Machine began

3.—Cigarettes Blaze the Way, 1932–1939

to manufacture and market a new hand lotion dispenser. It was recommended for "high-grade" department stores, theaters, office buildings, and other places frequented by women. A company spokesman explained that hand lotions had proved to be the only effective means of counteracting the "potent acids which are present in all forms of liquid soap." Many complaints were said to be made by women patrons to managers of these types of locations on the harshness of the soap in their restrooms. According to Utility, nine out of ten women used hand lotion and, after washing their hands in the public rooms, they would turn "automatically" to the hand lotion VMs.[92]

The men's restroom on the lower level of the terminal building in New York's Grand Central Terminal was checked for machines by a reporter in 1935. There were two Repeatoscope machines, one showing moving pictures of Sally Rand doing her fan dance and the other showing the Louis-Baer fight pictures. Each cost a nickel. "There is also a blood-pressure tester here as well as two or three pin-games, a handkerchief vendor, soap and towel vendors and much other automatic equipment."[93]

The Chicago fair of 1933 was seen as one of the most important events in vending history with regard to the publicity it could generate for VMs, especially in the move to modernize washrooms. A "Century of Progress," as the fair was called, opened May 27, 1933, and closed in October. Even prior to the opening, it was said that the restrooms and toilets on site would be ultra modern examples of the use of coin devices of all kinds in such locations. "The examples thus created will advance the idea of modernization of restrooms through the use of coin vending and service machines by at least five years, it is expected." Instead of using coin-controlled locks on the stalls themselves, the entrance to the facility was equipped with a coin turnstile that admitted the patron to the vestibule and restroom areas. Brooks Contracting had the concession for installing and equipping the restrooms throughout the fairgrounds, though some of the VMs were placed on a concession basis by other firms. Penny weigh scales as well as paper cup vendors were to be placed in all restrooms, but liquid soap dispensers were "furnished free as a part of the service given on general admission." Candy sales were confined to counter concessions in the restrooms. Also located in the women's restrooms were sanitary napkin machines, toilet seat cover VMs, and Midol units. A Brooks spokesman said, "we plan to use every type of high-grade machine that appears to be practical in such locations. By confining our concessions to strictly high-grade propositions it should be the greatest advertising possible for the idea of using vending machines in restrooms."[94]

Billboard heralded the official opening of the fair by declaring, "for the first time in the world's history coin-operated amusement and vending devices occupy a significant place in a major celebration." On the midway were two amusement arcades with modern coin-operated amusement devices. Some 50 comfort stations were located on the fairgrounds, filled with amusement and vending devices. The Brooks firm stated that it was a designed purpose to make those facilities "an example of coin-operated equipment for the modern restroom. Access to the pay stations is gained by depositing a nickel in the turnstile." In each of those restrooms, there was an assortment of amusement devices including, for example, an Atlas Indicator baseball machine, an Iron Claw, a Sportsman target, and Marble-Jax pin games. Installed vendors included dispensers for Kleenex tissue, Vend-Card toilet seat cover vendors, a shoe-shine machine, and other service devices. Penny weigh scales were operated at the fair both in restrooms and on the fairgrounds.[95]

From the start of the fair, however, there were complaints about the admission charge just to enter a restroom. Under the terms of its contract, Brooks was to provide free access to 20 percent of the restrooms. Complainants were from concession holders who sold, among other things, beer. They alleged that the free toilets were all placed under Soldiers' Field Stadium and along the beaches, clustered together and a long walk from most of the fair's action.[96]

VMs also made an appearance as part of the fair's attractions. Allied Coin Machine had a display exhibit in the Transportation Building that included a Seeburg jukebox, a Rock-Ola Loboy scale, and several penny merchandisers. Two or three models of a coin-operated Kotex vendor were on display in the regular booth of the West Disinfecting Company.[97]

Chicago's World's Fair returned for a second and final year in the summer of 1934. A wide difference in the type of VMs on site was noticeable. All of the amusement devices were gone from the 1934 edition — the two arcades themselves and all the amusement devices housed in the restrooms. Supposedly the disappearance was because of the high price asked for concession space. Also absent were the coin-entry restrooms. Merchandise and service machines were still found scattered liberally about the fair buildings: toilet door coin locks, 30 locations; 200 coin lockers; over 120 candy bar, peanut, and gum VMs; 28 coin telescopes and 25 coin binoculars; 75 Jergens hand lotion dispensers; 50 sanitary belt machines; 100 penny scales; 50 cold cream and cleansing tissue machines; 75 cloth towel and soap dispensing devices; 75 Kotex and paper towel machines; and an unspecified number of paper cup VMs. The obvious failure of the coin-operated, "modernized" restroom to catch on doomed the concept. It was a dream that did not die immediately, but rather faded slowly away. Never again would the public restroom be looked upon by the vending industry as a profit center waiting to happen.[98]

A popular location for VMs in the 1930s was in cinemas. The idea of wasted space appeared here also, in a 1932 *New York Times* editorial which read, in part: "Lobbies of movie palaces ... have for some time past been eyed resentfully as waste space by their owners ... they were not paying a penny for their existence." Someone "desperately" disregarded that atmosphere of luxury by installing a weight scale and a candy and chewing gum machine. Soon all the cinemas had them, "and though some have been discontinued, most lobbies are now supplied, for they have been found highly profitable." Reportedly, a few lobbies even contained sandwich and soft drink machines. One theater chain determined that its returns from the machines were far greater in proportion than the profits from the films. In an unnamed sanitarium town, the scales paid off handsomely because "The patients go to the movies in the evening and always get weighed to see if they are getting better."[99]

In 1934 columnist Silver Sam was asked for his advice on what machines to put in cinemas if an operator could get full coin machine rights to a group of theaters. First, he cited the experience of the Automatic Canteen Company which had placed an elite type of candy bar unit in a number of cinema lobbies. However, the slugging of those devices in Chicago theater lobbies became a serious handicap. Canteen head Nathaniel Leverone said that during the depression [apparently he thought it was over by 1934] it was impossible for merchandising machines to compete in places like big theater lobbies with counter sales of candy by attractive girls. "Salesgirls could be had for $5 a week and machines could not compete with that." Still, Silver Sam believed the elite cabinet type of candy VM was the most acceptable for lobby locations. He also advised the placing of cigarette vendors. Theaters with smoking rooms or balcony space offered very favorable space for candy bar machines, amusement machines, and cigarette machines unless prohibited by local ordinances. He also felt amusement machines had a place in cinemas, although they sometimes caused people to congregate around them to such a degree that building or fire regulations could be breached. Given his previously noted enthusiasm, Sam was also highly in favor of putting VMs in theater restrooms—machines such as scales, cosmetic vendors, Kleenex tissue units, aspirin machines, other medicinal devices, perfume vendors, and towel, cup, and toilet seat cover machines. The then-new type of nut vendor—which sold nuts in small envelopes or bags—would not be out of place in men's restrooms in cinemas, declared Sam.[100]

Offering somewhat different advice at the same time was vending trade executive William Gersh, who commented that it had been learned that more ornate machines must be designed for cinemas than had been used for the ordinary type of location. The slug evil managed to find its way into the theater and, at one period, "almost discouraged the operators pioneering in this field." At one point it was believed, he said, that coin-operated amusement devices would take the lead in theatrical locations, but time had proved that merchandising machines were best suited to the field. "The theater has therefore confined itself largely to using automatic merchandising equipment." Discussing the much earlier cinema experiments with back-of-the-seat devices, Gersh said they failed "since they were not only subject to slugging, but in many cases were actually ripped from the backs of seats and carried from the premises under cover of the darkness that prevails in theatrical houses." Other problems early vendors experienced included the use of below-standard merchandise and stale product. With regard to the time in which he was writing, Gersh thought one of the biggest obstacles to vendor success was competition from counter sales. "The machine can hardly compete with the attractive girls that stand behind these counters well located in theater lobbies." Low wages paid to these women "have certainly handicapped the expansion of merchandising machines in this field." In some cases, grumbled Gersh, operators had lost profitable cinema locations because management was able to lease the space formerly used by the VMs to a concessionaire for a candy counter.[101]

One large theater chain had accepted VMs to the extent that it bought its own machines, trained its own help to run them, and received the best wholesale prices on candy through its large buying power. Max Schosberg, director of merchandising machine activities for Paramount Theaters, was given the job by Paramount to develop and adapt automatic merchandising to profitable use in their cinemas. All VMs in Paramount houses from coast to coast were under his supervision. Home base for the executive was at the Paramount Theater in Times Square, New York City, where an average of 75,000 people paid admission every week. In that house were 10 of the "most modern de luxe merchandising machines," including a cigarette machine. Also located there were 10 ticket scales—tickets with weight and fortune on one side and a picture of a popular Paramount star on the other. An estimated 3,000 pennies—about four percent of the admissions—went into those scales every week. Only nationally advertised candy and confections were bought by Paramount for use in the VMs. Experience showed that the most profitable spots in theaters were the front lobbies where the machines greeted the patrons. Paramount's chief criticism of the devices was that "it is difficult to find machines to harmonize with the attractive surroundings of their theater lobbies." However, it was also noted that

3.—Cigarettes Blaze the Way, 1932–1939

counter sales were then being used in many of the cinemas and that the counter system was being extended.[102]

An example of an independent operator servicing cinemas was the Sanitary Automatic Candy company of New York, which looked after about 4,000 theaters throughout New York State where one or more VMs were in operation. Sanitary also ran candy counter operations in many of those houses, claiming it was "forced" to do so in order to make a reasonable profit. The VM system in theaters, said the firm, "has not yet proved to be generally successful." Most of the independent operators were reported to use private brands of candy (which wholesaled more cheaply than did nationally advertised brands) and to pack the product at their warehouse. "If the operator receives $2 to $3 net from each machine per week he is doing a pretty fair business," complained Sanitary.[103]

Transportation stations were usually, but not always, a popular spot for VMs. Perhaps expectations were too high. A 1932 inspection tour of the La Salle Street railway station in Chicago showed few types of coin-operated machines of any kind. Dixie drinking cup vendors, pay-toilet locks, coin-operated parcel lockers, and penny scales made up the list of devices. Although there were a dozen scales "well placed" in the main waiting room, the overall result disappointed Silver Sam. Sam drly noted that scales were sometimes accused of being amusement devices because of the variation in weight given. But he thought their proper classification would be as utility or health machines.[104]

Drug stores were another prime location for vendors, sometimes argued as being the most important of all. They began to receive consideration as acceptable locations for coin machines when weigh scales were in the limelight. The arrival of the modern pin game then found the corner drug store a "veritable mecca as a location. There are thousands of operators that would swear by the drug-store locations."[105]

The concept of the automatic

The Photomatic machine, 1936.

store surfaced only a couple of times—with no success and little publicity. A 1932 attempt was made to install multi-purpose vendors in apartment buildings, very much like the Delamat venture. It was the idea of Charles O. Johnson of Los Angeles, a distributor for National Sales Machine company of St. Louis (who also built the multipurpose machines). Just before Christmas in 1932, Johnson installed his "automatic commissary" in one of the "better class" apartment buildings in Los Angeles. Machines installed in the Chatham Apartments consisted of seven of the National units, four stocked with canned goods, two with bottled beverages, and one with bakery products. Vended products numbered 34 items, including ginger ale, lime cordial, bakery goods of all types, coffee, milk, sugar, staples, and canned goods of all kinds. Grocery items retailed for a dime, bakery goods for eight cents and 10 cents, candy bars for a nickel, and cigarettes at 10 cents and 15 cents. Johnson allowed the apartment house owner five percent of the gross as his commission. Each machine was serviced daily, except for the bakery unit that received two daily visits. The cigarette machine and the candy bar unit were separate machines, in addition to the seven National vendors. Failure of the automatic commissary was attributed to several factors, including that it could not make change, patrons found the 10-cent sizes of grocery items uneconomical, and the VMs were unable to compete with odd-cent pricing found in grocery stores. This idea was not a new impetus toward automatic stores. Rather, both Johnson's idea and the Delamat concept were simply latecomers to a field where the energy had mainly been spent by 1930.[106]

The only other happening of note in the direction

Actor John Barrymore stands inside a Photomatic machine in this 1939 publicity shot. Barrymore was quoted as saying, "Photomatic beats the wonders of Hollywood. And the pictures do justice to the Barrymore profile."

of automatic stores in the 1930s was not a true vending machine. Clarence Saunders, founder of the grocery chain Piggly Wiggly, planned a robot grocery store as early as 1935. Two years later he opened a prototype in the Piggly Wiggly outlets that surpassed his pioneering efforts in self-service. This somewhat automatic store was called the "Keedoozle" because a "key does all." It sold only dry goods and everything at only 0.5 to three cents over cost — a savings of 10 to 15 percent for the customer. However, the electrical system failed. Saunders closed the prototype, rebuilt the electrical system, and changed the type of key. The prototype was reopened, but electrical problems again resulted in its closure. Then in March, 1939, he reopened with a new key and new wiring. When this automatic store was opened in Memphis, public acceptance was said to be "tremendous." However, breakage was high and the electrical system remained unreliable. The first store had to be closed. Two more were opened later, but with similar results. Customers used a "key" loaded with a paper tape to purchase products displayed behind glass. When a customer put the key in the slot of the desired item, it punched and printed the name and price of the product on the tape. At the end of the shopping trip, the customer went to the cashier and paid while the tape went to an order desk in the back where the order was filled. The customer waited a few minutes until a clerk came with the bags and called out his order number. With all merchandise under glass, there was no spoilage by handling or theft by customers. Fewer employees were needed to load merchandise into chutes than to display it on self-service counters. Instead of a hundred cans of a product, one on display behind glass was enough. It should all lead to cost savings, thought Saunders. At the time of his death in 1953, Saunders was working on a semiautomatic food store called "Foodelectric." Customers carried a type of adding machine around with them. Merchandise was, again, all behind glass. After finding a desired item, the customer placed his adding machine on the slot. The price was recorded, the item dropped, and the customer put it in her shopping basket as usual.[107]

In time, factories would become one of the more important locations for VMs. However, that area was only starting to be touched in the very late 1920s and throughout the 1930s. An unnamed operator in a northern Ohio city had a concession in a large manufacturing plant. In addition to the many VMs he had in the plant, he operated a traveling unit. On a four-wheeled cart he had mounted peanut, candy, gum, five-cent candy bar, and other merchandise VMs. That cart was kept on the move through the factory by an attendant who wheeled it from department to department. Reportedly, it did a good business.[108]

Pioneering in placing machines in factories was the Automatic Can-

Charles Johnson, of National Sales Machine, is shown in his Los Angeles office with displays of his firms "automatic grocery stores," 1933.

teen company. After its modest start in Chicago in 1929, by 1938 it had grown to have 125 franchise holders who had exclusive distribution rights in most of the large communities of the US. Candy bars remained the principal product distributed. Although its VMs had selectivity for a maximum of five different bars, Canteen had 40 or 50 different brands in distribution to provide local favorites. With regard to locating his units in factories, Canteen president Nathaniel Leverone explained that the system had found favor because it performed a "valuable sampling and missionary service." He argued in some cases the use of vendors had enabled a manufacturer to break into a market from which he had previously been excluded. Getting to like a given product, the worker called for it outside the plant and the result was that dealers were soon asking their jobbers to supply if for their regular stocks. According to Leverone, this explained why dealers did not resent the appearance of Canteens in the plants from which their business ordinarily came, as they had been shown that in many cases the plant built business for them. Since the Canteen idea was to restrict distribution to products which could be consumed on the premises, the firm did not stock cigarettes. Chewing gum was handled, but Wrigley's was the only brand distributed. Initially, manufacturers and other employers who provided Canteen service found some resistance because of the impression formed by some workers that their employer intended to make a profit from their VM purchases. Leverone explained it was a good policy for the company profit from the vending operation to be contributed to some phase of employee activities, recreational or welfare. By doing so, all such criticism was eliminated. Explaining, incidentally, a long-running trend to use mirrors in VMs, Leverone said; "We place a mirror in the center panel of each machine. This prevents any attempt to break the front in order to pilfer the contents. People are too superstitious—they won't break a mirror!"[109]

A 1939 article from a trade publication titled *The Manufacturing Confectioner* said that one of the largest new fields for candy sales that had been opened as a result of vending machines was the modern industrial plant.

It was a "virgin field" in which the machine merchandiser had not only aided the candy manufacturer, but also had been of "inestimable value to the managements from industrial relations and efficiency standpoints." Workers in heavy industries were not candy eaters prior to the advent of the current mechanical merchandiser, according to the argument. Many plants had their special fruit and candy peddlers, but management often frowned upon them for several reasons: the efficiency of an area was said to be "often demoralized" during the time the peddler was in an area—the candy was only available at a specific time, the stock was not always fresh and clean, and stock was sometimes depleted before the peddler finished his rounds. This article also argued that local stores gained business because of VMs sited in nearby plants. In other words, a worker who had eaten a candy bar at work might buy the same brand from the store when he was on his own time. Another argument believed that candy "has definitely increased efficiency." As an example, it was said that at one plant workers had an hour for lunch. In the last part of that time they went drinking, resulting in a high percentage of accidents occurring right after the lunch break. When a candy VM was installed where the men usually ate lunch, the accident rate fell noticeably. "An individual who has eaten candy has no craving for beer or liquor. The two tastes simply do not mix." It was also said that new products could be introduced through VMs with their resultant popularity spreading to regular retail outlets.[110]

When the New York City World's Fair of 1939 opened VMs again had a strong presence, but it was quite different from the 1933 fair in Chicago in which most of the focus was on restrooms as locations. Rather, in 1939 the machines were sited everywhere. Service machines, merchandise units, and amusement games could be found in a wide array. Exclaimed one article: "The sheer number of coin-operated machines that dot the grounds in itself bespeaks the high regard fair officials entertain for the industry whose products will silently and efficiently serve the millions expected to click

The Standard Automatic Luncheonette battery of machines, 1932.

thru the turnstiles from now until October." A battery of penny Dixie cup vendors were placed at every drinking fountain station at the fair. Coin-operated lockers—10 cents per 24 hours or part thereof—were built into the walls of various exhibits. Coin-operated turnstiles were to be found at all bus, railroad, and suburban transportation terminals, both inside and outside the grounds as well as throughout the amusement area. Restrooms were equipped with paper and cloth towel vendors. Two paper towels were vended for one cent, with a nickel charge for the cloth variety. Women's restrooms were also equipped with two kinds of sanitary napkin vendors. Absent were all the novelty VMs, such as perfume dispensers, comb units, and shoe shine machines. An exception was that, in some facilities, coin-operated turnstiles admitted one to a select group of toilets. Ten cents admitted one to a dressing room equipped with toilet, wash stand, whisk broom, and so on. However, these were few in number.[111]

By far, the largest number of VMs at the fair were the standard candy, nut, and gum machines, with the contract for them held by the Canteen company. Most installations consisted of a five-column, five-cent candy bar vendor flanked on either side by a one-cent nut vendor and a one-cent gum machine. Gum and nut machines were also sited around the fair by themselves. Approximately 125 candy bar VMs and 300 nut and gum units were dotted about the fairgrounds and in the railroad and subway station located on fair property. Nationally advertised candy bars and Wrigley's gum were dispensed. Canteen had about 50 servicemen working the fair machines. Two other firms had located some 100 cigarette VMs at the fair. Cigarettes were vended at 16 or 17 cents per pack, with the counter price at the fair as high as 25 cents. Finally, about 100 penny weigh scales were at the fair.[112]

In September, 1939, it was reported that coin-operated machines of all types, including amusement games, grossed $305,598 at the New York World's Fair from opening day, April 30, to August 15, totaling 108 days. One hundred penny weigh scales grossed $5,843 (the fair's share was 45 percent—$2,629). That worked out to 54 cents per scale per day. The Canteen company grossed $48,028 from its 393 machines (15 percent, or $6,745). Cigarettes sold through VMs grossed $19,112 (the fair received $1,969 from two contracts, one at eight percent, one at 12 percent). Coin-operated lockers grossed $30,258 (10 percent, or $3,026). Paper cup machines (Dixie cups) grossed $4,454 (25 percent, or $1,113); pay toilets grossed $4,317 (70 percent, or $3,022). Each of Canteen's machines grossed, on average, $122.21 over the period, or $1.13 per unit per day. Canteen's payment of $6,745 was actually credited against the $20,000 advance participation the firm paid before the fair opened. With only 76 days left, Canteen was likely to be well short of the $20,000 advance figure.[113]

A 1933 survey of service stations, tire dealers, and auto accessory stores in Canton, Ohio, showed them to be popular and profitable locations for VMs. In recent months, a majority of those establishments had permitted the placement of penny peanut and penny candy VMs. Garages with more employees had also installed nickel candy machines. Although the garage and store owners only received "a few cents a week" from the units, they were reportedly satisfied since they felt the VMs prompted greater efficiency among the workers because "the use of the machines puts an end to the employees running out several times a day to a nearby confectionery store for their needs."[114]

As many as 15 to 20 small merchandising machines were placed by an operator in beer taverns, according to J. H. Austin, head of Specialty Coin Machine Builders. One machine was placed on each table. The sale of salted peanuts from those units helped to increase the sale of beer, a fact which appealed to the location owner. Specialty marketed a line of petite VMs which could dispense nuts, breath pellets, ball gum, and other small items. It was a line designed for the beer tavern trade. All of the machines stood under one foot tall.[115]

W. E. Bolen was an operator of bulk penny machines. He advised that locations for penny vendors were plentiful in nearly every community, "and there is not the trouble in securing satisfactory spots for these machines as there is for the large games or chance devices." However, the only sure method was by a trial usually lasting four to six weeks. During that time, various types of merchandise should be used in the bulk VMs to find the type of product most popular in the location. Thus, all-product vendors were preferable to dedicated vendors since the former gave an operator a choice of 25 to 30 different items to vend. In Bolen's view, the commission to locations for merchandise machines should be 20 percent or never over 25 percent. "It is better to move a machine than pay a higher amount." Any drinking establishment should have machines sited there that dispensed salted nuts, advised Bolen, while in factories, office buildings, restaurants, theaters, and so forth, preferred items were confections such as chocolate-covered mints, coconut cubes, spicy gum drops, after-dinner mints, candy-coated raisins, and similar items. In locations with a lot of child customers, the VMs should dispense a mixture of candy and jelly beans. Bolen also urged operators not to use cheap merchandise "that you would not eat yourself," and to "Use the highest quality products you can buy even if you have to give slightly smaller portions. It will pay in the long run."[116]

Billboard correspondent H. F. Reves, pointed out that the coin machine trade was a different business than any other because the cooperation and goodwill of other business proprietors was needed. Reves talked to various location owners in Detroit. Louis Beal, secretary of the Detroit Retail Druggists' Association, said the penny nut, gum, and candy machines were a big help to a drug store. For example, when a customer wanted one stick of gum, he could be "referred" to the penny vendor. That way, the druggist did not have to both ring up a one-cent sale and break a package of gum, perhaps letting the other four sticks go stale on his shelves. It meant he could "satisfy his customers and receive his percentage of the sale without actually putting the merchandise on his shelves."[117]

When Reves spoke to office manager John Doyle, the latter said that peanut and hard candy vendors were the wrong type of machine for an office with mostly male employees. Men did not want pellets such as kids went for, but they would purchase mints. Where office employees were mostly female, roasted peanuts and pistachio nuts in shells were out. Chocolate and mint candies, and other fancy items, were what women preferred. J. Herron of the Herron Tire & Battery Company declared that the peanut vendor worked the best for him. It was filled once a week and regularly took in $1.65, which practically emptied the bowl. Customers used it while waiting to have a tire changed or a battery checked. William Young of the Greyhound bus line explained that, in the depot, the penny weigh scale was a popular favorite at all times. Small, single package candy vendors were described as doing a fair business. As well, the depot had a magazine vendor that sold out every week.[118]

Theater chain owner Frank A. Wetsman, told Reves he did not personally favor candy VMs in the cinema, but his partner did. He acknowledged that VMs had a place in the theater, especially to sell to children. Having a machine in the lobby allowed the kids to buy something to eat and saved the staff the bother of issuing pass-out checks to children who wanted to go out for a minute to buy something at the nearest store. Several industrial executives expressed approval to Reves about having VMs in their plants for the employees. At the Book-Cadillac Hotel, executive Jack Stember stated: "Pay locks on toilets have proved very good as revenue producers. They serve further to keep out undesirables from the better class hotels."[119]

C. S. Spooner was an executive with the Northwestern Corporation, one of the larger manufacturers of penny bulk vendors. In an article of advice addressed to the person starting a VM route, he said the best locations had transient patrons rather than regulars because the latter "get tired of buying the same thing from your vendor." Spooner advised the neophyte to load four to five ready-to-go VMs into his car, take a list of likely locations, and drive around to them. A sample sales pitch to a location owner might include the following: "Every time I come around to collect I give you 25 per cent of the gross take (emphasize this). It uses very little space and, while it won't pay the rent, it will help to pay the light bill. If the machine is not satisfactory after a month's trial I'll be glad to move it." He warned against letting a machine be heavily slugged, "because the next step will probably be breakage or robbery. Pull it."[120]

When it came to what item sold best in the penny machines, Spooner said they had tried every type of candy and nut possible with the best seller being the largest blanched Virginia peanut they could buy. Advice offered by this executive even included a method to "refreshen" merchandise. That is, he suggested doctoring stale product. A quart of Wesson's Cooking Oil was heated to a boil. Then a cupful of stale peanuts was placed in a sieve and lowered into the oil for 15 seconds. After they had dried the peanuts were spread out on brown wrapping paper and resalted to taste. "After cooling the merchandise is ready to go again, and if the process is done right the taste may even improve. The oil can be used again merely by straining thru a cloth and adding a little more."[121]

After a machine was sited, Spooner advised the operator to adopt a schedule whereby he went back in two weeks to fill and service the machine. Then, return in two more weeks to service as well as collect. Thus, when the location owner was given his 25 percent, "it will look like more than if you give it to him every two weeks." If a vendor was left in a spot where there were a few sluggers, Spooner said it was a good idea to get some little gummed stickers printed, saying: "WARNING. It is a penitentiary offense to slug, cheat or damage this machine. This machine is protected by the WESTERN DETECTIVE ASSN." Explained Spooner: "Many times these will cure a location by their mere psychological effect." Twenty machines was a suggested number of VMs to start a route with. Total capital outlay, including merchandise and other small equipment, would be $175 to $180 (at 1935 prices). In a comprehensive listing of possible locations, Spooner identified 16 outdoor spots and 57 indoor locations.[122]

Columnist H. F. Reves felt that in a typical city maximum density of VMs (in stores) would be

An elaborate penny vending machine, 1937.

50 to the square mile. Where multi-unit dwellings prevailed, the number could be doubled or tripled. He defined three types of locations: 1) places where the people who frequent them are unable to leave during working hours—factories, offices, and so on, 2) places frequented by the public where the merchandise placed in the machines would not otherwise be sold—hotels, gas stations, and so on, and 3) locations where the machines were in apparent direct competition with the store itself, which also stocked the same merchandise. Reves did not see a rosy future for VMs in the last category, unlike a handful of years earlier when the trade was generally very enthusiastic about vendors in such locations.[123]

Illustrating the difference in money making potential between different types of coin machines was that operators who installed pinball games in stores, depots, and so forth paid the location 50 percent of the gross. A popular pin game could gross from $2 to $15 a day. On the other hand, a penny gum machine—paying 33 percent commission—might make from $2 to $4 a week for the store owner. A game machine could pay for itself in a few months of operation while a vendor could take as long as a year. As journalist George Crook observed, "Amusement devices selling intangibles, such as music, games or gambling, are more lucrative than the vendors of tangible merchandise, but their popularity is shorter lived."[124]

When J. H. Hirsch, secretary of the National Automatic Merchandising Association (NAMA), assessed the state of the vending industry in the 1930s, he first noted the ill-advised hype and fanciful schemes of just a few years earlier. He said: "tons of money have been spent on experimentation, foolish exploitation, blind spending of fortunes without making a survey of conditions, kinds of goods to vend or taking overhead into consideration…. Remember that there are many products that cannot be sold thru vending machines." Acknowledging that the industry had no definite statistics, Hirsch nonetheless went on to estimate that there were 25,000 to 30,000 cigarette VMs grossing $30 million yearly. Next came candy vendors, taking about $20 million annually. There were at least 200,000 sanitary napkin vendors on location. Weigh scales were thought to gross $3 to $3.5 million yearly. As a grand total Hirsch estimated VMs took in $100 million annually.[125]

If amusement games were much more profitable, vendors were much safer and steadier. In 1936, operators in the New York area were said to be swinging back to the bulk merchandisers. Sales of games were at a low ebb due to results being awaited in important legal cases. "A great many operators are adding merchandise machines to their present routes of games. Very few operators are giving up their amusement game routes but feel that the merchandisers act as a precaution against any event."[126]

That year Silver Sam commented on the same thing, noting that more and more operators were learning that it was smart "to take the slower nickels along with the fast ones." Operators who handled VMs had a greater legitimacy and respectability in the community. They had an easier time siting other types of machines if they already had VMs in place. Dave Robbins, an operator and jobber, added: "Games are fine for big profits but until such time as games are considered absolutely legal in all States every game operator should also have some vending machines which he can depend upon for a steady income."[127]

Taking a somewhat different position was David Bond, head of the Trimount Coin Machine Company of Boston. He complained that progress in the merchandise vendor field had not been comparable to the rapid growth seen in the amusement machine field. With the exception of the cigarette VM, "on the whole the progress has been slow." One reason for this lack of growth, he felt, was due to the fact that many ventures "were largely promotional." There were many such failures.[128]

On the other hand, journalist George Crook argued that public acceptance of coin operated machines had been "universal and in many cases tinged with gratitude." It could be generally stated, he added, "that wherever enough people pass or pause on their daily business there is room for a coin-operated machine of some sort." H. F. Reves declared in 1937 that most of the experiments in vending over the previous six to eight years were made by now non-existent companies. Mortality in the field was high. Part of it was directly caused, said Reves, "by too fantastic ideas and no proper mechanical engineering.... Again, the vending machine will only be successful in selling some reasonably popular and standardized merchandise."[129]

At the end of 1938, editor Walter Hurd of *Billboard* said that the progress made in cigarette VMs had laid the foundation for new and modern candy bar machines. "It has been a greater problem, of course, to get the selectivity which the public desires in machine selling of candy." In other words, the greater problem was the ability to dispense several different brands of five-cent chocolate bars from the same machine. It was an area, Hurd felt, that was just getting started.[130]

A 1939 account argued that the vending of bulk candies and nuts still left much to be desired, and that branch of the VM industry had not risen very much above the "racket stage.... Many cities today prohibit the placement of mechanical dispensers on buildings, sidewalks, etc." These bulk vendors did not take business away from candy shops because they represented additional business, declared the article, "business which neither the shop nor the manufacturers would get in the ordinary course of things."[131]

VM maker Northwestern gave some fairly detailed advice on how to price merchandise for its bulk vendors. Spanish peanuts cost the operator 12 cents a pound and averaged 1,350 pieces to the pound. So, in order to sell them at 60 cents a pound, the portion dispensed for a penny would be about 22 nuts. A machine filled with five pounds would take in $3 for a sell out, less 20 percent commission, which left $2.40 from which the cost of the nuts, 60 cents, would have to be deducted. Remaining was a gross profit of $1.80 or 36 cents a pound to take care of the servicing costs, overhead, profit on investment, and so forth. When vending pistachio nuts, most operators gave five to six nuts per penny portion. Average count for pistachios was 550 to the pound, thereby bringing a gross profit of $1 per pound. After deducting 20 percent commission, 80 cents was left. From that was deducted the cost of the pistachios, 33 cents per pound, leaving a net profit of 47 cents per pound. As a rule of thumb, all bulk vendors, regardless of item vended, should be figured along the lines of 20 percent merchandise cost, 20 percent commission, and the remaining 60 percent for overhead and profit.[132]

Dave Robbins of the jobbing firm D. Robbins & Company believed that, after paying 25 to 30 percent commission to locations and after paying for the merchandise, an average of 30 cents profit per pound could be realized on peanuts, pistachios, mixed nuts, chocolate peanuts, cashews, and so on. Therefore an average penny bulk vending machine should net the operator from 25 cents to 50 cents weekly profit.[133]

Of course, income could be understated, especially if a jurisdiction was thinking about imposing a tax or license fee on the machines. When Massachusetts was considering a bill in 1938 to license coin machines, Stoughton Bell, a spokesman for the vending trade, appeared before a legislative committee to declare it was doubtful if 10 percent of the operators "clear over $5 per year per machine." Any tax or fee imposed on vendors, no matter how small, "would put everyone of them out of business." He declared further that a

A multi-purpose VM, 1934.

majority of the vendors showed a net profit for the year 1937 of "between $1 and $3 per machine."[134]

How much commission to pay location owners remained a problem for the industry. One way to poach, or steal, a location which already had sited another operator's machines was to offer the location a higher rate of commission. That was a practice the industry wanted to stop. Nathaniel Leverone, president of Canteen, complained that many operators paid too much commission for the placing of merchandising machines. Canteen paid 10 percent "and we insist that it is the highest rate which can be paid consistently on merchandising machines and continue to sell good merchandise in the machines. Those operators of vending machines who pay 20 percent are either forced to lower the quality of merchandise sold, or finally go out of business." Leverone added that "we are using our influence to get vending operators in general to adopt 10 per cent as standard commission."[135]

In 1933, the Automatic Merchandisers' Association of Michigan observed that in the past few years thousands of VMs had been sited without the payment of any commission to the location — something that should have a beneficial effect on holding down the amount of commissions payable in other spots. This organization favored paying a fair commission, "but not too high. The operator who pays high commission admits his own failure as a salesman and usually passes out of the picture a victim of his own folly ... if the operating business were dominated by 'commission cutters' there would be no operating business at all." Recommended commissions posted by this group were as follows: scales, 20 to 40 percent; bar candy, five to 10 percent; small confections, 10 to 20 percent; nuts, 15 to 25 percent; gum, 10 to 25 percent; cigarettes, 0.5 to one cent per package, all other merchandise, up to 25 percent, according to cost and retail price. On penny-operated amusement machines, the commission should be 25 to 33 percent; on nickel-operated devices, 25 to 40 percent. Operators were advised in all cases to "never exceed the maximum figures."[136]

Billboard said that, among amusement machine operators, the general practice seemed to be the 50-50 plan — 50 percent of the receipts to locations after awards had been deducted. Some used a 60-40 split — locations got 60 percent and took care of all awards from their share. A problem with that method was that some locations might stint on awards, causing play levels to fall. The publication seemed surprised that some in the trade advocated paying "as much as 25 percentof receipts" in awards. Commission rates recommended on cigarette machines by the National Automatic Merchandising Association were as follows: monthly sales below 100 packs, not in excess of 0.5 cents per pack; 100 to 299 packs, 6.66 percent of receipts; 300 to 449 packs, 7.5 percent; 450 to 599, 10 percent; 600 packs and over, 13.33 percent. For candy VMs (other than industrial locations), NAMA had two rates: on machines in use for less than four years, 30 percent of the gross; on units more than four years old, 35 percent. For industrial locations, the recommended commission on candy machines was 10 percent on the first $30 in monthly collections and 15 percent on all monthly receipts in excess of $30. For example, if there were 20 machines on a particular location, a sum equal to 10 percent would be paid on the total monthly collections up to $600, and 15 percent on all receipts over $600. For VMs dispensing drug sundries, notions, and other staple merchandise, the recommended commission was 25 percent of the gross; 10 percent for fresh fruits, pastries, sandwiches, and other perishable foods. NAMA advised operators to pay locations 50 percent on weigh scales. Noted was the fact that Canteen adhered to a straight 10 percent commission on candy bar machines. Veterans in the trade recalled that the old rule had been 20 percent on merchandising machines.[137]

During meetings in 1934 of the Western Vending Machine Operators' Association, the topic of commission rates was often a matter of debate since the group wanted to avoid operators "entering into ruthlessly competing or 'cut-throat' commission agreements...." Members complained that rates as high as 30, 35, and even 50 percent were known to have been paid. It was agreed that a "live-and-let-live" rate was from 15 to 25 percent, "and surely not more than 25 per cent under the most extenuating circumstances." The organization decided to ask members to bring cases of "exorbitant" commission to its attention, with the association then making "friendly representation" to the payer of such rates.[138]

In 1937, cigarette machine operators in Pittsburgh organized as the Cigaret Machine Operators' Association "for the maintenance of a uniform commission among the location owners and for increased co-operation within their own ranks." At a meeting the members agreed to pay location owners a maximum commission of two-thirds of a cent per pack. If a VM sold under 250 packs per month, no commission would be paid; 250 to 599 packs, half a cent per pack; 600 packs and more, two-thirds of a cent.[139]

A 1938 article stated that the accepted commission rate on the penny bulk vendors was 20 percent, "or 25 per cent on exceptional locations and no more." Many times less could be paid if the operator was "smart and tactful." Readers were told to beware of "cut-throat" competition. If a proprietor said he could get a higher commission rate from another operator, he was to be taken aside in order to be told the economic facts about VM operation. If the proprietor still demanded a higher commission, the operator was advised to remove his machine rather than yield to the demand.[140]

As coin machines spread throughout America, the industry received growing media attention. *Billboard*, one of the major trade publications covering the field, set up a coin machine section in its magazine in 1932. In 1934, it established a "Merchandising Machine Division" section within the coin machine section.[141]

With an increasing VM public presence, some urged those in the field to adopt more public-relations policies. Silver Sam urged all coin machine operators to tout merchandising VMs and to be an "evangelist" for them. Every opportunity should be seized to educate people to the fact that buying from VMs was economical, since the customer did not buy more than he needed. Because he bought only what he needed, the customer, over the course of a year, "usually accomplishes a large saving." With vendors there were no high pressure salespeople trying to get the customer to spend more money. Convenience was also stressed as a reason to use VMs. Recalling an earlier time, Sam admitted "You can find many persons today who after depositing a penny in a machine 20 years ago and getting nothing in return haven't risked a penny on a machine since." So every operator and member of his family and employees were urged to "spread the gospel" that coin machines were accurate, dependable, and always gave the customer good value for his money.[142]

Despite the growing presence of VMs in America, next to nothing took place with respect to promotion and hype for the machines that did exist. The Morton Salt company had spent time convincing industries and offices that in hot summer months workers became tired and less efficient due to loss of salt from sweating. This led to the installation of salt tablet dispensers in many locations (given free to employees). After conferences with Morton officials, the bulk VM maker Burel & Company developed a program to benefit both. Burel offered to operators of its machines placards to use with the units reading: "Avoid heat-fag with salt. Get your salt the appetizing way — Eat salted nuts every day. Morton's Salt — When it Rains it Pours."[143]

Leverone and his firm Canteen did engage in some promotion using premiums, coupons, specials, and so on. He felt all the methods of attracting business which the retail store used could be modified in some way to apply to machine selling. Starting in 1932, his Canteen VMs adopted new advertising signs. New Canteens had an arrangement on the front of the machine so that "attractively lithographed" cards in six colors could be placed on the machines, with new cards supplied about every six weeks. "It is modern advertising adapted to machine selling," said Leverone. He also admitted that machine selling could not be made to compete with retail stores—that machines belonged in locations where the stores could not go, such as factories and garages, where convenience selling was an accommodation to the customers.[144]

One of the reasons there was little in the way of promotion surrounding existing VMs was that they served a limited niche market. Another reason was that VMs were successful only with known brands. As reporter Bill Gersh concluded in 1937, "Many years ago it became known that automatic merchandising was dependent upon nationally known merchandise for its success. The vendors developed into emergency sales equipment of this nationally advertised merchandise. To a great extent they appeased a definite need for these items at odd times."[145]

Regarding the place of VMs as compared to clerks, the *Times* of London had a 1933 editorial that spoke about the great future ahead for "slot machines." One potential problem was thought to lie in the fact that women were the main shoppers and women did not get the same pleasure out of using a machine as did men. Shopping, said the editor, was not shopping if there was no scope for changing the mind, for asking searching questions, and demonstrating competence and knowledge. "The machine has not yet been invented which can reproduce a flustered and obedient shop assistant, and all machines are maddeningly calm and offhand, especially when they fail to function."[146]

Walter Hurd of *Billboard* thought that one fact had become increasingly clear: that VMs could "only do a limited job of convenience selling ... that they are very limited as to types and size of merchandise, that they cannot compete with clerks in the job of selling, that their real reason for existence whether in store or factory is to provide an extra convenience for the customer."[147]

As with all parts of the coin machine industry, it became a practice in the VM area that machines were sold to operators who placed them on a commission basis on location. That is, VMs were not to be sold directly to location owners. Historian G. R. Schreiber said that until the late 1920s, vending machine manufacturers often did sell direct to locations, mainly because the trade was not well organized. It was not until the operating company became a well established factor—starting in the late 1920s—that the vending industry settled down and developed "along substantial and profitable lines."[148]

A policy of selling cigarette VMs directly to location owners of beer gardens, confectioneries, and so on, brought the ill-will of operators down upon the Safeway Vending Machine company in Detroit in 1936. Safeway started up in February, 1936, and had its own finance plan for proprietors.

However, it was out of business about a year later.[149]

Henry Wertheimer, an executive with the National Cigaret Vending Machine Manufacturing company, in a 1937 address before the Cigaret Merchandisers Association of New Jersey, declared: "National policy is that of maintaining thruout the years the established custom of not selling cigaret machines to locations." Those who tried to make the cigarette machine business a location business had failed, he said. A location proprietor did not want to become a serviceman, a mechanic, a purchaser of equipment, and, above all, "he does not want to make the investment in cigarets and stand his own chances thru loss by his employees."[150]

For the first time, in the 1930s, the VM situation in foreign countries began to be commented on regularly. That European manufacturers were active and proficient in making machines meant that the American firms would never capture as large a share of the market as they would have liked. As reported by the Specialties Division of the US Department of Commerce, there were 15,041 coin-operated machines exported in 1932 (valued at $573,188). Within that total were 4,309 commodity VMs ($132,460) and 10,732 other machines (except musical—$440,728). In 1933 there were 25,125 machines exported ($669,969). Of those, 4,976 were commodity VMs ($219,815) and 20,149 other units (except musical—$450,154). In 1934 a total of 43,316 coin machines were exported ($1,478,990). Within that total were 8,681 commodity units ($456,777) and 34,635 other machines (nonmusical—$1,022,213).[151] For 1936 exports of commodity coin-operated machines totaled 8,899 machines ($398,997), while machines other than commodity were 28,860 units ($930,503). In 1937 those figures were, respectively; 17,981 ($899,834) and 36,894 ($1,615,896).[152]

In London, England, "slot machines" for newspapers appeared at two railway stations, Euston and Baker Street, in 1933 as a test to see if the public would accept them. The novelty of seeing a newspaper fall into the "very wide well" below in response to a coin brought the machines many

A pencil dispenser. Note the sharpener attached to the top of the unit, 1936.

customers but, said a reporter, it was still too soon to know whether the units were practical. Each machine had three display sections, with each holding about 40 papers. Those VMs, said the account, "are less likely to be tampered with than other machines, as the type of acquisitive person who seeks to empty a cigarette machine by means of 'token' coins is hardly the type from which newspaper circulations are drawn."[153]

William Rabkin was a vending trade executive who took an extended trip through Europe in 1935. In his report on France, he dealt almost exclusively with amusement games. He noted that there were very few merchandise machines in Paris. "In fact, this applies to all of France. Scales are not at all noticeable and do not seem to be popular."[154]

Rabkin was more enthusiastic about the VM situation in the Netherlands. Most noticeable, he said, were the cigarette and cigar machines, with the sales made through them greatly overshadowing "anything which has yet been accomplished in America." Aiding the popularity of cigarette machines was a national law requiring all businesses to close by eight PM and all day Sunday, except drug stores which sold only drugs. These machines were hung from the top front window of retail stores like a window shade. During the day, while the store was open for business, the machines were pushed up and were hidden away by the top part of the window. When the store closed in the evening, the shopkeeper pulled the machine down to the level of the lower window. Any change due as a result of odd-cent pricing was wrapped with the package the purchaser received. Featured also in these VMs were candy, hot sandwiches, pastries, and other food items. Machines were said to be common all over Holland. Stores with larger windows featured a larger number of machines, small windows in proportion. "Almost every storekeeper in Holland features the machines," declared Rabkin. Sandwich machines, most manufactured in Vienna, Austria, were also said to be popular and pervasive.[155]

A United States consular report for July, 1939, assessed the VM situation in the Netherlands. It noted that the after-hours use of cigarette machines had helped popularize vendors in general. Most tobacco stores still had a few VMs outside their outlets after closing hours, while a number of the larger concerns had "whole batteries of such machines covering their show windows during the closed periods." Most of those units were made in the Netherlands, Denmark, and Germany. Merchandise VMs in general were also said to be great favorites in Holland, being used for the sale of chocolate, candy, gum balls, fried meatballs and rolls, sandwiches, edibles such as pieces of cheese, tins of sardines, pieces of sausage, hard-boiled eggs, Russian salads, salted and fried peanuts, pastry and cake, and a wide variety of pharmaceutical preparations such as headache tablets, cough drops, photographic films, and perfume. Weigh scales, mostly made in the Netherlands, were found in large numbers all over the country. Scales used a pointer on a dial (instead of tickets or speaking machines, and were placed in public squares, lavatories, street car shelters, railroad stations, and seaside resorts.[156]

Reporter Jack Capaldi composed a lengthy round up article on the coin machine situation in Europe in 1933, focusing most of his article on amusement machines. Given the number and proficiency of European coin machine makers, currency exchange controls, and other factors, Capaldi was not optimistic about Europe as a market for American VMs. N. H. Herman, a Paris representative of several US vending firms since 1925, introduced a well-known make of American peanut vendor in Europe in the early 1930s. Since Europeans did not have a taste for American peanuts, roasted hazel nuts were used instead.[157]

Most of the coin machines in Europe were locally made, said correspondent Hans Ullendorff in 1938, with Germany, England, and Austria as the major manufacturing countries. With few exceptions, European nations had very strict curfew laws for retail stores—early evening closing and no opening on Sunday. England had a great number of cigarette machines standing in front of tobacco stores after the closing hour. He also noted VMs in the London train stations selling practically everything a traveler might need—razor blades, toothpaste, shaving cream, cough drops, soap, sanitary napkins, handkerchiefs, and other items. However, he thought Europe lagged behind America when it came to the distribution of weigh scales. In France he found the "cumbersome and ugly cast-iron chocolate and bonbon vendors which for years have occupied space in the subway and railway stations of Paris" had been replaced by more modern units. Some gum and candy vending machines (US) had shown up, installed in front of Paris stores. However, gum chewing was not a common habit in France. Aside from candy, gum, nuts, razor blades, and a bit of perfume, reported Ullendorff, few articles were sold through VMs. No cigarettes were sold, as the government had a monopoly on the sale of tobacco.[158]

When Dave Robbins, president of the vending firm D. Robbins & Company, returned from an extended European visit in 1939, he remarked that there was no such thing as a cigarette machine operator since machines were sold direct to tobacconists who put them outside their door after they closed. "One never sees a cigaret machine indoors." Other types of vendors in England like gum, nut, and candy bar machines were, said Robbins, "on the whole, conspicuous by their absence." Commenting on France, Robbins said candy bar machines were seen in great numbers and all were indoors. He didn't see one nut or gum vendor in France. In Belgium, he found candy bar VMs outside of "almost every building." What impressed Robbins the most on his European trip was the way so many vending machines were placed outside. He wondered if American operators were wrong in the presumption that outdoor locations were unprofitable because of slug difficulties.[159]

VMs in Europe, especially ones located outside, were severely affected by the war. According to a report in late 1939 from the US Commerce Department, sales from VMs in Germany had been severely reduced by the war. Rationed foodstuffs could no longer be sold from machines since no control on amounts was possible; the units could not be illuminated at night due to blackouts imposed; taxes on cigarettes moved prices too quickly to adjust machines properly; and some products such as chocolate—heavily sold through the machines—had become unavailable because of requisition for army use.[160]

Back in America, the 1930s was a period of great organization within the vending industry as the trade matured somewhat and formed its lobbying groups. The year 1932 was especially busy with organizations formed on the national and local levels. Among groups formed that year were the Coin Machine Manufacturers Association of America, while operators in Chicago, Brooklyn, Fort Worth, and San Francisco formed local groups. At the opening session of the Independent Coin Machine Operators' Association of Illinois, stated objectives were to limit poaching, to prevent unfavorable legislation, and to get favorable publicity in newspapers. The Automatic Merchandisers' Association of Michigan had an agreement whereby no member operator would place machines in locations already handled by another member. It also acted as the agency to notify an operator when that occurred and to enforce the removal of machines unwittingly placed in that fashion. Also, the group had as an objective to put "pressure" on nonmember operators to join the organization. Presumably, that would have made it easier to impose uniform commission rates on locations.[161]

How organizations changed over time in this period can be seen through the Michigan experience. On November 26, 1926, ten Detroit operators met and formed the Detroit Vending Machine Operators' Association. The first item was to agree to respect the rights of other member operators already in a location (i.e. no poaching). The second item was to have an understanding as to what was a fair commission to pay, and to not exceed that amount. Realizing later the need for a State organization, Detroit and other area operators met in Lansing on November 16, 1929, and organized the Legal Coin Machine Operators' Association of Michigan. In April, 1931, Representative Miles Callahan of Reed City introduced a House bill taxing VMs. Both organizations mentioned above fought the measure before the committee and succeeded in having it tabled. In November or December of 1931, these two groups merged into one, the Automatic Merchandisers' Association of Michigan, and pledged to fight vigorously all "confiscatory taxation" and unfair trade practices, to make war on the slug menace, to create and maintain favorable public sentiment, and to achieve a better understanding with law enforcement.[162]

The necessity for presenting a solid national front against legislative attacks caused a dozen vending industry leaders to meet in New York on September 14, 1936. By the end of that meeting, NAMA the National Automatic Merchandising Association (NAMA) had been formed. To this day, NAMA remains the industry's main lobby group.[163]

One of the main things these groups fought was taxes and/or license fees which officials tried to impose on the VMs. Silver Sam commented in 1932 that experienced operators all refrained from bragging about how much money their machines were taking in, because it only encouraged new competition and, more importantly, it encouraged "the taxing bodies to make new tax laws." Machines should not be opened and the money counted where the public could see, counseled Sam. Whether the earnings were large or small, "count the money in the back and you will encourage neither taxes nor competition."[164]

San Francisco's Board of Supervisors announced in 1932 that it was contemplating a tax of $10 per quarter, or $40 a year, on each coin-operated machine. Operators lobbied and succeeded in getting the measure postponed until they could present evidence to show the tax would be prohibitive. Six months later the measure was again before the Board of Supervisors, only to again be postponed to allow the vending trade to present arguments. In favor of the tax were "club women" who disapproved of VMs because children squandered their money on them. Fighting the proposal was the Vending Machine Association of Northern California, said to include practically all of the manufacturers, jobbers, and operators in that area.[165]

Kansas City, Missouri, passed an ordinance which assessed merchandise VMs and amusement games as follows: machines requiring one to four cents to operate, $2 a year; five to nine cents, $5; machines requiring 10 cents or more, $10. The Los Angeles city council initially proposed a license fee of $5 per machine per year on all penny and nickel amusement and merchandise VMs. The Western Vending Machine Operators' Association visited and lobbied the council with the result that a new ordinance was struck setting a license fee of $2 per year per penny machine and $3 per year for nickel machines on just pin and amusement games in both cases. As a result of lobbying, the tax on merchandise VMs was eliminated in the revised ordinance.[166]

In 1935 the city council of Flint, Michigan, passed a licensing ordinance which imposed the following annual fees: $5 for pin games; 50 cents for penny vendors; $1 for nickel machines; and $2 for all others. Pin game operators were satisfied with the measure, but some of the merchandise machine operators decided to contest that part of the ordinance. They were granted a temporary injunction that was later overthrown by a higher court.[167]

Speaking of the general trend to impose taxes and license fees on VMs in the 1930s, Nathaniel Leverone called it a symptom of the times. Lawmakers should be cutting the cost of government, he thought, not looking for something else to tax. He also worried about location owners bragging about how much money they made off their amusement games—which led to a move toward taxation. "The vending-machine people are having to suffer along with the amusement folks, though our earnings on vending machines are not nearly as spectacular as those of the games." J. H. Hirsch, secretary of NAMA, urged operators to stand up and fight against cities that were starting to institute sales tax on retail sales (to increase revenue in the Depression). Said Hirsch, "The legitimate operators of merchandise machines have been subjected to more confiscation, taxation, and unfair trade practices than any other industry in these United States." Retail stores could pass the tax on, he argued, but VM operators could not do so because of the fixed prices, "as all coin devices are made for even units of 1, 5, 10 and 25 cents."[168]

Slugs continued to plague the industry in the 1930s. Victor Cook, a 30-year-old sign writer in London, England, was sentenced to six months imprisonment with hard labor on a charge of stealing a pack of cigarettes from a VM and to six months imprisonment on a charge of being in possession of 14 pieces of counterfeit coins, sentences to run concurrently. The Lord Mayor said that cases of stealing from automatic machines were increasing rapidly and must be stopped, or sentences had to be drastically increased. Francois Derlot, first mate on a French steamer, was found guilty in London of stealing chocolate from VMs at Liverpool Street station by inserting French coins of about the same weight instead of pennies in the slot. A solicitor for the British Automatic Company said that, whenever this particular vessel came to London, French "pennies" appeared in the machines at Liverpool Street station. From February until the end of June, 1932, 862 of them had been collected at that station alone. Derlot was fined five pounds Sterling. Sentences of six months imprisonment with hard labor were imposed on Samuel Glover and Leon Sugar in London for unlawfully possessing counterfeit shillings and stealing three packs of cigarettes from vendors.[169]

F. R. Martin and two others of East Moline, Illinois, were arrested there on a charge of using lead coins to operate coin machines at Atkinson, Illinois. Martin took police to the basement of his home where he had coining equipment and handed over a cardboard box containing about $10 in nickels, dimes, and quarters of lead. Martin had scraped his molds to eliminate the words "United States of America" from the slugs, believing this action prevented the charge that he was counterfeiting government coins. Ed Knight, of Tacoma, Washington, used seven counterfeit nickels on a machine and later pled guilty to a charge of counterfeiting. He was sentenced to 18 months in the penitentiary and fined $500.[170]

Silver Sam reported about a Florida operator who placed a large number of de luxe candy VMs in theaters only to find that the school children became so expert at using slugs in his vendors that he had to remove his machines and hold his concession by installing counters with live attendants to make candy sales. In Regina, Saskatchewan, an epidemic of washers reportedly had descended on the VMs. One operator complained that he took no less than 67 from one machine and admitted that for some time more washers than nickels had been found.[171]

Rhode Island passed a bill in 1932 to make the use of slugs, including ice-slugs, illegal. Senator and Republican floor leader Harry T. Bodwell, of Cranston, exposed the ice-slug racket whereby ice was molded to the shape of coins, used to operate a VM, and then melted completely without leaving a trace.[172]

At the Chicago World's Fair in 1933, Leverone's servicemen were baffled by empty machines and empty coin boxes. Finally a friendly onlooker tipped them off: a man had drilled a tiny hole in the edge of a nickel and attached a fine wire so that he could drop his coin in the machine and then pull it out again. Leverone solved the problem by inserting a pair of snippers in each machine. "But the idea swept the U.S., and Automatic Canteen suffered heavy losses before it got all the snippers in." He added, "Funny thing about coin machines. When somebody hits on a way to beat them, the news travels coast to coast in a flash."[173]

Joseph Klein, an Indianapolis operator, brought suit in Cedar Rapids, Iowa, in 1932 against the Appleton Novelty company, a candy and gum machine jobber. The suit was for $5,488 on the claim that an agent of the Appleton firm sold VMs under an agreement that they were slug-proof and theft-proof. R. J. Biery, of St. Louis, the agent who sold the machines, testified in court that he told Klein the units would reject some slugs.[174]

A 1935 account told of the police dumping 1.5 million slugs into the sea. The slugs came from the Independent Subway System, which had been accumulating them in its turnstiles at the rate of 1,575 per day since the system opened in 1932. Total slug use in New York City was then estimated at 10,000 per day. The *New York Times* put much of the blame on pin games, claiming the slugs were made in Chicago—home of most coin machine manufacturers—and sold to operators who used them as test pieces in VMs. Operators then gave many of those pieces to proprietors for testing. From that system came "leakage." *Billboard* was irate at this tie-in, but after noting an increased use of slugs over the previous two to three years, the article went on to state that "In Chicago's Loop district I have seen stacks of slugs in the dime stores. Hardware stores in the Loop district have had window displays of high-grade slugs and in some cases placards advertising the non-magnetic qualities of the slugs." Reportedly, slugs could be bought openly and easily in New York City with the price being 40 to 60 cents per hundred.[175]

When the Mills Novelty company introduced a new cigarette VM in 1936, it was advertised to be slug-proof, as almost every maker advertised their machines. The sales pitch may not have been entirely accurate, but it probably gave a good indication of what items people tried to use instead of valid coins. "You can slug it all day with brass, aluminum, iron, die-cast metal, lead, copper, tin, foreign coins, street-car tokens, tax tokens, purchase tokens, wood, linoleum, paper, candy, asbestos, mica, cardboard, center-hole slugs with both large and small holes, slugs with spokes and sticky coins" and all were rejected. If that claim was exaggerated, VMs did become dramatically more efficient in the rejection of slugs in the 1930s. The industry would not be plagued in the future by slugs to the extent it had been in the past.[176]

Unemployment, as caused or exacerbated by the vending industry, remained a sore spot in the 1930s. Although the hype of the late 1920s had not come to pass in the form of fully robotic stores, the vending industry remained sensitive and defensive to the charge. Silver Sam believed that even if mechanically perfect devices for vending some of the more offbeat items such as hot-cake vendors had existed, they would not have merited encouragement because "they have the appearance of taking away jobs from people who might work as attendants for noncoin-operated machines."[177]

Walter Hurd ran a full page editorial on the subject in September, 1937. He felt it all went back to the machine age. Whatever marvels the machine had accomplished, "the fact still remains that the machine age in all its glory let one of the worst depressions in history come upon the whole country and, worse than all, has let a growing army of unemployment accumulate during the past 20 years until it now runs into the millions." He felt that you could not tell a jobless man that there wasn't something wrong with the machine age. The vending machine and music divisions of the trade were the ones Hurd felt were most open to attack, and those divisions were also most easily made the victims of "cleverly devised propaganda." Any group opposed to or in competition with VMs or jukeboxes could easily develop propaganda "to show that such machines add to unemployment by replacing human beings with mechanical devices. That such propaganda can be very damaging to coin machines has already been demonstrated." It had all started, he thought, with the hype of the 1920s that stirred up opposition to VMs. Only the coming of the Depression saved the VM trade "from an organized drive by labor that might have driven vending machines completely out of the country." Time had proved, wrote Hurd, that VMs would never displace clerks in stores, and that vendors "exist only in those places where such machines offer a special convenience to the customer that could not be had in other ways." Hurd also stated that, as late as 1938 there were still a few labor groups, as in Massachusetts, who still opposed the devices.[178]

Journalist George Crook declared that the most prevalent misunderstanding in the industry was the mistaken idea that a "mechanical robot" was filling a job that rightfully belonged to a human. Crook argued that VMs were primarily conveniences that eliminated much of the unprofitable detail work of the busy retailer. "By their very nature they increase employment, for men must be employed to service them. These machines are servants of man which give birth to profitable sales where a clerk or salesman would be unable to earn a livelihood."[179]

During this period the vending industry abandoned large, grandiose plans, settling instead for more specific, narrowly focused hopes. There were more failures than successes. Despite the Depression dominating the decade, there still seemed to be a fair amount of money around for vending experiments. Notable failures were popcorn machines, the washroom as a major location, and any vendor designed to dispense frozen or cold items. The most successful new development was the arrival of the beverage (soft drink) vendor, although its major impact was probably not apparent at the end of the 1930s. Cigarette and candy machines dominated the trade, taking perhaps 50 percent or more of the vending market. Other advances included better slug rejection mechanisms and, in a minor way, the opening up of factories as machine locations.

4

The War on Slugs Goes Federal, 1940-1944

"The filling of [automobile] tires [with air] is just a courtesy service and any customer would be willing to pay one cent for the service."
H. F. Reves, 1940

"A great portion of the peanut crop is moved through these machines."
Representative Charles S. Dewey, 1942

As World War II enveloped the world, a little bit of unbridled optimism crept back into the vending industry. Reporter H. F. Reves pointed out that the hype of 1928-1929 was premature — machines of that era were not ready. He then noted some recent advances in the trade and concluded, "there is no reason why the age of machines should not arrive, as predicted for the past 10 years." Robot stores, despite their earlier failures, were still coming. A first opening for such installations might be in wayside stands, he declared, since there were tens of thousands of roadside stations spread along the highways of America.[1]

Six months later, Reves returned to state that Americans had long been coin-machine minded. An upward trend in that direction had set in, he said, with people turning more and more toward the use of all types of coin machines, especially VMs. However, Reves cited no evidence to support that contention. With a widespread interest in things mechanical, such as the automobile, Reves felt a coin-operated air hose for gas stations "would be a desirable and probably very possible innovation. The filling of tires is just a courtesy service and any customer would be willing to pay one cent for the service." Again, he saw the coming of robot stores as very possible. He predicted that one stimulation to VM use would be due to a labor shortage from war preparation and war economies.[2]

Some of that enthusiasm was on display at a 1940 coin machine show.

About 6,000 coin men registered for the event. *Billboard* editor Walter Hurd declared that there were a greater number of miscellaneous products on display at this assembly than at any previous convention. For example, two machines for vending cookies, two foot massage units, a machine for making voice recordings, a coin-operated electric razor, a VM for spraying sun tan oils, and a blood pressure measuring unit.[3]

Articles lauding the VM industry — and concentrating on the more unusual and hard-to-find devices — appeared around the time of this coin machine convention. A couple of those articles were reprinted verbatim in *Billboard*. One from *The Eagle Magazine* started by describing the complexities of the popcorn machine, where a customer inserted a coin and caused things to happen. "The show is as good as the hot corn." Next the article followed the mythical Joe, a traveler bound for New York City. At the station, he dropped a penny in the parking meter. Entering the station, Joe spotted an insurance machine and inserted a quarter, causing a glass panel to slide back to reveal part of an insurance certificate. After filling in some blanks with name, address, and beneficiary, the machine date stamped the original policy. Then, after a lever was pressed, a duplicate certificate dropped down while the original remained on file in the machine. Good for 24 hours, the policy paid a maximum of $7,500. On the train itself, the only "slot machine" Joe could play was the one dispensing paper cups for a penny.[4]

Once in New York City's Grand Central station, Joe found a VM that sent telegrams. After breakfast at an automat and inserting coins in subway turnstiles, he arrived at the post office where he discovered a Mail-O-Mat — then installed in several post offices, hotels, and railway stations. A customer put an unstamped letter in the slot, whereupon the machine weighed it and registered on a dial the amount of postage needed. When the correct coins were deposited, the machine printed a metered stamp on the letter. Ven-

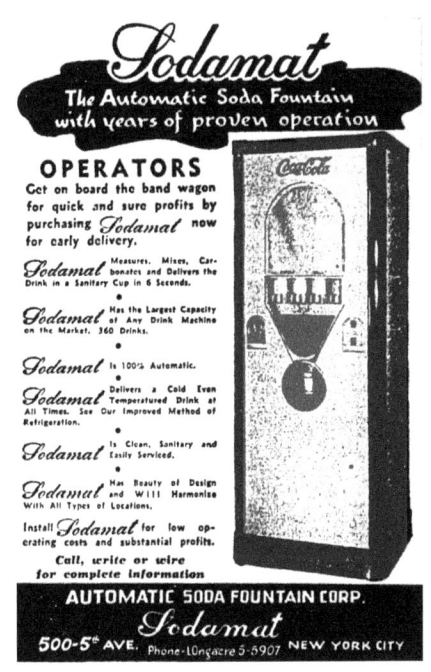

A Sodamat, 1940.

turing farther afield, it was noted that in Denmark a coin in the slot allowed a patron to enter a booth where he found a typewriter, stationery, carbon paper, and stamps, while in Germany and Holland there were automatic "talking letter" machines wherein a patron deposited a coin and spoke his message into a microphone. Within a short period out came a phonograph recording of the "letter," neatly wrapped and ready for mailing. Returning to Joe, the traveler next stopped at a department store where he deposited a dime and gave his feet a treatment at an oscillator (massage unit). Back at Grand Central, Joe discovered a newsreel VM, inserted five cents, and chose from four newsreels. When he arrived back at his home city, Joe bought a package of cigarettes and a box of candy, both from VMs.[5]

Chicago reporter David Teague wrote a similarly laudatory piece on the industry at the time of the 1940 coin show. His long list of goods and services available automatically in some 90 cities included cigarettes, cigars, candy bars, chewing gum, books, bottled carbonated beverages, carbonated beverages mixed at a central plant and dispensed in a cup, carbonated drinks mixed by the machine, cups, sticks, bars, and cartons of ice cream, pop corn, pencils, razor blades, hard-boiled eggs, fresh fruit, orange juice, milk, postage stamps, perfume, powder, aspirin, cough drops, social security plates, identification plates, postcards, breath sweeteners, sandwiches, cakes, slabs of pie, horoscopes, handkerchiefs, shoe laces, telephone calls, toilets, telescopes, shoe brushings, the use of washing machines, weight and fortune, subway entrance, and parking meters. Recent cigarette taxes had increased prices two cents above the usual 15 cents. Teague saw two solutions to that problem: One was a machine that made change from 20 cents. "The other, and more practical, is a cigaret package with three pennies pre-inserted into the cellophane jacket."[6]

A year later Sidney Shalett followed the same pattern with a piece in the *New York Times Magazine*, detailing a long list of goods and services available from VMs in the "slot-machine age." All these lists had in common the fact that they listed items such as popcorn, fruit juice, shoe shines, and ice cream. None of the devices dispensing these goods or services actually worked. The numbers of them on location were small, limited to an experimental group which came and then disappeared — sometimes repeating the cycle as model after model failed to deliver an acceptable product.[7]

A more accurate assessment came from G. R. Schreiber who remarked that, when the War Production Board suspended the manufacture of vending machines in April, 1942, the industry consisted for all practical purposes of devices to vend candy, cigarettes, gum, and soft drinks. Operating companies numbered less than 3,000, he estimated.[8]

One bright spot for the industry in this war-limited period was the continued quick development in soft-drink vending, at least until VM production was completely halted. Another new machine introduced at the 1940 coin show was a new bottled beverage dispenser from O. D. Jennings & Company. It had a capacity of 120 standard size bottles and could handle bottles ranging in size from six to twelve ounces.[9]

Walter Hurd wrote both an article and a full page editorial on the topic of beverage vendors in the same issue of *Billboard*. Describing the field as then "just in its infancy," he remarked that just 10 years earlier refrigeration was so serious a problem in VMs that some industry watchers said a successful machine could never be built. In those days, refrigeration applied to VMs even "froze" the coin mechanisms so they would not operate after about 24 hours of refrigeration. Hurd also considered what name should be applied to the units. Refrigerated vending machines struck many as cumbersome, so some were saying simply "cold vendors." "Drink dispensers" was an earlier term, but the trend seemed to be to use the "more dignified" term of beverage vendor. Machines vending bottled drinks were then on the market in sufficient numbers so that they were a "commercial reality." Such units were either selective or non-selective. One machine on the market offered customers a choice of 10 different beverages by simply turning a knob. However, said Hurd, most selective vendors, were limited to a choice of two or three items. He credited Coca-Cola for giving bottle VMs a long and worthy test: "The bottle vendors have now been tried for four years and the present national interest in bottle vendors is largely due to what this one firm has done in the field." With bottle vendors no longer an experiment, Hurd felt the only question that remained was whether the soft drink bottlers or professional operators would site the units. Not surprisingly, the editor felt it would be the operator. However, the soft drink

Another soft drink cup vendor, 1940.

companies, recognizing the profits to be made, moved quickly to purchase, site, and service their own vendors, leaving only a marginal place for professional operators.[10]

Slightly newer and less firmly established were machines that dispensed soft drinks in cups. These bulk VMs could have pre-carbonation, or the gas and the water could be mixed (carbonated) directly within the machine. Not much selectivity existed in the bulk drink vendors—one unit offered a choice of three drinks in the same machine. In any case, when it came to refrigerated soft drink machines Hurd declared the "missionary work" for the vending method had been done. "Public acceptance has already been assured; vending mechanisms have been perfected."[11]

Herb Jones, advertising manager for VM maker Bally Manufacturing Company, offered advice on where to place soft drink machines. The first choice was commercial locations in which beverages were not ordinarily sold such as theater and building lobbies and garages. The second choice was commercial locations in which beverages were sold such as drug stores, department stores, and depots. The idea was that the machines offered quick self-service for patrons who would not ordinarily wait for table or fountain service. The third choice was industrial locations such as factories, mills, and warehouses. Since no plumbing was involved, the Bally Beverage Vendor could be placed on sidewalks outside of stores. Product in the Bally machine was pre-mixed and pre-carbonated in a central unit serving 20 to 30 VMs, located in the operator's headquarters, with the beverage transported to the VMs in stainless steel barrels.[12]

Baltimore had about 500 coin-operated beverage machines in operation in 1941. Bottle machines had been in operation for the past three or four years, whereas the bulk vendors had been on the local scene a little over a year. In the bottle vending field, the Coca-Cola bottler was described as the largest operator, using Mills Novelty company machines. Dr. Pepper also had VMs in the bottle dispensing field.[13]

The year 1940 was also reported to be a good period for the makers of VMs for marketing milk, both plain and chocolate, in bottles. In the beginning most of the sales were made to diary companies, but more private operators were purchasing these units in 1940. Private operators used the vendors as their main line of business, whereas some of the dairies looked upon the machines as a side line and thus did not go after locations with the same vigor. One factor helping to move more vended milk was the attitude of factory owners, personnel managers, and so on, who were said to be mostly in favor of selling dairy products. Long before the VMs for dispensing milk were developed, the National Dairy Council worked to induce delivery of bottled milk to factories so it could be made available to employees. Thus some groundwork had been done when VMs arrived, and in many cases a market had already been established.[14]

When the New York World's Fair opened in 1940, it had about the same number of VMs as in 1939. One change was that the fair abandoned its use of coin-operated turnstiles for restrooms, contenting itself with pay locks on the stall doors. Final figures for the 1939 fair showed that coin-operated machines grossed in excess of $400,000. Individual grosses included: Photomatic Studios, $47,942; penny arcade, $40,449; scales (100 machines), $12,485; Skee ball and Chime ball, $68,173; gum, nut, and candy machines (393), $96,742; cigarette vendors, $31,556; coin-operated lockers, $53,156; and coin-operated toilets, $8,439.[15]

Leon Silver, a Los Angeles operator of penny gum and peanut machines, and many other operators liked ideas such as the three percent sales tax and the seven cent street car fare in his home city because they added odd pennies to the pockets and purses of his customers. Silver installed many of his machines at street car transfer points. He also sited many in defense plants and saw his business grow dramatically.[16]

World War II also had the effect of opening up industrial locations to the vending industry. While VMs could be found in some plants prior to the war, industrial plant managements had been, at best, tolerant of vending. Machines were generally not embraced or welcomed. With the war underway, employees in industrial plants worked 10 to 12 or more hours per day. Management suddenly discovered that the vending machine was an important tool for keeping workers on the job. Where industrial managers once worried that the installation of VMs would cause workers to dawdle on the job, they now found men and women could work 12 or more hours at the job, said Schreiber, "if they were refreshed occasionally with a candy bar or a soft drink."[17]

A 1940 ad for the Bally soft drink machine.

Statistics for the industry began to appear for the first time, although, since the numbers were industry estimates, their accuracy was unknown. As of January 1, 1941, there were reportedly three million penny vendors on location in America with a total annual sales volume of $78 million and a total investment in equipment of $21 million. Of that total number, 1.8 million were nut machines, 750,000 were gum vendors, and 450,000 were candy dispensers (250,000 of those were nickel VMs). Average investment per penny machines was just $7. Nickel candy units went through the war years serving many types of substitute products, such as packaged cookies, when the candy bars for which they were designed were not available. Their annual sales volume was $12.5 million, an average of $35 per machine per year. Penny vendors had an average yearly gross of $26 apiece, 50 cents per week. Cigarette vendors totaled 126,500, with total yearly sales of 657,800,000 packs of cigarettes. At 15 cents per pack, that amounted to some $98 million, but lower prices were in use in some States so a more realistic yearly dollar figure was put at about $75 million. Using the higher figure, cigarette machines had an average yearly take of $780, $15 a week. Five-cent candy VMs sold 625,000,000 chocolate bars in 1941, a gross of $31,250,000, or $125 per year per machine, $2.40 a week. Beverage (soft drink) vendors numbered 28,000, with a sales volume of $12,096,000, or $432 per machine per year, $8.31 per week. For 1941 it was estimated there were 4,879,500 coin machines in the US, of which 3,329,500 were VMs.[18]

Operating companies were mostly small businesses with an estimate in 1943 that 70 percent of US operating concerns were one-man outfits. A typical one-person route was one of the following: 80 to 100 jukeboxes, 100 to 150 games, 200 to 300 penny vendors, 100 cigarette machines, and 100 five-cent candy machines, or a combination thereof. People in the trade regarded cigarettes as the most practical commodity for vending because of package standardization, universal acceptance, and repeat buying. Those 125,000 cigarette machines in use accounted for as much as 11 percent of all cigarette sales in some parts of the country, mainly in eastern areas.[19]

The policies of the US Mint became increasingly entwined with those of the vending industry. A record number of coins were produced in the 1940 fiscal year, more than double the preceding year's output. Stating the record was made in the production of pennies, nickels, and dimes, US Mint director Nellie Ross said the unusually high demand for coins was due primarily to "the increasing use of coin-vending machines as well as other devices operated by coins."[20]

Due to a shortage of nickel, in the second War Powers Act of 1942 there was a direction to the Mint to eliminate the metal known as nickel from the coin with the same name and turn out nickels composed of equal

4.—The War on Slugs Goes Federal, 1940–1944

parts of copper and silver until December 1, 1946. Representative Charles S. Dewey of Illinois was told by a vending machine manufacturer that the devices "which have become an American institution" would not work with the new coins. Dewey argued against the new coin, declaring that the Treasury department was thinking solely of the monetary aspect of the nickel and not at all of its economic and social significance. The economic aspect came from the development of the VMs, said Dewey. "Thousands are installed in manufacturing plants, including those doing war work, where, for security's sake, human vendors are not wanted, and wherever the American people congregate. A great portion of the peanut corp is moved through these machines." Social significance was found in the fact that the nickel was the coin most

Lucille Warran, cigarette girl at the Sky Way Roof in the Peabody Hotel, Memphis, Tennessee, beside a DuGrenier cigarette VM, 1940.

used by the public. "It brings food and nourishment to war workers and other toilers;" stated Dewey, "it brings a relaxation through 'canned' music; and it pays for transportation in many places." Because of Dewey's lobbying effort, a new formula for the coin was worked out. Thanks to Dewey's efforts, observed journalist Arthur Krock, "the new five-cent pieces of lowly commerce will continue to evoke, when dropped in the slot, that cheerful and fruitful clang which forecasts prompt delivery of the small goods by which citizens of the United States enjoy a large portion of their daily existence."[21]

Editor Walter Hurd continued to lash out against taxation of VMs. In a 1943 editorial he again noted the mistakes made in 1928 and 1929 when the VM industry bragged it would soon replace clerks. That led to labor opposition and "a strongly organized movement in those days to tax vending machines out of existence." Speaking of the time in which he was writing, Hurd believed the promotion of plans for taxing machines came from retail circles because many retailers were led into the mistaken idea that

VMs took a lot of business away from them. A machine tax in one State, he said, was promoted by as many as four retail organizations, while cigarette vendors had been kept out of another State for many years by the pressure of a strong retail drug association. Hurd concluded, "Taxing bodies should be aware of one of the greatest evils of modern business and kill any tax promoted for ulterior reasons by some competitive business."[22]

World War II could only be described as beneficial to the vending machine industry—even though production of new coin machines was halted in April, 1942, and even though there was a shortage of candy and soft drinks—two vending staples. In spite of these problems, business was up because the public had more money to spend and machines were easy to place. Prize locations were in war plants or small stores across the street from those factories. The outlook brightened further for manufacturers of jukeboxes, games, and VMs in May, 1945, when the federal government gave them one of its first go ahead signals to resume regular peacetime production as soon as material and manpower supplies permitted. By October of 1945, Rowe Manufacturing had started production of its postwar cigarette vendor. Deliveries were to start on January 1, 1946.[23]

Slugs were rapidly becoming less of a problem to the industry for two main reasons. One was the trade's lobbying efforts to have laws enacted and enforced. The second reason was an improvement in the machine mechanism to reject slugs. As the 1940s began, the better mechanisms subjected the deposited coin to several tests. First it was tested for physical dimensions by the size of the slot which received it—too small and it would return. Then the coin passed through a horseshoe magnet which tested for iron and steel. If the coin had magnetic properties, it would return. Next the coin was directed against a spring-loaded pendulum. A light coin would not operate the pendulum. Fourth was a metallurgical test designed to catch coins of the proper size and weight but which did not have the correct composition, such as foreign coins. As it passed a permanent magnet, a coin of improper composition set up currents which delayed the coin in its path and diverted it to the return chute. Any genuine coin could pass through those four tests in less than five-eighths of a second. Then it faced a fifth test, wherein it was dropped at an angle onto a hard steel "anvil" that bounced it over a hurdle into the "pay" slot. If the coin did not bounce high enough the hurdle caught it and dropped it into the return area.[24]

A major precedent was set in December, 1940, when the Federal Court in session at Omaha handed down the first ruling and conviction against a seller of slugs on the charge of counterfeiting. This meant that federal authorities—the FBI, Secret Service, and the Post Office—could enter the fight against slugs as it now violated a federal law. Until then, any prosecution had to be left to local authorities. The decision led to a major attack on slugs with many arrests and prosecutions around the country. More laws also continued to be enacted. For example, Ohio and Minnesota both passed anti-slug laws in 1941.[25]

Acting on order of the US Attorney General, the US Secret Service swept the country of all important manufacturers of slugs. As a result of evidence obtained by agents of the Secret Service and the Post Office Inspection Service in cooperation with local police, seven firms alleged to be manufacturing or distributing slugs were indicted before a Federal Grand Jury, convened in New York in May, 1941. It was a nationwide market said to be costing American business some $5 million annually. In case anybody was naive enough to not understand their purpose, these counterfeit items were advertised as follows: "These slugs are not intended for use in vending machines." Action was begun by the federal government in answer to complaints made by the Rowe company, NAMA, and influential operators throughout the nation. Late in 1940, George Seedman, acting for Rowe, brought the problem to the attention of Senator Lister Hill of Alabama, who brought it to the attention of US Attorney General Robert H. Jackson. Seedman also wrote to "important" operators, urging them to bring the slug problem to the attention of their Congress representatives. This caused the Secret Service and the Post Office to mount a joint action, wherein letters were sent to all the major slug makers for prices and samples. Slugs were then ordered and received. On several occasions it was specifically stated that the slugs were wanted for use in cigarette VMs. Agents visited the largest of the seven manufacturers—De Vere Novelty Company in Dayton, Ohio. Posing as customers, agents were shown how the slugs were used in VMs. Those agents also purchased slugs, which were tested in Rowe cigarette and candy machines, in Pitney-Bowes Mail-O-Mats, in telephone coin boxes, in subway turnstiles, and in Horn & Hardart Automats. The slugs performed like real coins.[26]

Nothing entirely eliminated slugs. Ohio cigarette machine operators donated a ton of slugs in 1941 to the country's defense collection plate. The metal, taken from VMs in that area in the previous two years, was turned over to a government agent for war preparedness use. Anthony Lombardi pled guilty in New York to using slugs to obtain five sticks of gum from a subway vendor and was fined $50 or 30 days in the workhouse.[27]

On April 3, 1944, President Franklin D. Roosevelt signed into law an act providing that any person making or selling slugs to be used to obtain free cigarettes, stamps, admissions, or other goods or services from coin-operated machines was subject to a maximum penalty of a $3,000 fine and a year imprisonment.[28]

The years of World War II were good years for the vending industry. Profits were likely higher than usual as, for one thing, machines did not have to be replaced by new models. Unemployment was negligible and war plants welcomed VMs to an extent that peacetime factories never had. Governments took far more rigorous action against slugs than they ever had before. And more people had extra money to spend during their extended hours on the job. Post-war America was highly anticipated by the vending industry. Enthusiasm was strong.

5
Optimism Returns, 1945-1949

"Nickel paradise."
Business Week, 1945

"The ultimate perfection in self-service is provided thru the vending machine...."
Walter Hurd, 1946

"... the public has always expected its table water to be relatively free."
Billboard, 1946

"Robot salesmen save money."
Paul Cohen, 1949

"So many [vending] machines today remind me of Victorian bathing suits."
Egmont Arens, 1949

Following the end of World War II, the remainder of the 1940s was a very optimistic period for the vending trade. In the immediate post-war period, that enthusiasm was mostly directed at the idea that items not yet vended soon would be. Actually, many of these "new" ideas had been tried in the past. Later in the 1940s, that optimism would turn to more grandiose dreams. When *Business Week* commented on a NAMA meeting in November 1945, it remarked that super-gadgets on the drawing boards included a dispenser that squeezed fresh orange juice, a unit that furnished hot coffee, a doughnut vendor, and an electronic grill that automatically produced a choice of hamburger, hot dog, or toasted cheese sandwich. Coin changing attachments were also expected. Further into the future some trade observers foresaw VMs for frozen foods, cosmetics, combs, handkerchiefs, hosiery, newspapers, and magazines. One "daring" item for entrepreneurs, said the article, was a chain of comfort stations to be operated as independent enterprises for profit in traffic-counted best locations—distinct from the coin-operated toilet stalls found in hotels and railroad stations. These stations were to be completely maintained by their revenues. Balancing these optimists were skeptics and conservative operators who believed that their future continued to lie in such stable lines as cigarettes, candy, gum, peanuts, and soft drinks. The statistics that existed for the industry, *Business Week* admitted, did vary. There were perhaps two million VMs on locations that were thought to account for 18 percent of total cigarette sales, and 10 to 20 percent of five-cent candy bars. One manufacturer advised that the net monthly profit per cigarette machine was $4, while a penny gum and candy machine operator was said to need 400 or 500 machines to net $300 a month. In conclusion the magazine stated: "Though Simon-pure merchandise vending-machine men dislike to admit it, big money in coin-operated devices still comes from the juke boxes, pin-ball games, and one-arm bandits." Still, the VM future was written as decidedly upbeat in this article about "Nickel Paradise."[1]

A few months later *Billboard* declared that products sold or soon-to-be sold by vendor, ranged from ice cream, popcorn, cookies, fruit juice, newspapers, ice, magazines, and shoe shines to hot sandwiches of all sorts

Left: Popcorn unit, 1946. *Right:* Another popcorn machine, 1947.

and frozen foods. Those new items, along with great improvements reported in vendors of such standard products as soft drinks, candy, gum, and nuts, supposedly held the promise to open many entirely new locations to the trade. "Each of the new vendors can be expected to gain entry into business houses such as banks, offices, and stores that had hitherto been virtually closed to other coin machines." The easiest and most convenient way of providing people with snacks was through VMs, argued the report. Coffee vendors had long been a dream, but "So far, however, no successful coffee vendor has been reported on the market." Industrial locations were felt to be the richest immediate market for VMs, followed by bus stations, railroad depots, office buildings, and department stores. This account even expected the popcorn VM to stage a comeback as "most of the bugs" which hampered the machine before the war had been eliminated.[2]

James Kirk Paulding II demonstrates his railroad ticket vendor, 1948.

In a 1946 editorial about the growing use of self-service by retailers in general, Walter Hurd asserted that "The ultimate perfection in self-service is provided thru the vending machine, and all progress in the field of self-service will lead to wider and wider use of coin-operated devices to sell goods." He did acknowledge that one restriction placed on the patron by the VM was that he could not handle the merchandise before buying. But since the vending machine was largely limited to well-known, standardized items, "the desire to handle the goods is not important to the customer." VMs performed well as display devices and at other functions of selling. "The vending machine is a much more complete self-service device than the usual stand or table," concluded Hurd.[3]

A 1947 US Commerce Department report estimated $500 million in sales annually through vendors. This report also looked to the future, stating that the sale of books and phonograph records through machines was being tested. In addition, milk in paper cups and beer in bottles or cans, cooled to just the right temperature, were under consideration while the sale of frozen vegetables, fowl, and fresh fruits or fruit juices is "a certainty."[4]

At the 1947 annual NAMA convention, Nathan Cummings, president of the wholesale and retail firm Consolidated Grocers Corporation, delivered an address in which he got a little carried away. Cummings predicted that in 10 years retail sales through VMs would total $3 billion annually, and that "It is possible to foresee completely automatic grocery supermarkets and automatically operated service stations." He also felt that automatic merchandising would grow more rapidly in the coming five years than it had in the previous 20 years. Conventional retailers, he argued, had to be shown that VMs helped human salespeople and did not replace them.[5]

The industry was getting bigger and growing more important. In November, 1946, a new magazine for the coin-operated VM trade, *Vend*, was introduced by Billboard Publishing Company. That periodical — with a later name change to *Vending Times* — is still being published today.[6]

Cigarettes remained the dominant item in the vending industry. The largest maker of cigarette vendors was the Rowe corporation, which was also an operator with around 17,000 units on location — with annual sales of 95 million packs of cigarettes worth $16 million. In 20 years Rowe had manufactured approximately 165,000 cigarette vendors. Over the previous 10 years, Rowe had studied plans to dispense other items, but in the end rejected

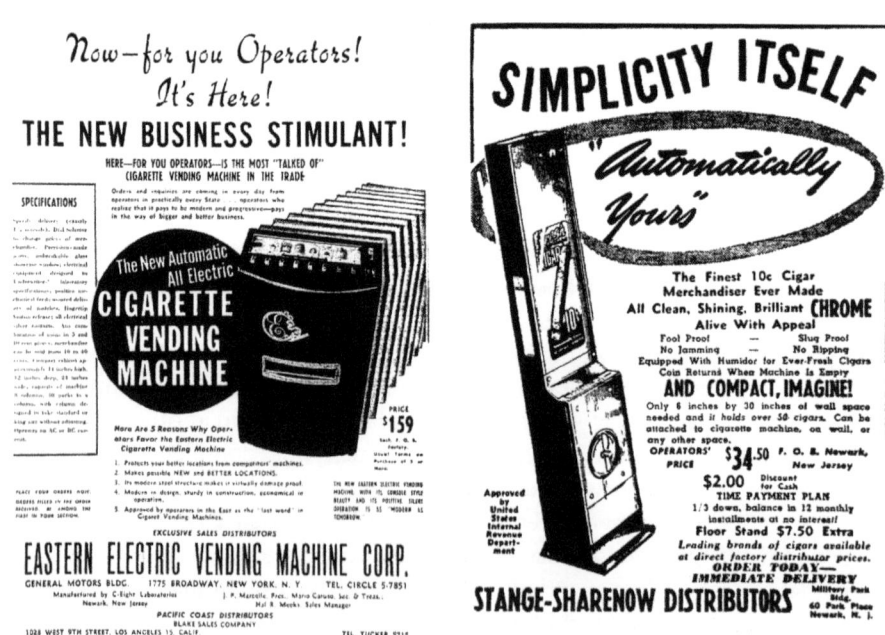

Left: An early electric cigarette machine, 1946. *Right:* A cigar VM, 1947.

them all. Rowe did turn out a small number of penny and five-cent gum machines and was thinking of going into nickel candy devices when war intervened. Mainly, the company stuck to making cigarette dispensers. Its new post-war model, Crusader, had 10 columns, held 475 packs of cigarettes and 500 books of paper matches, and required much less frequent servicing than did the first Rowe unit, which held only 100 packs. Prices for Rowe machines had remained fairly stable, at least through the 1930s. The 1941 Rowe President sold for $109—an increase of only $34 over the cost of Rowe's $75 1927 model. Crusader sold for $175.[7]

The Rowe Crusader, 1946.

Rowe got into the business of also being an operating company quite by accident. That division started in 1928, shortly after Robert Greene first came to New York as a cigarette machine salesman. Since it was such a large city, Greene decided to refuse an order for less than 100 machines. However, tobacco jobbers claimed the devices would hurt their retail clients and would not listen to the argument that VMs could only supplement counter selling, not replace it. Resultingly, Greene got orders for only small numbers of machines, such as 10 or 15. He phoned Los Angeles and convinced Rowe they should operate themselves. By 1947 Rowe operated around 3,000 cigarette machines in New York, selling 450,000 packs a week, 23 million per year. The other 14,000 machines operated by Rowe were spread around 11 States. The biggest areas outside of New York were Philadelphia and Pittsburgh, where Rowe operated 2,000 units in each city. Rowe's net per-pack profit was reported to be slightly more than half a cent. Fifty machines was said to be the minimum required to support an individual operator, and 100 was the most a single operator could handle. The best spots to locate cigarette VMs were in bars and eating establishments. Commissions to locations were said to average about one cent per pack. If an operator could not buy packages of cig-

Traveler purchasing a life insurance policy from a VM, 1948.

arettes that already had change pennies inserted under the cellophane cover, he had to do the job himself. VMs were reported to need to sell 70 packs or more to be profitable, and the figure for a weekly industry average was 150 packs per machine. Therefore, a 50-machine operator would handle 390,000 packs a year, paying about 15.5 cents apiece in New York and selling them for 20 cents. After deductions, profit dwindled to slightly more than one cent per pack. Yearly profit thus worked out to $4,000, or $330 per month for a 50-unit operator.[8]

Direct-to-location sales of cigarette machines reportedly had made inroads in New England in 1949, with a worry it could spread to other areas. For a year, the situation had been a thorn in the side of cigarette machine operators, who continued to argue that the direct-to-location sale of VMs had never proved profitable for locations over the long run. It had started in Boston when the J. P. Manning Company, one of the city's largest tobacco wholesale companies, began to handle a cigarette machine made by the Yeaton Manufacturing company of Lawrence, Massachusetts. Manning sold directly to proprietors and also ran its own operating route in which it offered locations three cents a pack commission — much more than regular cigarette VM operators paid. Yeaton's machine stood 29" high, 16.5" wide, 9" deep, and weighed 45 pounds. Capacity was 20 packs of each of five brands, for a total of 100 packs, with storage room for some additional cartons. Manning sold the unit to Boston locations for $60 without the slug ejector or $82.50 with the slug mechanism. Machines were quarter-operated and were equipped with penny tubes that kicked out one, two, three, or four pennies. The number of pennies returned with each purchase was controlled by the location: if only two of the penny tubes were filled, two pennies were kicked out, if three, then three, and so on. Some locations were able to buy the machines for $1 down and $1 a week, and pay from receipts. Operators stressed they offered service and convenience and that location staff would have to stock the VM, leaving the location vulnerable to theft. Still, as one article admitted, "On the face of it, operators are not able to compete on a dollars-and-cents basis with location-owned equipment."⁹

In 1946 Eastern Electric introduced the first electrically-activated console cigarette machine, and subsequently sold it to the Seeburg company. Electrically-activated machines had existed since the 1920s but had always been a very minor, almost novelty, part of the industry. Starting in this period, these VMs became more common as they began replacing more and more of the non-electric mechanical machines which utilized a simple gravity drop principle to operate.¹⁰

A US Department of Commerce survey released in 1946 looked at confectionary sales. According to this survey, 78 major candy manufacturers sold confections worth $11,766,000 (at wholesale prices) through VMs in 1944. At retail prices, that worked out to more than $23 million worth of candy bars, penny pieces, and 10-cent boxes. The figure represented nine percent of their sales of goods especially adapted to VM distribution, or about seven percent of their total sales of all types of confections (comparable numbers for 1943 were, respectively, six percent and four percent).¹¹

That survey report caused

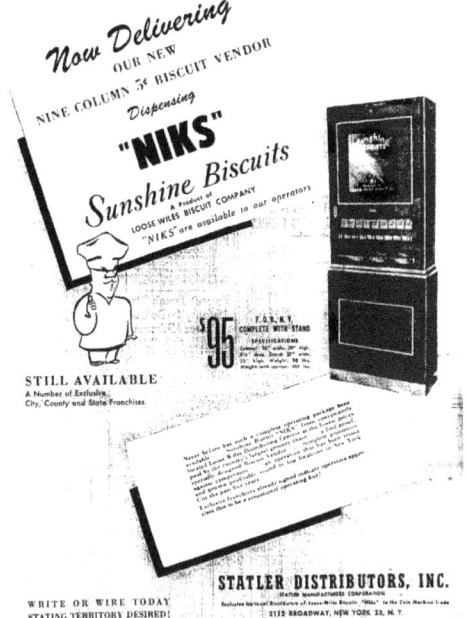

Top: A nickel biscuit machine, 1946.
Bottom: A multi-purpose machine to deliver candy and gum, 1946.

Billboard to take issue with the numbers and declare the Commerce report figures as too low. One company alone, Automatic Canteen, was reported to have 87,750 candy VMs which retailed 385,639,000 candy bars in 1944, worth $10,026,000 wholesale. It was estimated by trade sources that at least 90,000 candy bar VMs were in operation in America besides those of Canteen, in addition to the penny candy vendors which had been estimated at nearly one million. On that basis and the "common trade knowledge" that a vendor must sell 70 or more bars per week to be profitable, sales of candy bars by other vendors must have amounted to approximately 327 million bars in 1944, worth about $8,520,000, said *Billboard*. These figures would bring the grand total of vendor sales of five-cent bars and packaged candies in 1944 to about $18,546,000 wholesale. To that figure had to be added the amount sold through penny candy machines and the amount of 10-cent product — estimated here at another $3 million. That brought the final grand total to about $22 million worth of candy at wholesale prices, nearly 18 percent of total candy sales.[12]

Sam Kresberg, vice president of a VM manufacturer called Drink-O-Mat Industries, said that in the course of a year the annual volume of cup beverage VMs had risen from about $9 million in 1947 to $19 million in 1948. According to Kresberg, approximately 20 percent of all the Coca-Cola syrup then being used was sold through these machines. To that date,

Left: A 1947 soft drink unit. Right: A Mills cup unit, 1949.

the most successful operation of cup dispensing soft drink machines had been in the New York subways where, during certain periods, their popularity had been so great they were unable to give adequate service to the crowds. Kresberg stated that when a machine dispensed more than four drinks per minute it did not maintain the cold temperature it was expected to have during warm weather. One problem identified by Kresberg was price. The average top-grade soft drink cup dispenser then cost nearly $1,500, and had to vend 125 drinks per hour to break even. He hoped to see a machine developed that sold for no more than $500, thereby needing to vend only 60 drinks per hour. Average gross income to operators was said to be two cents out of each nickel drink, and the maximum commission paid out to locations was 25 percent. Kresberg enthusiastically predicted that these VMs would be used in buses, trains, and so on — not just in the transportation depots. He also predicted the wider use of many other types of VMs, stating "It is impossible to measure the potential for this business."[13]

By far, the most important development of this period was the coffee VM. It arrived from two different sources around the same time. One came from Chicago's Bert E. Mills company (separate from Mills Novelty), which unveiled its new device in 1946. From piped-in water and powdered coffee, the machine made an electrically heated brew for five cents. Its four buttons allowed customers to receive a paper cupful of coffee with cream, sugar, both, or neither.[14]

At Wright Air Field one morning in 1944 Lieutenant Lloyd Rudd and Sergeant Cy Melikian took a break from work to get a cup of coffee. At the cafeteria, they were met by a sign saying henceforth coffee would not be served between meals. The men went to a VM and got two cokes instead, thinking "wouldn't it be good if you could get a coffee that way." Working on their off hours, they built just such a machine, constructed of old auto parts. After leaving the army, the pair established a factory in July, 1946, to produce their VM. The device measured two feet by three feet by six feet high, had a 425 cup capacity and was called "Kwik Kafe." Like the Mills machine, this device dispensed powdered coffee and the desired condiments for a nickel. By April, 1948, Rudd and Melikian had 53 employees and sales of nearly $1 million. The machine not only electrically heated a five-gallon tank of water, but also refrigerated the cream. When a nickel was inserted the machine handed out a wooden spoon, dropped a paper cup into place, and filled it with hot water and coffee concentrate. Over 400 of their coffee VMs were in use by April, 1948, with orders on hand for 3,000 more units. One of the machines located at Upsala College sold 350 cups a day to students.[15]

The City Milk company of Maspeth, Queens, announced in 1949 that

Left: This 1948 unit delivered coffee or hot chocolate. *Right:* A 1948 coffee VM.

it planned to use VMs to sell milk and to place them in apartment houses and housing projects in various parts of New York City. A trial of the idea in one Queens housing project was said to have produced "excellent results." Each machine was refrigerated, serviced daily, and carried a maximum of 150 paper quart containers. Quarts were dispensed for 20 cents each during the trial, but the device could also make change in pennies. Plans called for a vend price of 19 cents when the trial was expanded. Machines were to be placed on a commission basis, like washing machines in apartment buildings. One advantage touted for this method, said City Milk, was that the consumer was able to purchase refrigerated milk near the door in the needed amount, avoiding the possibility of hand-delivered milk standing in hallways for long periods. Many similar experiments to vend milk were attempted, though none succeeded. While vending milk in small one-person, one-portion containers to be consumed on the spot worked, vending milk in large containers to be bought and taken home for use in the future did not.[16]

An attempt was even made to vend fresh orange juice. The VM automatically sliced the orange and squeezed the juice from each half. Trouble arose because the device could not assure each customer a full measure — oranges could be selected that were fairly uniform in size, but oranges were not uniform in juiciness.[17]

A beverage far ahead of its time was introduced in 1946 when the Pepsi-Cola company pushed a new carbonated drink called Everess. It was a sparkling water that came in a 12-ounce bottle and sold for a nickel. It could be used as table water in localities where the water was not palatable. Reportedly, it was successfully vended at an industrial plant when supplies of regular Pepsi could not be obtained. However, observers were skeptical of the company's plans to supplant regular city table water with the new carbonated beverage because, they said, "the public has always expected its table water to be relatively free." Those skeptics were correct, and the idea quickly failed only to resurface much later.[18]

Although laundromats dated to the 1930s, very few seem to have been around until near the end of World War II. Chicago's first launderette reportedly did not open until March, 1946, with 22 automatic washing machines. Promoted as a "self-service" laundry, the charge was 25 cents to wash 10 pounds of clothes. Soap was provided free. In New York City, first appearance of these outlets was said to have been in 1944. Laundromats proved their efficiency during the wartime washing machine shortage. From their beginning, the outlets in New York operated six days a week—from seven AM to nine PM. It was reported that, concurrently with the Chicago development, laundromats were being introduced outside of New York in major cities from coast to coast.[19]

Yet another attempt was made to vend books when, in 1946, the first book VM was placed in operation in the subway arcade of the Lincoln Building on East 42nd Street in New York. Designed for the pocket-book buying public, the device was financed by the publisher Pocket Books. Each unit was 18 inches wide, two feet deep, 4.5 feet high, and displayed two books at a time through a glass window. Capacity was a maximum of 96 books, or six copies of each of the 16 titles. Customers inserted 25 cents on either side of the unit—depending on where the desired

Unidentified model posing with coffee vendor, 1947.

Bert Mills beside his coffee machine, 1948.

title was situated — and pulled down a short lever to receive their book.[20]

The automatic shoe shine machine also resurfaced, with two units of the latest incarnation placed on trial in the New York subway in 1949. The city's Board of Transportation was to receive 50 percent of the gross income. In an industry that never had a shortage of bad ideas, the shoe shine VM was surely one of the worst. Over roughly a 20 year period, the trade produced at the very least three or four different shoe shine vendors. All quickly failed for the very obvious reason that when the machine applied the shoe polish it did not always limit itself to the customer's shoes. After 1950, the idea of a shoe shine VM seems to have mercifully been allowed to die.[21]

Just before Christmas, 1945, the General Electric company announced it would build several thousand VMs to serve hot dogs, hamburgers, and grilled cheese sandwiches (all three products could be in each unit) heated by electronic tubes. These machines were to be built for Automatic Canteen Company of America, whose engineers collaborated with GE. Patrons dropped in a dime, whereupon a wrapped sandwich dropped down into an electronic oscillator coil. High frequency radio waves were then employed to heat the previously cooked item to the proper temperature before it fell into the receiving compartment. The first machines were expected off the GE production line in January, 1946. More than 1,000 different types of oscillators were built during development before the problem of heating both rolls and meat uniformly, without burning, was overcome.[22]

Rivaling that machine was "Speedy Weeny," an electronically cooked hot dog VM first used in February, 1946, at the W. T. Grant store in New York City — the first of 21 test locations. It served a cooked hot dog wrapped in cellophane for 10 cents. After insertion of a dime, the machine cooked the hot dog "in a matter of seconds and delivered it in an oven-fresh roll wrapped hygienically in cellophane, ready to eat." The unit on site held 180 hot dogs in a cabinet 28" deep by 30" wide by 78" high, but plans called for future models to hold between 300 and 400 hot dogs. The items were wrapped and sealed by the operator or location owner in cellophane bags and then placed into the machine, which maintained a temperature constantly under 45 degrees F. The maker said the machine would also dispense other types of hot foods and sandwiches, and that a battery of them could be installed in one location — each with a different product.[23]

With regard to locations, J. Edwards, a Kansas City, Missouri operator, told a convention of tobacco distributors that the war greatly added to vending machine popularity. In shipyards, hospitals, industrial plants, and in hundreds of other locations, he said, the consuming public met

An ice cream bar vendor, 1948.

the automatic merchandise machine and liked it. "They are no longer a novelty or a fad, but have become a part of the American way of purchasing."[24]

A survey conducted in 1944 by the federal government's War Food Administration covered 2,416 industrial plants and revealed that coin-operated VMs were in use in 35.8 percent of those plants; 39.8 percent had permanent canteens or cafeterias; and 16.4 percent used mobile canteens. For industrial plants, one national distributor of VMs suggested siting one machine for every 50 to 75 employees.[25]

For the first time since 1940 when most of the larger theater chains imposed a ban on popcorn eating inside their cinemas, the kernel was said to be staging a comeback in 1947. However, the Showcase, a movie house on 42nd Street near Broadway in New York, was to that point the only one in the Times Square movie belt that had approved popcorn. All the other first-run houses there such as the Palace, Astor, Capitol, Roxy, and Music Hall still required patrons to check their popcorn before entering. Candy was allowed in all cinemas, and the counters and VMs located there were all reported to be doing well. Some smaller cinemas away from the first-

This automatic store in New York, a Sodamat, sold several different kinds of soft drinks from this battery of machines, 1948.

run Times Square area also allowed popcorn — available at their counters. One account admitted there were few, if any, popcorn vendors within the city. Nonetheless, the article believed it was just a matter of time before the appearance of coin-operated bulk and automatic popcorn machines in the "better" movie houses. But ultimately, popcorn would be dispensed by a live attendant in counter sales. Popcorn VMs were another of the industry's bad ideas.[26]

Robert S. Curtiss, director of the Department of Concessions and Revenues of the Port of New York Authority, reported that for 1948 gross revenue from VMs approached $500,000 from La Guardia Field, New York International Airport, and Newark Airport — the majority collected mainly from La Guardia. Curtiss wanted to extend VM use at all three locations. Three types of VMs at La Guardia produced gross sales in excess of $2,000 per machine for the year and five others exceeded gross earnings of $1,000 per machine. A machine vending nylon stockings sold 1,000 pairs in one month. Curtiss said an effort to avoid direct competition with shops and other concessions was made by placing machines in "studied positions." The Port Authority learned that by shifting the location of a machine as little as six feet its income could be doubled. Also, the Authority maintained VMs at the Holland Tunnel, Lincoln Tunnel, and George Washington Bridge, with reportedly excellent results.[27]

Subway locations in New York City remained the most lucrative. The city's share of VM revenue from the subway locations totaled $1,169,734 in 1947 and $1,173,863 in 1948. Plans were made to have more VMs installed — for example, two more five-cent gum VMs, five-cent cracker machines, and nickel Life Saver dispensers as well as five more shoe shine vendors. Through the Board of Transportation, the city of New York collected 70 percent of the gross regular advertising in the subways, 40 percent of the gross on weigh scales, 70 percent of the gross at flower stands, 30 percent from each of the five-cent cracker and nickel candy VMs, 40 percent from the coin-operated lockers, 75 percent from the pay toilets, and 25 percent of the gross revenue from the relatively new soft drink vendors. For comparison, New York City's share of subway advertising revenue in 1948 was $2,754,050.[28]

Board of Transportation figures for the 11 months ending May 31, 1949, revealed the city's share of receipts from advertising and vending in vehicles and stations throughout New York's rapid transit system was $3,932,333 from a total gross of $12,851,446. Advertising brought the city the most at $2,601,026. Other totals included: newsstand sales, $390,688; VMs, $548,836; luncheonette sales, $42,137; eight candy stores, $28,715; weigh machines, $53,841; bootblack stands, $7,812; shoe shine VMs, $425; flower stands, $21,305; cracker and candy machines, $1,511; soft drink VMs, $131,587; coin-operated lockers, $31,290; pay toilets, $16,831; and pay telephones, $56,323. High bidder American Chicle was awarded a five-year contract in 1949 for the installation and maintenance of VMs and weigh scales in 527 stations of the transit systems, as well as car shops, garages, barns, and employees' recreation rooms. American Chicle agreed to pay the city the following rates: penny gum and chocolate machines, 28 percent; peanut dispensers, 30 percent; weigh scales, 50 percent; five-cent gum units, 28 percent; and nickel candy vendors, 20 percent. A monthly minimum commission payment of $65,000 to the city was guaranteed.[29]

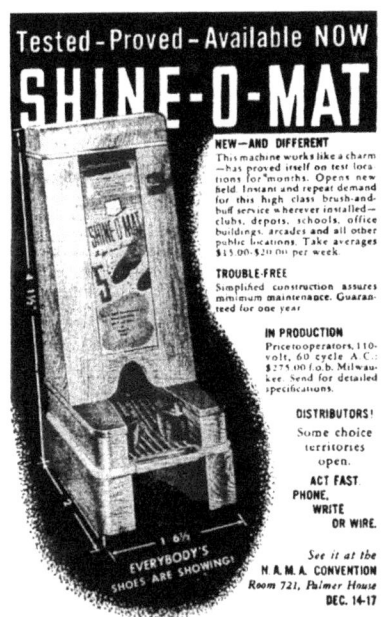

A brush and buff shoe machine, 1947.

Installation of soft drink dispensing machines in New York's subway system began on May 26, 1948, and was completed on August 20, 1948, when the last of the initial 112 machines was sited. In the fiscal year ending September 30, 1949, beverage VMs grossed $881,232 (the city received 25 percent, or $220,301). In the last three months of 1948, those units grossed $166,342. That amount increased to $261,612 in the last three months of 1949 as more units were sited by then.[30]

New York's Long Island Railroad placed an automatic ticket VM on

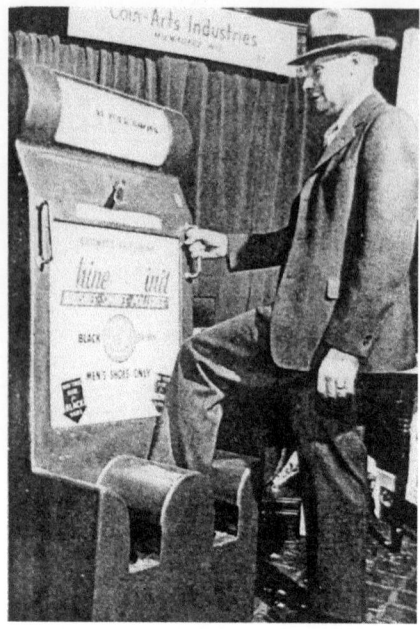

A shoe shine machine, 1947. Note that black shoes went in on one side, brown on the other.

a six-week trial in its station in 1949. Reportedly, this "mechanical sales force" drew crowds of the curious. Similar machines had been used to sell theater tickets and pari-mutuel tickets at race tracks, but this unit had a change-making device for amounts up to $2. Patrons operated the machine by a hand dial that could be set for any one of 50 destinations—the most frequently requested destinations out of 150 in total were chosen—listed on a printed chart along the dial. After coins were placed in the slot, a bar was pressed and the customer received the ticket from one slot and the change, if needed, from another. The machine recorded the total number of sales, total money deposited, number of tickets sold, and net amount in fares, holding $500 in cash to make change. Six weeks later the machine was removed from the Long Island station. Passengers were said to have "cooperated willingly in the experiment until the device produced tickets but balked at returning change."[31]

According to *Business Week*, sales from VMs totaled $500 million in 1945 compared to $300 million in 1941. Continuing the upbeat trend, *Time* magazine reported that there were almost 200 VM manufacturers with the larger firms being Rowe (cigarette machines), Du Grenier (cigarette and candy machines), Mills Novelty (units for Coca-Cola and gambling machines), and Automatic Canteen (snack dispensers). More firms were also going into the business: Bell Aircraft was working on a coin changer and General Electric was involved in developing a hot dog vendor.[32]

Reporter Haviland Reves thought the spotlight of interest in the coin machine industry had long been trained on the "glamour girls" of the trade—jukeboxes and game machines—while the VM had played the role of Cinderella. He thought there were about 3.3 million vendors on location prior to the war, but that number had taken a sharp drop during the war as the penny candy vendors "virtually disappeared" under the pressures of rising prices and a scarcity of candy. Of those pre-war units, Reves said three million were penny VMs while just 300,000 units comprised all others. Sales from VMs, he said, accounted for over one percent of the retail trade of the entire United States. One major drawback noted was the relative inflexibility of the average vending machine as far as price selection was concerned. Coin chutes, in general, could not readily be changed to accommodate various priced items, and the typical machine was "restricted to the familiar penny, nickel or dime. In-between prices are difficult to handle on machines."[33]

Robert Greene, president of NAMA in 1947, bristled at the word "slot," a term still sometimes applied to VMs. He wanted the public to understand that any relationship that had ever existed between VMs and gambling devices had long been "terminated by absolute divorce." When NAMA was formed, its membership rules drew clear attention to the division, stating that membership was limited to those firms that made or operated machines for selling goods. NAMA estimated that there were 2.5 million merchandising machines on location in America in 1946, with sales that year as follows: chewing gum, $10 million; nuts, $20 million; beverages (soft drinks), $52 million; candy, $70 million; and cigarettes, $300 million. With firm determination to establish the industry as legitimate in the public mind, NAMA admitted that in the fairly recent past "gamblers often used vending machines as cover for their more lucrative trade, running an honest gum seller in the front of a store and an outlaw slot machine in the back room."[34]

A Pocket Book vendor, 1947.

Business Week ran yet another rosy article about the industry in 1947, in which it estimated VM sales for that year at $500 to $600 million, with projections of $2 billion a year by 1952. Estimates for 1947 showed that there were 200,000 cigarette machines, 750,000 penny gum and peanut machines, 300,000 nickel candy dispensers, and many thousands of soft

A Speedy Weeny hot dog VM, 1949.

drink machines on location. Service machines like weigh scales, coin-operated lockers, and pay toilets ran to about 350,000. The new electronic cigarette machines cost slightly over $200, compared with $175 to $180 for mechanical units. Soft drink cup vendors were popular in both industrial plants and cinema lobbies because they did away with the empty bottle problem. Newest cup dispensers had a capacity of 750 to 1,000 cups and ranged in price from $750 to $2,200. A Pepsi-Cola cup dispenser in a Detroit bus terminal sold an average of 900 cups a day. With each cup dispensed, the machine played Pepsi's familiar radio commercial. The only problem this article could forecast involved change making, for example, pennies in cigarette packs. With changing taxes at both the state and local level, the amount of returned change differed, and at a price of 21 cents, providing four pennies change was not easy.[35]

Writing in *Science Digest* in 1949, Paul Cohen argued that 60 percent of the price paid to the retailer went to cover the expenses of distribution. A trend toward lower distribution costs was self-service, which started with the rise of supermarkets in 1930s and through the use of VMs. Cohen felt perhaps half the US population, or 75 million people, used some form of coin-operated device every week. Sales from VMs for 1948 were estimated here at $750 million, with cigarette machines responsible for 15 to 25 percent of all cigarettes sold in America. Just as it depended on a standardized coinage, the VM also required standardized packages, goods, and buying habits, noted Cohen. "Nevertheless, the customer still enjoys the illusion of making a free choice." His estimate of around three million total VMs broke down as follows: penny gum, peanut, and other bulk items units, 1.5 million; bottle soft drink machines, 385,000; cigarettes, 250,000; candy bar, 230,000; weigh scales, 200,000; postage stamps, 150,000; gum, 100,000; popcorn, 45,000; soft drinks in cups, 22,000; milk, 15,000; cookies, 12,000; ice cream, 3,500; shoe shine, 3,000; cigar, 3,000; apples, 2,500; aspirin, 1,000; fruit juice, 500; and coffee, 500 machines.[36]

5.—Optimism Returns, 1945-1949

Once the war ended exports of coin-operated machines increased dramatically, only to then decrease as countries began to impose import restrictions and currency controls. For 1945, 7,233 coin machines (worth $552,119) were exported: 1,364 jukeboxes ($309,152), 3,832 games ($188,546), and 2,037 vendors ($54,421). In 1947, 26,542 ($5,120,102) machines were exported: 12,379 jukeboxes ($3,967,859); 7,378 games ($681,009), and 6,785 vendors ($471,234). For 1948, 14,183 ($2,309,581) units were shipped abroad: 3,894 jukeboxes ($1,623,978), 3,852 games ($353,544), and 6,437 vendors ($332,059).[37]

Slugs were less of a problem due mostly to a company that made next to no complete vending machines but remained a major force in the industry. John Gottfried, president of National Slug Rejectors, Inc., of St. Louis, headed a firm that made only the part of the VM that rejected counterfeit coins and slugs. Gottfried had tinkered with gadgets for years before he stumbled across the system for his rejecter, and he began to find a ready market for his device in the 1930s. By 1947, his factory of 283 employees produced 96 percent of all the slug rejecters made in America.[38]

Vandalism, however, remained a problem for the industry though, as in the past, it was a problem rarely mentioned. An exception occurred in a 1947 account in *Fortune*, observing that the VM was considered fair game for small boys, disappointed customers, drunks, vandals, and plain thieves. Non-criminals who would scorn to pocket an unguarded dime would cheerfully spend "untold energy, ingenuity, and animal cunning to beat a vending machine out of a nickel bar of candy." It was a form of petty thievery which this publication thought topped "wet-fly fishing as a national pastime." When a penny went unrewarded with a piece of gum the irate customer might attack the machine, the drunk poured beer into the coin chute, small boys smashed mirrors on the devices for fun; and schemers pulled units from the wall in order to claim physical injury.[39]

A Kleenex tissue machine, 1949.

Perhaps the greatest difficulty for machines in this period was in change making. Devices for making change had been around in experimental form for some time, but did not perform that well. Stand alone machines usually only changed quarters into smaller coins and did not deal with odd-cent pricing. Moreover, these units had limited appeal since they cost money but did not actually make any money. It was a hard sell convincing operators that with a change maker on site total sales could increase. What was needed was a change making capability built directly into each vendor. With frequent price changes in products in the post-war period—compared to the more stable 1930s—the problem of making change became more serious.[40]

In the oddities category was 10-year-old Antoinette D'Angelo who went to the movies in Brooklyn in 1947 with her two sisters. Feeling thirsty, she went to get a drink of water. She inserted a penny in the Dixie Cup dispenser, the cup failed to drop down, and, in trying to extract it, D'Angelo got her left hand up to the wrist imprisoned in the device. The VM was removed from the wall with her hand still attached and placed on the desk in the manager's office. Members of Police Emergency attended and spent half an hour freeing her hand.[41]

Morton Krouse regularly bought gum and chocolate from the penny VMs in the New York subway system. From September 1948 until around the end of that year, he lost 46 cents a penny at a time on VMs that failed to deliver the goods. Finally, he sent the company responsible for operating those machines a letter requesting the return of his 46 cents. The letter was ignored. Krouse then sued in Small Claims Court where he won and was awarded $1.71. The other $1.25 was for the cost of serving the company with a summons.[42]

A more grandiose optimism for the vending industry emerged during the latter part of

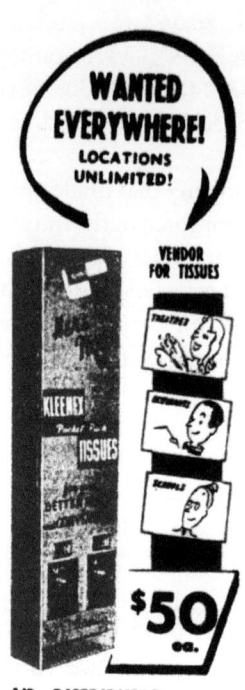

A different model Kleenex VM, 1949.

5.—Optimism Returns, 1945-1949

this period. It matched the late 1920s in terms of its uncritical, impractical dreaminess, but was nowhere near as pervasive. In its 1947 celebration of a VM "jackpot," *Business Week* observed a belief that coin machines would supplement both cashiers and grocery clerks and there would eventually be coin-operated drive-ins along America's highways. The motorist of the future would be able to drive into a gas station at night, "put coins in the gas pump to fill his tank, and then put more coins in food and beverage machines to fill his stomach."[43]

An executive with the vending firm Telecoin predicted that within a few years there would be stores devoted entirely to mechanical merchandising devices—what he called "vendormats." The key to success for such ventures lay in the "constant perfection" of VM design. Additionally, the machines of the near future would be used more to display and advertise products.[44]

Tom Bernard authored a long piece in *American Magazine* in 1948, claiming that sales through VMs in 1947 reached $1 billion [highly exaggerated]. His availability list included articles such as coffee, insurance, towels, tooth brushing kits, aspirin, books, newspapers, milk, frozen foods, fruit juices, soup, ice cream, golf balls, fishing tackle, hot sandwiches, stockings, vitamins, gasoline, cosmetics, railroad tickets, "bacteria-free" soft drinks, and fresh fish, and services such as a shine shoe, send a telegram, mail a letter, rent a typewriter, wash and dry clothes, massage feet, and acquire a sun tan. However, in the near future he predicted there would be banks of food dispensers lining apartment building lobbies, drugs and sundries would be available in the outer walls of pharmacies after closing time, supplementary feeding units vending complete meals from soup to dessert would be found in industrial plants, and batteries of machines at parks, beaches, and picnic grounds would supply everything essential to a family outing—from insect repellent to kindling wood. Possibilities were "unlim-

VM models on display at a 1947 trade show in Chicago.

ited" and that long touted automatic store would soon be everywhere. It all meant greater shopping ease for customers with more products available in handier form. Concluded Bernard: "The machine as a salesman has definitely come of age, and in a few years it is entirely possible that any product that's reasonably small, packageable, salable at a modest profit, and available in quantity will be yours for a few coins in a slot and a thumb on a button."[45]

Speaking at a 1949 session of NAMA in New York City, industrial designer Egmont Arens predicted that within another 10 years the coin machine would be as much a symbol of American life as the hot dog. He also predicted that vendors would become a major source of income for department stores and supermarkets. Extending the frontiers, he said, were the rapid development of plastic packaging materials and the rise of prepackaging. Arens urged his listeners to use VMs more for display. "So many machines today remind me of Victorian bathing suits. They hide the product or let it peep out of an obscure corner."[46]

Perhaps the most noteworthy happening in this brief period was the development of the hot coffee vending machine. It would in time have a significant impact, but not as much as the cigarette machine or soft drink vendor. While some fanciful dreams and predictions emerged, no physical attempts were made to bring them to reality. That would have to wait for the 1950s, when another technical era (the space race) would prepare a foundation for another attempt at the automatic store.

6

The Four C's Dominate: Cigarettes, Coffee, Cola, Candy, 1950s

"Rows of monstrous, coin-operated refrigerators ... have been installed in apartment houses to compete with the milkman and the grocery store's dairy department."

John Sharnik, 1950

Milk VMs on the streets "are not in keeping with Union [New Jersey]'s policy of gracious living."

F. Edward Biertuempfel, 1954

"Robots ... at your service."

Andrew Hecht, 1956

Although much attention was often devoted to stories and predictions about how vending was going to expand into dispensing items it was not then vending, or into more elaborate robotic stores, the industry settled into a pattern where it depended on what were sometimes called in the trade the four Cs. Vending received the vast majority of its income from cigarettes, coffee, soft drinks (cola), and candy. This pattern became well established in the 1950s and would remain the prevailing situation for several decades. Amidst the many failed vending experiments, the trade had found one huge success in each decade from the 1920s to the 1940s: cigarettes, cola, and coffee, respectively. However, no such future hits would be forthcoming. So well entrenched were these four items, and so much taken for granted, that they received few media mentions. Rowe continued to be one of the largest manufacturers of cigarette VMs in America. The idea of the talking machine surfaced again when Rowe introduced a talking cigarette machine in 1954. It said things like "Hello" and "Don't run short. Better buy two packs while you're here." The voice came from a battery-operated miniature record player that went into its sales talk as soon as the customer pulled the plunger. Supposedly, this machine was then installed in a few Manhattan locations.[1]

One development that helped the coffee VM was the institutionalizing of the coffee break in the 1950s, which generated an outside business to cater to that need including, but not limited to, VMs. For example, in 1950 Schrafft's, an east coast restaurant chain, was called in by the Mutual Life Insurance Company of New York to do something about the daily chaos caused by 1,700 coffee-seeking employees on 13 floors, all trying to go up or down the elevators at the same time. Schrafft's sent a battalion of waitresses with specially equipped carts rolling from desk to desk, reducing coffee break truancy so efficiently that 500 other employers were soon signed up for the service. By 1956 Schrafft's grossed $4.2 million a year from its coffee break service, employing 500 waitresses to deliver 20 million cups of coffee and 13 million pastries a year to offices in Manhattan, Philadelphia, Boston, and Newark. And, of course, many other companies solved their coffee break chaos by using vending machines.[2]

Some 10 years after Rudd and Melikian introduced their first coin-operated coffee machine, *Business Week* commented that "Only a few manufacturers have been able to crack the problem of dispensing a palatable cup of coffee...." However that seemed to have no effect on the rapid growth rate of the devices.[3]

At the end of the 1950s, reporter James Nagle estimated that there were 1.2 million soft drink vendors in the nation selling $570 million worth of product annually. This represented about 20 percent of all soft drink sales — total VM revenue was $2.1 billion per year. Bottle VMs then cost $275 to $625, while cup units retailed for $500 to $1,500. The earliest metal soft drink vendor, which carried a list price of $60, came with the added inducement of 20 free cases of the soft drink of the buyer's choice.[4]

Candy bar popularity could be seen from the experience of the Boeing plants in Wichita, Kansas, where it was reported that employees purchased 3,156,473 chocolate bars in 1951. That amounted to 13 bars per worker per month, or 263,039 bars sold each month through the plant's vending machines.[5]

Milk vending also remained in the news in the 1950s. As machines vending quart bottles were installed in 1949 in a few apartment buildings, reporter John Sharnik was moved to write that "Rows of monstrous, coin-operated refrigerators, combining the design of a restrained juke-box with the architecture of a bank vault, have been installed in apartment houses to compete with the milkman and the grocery store's dairy department."

It was all part of a move by the "robots" to replace not only the man behind the shop counter, but also "the ... counter itself, and even the shop."[6]

City Milk apparently abandoned their experiment and then restarted it because it was reported in 1953 that milk delivery had been stopped at 70 apartment buildings in New York City where "mechanical milkmen" had been quietly tested in lobbies for a year. Machines held 140 quart cartons of milk and vended a quart for 22 cents—the same price charged in retail stores and four cents below the usual home delivery price. Each unit cost $845 and would not be sold or leased to apartment house owners who, "if they insist, will receive a percentage of the receipts," said Rowe vice president John S. Mill. So far the devices had been accepted by the landlords as a "service to tenants." That is, no commission was paid.[7]

John R. Humphreys, a dairyman in Glenside, New Jersey, had no thought of being a pioneer in November, 1953, when he bought six milk VMs and placed them in nearby communities. He did not install them in the usual indoor locations, but rather outdoors in gasoline stations, bus stops, and in residential areas where no store was nearby. Rowe watched closely, since a worry was that any sales through the VMs would merely be transferred from conventional retail outlets. Rowe found that store sales and home deliveries in the areas served by Humphreys's machines were unchanged. Therefore, the milk sold through the vendors represented extra sales. According to Rowe, 16,000 milk VMs grossed $22.5 million in 1954.[8]

One argument in the field of milk vending that came to dominate in the 1950s was that quart vending sales did not enlarge the market; it merely altered the distribution patterns. However, any sales picked up in the half-pint machines found in locations such as factories, schools, or offices might be sales that would not have been made. Therefore, if the dairyman was looking for more sales, he had better forget quarts and concentrate on half pints. It was the old VM dilemma of impulse buying (immediate consumption) versus cracking the take-home market. Journalist Andrew Hecht called 1953 the year of the milk vendor, with the machines widely hailed as a means of eliminating the country's milk surplus—and heavily attacked by retail grocers and the Milk Drivers and Dairy Employees' Union, AF of L, as cutting into their livelihood. "They sabotaged the milk machines by any and all means," wrote Hecht, "from pouring molasses down the mechanism to having prohibitive local ordinances passed against them."[9]

When Land O'Lakes Creamery set up outdoor vending stations in Austin, Minnesota, local dairies retaliated by pushing through an ordinance specifically forbidding the sale of milk in coin machines. In September, 1954, the Union, New Jersey township committee approved an ordinance banning milk VMs on the streets, but allowing them at indoor locations such as stores, factories, and schools. Mayor F. Edward Biertuempfel declared that the machines "are not in keeping with Union's policy of gracious living." He condemned as unsightly the "slot-machine method of selling products."[10]

Secretary of Agriculture Ezra Benson saw VMs as a possible cure for one of his biggest headaches in 1954—the federal government's 600 million gallon milk surplus. In an effort to promote milk consumption, he had machines installed in various government buildings in Washington, including his own Agriculture Department. He wanted to put milk vendors in every department in the government, even the White House. Also involved were the National Dairy Milk Producers Federation and its local member groups, who were sponsoring an education program, the "Dairy-Vend-Caravan," then touring the country. It featured slide and film demonstrations and talks on how the automatic vendors worked and could be used. The effort was to induce milk drinkers to drink more, and to create a new market among the estimated 50 million Americans who did not drink milk at all.[11]

Governor Thomas Dewey of New York, who had christened almost every kind of building and monument imaginable, broke new ground when he joined Benson's campaign by christening a milk VM located in the first floor lobby of the Capitol. He bought a container of white milk (chocolate was also available) for 10 cents and gave the media a photo opportunity.[12]

Early in 1955, Benson had the VM removed from the entrance to his office in the North Agriculture Building in Washington. The machine dispensed 213 half pint cartons in a 20-day working month—an average of only 10.6 cartons a day. Reason for the poor sales figures was thought to be that there were not enough visitors to Benson's office area. Moved one floor up to a busy corridor, the unit was said to be doing well. Across the street in the South Building, seven milk vendors were each dispensing 1,300 to 1,500 cartons a month.[13]

One product not vended in the 1950s was water. Reporter John Sharnik observed that in the early 1950s manufacturers of VMs were approached almost every week by business people or inventors who wanted the makers to develop new machines. However, among the proposals those manufacturers had "stoutly refused" to develop was one for "coin-vended water, a commodity held in high esteem almost everywhere but not usually felt to have much commercial value."[14]

Juice firms active in vending at the beginning of the 1950s were Minute Maid and Welch Grape Juice. By the end of 1951, they hoped to have a total of 1,500 machines vending their products, consisting of orange, lemon, grape, and apple juices. These and other juice producers hoped to expand the market further in 1952. First of the frozen juice producers to try serving its product in cup machines was Minute Maid, opening the field in November, 1949, when it signed a contract with Mills Industries for 1,000 vendors. The original contract called for single-drink, non-selective units priced at $750. However, when 225 units had been delivered, Minute Maid decided to switch to a selective machine. Mills built the remaining 775 units as dual-flavor dispensers, listed for between $1,050 and $1,150. One reason for the model change was that rising production costs would have boosted the price of the single flavor unit to $900 — a price Minute Maid felt was too high for a non-selective machine. With the introduction of two-flavor equipment, a lemonade drink was added to the juice menu. Commissions on juice machines proved to be a major problem in juice vending, according to Minute Maid executive William Burke. Due to costs, commissions on the 10 cent juices could not exceed 15 percent. Only in a few cases were they higher, as in New York's subway system. Thus, said Burke, locations used to receiving 25 percent on nickel soft drinks balked at a lower percentage. When Minute Maid orange juice vendors went into test operations in December, 1949, it was found that 100 drinks a day was the average vended by the single-flavor machines. However, both New York subway and Chicago railroad locations achieved averages of 250 to 300 drinks daily. Welch, which started its vending program in 1951, designed and manufactured its own two-flavor unit. Based on test locations, the company predicted average sales of 1,000 drinks per week. Unlike the Minute Maid machines, Welch units were not sold outright. Operators paid $88 down per machine and leased them for a three year period at a rate of $22 a month. After three years, operators had the option of buying the machine at the prevailing market price or of continuing to lease the unit, with the monthly payment dropping to $10.[15]

Attempts also continued to automatically vend books and magazines. The automatic "VendAvon Book Machine," which held from 350 to 650 copies of 24 Avon 25-cent reprint titles, was introduced in 1950 in the New York area by Avon Publishing Company at a cost of more than $30,000 in development expense. A non-electrical unit, the device was three feet wide, 1.5 feet deep, and 6.5 feet high. When considering locations, Avon thought the best ones would be in areas such as hospitals, hotels, docks, supermarkets, and ferries. A test model had been in use for several months at La Guardia Airport, followed by the siting of four more at Long Island's Idlewood Airport. Avon believed the new VMs would give first a clear idea of what sort of book people would buy without the opportunity of examining it; a book's appeal had to depend even more on the title, author, and cover

The VendAvon Book machine, 1950.

art. One account noted that previous experiments in vending books by VM had been "impractical." The Pocket Books experiment had failed by this time.[16]

One year later, Avon had about 120 machines in operation in New York, Maryland, Massachusetts, Arizona, and other places. Maurice Diamond, vice president of Avon Books, said they returned a "fair" sales volume. Avon owned the vendors and lent them without fee to several franchise operators who accepted books from the publisher on consignment, paying only for the number actually sold. Average weekly sales volume per machine was reported to be 75 to 100 books. Diamond said the best locations were air terminals and other spots where traffic was heavy — provided that traffic was transient. If the same people returned over and over to the same locations, then the volume dropped. Thus, heavily-patronized supermarkets did poorly when it came to automatically vending books. Diamond also felt book vending as then set-up would only be financially attractive to operators with substantial routes of diversified equipment, since sales from book VMs stacked up poorly against the overhead required to run a specialized book vending route. By the spring of 1952, Avon reported it had 210 machines on location and was "doing well."[17]

In the magazine area, *Reader's Digest* committed itself in the fall of 1951 to more elaborate testing of VMs, ordering a new batch of units from manufacturers to be placed in a wide variety of locations. Two *Digest* machines, one holding 50 copies, the other 75, had been on continuous trial in New York and Chicago air terminals since January, 1951. However, Cowles, publisher of the picture weekly *Quick*, expressed doubts that any further steps to promote magazine vending would be taken by it. Cowles circulation chief Abner Sideman remarked that, "the economies of selling for *Quick*, at least, would leave little profit for operators were it thrown open to route placement." He added that there would be little potential in restricting placement to newsstands for after-hour sales. While *Quick* had been vended experimentally through 10 machines no further orders for units were planned. *Life* magazine had expected to be in the experimental vending phase at this time, but delays had kept it in the preliminary stage. A pilot machine was returned by *Life* to the maker for redesign. *Time* magazine was moving ahead on a related project of its own — the sale of magazine subscriptions via VMs. Patrons would insert the proper number of quarters, write out their order, and tear off a receipt. Cost for a four-month subscription would be $1.25 in military installations and $1 on college campuses. Test units were expected to be in the field by the fall of 1951.[18]

Still in a testing phase, *Reader's Digest* installed a VM in the Chappaqua, New York, station of the New York Central Railroad. By 1952, the *Digest* had 102 machines in high traffic spots. However, both Curtis Publishing and Crowell-Collier Publishing had given the idea a try and dropped it as impractical. Time was still reportedly tinkering with prototype units for *Life* and *Time* magazines. One main catch was the high cost of servicing machines that sold such a low profit item.[19]

When *Billboard* analyzed the magazine vending situation in 1955, it declared it seemingly unlikely that any widespread installation of vendors for magazines and newspapers was imminent. "One thing seems fairly certain though: Whatever development does take place in the vending of periodicals will be done by the publishers; operators just don't fit into the picture." The deterrent to operators was obvious: there was no money in it. Any location with a high volume of traffic probably had a newsstand nearby; any location with a low volume of traffic would not generate enough sales to warrant installation of a machine. *Life* finally got two test models on location — electric VMs with a capacity of 100 copies. However, one of the units had been out of commission for most of the year it had been on trial due to mechanical problems. Vended products such as cigarettes, coffee, candy, and soft drinks made a profit because they could and did achieve several sales a day to the same individuals. When an individual made a purchase, he did not cease to be a prospect for the next seven days, as he did in the case of a weekly magazine.[20]

One tradition started to die in 1957 when the American Scale Manufacturing Company of Washington, D.C., introduced the first two cent weigh scale. Putting on a brave face, the firm declared that selected tests of the new machines showed no drop in patron usage. However, the weigh scale, at whatever price, was rapidly disappearing. With postwar affluence came the development of many gadgets, for example, the accurate and inexpensive household bathroom scale. Households interested in weight could and did purchase home scales and the public weighing machines passed into history.[21]

Perfume VMs proved another industry bad idea. They, too, kept returning. Around 1950, Lawrence Hoffman of Toronto formed a company, Perfumatic of Canada Limited, to make a contraption he had spent three

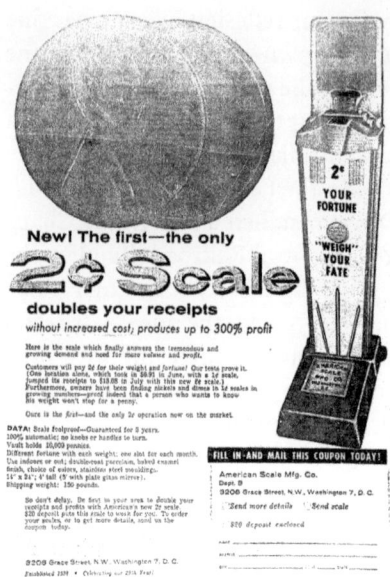

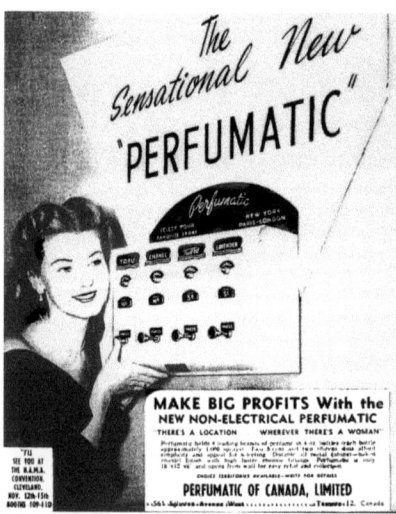

Top: First of the two-cent weigh scales, 1957.
Bottom: Perfume vendor, 1951.

years in devising. He believed his company was then the only one making perfume dispensing machines. Most of his units were shipped to the US and, by the end of 1953, he hoped to have 10,000 machines sited in America. Units sold to distributors for $93.75, and to operators for $125. From one four-ounce bottle of eau de cologne, a machine could dispense from 600 to 1,000 sprays at a dime apiece — depending on how hard the plunger was pulled. Thus, the return on one bottle was $60 to $100. Since each VM held four such bottles, the total gross return from one machine could range from $240 to $400. With an original cost of $10 for filling all four bottles, Hoffman declared the profits were enormous. For her 10 cents, the customer had her choice of four perfumes — Dana's Tabu, Chanel No. 5, Lentheric's Tweed, or Yardley's Lavendor. Actually, the product was not perfume, but eau de cologne. Perfume was said to evaporate too readily and was apt to stain clothes. Perfumatic machines were found in washrooms in hotels, restaurants, night clubs, department stores, bowling alleys, dance halls, air line terminals, and bus stations. Said Hoffman, "Where there's a woman there's a location." Commissions paid to locations started at around 15 percent. Installation was financially justified, argued Hoffman, even if the VM dispensed only 10 sprays a day. That would bring in $7 weekly, with $1.05 to the location owner.[22]

In Detroit the G. J. Vending company was established in 1951 to operate hair oil vending equipment. With no machine available to dispense their chosen item, the firm acquired an older type of vendor said to have been originally planned to dispense Jergens' hand lotion and adapted it for hair oil dispensing. As well, the company began to also dispense hand lotion through units operated by a penny. Favorite locations were in washrooms and wherever there was a swimming pool or a shower. Hand lotion machines were said to be proving a favorite in women's washrooms in department stores.[23]

Brylcream had a hair oil vendor being used in England and other foreign countries before being introduced in America around 1951 or 1952. The Brylcream machine operated in pool, beach, and gymnasium locations. A patron placed a hand beneath a delivery nozzle on the face of the wall-mounted vendor and, for a nickel, received a quantity of oil in his hand by slowly depressing a plunger to activate the mechanism. Capacity of the unit was one-half gallon of the hair preparation, sufficient for about 400 portions. Brylcream could be purchased by operators in two-gallon containers, to be pumped into the VM product compartment. Locations received a commission of 25 percent of the gross receipts.[24]

Stranger still was the machine installed in San Antonio, Texas, bars to cure hangovers. For 25 cents it gave patrons a 10-second whiff of pure oxygen. Another oddity involved the unnamed Atlantic City, New Jersey tavern proprietor who applied for permission to operate an alcohol-serving VM. William Howe Davis, director of the New Jersey Division of Alcoholic Beverage Control, delivered a ruling that forbade the sale of alcoholic drinks from coin machines. It was an emphatic "No." He said: "I have not yet heard of a machine that can say 'no' to a minor or a drunk or any other who should not be served."[25]

With respect to locations, the coin machine industry was large enough by this time to have developed a specialized occupation. Ontario, California-based Frank F. Barreras had placed hundreds of machines during the 15 years he had been associated with the coin machine field. Known as a "locator," his business was getting locations for bulk merchandisers, cigarette machines, jukeboxes, and amusement games. When he had a location sold on the idea of accepting a machine, he notified either a distributor or an operator for work on speculation. However, most of his work was on order, the operator designating the number and type of spots—even the area—that he wanted. Barreras was credited in the industry as having a knack for getting locations. For obtaining a location for a bulk merchandiser, he charged $3 per machine; if two machines were placed in one location the charge was $5, for three machines, $7.50. A cigarette machine location cost the operator or distributor 10 cents per pack on the first week's sales—

usually $10 to $12. When he located a jukebox or a game, Barreras received the first two weeks' receipts. Before working on his own for four years, he had worked exclusively on salary for distributers as a locator. Barreras got his start 15 years earlier, around 1942, when he wanted to buy a coin machine route in the Midwest. The distributor asked him if he would like to locate machines and, while he accepted the challenge, he never bought the route.[26]

According to a 1950 film industry census, approximately 32 percent of the nation's theaters had some sort of VM service in their houses for confectionery sales. Small theaters tended to use lobby stands and counters exclusively, while the intermediate and larger houses used vendors to serve balconies and remote areas, such as lounges, as well as for hours when the counters were closed. Some 5,933 American cinemas used VMs while 12,647 had manual stands or counters. An average of 3.4 percent of all movie houses depended entirely on VMs. Only 2.7 percent of houses having 500 seats or less relied completely on VMs; 4.1 percent of houses with 501 to 1,000 seats; 7.1 percent of the 1,001-seats-and-over theaters used machines exclusively. The trend was toward theater-controlled sales of confections and beverages. Outside concessionaires controlled sales in 19.5 percent of the cinemas while in the other 80.5 percent of the houses such sales were theater-owned and managed. It was big business. A confectionery or beverage sale was made to 56.6 out of every 100 people who purchased tickets, with an average sale of 8.5 cents. Assuming 90 million people attended the movies every week, this meant there were 50,940,000 purchases worth $4,329,900, or $225,154,800 annually.[27]

Vending in the New York City subway system in 1950 produced the following results: one-cent gum machines ($1,306,211 gross, 28 percent of that to the city); five-cent gum ($60,033, 28 percent); one-cent candy ($339,639, 28 percent); five-cent candy ($139,635, 20 percent); five-cent cracker ($70,213, 20 percent); one-cent peanut ($266,922, 30 percent); one-cent weigh scales ($125,724, 50 percent); five-cent tissue ($1,845, 10 percent). The grand total was $2,310,222. At the end of December, 1950, the system had 7,857 penny gum, chocolate, and peanut units, 2,090 scales, and 938 nickel gum, candy, and cracker vendors. Additionally, drink vendors grossed $1,022,973 from 395 machines—all cup units. They included 80 four-selection dispensers, 146 single-flavor units, 123 three-selection devices, and 46 fruit juice dispensers.[28]

Reporter Meyer Berger commented in 1953 that the New York City subway system supported 11,700 VMs, while the combined railroad stations of the US supported fewer than 10,000 machines. American Chicle still held the subway vending contract, but assigned actual operation to the International News Company which kept 145 men underground all day collecting, stocking, and maintaining the machines. Company executives were unhappy about the public response to pennies lost in their dispensers. Each day some eight to ten people wrote to complain of one-cent losses. It cost the company about eight cents to reimburse the patron — a penny was taped to the return letter. Chewing gum accounted for about 65 percent of the total merchandise sold, five-cent candy was second, one-cent chocolate placed third, and one-cent peanuts finished in fourth. According to Berger, "The company maintains a list of psychopaths who stuff machines with paper or cardboard, then fish out pennies put in by customers." For a long time International News used a distinctive slug with the inscription "Inco" which its weigh scale adjusters were to put the Inco slugs in to test the machines. If the slugs did not turn up in the collector's gathering, it was plain the adjuster had skipped the machine. One day it dawned on company executives that they were violating the federal anti-slug law themselves by using the slugs. On their lawyers' advice they dropped the practice.[29]

The Chicago Transit Authority (CTA) reported that it had the following number of VMs in its subway and el stations: one-cent candy (143 in 1948, 221 in 1951); gum (223, 310); nuts (116,178); scales (250, 267); beverage (0, 85); total (732, 976). Included in the 1951 total were 111 units added to a new four-mile, 12-station system extension opened in March, 1951— 25 penny candy units, 33 nuts and 43 gum vendors, and 10 beverage units.[30]

For 1953, the CTA reported that the 920 VMs located in its subway and el system earned a total of $74,683, from a gross total of $292,250. In 1952 1,018 machines earned the CTA $89,177. That drop was attributed to less passengers, a result of higher fares and a general downward trend in transportation system earnings. Penny vendors, including 184 chocolate, 250 gum, 166 nut, and 184 scales grossed $133,524 in 1953 (CTA's share was $35,414); 44 nickel gum and 21 dime candy VMs grossed $48,074 ($8,615); 51 cup beverage dispensers grossed $93,176 ($25,718); 18 ice cream machines took in $17,988 ($2,697); two photo machines grossed $4,488 ($1,239). CTA vendor income was $55,196 in 1949; $84,155 in 1950; $84,539 in 1951; $89,177 in 1952; and $74,683 in 1953.[31]

Attempts were even made in the 1950s to install VMs on railroad cars and city buses, with no success. The Pennsylvania Railroad tried out food-dispensing VMs in 1951 when five trial machines were placed on the heavily used, hourly New York to Philadelphia run. The idea was to broaden the service if it proved popular. Seen as a supplement to the regular dining car service, those VMs could, in combination, dispense an entire light meal: fruit juice, 15 cents; ham sandwich on rye, 35 cents; pastry 15 cents; coffee,

10 cents; total 75 cents. Milk, ice cream, and candy were also available. Built by Rowe, the five machines cost about $3,500 for the set and were given special shock absorbing protection.[32]

So intriguing was this idea that the *New Yorker* magazine sent its reporter "Stanley" out to cover the media test run. On board were two publicity people with the Pennsylvania Railroad and Charles Brinkmann, vice president of Rowe Manufacturing. Signs all over the cars read "Food and Drink Machines Straight Ahead," while pamphlets about the vendors were on every seat. Right above the machines was a big sign: "Automatic Buffet." Five seats had been removed from the end of one car to make room for the five dispensers. A milk machine, a coffee unit, and a sandwich dispenser priced 25 to 50 cents were on one side, while on the other side of the aisle stood another two, one for ice cream and the other to vend candy-cake-pie-pastry. A change making device gave nickels and dimes for quarters, but there was no way of changing bills. Talking to Brinkmann, Stanley inadvertently used the term "slot machine," causing Brinkmann to hit the ceiling. He asked Stanley to never say slot machine to a Rowe man; the proper term was "automatic food dispenser." Those slots in dispensers through which coins were fed were officially called, emphasized Brinkmann, "coin inserts." Rowe admitted it had a hard time adapting dispensers for use on trains because of the constant jarring from the motion and because jiggling kept causing dispensers to give out merchandise free. However, Rowe insisted it had overcome all such problems. Within a short time, though, the Pennsylvania Railroad had to drop its VM idea when it found the machines were being constantly shaken loose from their moorings.[33]

Springfield, Ohio's municipal bus system, Springfield City Lines, installed penny gum VMs on its buses in 1953. After the six-selection, 315-capacity gum vendors had operated for a time, bus company president C. E. Baker declared: "Penny gum vending machines installed on all our buses have been amazingly successful in producing additional revenue." Gum units on the Springfield line were said to be doing their best volume on buses used for factory and school runs. The machines were mounted on metal support posts near the entrance and exit doors with special grommets that absorbed vibration and noise. Springfield City Lines started slowly by installing just one machine on one bus. After a year, gum VMs were installed on all 62 buses. Each vendor grossed $3 to $6 a week, with the bus company receiving 15 percent commission. In March, 1954, the bus line bought the VMs.[34]

Industrial locations continued to be an important growth area for the vending industry. Research done by the Paper Cup and Container Institute, covering 118 industrial plants, reported VM presence both for 1950

A typical VM installation at an industrial or office location, 1957.

and the wartime peak (year not given). Bottled soft drinks were vended by 65 companies in 1950, 64 in the wartime peak year; cup soft drinks (64, 32); milk (29, 21); coffee (23, 3); cookies (15, 2); ice cream (15, 5); fruit juices (13, 2); cakes and pies (6, 3); and sandwiches (3, 2).[35]

Reporter Cedric Larson said in 1954 that 90 percent of all manufacturing plants employing over 75 people then had one or more VMs, as did 98 percent of all plants with 1,000 or more employees. There were then said to be 75 percent more vendors in industrial shops than even at the peak of World War II. Said one unnamed factory manager: "Without the vending machines we would certainly have to set up refreshment stands within the plant and add to our growing losses from restaurant operations."[36]

Business Week argued, in late 1954, that it was only since the Korean War that a worker could buy himself a meal in his plant by dropping coins into a long battery of VMs. In-plant feeding then looked like the richest mine for the vending industry to tap. Many plants were said to have installations similar to that found in the textile firm of M. Lowenstein & Sons, New York, where rows of 10, 12, or more machines, collected in one spot, sold everything—hot and cold sandwiches, soups, pastries, coffee, milk, soft drinks, and ice cream. Some operators even installed their VMs behind a uniform front to make them more attractive. One reason for the success of machines in industrial locations was that many plants were industrial islands with few, if any, restaurants nearby. VMs were good for the companies because they required no capital outlays—cafeterias generally lost money but were supplied because of employee need. Operators usually (but not always) gave a plant a five to ten percent commission on the VM receipts. Also, vendors were available 24 hours a day while cafeterias usually were not. Nevertheless, some plants were proud of their cafeterias serving hot, full meals. That was something the VMs did not do, despite their many claims to the contrary.[37]

A survey of 5,000 factories in 1955 made by the Paper Cup and Container Institute — 1,200 plants completed the questionnaire — disclosed that 55 percent of the respondents were offering some food service to their employees. Of those, 84 percent used some VMs. Almost 40 percent of the plants using VMs said they had introduced them within the last five years. Still, machines were considered a supplementary service in most cases. Many of the plants with VMs said that they also had cafeterias, canteens, or mobile food units. Of 382 companies operating cafeterias, 308 also used vending machines.[38]

Office locations in New York City were not doing that well for VMs, according to journalist Aaron Sternfield. Operators needed a large number of employees, and a high number of Manhattan offices employing from 10 to 50 people did not meet that standard. Also, the average office worker in Manhattan had a choice of many restaurants and delis very near his office. Any office in Manhattan with 200 or more employees was considered a good prospect. If an operator estimated there were enough employees or traffic to gross the $90 weekly expected on the average three-unit installation, then he would try and place the machines. An average office location would have a milk machine, either a juice or sandwich machine, and either a candy, cookie, or pastry vendor. Cigarette VMs in Manhattan office buildings tended to generate low volume because employees were close to many chain and drug stores, which sold cigarettes cheaper.[39]

Somewhat bizarrely, VMs even made an unsuccessful attempt to establish a serious presence in shopping centers. Opening in 1955 in St. Louis, the $15 million Hampton Village Shopping Center included 210 retail stores, a medical center, a sports center, several cinemas, a huge supermarket, doctors' and dentists' offices, and a few taverns. It was also home to about 500 VMs operated by 11 different operators — not including several pin games and jukeboxes. About 90 cigarette vendors alone had been sited in the retail stores, taverns, and entertainment centers, as had candy, cookie, bulk confection, and nut vendors. Cup soft drink machines were placed in the bowling alley, theaters, some of the big offices, and in the supermarket.[40]

Schools at all levels would soon be a lucrative and controversial location for the machines. At this point, though, such placements were in their infancy. One who did take note was Dr. William Humphrey of Denver. Writing in the American Dental Association's journal in 1956, he said that public schools should remove vending machines that dispensed candy and sweetened beverages. He concluded: "Schools should practice as well as teach good nutrition."[41]

Existing retailers of various types also launched experiments. Robert

Greene, president of the Rowe Corporation, told the Greater Buffalo Advertising Club in 1950 that a well-known drug store chain had plans for a revolving store front. During the day one would see the usual display windows, but after closing hours the front would become a battery of coin-operated machines for emergency items. The example cited by Greene did not happen, but the concept was clearly modeled on the European situation, a success greatly envied by the American vending trade.[42]

Six years later, the revolving store front method was in use in at least one store. More than 1,000 packages of 25-, 35-, and 50-cent candy were reportedly sold each day through an "automatic window" at the Loft Candy Shop at 11 East 42nd Street, New York. Purchased from the Window-Matic Corporation, the window had two VM devices (one at each end) from which passers-by could make purchases 24 hours a day. Thus, it was a combination display window and VM. The six-feet wide units were made in West Germany, assembled in America, and, according to store officials, had increased the sale of the vended items "considerably." Although similar automatic windows were being used throughout Europe, the one installed at Loft's was said to be the first in the US.[43]

One year later, Loft had a total of three windows installed. Also, one was placed in G. C. Murphy's department store in Pittsburgh. Machines were manufactured to vend from eight to 30 items, took coin deposits from a quarter to a total of $3, and were priced at $2,000 to $3,000.[44]

A somewhat similar experiment began in 1956 in East Paterson, New Jersey, at a new supermarket opened by the Grand Union grocery chain in the Elmwood Shopping Center. Included in the store were eight VMs stocked with milk, eggs, bread, margarine, frozen fish and meat, coffee, tea, and cold cuts. Able to make change, these units were built into the front wall of the supermarket and were accessible from the street 24 hours a day. The supermarket was the largest in Grand Union's 350-unit chain — it was greatly expanded when it replaced one that burned down three months earlier — with 48,860 square feet, company officials calling it "the store of tomorrow." With this experiment it was hoped that "grocery resistance" could be broken down, leading to a whole new area for automatic merchandising.[45]

Business was reported to be good the first week of Grand Union's experiment, though that was not uncommon for any unusual VM placed on location. The first week or so often generated a great deal of business, but much of that was from the novelty factor, which quickly dropped off. During the first Sunday the machines were on site (the store itself was closed on Sundays), the VMs sold out — taking in more than $700 — vending 480 quarts of milk and 180 loaves of bread. A sign over the battery of eight machines said "Nite and Day Quick-Pik." Rumor then had it that Grand Union planed to add outdoor VM batteries to at least 200 of its outlets. Other major supermarket chains reportedly were signaling their intention to enter automatic merchandising. Machine number one in the battery vended two 48-bag selections of tea bags, 61 cents and 50 cents; five selections of one-pound coffee tins, $1.07 to $1.55; three selections of two-ounce instant coffee, 49 cents to 53 cents; and two-pound bags of sugar at 23 cents. Unit number two held marble cake, 35 cents; cans of evaporated milk, 13 cents; doughnuts, 25 cents a dozen; 12-ounce cans of Spam, 40 cents; canned corn beef, 45 cents; corn beef hash, 30 cents; canned salmon, 35 cents; and canned tuna, 29 cents. Machine number three had four brands of margarine in one-pound packages at 23 cents to 29 cents; various cheeses and cheese mixes at 30, 33, 50, and 55 cents; cinnamon rolls, eight for 25 cents; and jars of creamed herring for 69 cents. Unit number four sold half-pounds of butter, 39 cents to 43 cents; pounds of butter at 69 cents to 71 cents; cottage cheese for 32 cents a pint; heavy cream at 39 cents a half pint; light cream for 24 cents a half pint; and American, Swiss, and cream cheeses at 30, 33 and 36 cents. Dispenser number five had bread at 21 cents a loaf; number six vended eggs at 65 cents and 70 cents a dozen; number seven sold milk at 25 cents a quart. Machine number eight held five selections of cold cuts vended in six-ounce packages for 25 cents to 30 cents.[46]

Three years later, at the end of 1959, Grand Union was still conducting its experiment. No expansion had taken place. Not too much longer after that, Grand Union abandoned the idea.[47]

Nevertheless, this and other experiments caught the attention of the British business publication *The Economist*. It commented that America had 3.1 million "automatic salesmen" on location. The surprising thing was not the number of VMs in existence, but that the industry had been "so slow to move outside proven paths." Mentioned specifically were the Grand Union test and another by the IGA grocery chain. The latter experiment was a variation of the Keedoozle sys-

The Nite and Day installation, 1957.

tem, with the customer again carrying around a key mechanism which recorded prices and caused selected items to move to a conveyor belt. Also catching the attention of this publication was the attempt to introduce "full-line feeding batteries" in plants and as free-standing stores to serve a wide range of food items for immediate consumption. Commenting on the technical difficulties for VMs quickly serving and storing meals hot or cold, the publication concluded "The success of these dehumanised feeders lies, of course, in the public acceptance of their offerings ... [Americans] may be willing to pay for it — even in terms of the lower quality that too often seems inevitable when food factories replace individual kitchens. On the other hand, they may decide that the price is too high."[48]

Department stores became involved just before the Christmas period in 1949, when Detroit's J. L. Hudson company installed a battery of VMs inside its store. It wanted to see how successfully "robot selling" would work for hosiery, Christmas cards, and other low priced items with a heavy turnover. As of May 1950, the store had not made up

Top: Another view of the IGA key invention, 1957.
Bottom: A partial view of the IGA proposal, 1957.

its mind about the machines' performance, or if it would use them in the coming year. However, Hudson found that even during peak hours of the peak season the machines did not get much play. Hudson admitted it made no effort to advertise or promote the machines. The only other major test made by a department store was made by Rich's in Atlanta. They also tried vending (from units inside the store) a variety of merchandise costing up to several dollars. Rich's concluded that the public did not respond, so it took the machines out. The failure was explained on the basis that customers liked to see and feel goods out in the open before purchasing. Therefore, the main area for VMs of this type would continue to be in air, rail, and bus terminals. Usually *Business Week* wrote glowing, upbeat accounts of the vending industry but, in reporting on these two failures, the magazine delivered one of the first critical, discouraging articles on the field.[49]

A step described by a reporter as "One of the most revolutionary experiments in recent retailing history" was taken in May, 1950, in Boston by Filene's department store when that firm opened a completely "automatic merchandising department" in the city's new Greyhound bus terminal. Officials of Federated Department Stores (New York City), an eight-store group of which Filene's was a member, said that this was the first time a well-balanced merchandise stock had been offered by a department store to the public in one location through VMs. If the test proved successful additional product lines could be added and other Federated members might adopt the practice. Filene buyers selected best-selling items, with a simplicity of style, size, and color range, and which could be packaged and sold by machine. This new section, called the U-Serv-U department, employed uniformed attendants who made change and kept the machines stocked. Among the original 18 items offered were lingerie, toys, jewelry, men's furnishings, baby supplies, and nylon stockings. U-Serv-U supposedly had special appeal to commuters and office workers because it eliminated waiting.[50]

Within a couple of weeks, Filene's installation consisted of three batteries of VMs that sold 23 different items of merchandise — from 23 machines. Products included men's hose (75 cents), men's ties ($1), ladies' panties ($1.65), and baby rattles ($1.75). At times there were as many trade observers around the units as there were customers. All were anxious to see if the experiment would work. While VMs were said to then gross about $1 billion a year, it was noted that everything other than cigarettes, gum, candy, and soft drinks accounted for only a tiny fraction of the total. Filene's looked on VMs as an extension of the store, rather than as something that would replace current selling methods in the store. It was then working on the assumption that there would probably always be several limitations to robot selling — including a limit on how many coins a customer would bother to insert, the size range of items that could be carried, and the physical size of the item.[51]

The U-Serv-U was the first major test of what the trade referred to as "merchandise vending." Nothing existed on that scale before as the test got underway with considerable fanfare. Later Filene's installed another battery of 24 machines at Logan International Airport in Boston. Around the beginning of 1952, Filene's very quietly abandoned its experiment. In analyzing what went wrong, Filene's offered the following reasons for the failure: traffic was not heavy enough at either location, people did not want to buy the higher-priced items ($1 or more), and people did not want to buy style goods in a VM. It was the cheaper trinkets — the small toys, key chains, and puzzles — that sold well and finally dominated U-Serv-U. The vending industry relied mainly on two things: traffic and impulse buying, which together spelled volume. Most people drank coffee every day, so if an operator found a spot with enough passerbys, he would do alright. But no one bought socks every day. Other problems that could not be handled included what to do about change when the price went over $1 and how to handle the array of sizes, colors, and styles needed in garments. There was also the psychological question of how to sell the kinds of goods people liked to handle and touch before they bought. Based on the Filene experience, one account concluded: "But the fact is that there are very definite limitations to automatic vending."[52]

All-in-one, multi-purpose machines also made a reappearance in the 1950s. At a NAMA exposition in 1951, it was pointed out that there were nearly half as many VMs as retail sales personnel in America and a prediction was made that the time was approaching when the machines might outnumber live salespeople. Also, delegates were told that a new "giant multiple vending machine" had been invented in Australia that could handle 25 different packaged items, up to something as large as a box of cornflakes. Known as Elmer (short for Electrical Merchant) the device accepted pennies, nickels, dimes, quarters, and half-dollars up to a total of $1.99 for a single purchase.[53]

A VM that could handle 192 items was tested in 1953 in Pennsylvania Station, Newark, New Jersey. With the device being weatherproof and tamper-proof, the machine was reported to be useable unguarded 24 hours a day. It dispensed toys, toilet articles, wrapped foods, handkerchiefs, socks, baby bottles, nail polish, bobby pins, and similar small items. Reportedly, the device had been successfully tried out in Denmark.[54]

After three years of extensive experiments and tests, Lunch-O-Mat Corporation of America, headed by Mrs. Lawrence Reiss, unveiled its seven-section automatic merchandising unit in 1952. The seven divisions, containing 11 different food types, could be operated by as many people simultaneously, if necessary, since each division contained its own coin mechanism and operated independently. Measuring 48" wide, 31.5" deep, and 72" high, Lunch-O-Mat contained 298 separate food items and held 150 cups of coffee. Sandwiches were heated by microwave radar and the company declared that "A special wave length has been assigned by the FCC to eliminate any possible interference by the electronic equipment with television or radio reception." A change maker broke quarters into dimes and nickels. Products retailing at 10, 11, 12, 15, 20, 25, 30, 35, or 50 cents could be accommodated. In addition, Lunch-O-Mat had a condiment tray attached to one side so that patrons could season their food. Hot sandwiches were heated from 10 to 15 seconds depending on the type. Reiss believed Lunch-O-Mat had the potential to do a gross of $100 per week serving only 75 people. One of the reasons to try and develop multi-purpose vendors (most robot store concepts had a separate VM to dispense each item) was to overcome the resistance held by some building managers against batteries of VM units—a resistance that would not be transferred to the single, and compact, multi-purpose units such as Lunch-O-Mat. However, none of these types of machines had any success.[55]

Articles that appeared in the general media in the 1950s tended to be very upbeat and optimistic about the vending industry; they still sometimes spoke about robots. Writing in the *Reader's Digest*, Risdon Tillery told of the wide variety of items available from VMs and that modern models were mostly slug and vandal proof. The *New York Times* hailed 1952 as the best year in history for vending machines, due in part to the increasing variety of items sold through machines and to the growing placement of VMs for in-plant feeding.[56]

Cedric Larson wrote enthusiastically about "Our growing robot army," declaring that no field in merchandising was growing more rapidly at the time than automatic merchandising. While Larson acknowledged that the machine would only supplement person-to-person selling and never replace it, he did conclude that in the future "it is possible that thousands of products ultimately will prove practical for machine selling.... Tomorrow the public demand for push-button convenience may lead to markets whose every operation is controlled, swiftly and economically, by coins and levers."[57]

Emphasizing technology, a 1955 piece in the *New York Times* discussed the talking cigarette machines and how they changed the VM from a passive to an active salesman. This account also focused on the robot restaurants and multi-purpose devices. Concentrating on most of the same developments in an equally uncritical way, journalist Andrew Hecht wrote about "Robots ... at your service" in *American Mercury*. Writing in *Newsweek* in 1957, Sandford Brown talked about the blue-chip future of the industry: "the machines are moving into supermarkets, drugstores, and department stores on the Main Street of retailing."[58]

Printers' Ink also did a lengthy piece predicting large future growth for the industry as it rapidly expanded to vend items other than the staples of cigarettes, candy bars, gum, coffee, and sandwiches. Robert Greene was quoted as stating that machines did not need to know the psychology of selling because they could only sell presold items that people already wanted.

A hot beverage VM, 1953.

"They do that job just as well as the human salesman. They don't go out to lunch nor do they keep customers waiting or ask for a raise." Coffee breaks were then an institution with 36 of every 50 firms, giving employees two coffee breaks a day of 10 to 15 minutes each. Norris Willatt penned an article called "Robot salesmen" for *Barron's* in 1958. Most of these pieces, including Willatt's, were very optimistic about the future of robot restaurants, or at least about VMs capable of serving full hot meals—a meal closer to what one received in a restaurant.[59]

Statistics on the industry were now more available than in the past. However, figures usually came from a yearly survey the industry conducted of itself, in which questionnaires were mailed out to most operating companies. Returns usually were in the range of 10 percent and then extrapolated for the industry as a whole, meaning the numbers could be less than reliable. In 1949, there were one million VMs on location in America, averaging 100 sales per week per machine. 347,000 nickel candy bar machines each made 140 sales per week, accounting for 15 percent of the nation's total candy bar sales. Cigarette machines numbered 364,000 and sold on average 150 packs per week per machine. Some 16,000 cigar VMs sold 40 cigars each per week. Bottle soft drink vendors numbered 410,000 and vended 180 bottles each per week, while the 15,000 cup soft drink units averaged 850 drinks per week. Counter prices for cigarettes stood at 19.9 cents in both 1948 and 1949, while the VM prices for those years were, respectively, 20.7 cents and 21.4 cents.[60] Responses to this survey came from 455 operating firms, representing about 10.5 percent of the total operating group.

VMs grossed $1,573,000,000 in 1953, up from $1,370,000,000 in 1952. One-man routes were 31.6 percent of all operators in 1951, 26.04 percent in 1952, and 21.3 percent in 1953. Coffee machines grossed $65 million in 1953 — there were 9,100 units in 1951, 16,720 in 1952, and 25,900 in 1953. Cigarette vendors moved 3.47 billion packs in 1953, for a gross of $750 million or 16 percent of the total US cigarette dollar market. There were 473,770 cigarette units in 1953 — 124 packs were sold per week per machine in 1951, 120 in 1952, and 119 in 1953. Candy VMs sold 4.6 billion nickel bars in 1953 for a gross of over $230 million, 20 percent of total candy bar sales in America and four percent of the entire candy market. There were 396,850 candy bar VMs in 1951, 421,360 in 1952, and 451,550 in 1953. Ice cream vendors numbered 12,325 in 1951, 16,075 in 1952, and 22,045 in 1953, when they vended $2.6 million worth of ice cream novelties, averaging 228 sales per week. Cup soft drink machines totaled 32,125 in 1951, 38,475 in 1952, and 44,670 in 1953. Average sales per week per unit in 1951 were 810 cups, 830 in 1952, and 820 in 1953. Penny vendors numbered 1.34 million in 1951, selling $69.68 million worth of items, 1.35 million in 1952 selling $70.2 million, and 1.5 million units in 1953 made sales totaling $78 million.[61]

Slightly different sales figures for 1953 came from *Business Week*, which put the total at $1.405 billion: cigarettes $650 million, soft drinks $370 million, candy (packaged) $200 million, coffee $50 million, postage stamps $40 million, bulk (penny machines) $25 million, milk $17 million, ice cream $13 million, cookies and crackers $13 million, chewing gum $11 million, and all other $16.2 million. Either set of figures showed the almost complete reliance on the four Cs which, in the last case, amounted to $1.3 billion of the $1.4 billion total (when penny totals were also included). The figures also showed the very narrow and limited range of items sold through the vending machines.[62]

NAMA estimated sales of the industry in 1957 at $2.225 billion, the first time over the $2 billion mark — the total was $1.9 billion in 1956. Total number of VMs was 3.5 million in 1957, up from 3.2 million in 1956. Cigarette sales were $825 million in 1957, soft drinks $550 million and candy $240 million. Robert Greene said the industry was working on the toughest problem yet: the production of a true robot restaurant, capable of delivering complete meals from frozen storage to the hot, ready-to-eat stage, in less than 20 seconds at the drop of the coins, and operating 24 hours a day.[63]

Somewhat different figures for 1957 put the total sales at $2.052 billion: cigarettes $760 million, bottled soft drinks $258 million, soft drinks in cups $101 million, packaged candy $244 million, coffee $94.7 million, penny machines $57 million, milk $50 million, ice cream $22.7 million, and hot canned foods $14.8 million.[64]

For 1958 VM sales totaled $2.132 billion from machines numbered at 3.716 million. Cigarette machines numbered 690,000 and took in $830 million, 865,000 soft drink units sold $448 million worth of product, and 485,000 candy VMs took in $303 million. In comparing sales totals with the UK, American total sales figures for 1958 converted to 750 million pounds Sterling, whereas sales from VMs in the UK in 1957 amounted to 2.3 million pounds Sterling from 42,479 machines, an "unimportant fraction of retail sales." Actually, the given UK figure was lower than in reality because the comparison excluded machines used by retailers in association with shops. That is, units owned by shopkeepers were excluded from the figures.[65]

Export markets for American vending machines never did open up, at least outside of Canada. Europe was well serviced by local manufacturers. In 1950, for example, the US exported 2,708 VMs worth $501,843, 975 of these units worth $221,775 went to Canada. In 1951 total VM exports were 7,753 ($543,635) of which Canada took 5,381 units ($284,063). In 1952, of the 38,350 machines ($1,073,708) exported, 34,168 ($752,704) went to Canada.[66]

Some indication of the devastation of the vending industry in Europe can be seen in a situation in France. By 1939, there were about 4,300 candy machines in the country, of which 3,700 were located in railroad stations and 600 in subways. In 1950, there were around 2,000 candy machines and 2,783 scales on location in French railroad and subway stations. Route men were on call to repair equipment, but the actual stocking of machines was left to the station managers. Location commission was 20 percent. Weigh scale prices had been increased from one and two francs (one franc equaled 2.8 cents) in 1949 to two and five francs in 1951. Straight dial scales (2,089 units) operated at two francs, while the 694 ticket scales were set for five franc operation. All these scales were pre-war models, with commissions set at 48 and 50 percent.[67]

European multi-purpose VM units, and vending in general, were presented in the American media as more advanced and pervasive than in the US. A 1952 account reported that throughout Scandinavia canned meats, fruits, vegetables, and other groceries were sold through, in some cases, huge machines that could hold up to 70 separate items. Also available automatically were first-aid kits, photographic film, and snuff. Four years later another account reported European vending as more advanced with many retail stores in Germany, Holland, and the Scandinavian countries having VM fronts, as they were obliged by law to close at 6 P.M. and remain closed on Sundays. Germany even had a lonely hearts vendor. With separate columns for men and women of various age groups, it delivered for two German marks (47 cents) the photograph and description of a prospective companion.[68]

Canadian vending totals stood at an estimated gross of $15 million in 1953 — at roughly one-tenth the size of the US, it was disproportionately behind its southern neighbor. Some 2,500 cigarette machines grossed $7 million, 3,000 bottle soft drink VMs took in $2.750 million, 600 cup soft drink units made $2 million, 500 candy bar units: $0.4 million, 250 coffee machines received $0.8 million, and 1,100 miscellaneous VMs grossed $1.5 million.[69]

Automatic Canteen Company of America remained the largest concern in the vending industry. In 1943 it grossed $14.7 million, in 1951, $36.7 million, and in 1955, the figure was $99.7 million. Still, Canteen was responsible only for five or six percent of the total vending gross. It operated about 275,000 VMs in 1956 and concentrated almost entirely on placing machines in factories and offices where employees were "captive."[70]

Canteen ran afoul of regulatory agencies when, in 1950, the Federal Trade Commission ordered the company to stop alleged practices that violated the anti-trust laws. In particular the FTC ordered the company to cease making exclusive contracts with VM distributors and to stop accepting cut-rate prices from confectionary makers. Stating the company had violated the Clayton and Robinson-Patman anti-trust laws on those two counts, the FTC said Canteen had increased its sales from $1.937 million

VMs located outside a gas station, 1957.

in 1936 to $12.899 million in 1945 largely through its allegedly illegal practices. Those exclusive contracts provided that distributors who handled Canteen-made VMs had to buy all candy, gum, nuts, and other products from Canteen. As an example of cut-rate prices, the federal agency said the Wrigley company sold Canteen $8.823 million worth of gum between 1937 and 1945 at 38 cents per hundred sticks. Canteen resold the gum to its dealers at 56 cents, giving it a gross profit of around $4 million. The FTC asserted that 96 percent of the profit was the difference between Canteen's preferential price and what others had to pay Wrigley.[71]

In 1958 the FTC ordered Canteen to divest itself of 14 subsidiary companies and to refrain from acquiring any VM maker for the next 10 years. Those subsidiaries formerly were part of the Rowe Corporation, a major competitor acquired by Canteen in 1955. Canteen consented to the order issued by the FTC. The commission filed anti-trust charges, stating that the merger with Rowe endangered competition. Since it bought Rowe, said the FTC, Canteen had been able to manipulate the supply of machines to competing operators.[72]

Slugs again surfaced as a problem for the industry, but not nearly as often as in the past. Solomon Schnapp, a Parks Department recreation director in New York City, was found guilty in court in 1950 of using slugs in drug store postage stamp vendors. He was sentenced to 30 days in the workhouse, but final passage of sentence was postponed for a week if he would tell where he had obtained the slugs. Charles Rubenstein, a VM operator, observed Schnapp deposit 10 slugs in a machine in a Walgreen's drug store. Rubenstein then tailed Schnapp to another Walgreen drug store in the area where he deposited 15 more slugs. Upon his arrest, 25 10-cent stamp packages were found in his possession. Rubenstein had stationed himself near the VM because his company had been losing "large amounts" of money due to the use of slugs. Rubenstein later told the court that Schnapp had admitted to him after the trial that the slugs had come from stamp VMs that Schnapp himself owned.[73]

In Pittsburgh in 1953, slugs were reportedly becoming an increasing problem with operators finding many brass washers. When managers of industrial plants where machines were sited were told of the situation, they explained that the washers could be purchased in any neighborhood hardware store.[74]

For the fiscal year ending June 30, 1955, in New York City the Transit Authority reported that 433,807 items other than authorized tokens had been used in the subways. Of those, 125,359 were tokens of lesser value for other transit systems and 36,080 were of the same 15 cent value as the New York tokens. All tokens were redeemed by the issuing transit systems.[75]

Vandalism remained a problem to some extent, but as in earlier periods, the issue was rarely mentioned. One member of the vending industry told reporter John Sharnik in 1950: "You've no idea what our machines go through. They turn up with hairpins, wads of gum and chunks of steel jammed into the coin slots. They're kicked, they're banged, they're battered." Six years later, journalist Andrew Hecht observed that "Vandalism in general is quite a problem. Instead of asking for their money back, disgruntled customers often take it out on the machine."[76]

Scams continued to be worked in the vending industry. Even though the methods of the blue sky promoters remained the same decade after decade, there always seemed to be no shortage of people ready to fall for the pitch. A woman in Texas bought five VMs in 1952 for $550 from a salesman who promised her she would make from $100 to $150 a month from these pre-located units. Her average was, in fact, $8 per month. When she asked the promoter to buy the machines back, she was offered $75 for the five machines. Philadelphia newspapers were then refusing to take VM advertising unless it had received the stamp of approval of a known organization such as the Philadelphia Coin Machine Operators' Association. Promoters promised $2.50 net per week from penny nut dispensers while legitimate operators with such units on location were agreed that the real net was about 35 cents per week per machine. Pre-located machines often promised the proprietor a high commission.[77]

New York City's Better Business Bureau had warned for some time that some VM promoters were selling their machines by means of highly exaggerated promises of potential earnings. It sent a questionnaire in 1953 to 50 people who had, during the previous year, inquired at their office regarding specific VM promotions. Twenty-five replied — 18 said they did not purchase the vendors as a result of the bureau's report. Those seven who did invest all reported disillusionment and failure to earn even a fraction of the amounts promised. Highest earnings came to one purchaser who received a total of $250 from 12 machines over a 15-month period. He had been promised earnings of more than $200 a month.[78]

James Nelson gave up his job as illustrations editor at *Business Week* in the early to mid 1950s, heading west to California to seek his fortune. He chose to look into the VM industry and detailed his ordeal in *The Trouble with Gumballs* (1956). Nelson found a company willing to help him enter the vending industry. Their promises were typical — for a cash investment of $1,000, work eight hours a week and net $100 a week, invest $2,500, work 20 hours a week and net $250 a week, and so on. He purchased 100 gumball machines for $5,200 plus $156 tax. Soon he discovered he had paid $52 for machines listed for $17.35 each. For 45 cents, he got 100 pieces of gum that brought in a gross of $1. After paying out 15 cents to the location owner, Nelson was left with a gross profit of 40 cents. Most of his machines grossed in the $2.50 to $4 range per month. After months of struggle, he reached his peak one December when his machines grossed a grand total of $633.38, or a net to him of $249.51 for the month.[79]

In the area of strange happenings, fell a 1952 police investigation in Wheeling, West Virginia, of 50 "subversive" VMs. Police seized those machines after it was discovered that they had been doling out Communist trinkets along with the candy. After it was found that some VMs dispensed trinkets bearing the hammer and sickle and that some gave out cards containing data about the Soviet Union, Wheeling City Manager Robert Plummer ordered all penny candy machines in the city to be seized. Irving Marrick, owner and operator of the machines, explained that he purchased the candy from a New York firm and had not known that the packages contained propaganda.[80]

There was also the unidentified citizen of North Wilkesboro, North Carolina, who got angry after losing a penny in a weigh scale. He threw the vendor through a department store window and, after cooling off in jail, he proceeded to destroy all the plumbing in his cell. Repairs to the store and the jail cell were estimated at $500.[81]

By the end of the 1950s, the vending industry had failed to live up to the hype and expectations of the earlier part of the decade. After the hype of the late 1920s, the industry put the failure down to a technological problem not then solved — slugs. However, this time around the blame could not be placed on slugs. Instead, another technical problem still out of reach was singled out — lack of a bill changer. Much of the industry's hopes were placed on the supposed revolutionary changes the industry would undergo once a bill changer arrived. By 1957, a prototype was on display. Made by the ABT Corporation, the unit could make change for a one-dollar bill but no other denomination.[82]

The dollar bill changer was tested at Chicago's Illinois Central Station, Midway Airport, and other points around the city. After a bill was inserted, there was a three-second pause during which the machine checked to see if the bill was genuine. Then it dispensed three quarters, two dimes, and one nickel. One problem occurred when people failed to read the instructions and inserted a bill of greater denomination than $1— they received change for only one dollar. The device also had a tendency to assume that torn bills were counterfeit and to confiscate them. Several other firms besides ABT had bill changes in the prototype stage. Reporter Norris Willatt noted that the industry expected to break out of cigarettes, food, and confections into a great many other lines once the bill changer arrived.[83]

Even more enthusiastic was E. B. Weiss, columnist for the trade publication *Advertising Age*, who wrote that, with the advent of a device that would accept paper money, "I think the age of robot retailing will be ushered in. This does not necessarily mean an age of vending machine retailing, although the vending machine will leap ahead ... and will also appear in forms far more advanced than any now on the drawing boards."[84]

Toward the end of 1959, ABT was ready to start leasing its dollar bill changer to operators at a monthly charge of $30 a unit. Meanwhile, *Printers' Ink* noted some of the other problems facing the industry at the end of the 1950s. It wanted to serve full, hot meals, but all such experiments had failed. Hot foods could not be dispensed successfully in cans and aluminum trays, presented as one possible solution, cost too much. There was no solution seen on the horizon to this problem. Vending's future in general retailing was also clouded, especially in light of failures such as the one at Filene's. What was needed, said the article, was a degree of automation still beyond the horizon—a machine or machines capable of offering a customer a wide range of vended items to choose from. "Such a machine (or battery) would assemble and wrap several purchases in one package, totting up a single bill that could be paid with one piece of paper money, for which the machine would provide change. That's in the future—how far it is difficult to estimate." Hopes that a technological fix would send vending to unheard of levels—as opposed to accepting that it was limited to certain niches—would remain a factor in the early part of the period 1960 to 1985 but would then dissipate as the industry fell into a period of stagnation.[85]

7
Dreams Placed on Hold, 1960-1985

"Installing a coffee machine is a fairly simple operation, but when you start vending rolls to go with the coffee, you are already in trouble."
Ronald Wolff, 1961

"In the near future American men may be buying their shirts made out of paper from vendors for 25 or 50 cents ... virtually every hotel lobby will have a paper shirt vending machine."
James Suffridge, 1961

"The era in which the shopper brings her purchases to a checkout point must wane."
E. B. Weiss, 1963

"Now that they can't charge people to go to the bathroom they want to charge people for air."
Alfonse D'Amato, 1978

After the arrival of the bill changer around 1960 and its supposedly becoming bug-free in a couple of years after that, there was a renewed burst of optimism and big dreams. Business columnist E. B. Weiss declared in 1960 that the vending machine era had then begun, partly because of the advent of the bill changer. It was therefore logical for large manufacturers of "pre-sold" brands to start mature planning for "the coming age of automatic vending of a remarkable variety of pre-sold brand classifications." Trade publication *Iron Age* offered the opinion in 1961 that "The industry is exploding in a hundred different directions. Technical breakthroughs are coming rapidly. The push-button supermarket is already on the drawing boards." E. B. Weiss, both a marketing executive and a columnist for *Advertising Age*, stated in 1963 that: "The era in which the shopper brings her purchases to a checkout point must wane. It is no longer necessary. It is archaic." Although automation had come to manufacturing and warehousing, he felt the retail selling of general merchandise remained manual.[1]

Time magazine also featured the industry's optimism in 1960. Underlying this sentiment were changes in the US economy such as automation, high labor costs, and increased leisure time. Kansas City's Vendo Corporation had set up completely automatic snack bars at the University of Kansas and the University of Wichita, offering sandwiches, milk, coffee, pastry, and juices. Said Vendo board chairman Elmer F. Pierson: "In America today nobody wants to be a servant and vending machines free people from being servants." Even then, work was underway on several fronts to develop machines that could handle more denominations of bills. Delbert W. Coleman, head of the VM manufacturing firm Seeburg, remarked: "Just open up a suitcase and try to sell in the lobby of a big office building. They'll throw you out on your ear. But with vending machines they welcome you because you're rendering a needed service." Taking advantage of the leisure-time increase, operators had moved VMs into sports arenas, bowling alleys, and stock-car racetracks. At Squaw Valley's 1960 Winter Olympic Games, the ABC Vending Corporation did $280,000 worth of business in 10 days, deciding to keep its snack bars in the area permanently.[2]

Another account from that year discussed a new "Moto-Mat" experimental gas station opened by Esso Standard Oil at Gramercy, Louisiana, which featured a bank of VMs that made change automatically and dispensed soup, sandwiches, canned foods, fruit juices, ice cream, soft drinks, candy, coffee, and pastries. It was designed to attract motorists who did not like to delay by stopping at restaurants. In conjunction with the Vendolator company, Pepsi-Cola had developed a coin-operated machine that vended the six-pack Pepsi cartons. The vended hot food platter was reported to be "just around the corner."[3]

When in 1960 W. J. Manning asked what made a product vendable, he came up with four basics 1) the product must be pre-sold through advertising or wide consumer acceptance; 2) the product must be vendable in sufficient volume to justify the cost of the selling machines and the expense of servicing them — servicing costs took up more than 30 percent of gross sales; 3) the product must be consumable or usable within a relatively short distance of the VM, otherwise the customer will probably prefer buying at an attended store; and 4) the product must be so standardized that the customer will not wish to feel or test it before buying.[4]

Despite the enthusiasm, the vending of hot food was close to nonexistent — certainly it was in the area of hot meals. Some VMs heated up sandwiches or cans of soup and so on, but anything more elaborate presented the industry with great problems. For instance, hot food involved

7.—Dreams Placed on Hold, 1960-1985

enormous waste at the end of the day. *Time* pointed out in 1961 that the problems had not been solved and the industry was still trying to deliver a method of heating and serving a complete frozen meal in 15 seconds. Interstate Vending Company president Ronald Wolff remarked: "Installing a coffee machine is a fairly simple operation, but when you start vending rolls to go with the coffee, you are already in trouble."[5]

Sales of hot foods in 1959 amounted to only one percent of vending's total receipts for that year. Two major types of hot food VMs then existed: one was filled with food in the morning, heating it gradually. The other dispensed frozen meals that had to be manually inserted in a quick-cooking oven. In the gradual-heat units after about four hours the hot meals were inedible. Machines that automatically moved frozen foods into a fast-heat oven and then dispensed the meal — all in a matter of seconds — would have to wait, thought the trade publication *Advertising Age*, for the packaging industry to catch up. "Attractive packaging of complete meals in materials which can withstand both temperature extremes is sorely needed."[6]

Meanwhile, one of the pillars of the vending industry started to run into serious trouble. It all began in 1964, when the US Surgeon General issued a report declaring cigarette smoking to be a health hazard. To show itself to be responsible, NAMA quickly sent a telegram to Surgeon General Luther Terry notifying him of its program to prevent the sale of cigarettes to minors. According to the telegram, operators of cigarette machines in every state had ordered more than 260,000 "Minors Are Forbidden" labels for their machines in the past year. Also, it said, the program provided a constant survey of the machines' accessibility to minors.[7]

In the wake of the Surgeon General's report, hospitals wrestled with the idea of cigarette availability in hospitals. In dozens of hospitals by early 1964, cigarette VMs had either been moved to obscure spots or placed near anti-smoking posters. There were few outright bans at this time. Said Carroll Ogren, administrator at Washoe Medical Center in Reno, Nevada, "As a service to the patient I will have to insist we have cigarette machines in the hospital."[8]

The position of cigarettes as the single most important item dispensed by VMs (by dollar volume) began to slowly erode. In 1985, the American Medical Association (AMA) called for a complete ban on the advertising and promotion of all tobacco products. Current federal law then banned cigarette advertising only on radio and television. Additionally, the AMA called for new laws banning VM sales of cigarettes and for setting a minimum legal age of 21 for purchasing tobacco products. Cigarette machines comprised 21.1 percent of all VMs in 1960, yet generated 44.2 percent of all vending revenue that year; in 1983 those numbers were, respectively, 14.0 percent and 19.7 percent.[9]

Talking VMs emerged again in 1981 when Coca-Cola introduced its version. Using a speech synthesizer, the machines played Coke theme music, plugged the company's products, and reminded customers, "Don't forget your change." Coca-Cola claimed the talking vendors had increased soft-drink sales by as much as 400 percent. Reportedly, the company had installed 3,000 of these vendors in the space of one year. The model for 1981 allowed distributors to change the background music and the messages by using different computer chips. Also, Coke was then introducing new VMs with built-in video screens that allowed customers to play one or two short video games for free after buying a soft drink — simple games that lasted less than 30 seconds. Yet another unique model offered customers volume discounts: one Coke for 40 cents, two for 75 cents, and three for $1.05. Another machine provided change for a dollar bill from a built-in changer.[10]

In 1982 VM sales accounted for about 15 percent of the $18 billion worth of soft drinks sold each year in America. Profit margins were high. For example, you could then buy a two-liter bottle of pop for about $1.49 at the supermarket; Coca-Cola was then testing a VM that would vend the same bottle for $2. Coke then offered its bottlers nine different VM options, including those mentioned above. Said Brian G. Dyson, president of Coca-Cola U.S.A.: "The standard machine was like a clerk. It was static at the point of sale. We are trying to make that old machine more dramatic, more vibrant. Instead of being the clerk it is now, it should be a salesman that reaches out and grabs the person's attention."[11]

Reddi-Wip joined the list of companies trying to automatically sell unusual items in 1965 when it announced that it was testing new coin-operated peanut butter VMs in nearly 40 supermarkets in Southern California. For 59 cents the unit dispensed a pound of peanut butter into a plastic container.[12]

Another idea that did not catch on was the coin-operated dry cleaning unit. By early 1960, one company already had a machine in the field while a couple of other manufacturers were working on their own models. Already on the market was a unit made by Standard Incorporated of Dallas, Texas. It was a twin tumbler unit with a total capacity of 18 pounds, a weight of 1,300 pounds, and a price tag of $6,000. For about $1 a customer could give nine pounds of clothes a 40-minute cleaning in perchlorethylene. A typical nine-pound load was three snowsuits, or three or four pairs of trousers with one sport coat. Handicaps were the machine's high price and bulk. Other firms were looking to develop a cheaper model.[13]

Within a few months, both the Whirlpool company and the Norge division of Borg-Warner also had dry cleaning VMs on the market—all charged $1 for nine pounds. At a conventional dry cleaner, the same weight of clothing would cost $6 to $8 and take three to five days before the clothing was returned. One Whirlpool executive thought coin-operated dry cleaners would be in as wide a use in 18 months as coin-operated automatic washers—there were then 37,500 launderettes, with many of them being fully automatic coin-operated establishments.[14]

Book vendors made another appearance, and a quick exit. A division of the company called Bookshelf of America unveiled its "Vend-A-Book" in 1962. With its large glass front and 40 pockets it could hold up to about 400 mass-market books, depending on the thickness of the titles. The unit could take any combination of 5-, 10-, 25-, and 50-cent pieces, but did not give change, stood 52" wide, 24" deep, 72" tall, and cost $895. Machines had been placed in several hospitals, airports, and one supermarket in the New York metro area. Commission paid to locations ranged from 10 percent to 25 percent, depending on the quantity of books sold.[15]

The Vend-A-Book unit, 1962.

Around the same time, the Read-O-Mat paperback book VM was also introduced. It had a capacity of 40 titles and held 15 copies of each, for a total of 600. Standing 36" wide, 23" deep, 71" high and costing $667, this device could handle books priced from 25 cents to $1.45 in five-cent increments. A change machine could be provided at extra cost.[16]

Coin-operated gas pumps had been in operation for some time. Apparently Oriental Refining outlets in Denver, Colorado, had been coin-operated "for years," as of late 1961. When Sutcliffe Oil Company (Pennsylvania) opened a coin-operated gas station that year at Clarks Summit, state police tried to close it on the grounds that it was a fire hazard. Sutcliffe argued that state police had no authority in that area and, in any event, no hearing on the matter had been held, as required by law. Court decisions in the early rounds favored Sutcliffe. At the station during the hours live attendants were on duty (daily from 7 A.M. to 10 P.M.), the one bank of coin-operated pumps was attendant-controlled. The coin-operated feature did not operate until the station was closed (nightly from 10 P.M. to 7 A.M.). Sutcliffe said the main idea of the coin pumps was not to do away with attendants during the station's open hours, but to offer motorists a chance to buy gasoline during the night when the station normally was closed. As the legal wrangling continued, Sutcliffe did follow some police recommendations that "No Smoking" signs be painted at the coin-operated island and that a fire extinguisher be installed.[17]

Sanitary Vendors of Newark, New Jersey, briefly sold contraceptives from VMs in 13 counties in that state in the early 1960s. The company then brought a court action because of what it called "harassment" by prosecutors in those counties. Those condom machines were placed in gas stations and diners. However, the State Supreme Court of New Jersey unanimously upheld a 90-year-old State law that restricted the right to dispense contraceptives to physicians and druggists.[18]

Jero Sales of Drexel Hill, Pennsylvania, offered a machine in 1964 with a selection of 15 separate stationery items, all individually wrapped and visible: loose leaf fillers, pens, pencils, pencil and ink erasers, index cards of several sizes, reinforcements, rulers, note books, dictionaries, file folders, and paper clips. Holding up to 315 items, the unit permitted a choice of 12 different price settings from five cents to $1.50 for each of the 15 items. Standing 31" deep, 31" wide, and 72" tall, the VM accepted nickels, dimes, and quarters, but did not

Another book vendor, 1962.

7.—Dreams Placed on Hold, 1960-1985

give change. One unit was then in the Free Library of Philadelphia, which received a 10 percent commission on the gross sales.[19]

There was also the 10-cent candy bar VM in 1971. What was unusual about this device was that, along with the chocolate bar, the customer received a talking joke from comic Henny Youngman, who had taped 230 of his jokes for the machine's benefit. For example: "Hey! My mother-in-law tried a mudpack treatment on her face, and for two days she looked great. Then the mud fell off." The company that had developed this machine predicted it would have 5,000 of them on location in a matter of months.[20]

In 1978 the Hempstead, Long Island, Town board unanimously approved an ordinance requiring gas stations to provide air free of charge. As well, the ordinance required all stations that did not then have air pumps to install them and to provide free air, even to motorists who did not make purchases. Alfonse D'Amato, Hempstead Town presiding Supervisor said that, although the board knew of no station in the town that did charge for air, the ordinance was an attempt to "head off the problem which had cropped up in other jurisdictions." He added that it was part of the traditional aspect of service stations to provide such necessary services as free air. D'Amato drew an analogy between the charging for air, which was usually 25 cents for the coin-operated air pumps, and pay toilets, which were outlawed in New York State in 1976. "Now that they can't charge people to go to the bathroom, they want to charge people for air," said D'Amato, referring to the Nik-O-Loc company of Indianapolis, which made many of the locks for pay toilets and designed the devices installed on the coin-operated air pump. At Hempstead's hearing on the ordinance, no one was opposed — even gas station owners supported the measure.[21]

In certain rural parts of 21 states in the mid 1980s could be found a coin-operated VM that dispensed live bait to fishermen. Vend-A-Bait was devised from old sandwich machines by Glenn McClintic of Des Moines. He was involved in selling sandwich VMs when the market for such devices dried up. Worms and other slithery kinds of bait were packaged in ventilated eight-ounce cups with a bedding of moist paper shot through with feed and conditioner. Minnows, goldfish, and the like were packed in water-filled plastic bags with a chemical that slowed their metabolism. However, after seven days minnows had a mortality rate of about 50 percent. "What kills them is their own waste. They pollute the water," said McClintic. He had 1,200 units on location in 1985. Machines sold for $3,800: $300 down, with payments on the rest at $120 to $150 a month. He told potential buyers that, if they sold six or seven cups of bait a day (priced from $1.25 to $2.75), the business was self-supporting.[22]

Concerns for the environment led to the development of machines that came to be known generically as reverse VMs. Scottsdale, Arizona toy maker Tike Miller developed, in 1977, what he called the "Golden Goat." It was a VM into which you inserted items and got money back. Within a year Miller had 20 units on test in Phoenix shopping centers—the device was small enough to fit into a single parking space. Miller was moved to develop it after learning that 75 percent of the 27 billion cans made annually in America were not recovered. A patron put a can into the hopper and pushed a button. First it separated out non-magnetic metals; aluminum cans were extracted by another operation and blown through a crusher that reduced them to 17 percent of their original size. Crushed cans were then weighed on an electronic scale and coins poured out. The payoff price could be adjusted up to 99 cents a pound.[23]

Some six years later, there were many more of the reverse machines on location, though commonly they dispensed redeemable coupons, tokens, or chits instead of cash. Recycling centers often incorporated them in an effort to reduce labor costs. Usually, the VMs paid slightly less for the scrap than did the recycling centers. In Denver, Colorado, 20 reverse VMs reportedly paid out more than $1 million in an 18-month period.[24]

Amazingly, penny gumball machines could still be found in 1975, but inflation threatened their very existence. Said Gene Serva, of Detroit distributing and operating company A. C. Courville: "We've still got penny jawbreakers. But that penny gumball has gotten just about as small as it can get. In fact, if something doesn't happen, it won't be around much longer. It's still got gum in it, but not very much." With more oil price shocks and inflation awaiting America in the remainder of the 1970s, it seems certain that the penny bulk vendor disappeared sometime that decade. Of course the bulk vendor still exists to this day, but it doesn't work for a penny.[25]

Department stores continued to experiment with elaborate units placed within their outlets. Macy's, 7th Avenue and 34th Street, New York, unveiled such a machine in the summer of 1960 that accepted paper currency from $1 to $5 as well as coins, could make change, and could hold up to 684 soft goods items. Made by Universal Match of St. Louis subsidiaries, it was still regarded as a prototype. Universal planned to lease it to retailers rather than sell it to them. It was equipped with 36 columns and, with 19 items to a column, different sized and priced items could be placed. Enormous in size, the unit stood 7'4" high, 7'8" wide, and 43.25" deep. Fully stocked with cash, the machine held $700 in currency and $700 in change. Trade officials hailed the introduction of this new device "as a major step in the application of vending machine selling to the retailing field." Earlier failed experiments, such as the one at Filene's, were specifically mentioned, with the difference seen to be a lack of change making abilities in the failed tests. Macy's believed they had solved that problem.[26]

Printers' Ink looked at the Macy's experiment, especially its bill changing capabilities, and concluded that every other machine the vending industry had dreamed about "(and they are expansive dreamers) is within reach, or soon may be ... we will see machines that cook and serve a variety of hot meals and offer other merchandise from hose to hardware, in a range of sizes and prices."[27]

A bank of six VMs went to work for the big Atlanta department store Rich's early in December, 1960. Shortly thereafter, Montgomery Ward installed three machines in three of their stores. Those machines were all made by Universal Match and were essentially the same as the one tested at Macy's. Rich's was selling items priced from $1 to $3, but the machine could handle anything up to $9. Rich's gave the bank a high-traffic location — the so-called Crystal Bridge across the street that separated the two Rich's buildings. A lunch counter formerly occupied that spot, but was closed after Blacks demanded to be allowed to eat there. The store drew up a list of fast turnover items likely to catch the eye and, since the machine could handle only small boxes, some merchandise was eliminated from the start. Rich's opted for small, fancy gift-type items, things that could be attractively displayed — hosiery, cosmetics, soft slippers, men's socks, handkerchiefs, costume jewelry, and perfumes. Machines were not left to do their own selling. Instead, several young saleswomen stood by to explain the devices to customers. There was a worry at Rich's that the large machines looked complicated and might scare shoppers away.[28]

Those experiments were all deeply disappointing for the vending industry. Macy's test was limited in the end to two products: men's T-shirts and boxer shorts in three sizes, all offered at one price, 97 cents. For four weeks the machine was located in the third floor toy department; then it spent its last two weeks placed in the second floor men's wear department. The only publicly revealed result indicated that, at the time of removal in mid-August, the machine was making 100 sales each six-day selling week and was giving no mechanical difficulties. Montgomery Ward placed its three units in three catalogue stores in the Eastern US to sell men's T-shirts, athletic shirts, briefs, and boxer shorts in a range of color and size selections. Only two prices were used: $1 and $1.25. Results of that test were not made public, but all the dispensers were removed less than a year after installation.[29]

Rich's six test machines were installed in one bank on the bridge on December 5, 1960, where they remained until March 2, 1961. Midway through the test, on February 13, two machines were removed and the remainder were canted to test the sales effects of a nonuniform machine layout. Also at this time, a bolder display panel background was installed. For the first 10 weeks, one machine was stocked only with hosiery, one with women's scuffs and gloves, one with men's socks and handkerchiefs, one with cosmetics, one with men's accessories and candy, and the sixth with ladies' jewelry, leather goods, and handbags. Later the machines were restocked to test drugs, stationery, household items, brand name children's socks, women's brassieres, and packaged cookies. No machine assortment was left unchanged longer than a month. Prices ranged from a low of 25 cents to a high of $6.90. Rich's was disappointed with the sales results and terminated the experiment completely on March 30, 1961.[30]

The two machines removed from the main store were located outside Rich's suburban store in the Belvedere Shopping Center, where they remained until March 30. One unit was stocked with cookies and candies, while the other held a line of sundry items—shampoo, razor blades, hand lotion, toothpaste, and so on. In analyzing the failure of the VMs to catch on, one reason was thought to be that the bank of six machines were "imposing" and "confusing." The use of sales help stationed near the machines to help customers continued at the second location, but only during store hours. During the three-month downtown test phase, three full-page newspaper ads were devoted to pointing out the presence of the VMs downtown. It was also believed that the inability of the VMs to take charge accounts was a "great deterrent to their increased use." Lower-priced items generally moved the best in the dispensers, with customer hesitation starting at around the $3 mark.[31]

The reality of these experiments was in stark contrast to some of the blindly enthusiastic pronouncements of the period. Speaking in 1960 before an international conference in Tokyo, Japan, Lincoln Theismeyer, president of the Pulp and Paper Research Institute of Canada, said: "In the near future American men may be buying their shirts made out of paper from vendors for 25 or 50 cents ... virtually every hotel lobby will have a paper shirt vending machine." James A. Suffridge, president of the Retail Clerks International Association, in a 1960 appearance before the Joint Economic Committee of Congress, stated: "Clearly, with the development of automatic vending machines the possibility of a completely automatic retail store is virtually upon us ... selling goods to shoppers ... who never see a clerk or a check-out counter." Frederick L. Schuster, chairman of the board of Automatic Canteen Corporation of America, at a press conference to introduce a new multi-purpose VM, remarked: "This new marketing concept can automate up to 90 percent of supermarket operations [enabling] the automatic vending of staples, canned goods, meats, drugs, sundries, textile products, housewares, or ready-to-eat hot foods...."[32]

An automatic drive-in restaurant and grocery store, said to be the first of its kind in America, was in full 24-hour-a-day operation late in 1960 in Kansas City. It was a pilot installation of the Vendo company (a VM maker) and dispensed hamburgers, cheeseburgers, and milk shakes as well as dairy products, eggs, bread, candy, frozen foods, bacon, bologna, soap, toothpaste, tissue, and other products. Items sold varied in price from five cents to $1.50. Although the VMs did not make change, separate units for change making were part of the facility — a 1,400 square foot heated building with 400 square feet of outdoor patio for limited dining, plus parking for 40 cars. Fifteen individual VMs, each 7'9" high and 36" wide were contained within the facility. Nine sold prepared foods and selected packaged grocery items, six dispensed cigarettes, candy, coffee, ice cream, milk, and soft drinks. A kitchen on the premises provided most of the prepared foods. It was not a true robot store, however, as a manually staffed service counter was open from 11 A.M. until about midnight. Automatic service was available around the clock. Vendo head Robert Wagstaff predicted this new facility "will demonstrate the limitless uses to which automatic vending may be put."[33]

One year later, Vendo's experiment was still ongoing, with the company announcing it would open up a "completely automated, 500-item, 24-hour grocery store within a few weeks at an undisclosed location." A number of such installations would be in operation within a year, Vendo boldly predicted.[34]

Around the same time, an experiment was conducted by the Rand (disguised name) Supermarket, a 28-unit grocery chain that served five Midwestern communities. To explore the potential for automatic grocery vending, it did a 10-week controlled experiment in a shopping center adjacent to one of its largest supermarkets. The vending installation consisted of seven 10-selection coin-operated "Grocerette" VMs — three refrigerated and four not cooled — plus a console cigarette machine, a fresh-brew coffee machine, a six-selection cold-drink unit, and three coin changers, all housed in a temporary 18' by 40' building. Forty staple grocery items were chosen for the initial product assortment. All products were nationally advertised brands, except for butter, which carried a private label. One machine was devoted entirely to the sale of three varieties of canned soft drink singles and to six-pack cartons of a popular cola. Prices were identical to those in the main Rand store, ranging from 10 cents for 10-ounce cans of the soft drinks, to 60 cents for a pound of wieners, and 70 cents for a dozen eggs.[35]

Rand held its test from July 24 to October 2, 1961. A decision had to be made by October 2 on whether to continue the program, since continuing meant a capital cost for building insulation and heating equipment for the winter months. For the first four weeks, VMs operated only when the main store was closed. Its hours were 9 A.M. to 6 P.M. daily, except until 9 P.M. on Thursday and Friday, and closed Sundays as were all grocery stores in the city. Sales during the initial four-week test period were described as "mediocre," so for the remaining six weeks, the machines were available 24 hours a day, seven days a week. This caused sales to increase almost 100 percent from week four to week five. Bread and milk accounted for about 50 percent of total unit volume, soft drink sales a further 18 percent. One observer of the experiment estimated that the VM installation "was probably losing from $100 to $125 a week, exclusive of the commissions from the cigarette and drink machines." Rand decided to continue the experiment for one additional month, but with no additional capital outlay. With the onset of colder weather after the middle of October, however, sales in the unheated building began to decline markedly and the installation was closed on November 1, 1961.[36]

Gas stations looked more to become locations for VMs in this period, but with little success. Shell Oil opened two automated restaurants in Illinois in 1962, with Automatic Canteen owning and servicing the food VMs. One closed quickly due to lack of business while the other lasted a year or so. Standard of Ohio and Stouffer Foods Corporation ended a joint experiment at eight Sohio sites as a result of poor sales after a test period of around two years. Sohio owned and operated the automatic restaurants and Stouffer suppled the food. In Sohio's VMs, hamburgers sold for 45 cents, compared to an average highway restaurant price of 35 cents (with waitress service) and a roadside stand price of 15 cents.[37]

A Colonial Oil gas station in Orlando, Florida, was using a grocery VM in 1963 to try to increase traffic and boost profits. The "Supermat 24" was made by Ventronics of Philadelphia and vended bread, milk, eggs, and other groceries 24 hours a day. The dual unit vended 36 items, stood 12' wide, almost 8' deep, 9' high, contained a refrigerated section, and sold for $9,950.[38]

Gas stations continued to look to VMs into the 1970s, although with less elaborate ideas. With stations in all 50 states, Phillips had models of buildings with space set aside for VMs. Humble emphasized outdoor banks of VMs that it termed "refreshment centers" while Texaco referred to its dispensers as "markettes." Mobil put special rooms in some of its stations, called Travel Centers, and equipped them with tables of various heights at which people could stand or sit to eat the food purchased from VMs lining the walls. Items sold from these VMs included: ice cream bars and sandwiches, malts, meat and cheese sandwiches, candy, soda pop in bottles and cans, pastry, pints of regular and chocolate milk, hot coca, hot coffee, hot soup, cigarettes, potato chips, and ice.[39]

Plants and offices, with their "captive" employees, grew more and more important as VM locations. Carl M. Loeb, Rhoades & Company, a large brokerage house in the Wall Street area of New York, installed an "automatic cafeteria" on its premises in 1960 where its 600 workers could obtain complete meals for less than $1. In addition to the usual coffee, soft drinks, sandwich, and soup dispensers, it also featured a newly developed machine to serve hot casserole dishes. Quick-frozen aluminum foil platters of veal cutlets and mashed potatoes, codfish cakes and rice or baked lasagna, prepared by the Brass Rail catering firm, were placed in the machine each night. At a designated hour, an automatic timer switched on the electric heating unit, and at noon they popped out, piping hot, as fast as the customers could each insert two quarters. Trade insiders at that time saw the fastest growing vending segment to be automated canteens for offices and plants. Any site employing 250 or more workers was a prime location. The biggest potential of all was foreseen for machines capable of heating and dispensing quick-frozen dinners, made possible from a unit on the order of the device that was part of the Loeb installation. Other manufacturers working on similar devices admitted there was a great deal of difficulty involved and a lot of problems to overcome. Skeptics believed the unit at Loeb's was not practical because food that remained unsold a few hours after it was heated became inedible. Nevertheless, when reliable VMs of that type became generally available, said reporter David Loehwing, "the automatic vending industry expects to graduate from the snack business and take over the lion's share of the 'at-work' feeding of the American people."[40]

One of the reasons many companies were reported to be switching from the usual live-service cafeterias and restaurants over to VMs in the 1960s was because the companies were achieving substantial savings. The New York Telephone Company received about $40,000 annually as its share of commissions from VMs installed in 10 of its Manhattan office buildings. Formerly it paid $20,000 a year in subsidies to feed the 5,000 workers employed in those locations. At the General Electric Company's huge River Works plant in Lynn, Massachusetts, there were about 12,000 workers employed in 50 buildings spread over 126 acres. Using VMs, the plant's entire feeding program was run on a break-even basis to the firm — compared to an annual loss of $80,000 when GE ran its own cafeteria.[41]

Automatic Canteen developed a battery of VMs that offered a complete snack line, including infra-red toasted sandwiches, hot soups, chili, baked beans, pastry, coffee, and cigarettes. Said company chairman Nathaniel Leverone: "The sales potential in in-plant feeding alone is at least as great as the entire automatic vending business is now."[42]

A 1970 account reported that VM operators had to pay a 10 percent commission to the plant or office housing the machines, a commission arrangement that Macke Company (an operator) treasurer Wesley LaBlanc considered "a curse to our industry."[43]

Schools became increasingly important locations for VMs in this period—and increasingly controversial. Around 1960, Frank Burge, director of the University of Kansas Student Union, was looking for ways to reduce the cost of maintaining snack bars on campus that catered to the 9,000 students. Burge's solution was to install eight "automatic cafeterias," using 170 VMs, in strategic sites around the campus. After machines were installed, his labor cost dropped from 35 percent to 15 percent. Vending trade people saw, at that time, an important potential market in the nation's schools, but focused more attention on office and plant sites.[44]

The vending industry was making some strides in 1964 in the $20-billion-a-year school-lunch area, where banks of VMs had replaced hot meals in many high schools and colleges. That year, 107 Southern California schools converted from cafeterias to vending machines.[45]

By 1968, Vendo company, one of the larger VM manufacturers, estimated that there were 750 schools in the vending camp around the country, more than 200 of them in California. Still, as one account said, the vending industry did not then "have a prayer of getting into more than a fraction of the country's 25,000 high schools, which represent the primary market." That was because, explained *Business Week*, the US government, state governments, most boards of education, and organized food service employees and administrators had put up a "solid front" to keep vending out. The National School Lunch Act, which offered cash and foodstuff subsidies to schools in return for a non-profit hot lunch program for children, was described as the legal underpinning to the machine opposition. Vendo's approach was to use low-key persuasion — schools could use VMs and still keep the federal government subsidy. Also stressed was the idea that vending was a good supplement, and that partial-use vending without infringing on subsidy regulations could be profitable for schools. NAMA claimed it had scrupulously avoided lobbying on the school lunch issue because the opposition was so adamant "that pressure is unlikely to work." The National School Lunch Act was administered by the School Lunch Division of the US Agriculture Department. Passed in 1945, the act was a direct descendant of the farm surplus removal programs of the 1930s. Originally, only surplus commodities were distributed to the schools, but, starting in 1946, the program included cash. In the late 1960s, the act provided a 4.5 cents cash subsidy for each school lunch and between 8.5 and 9.5 cents worth of food commodities. That legislation, adopted to aid states, stipulated that a school that operated its lunch program under a fee concession or contract would not be eligible for participation. In other words, no one was permitted to make money from the lunch program, such as outside service contractors. Under the terms of the program, schools could have VMs in the building — for snacks and drinks — but most of those dispensers were hidden away in teachers' lounges.[46]

In 1970, the US Department of Agriculture agreed to amend the national School Lunch Program to allow vending and food-service companies to participate.[47]

During a 1973 hearing of the US Senate Select Committee on Nutrition and Human Needs, school lunch officials warned that VMs that dispensed "junk food" threatened to undermine the school lunch program. Criticized was an amendment to the School Lunch Act passed in 1972 that allowed the sale of "competitive foods" at the same time and place in which federally subsidized school lunches were served. Regulations that would "result in exploitation of children's nutritional needs by people whose interest is profits" were then being drawn up by the Department of Agriculture to permit normal use of the machines, said Josephine Martin, chair of the legislative committee of the American School Food Service Association. Agriculture department officials declared it was "against our regulations" to have operating VMs in lunch rooms during lunch hours, but critics claimed VMs in lunch rooms were already in use in some states. Gretchen Plagge, director of New Mexico's School Food Service Program, said that student participation in the federal lunch program in a Santa Fe junior high school had dropped from about 350 to 235 and participation in the breakfast program had been cut from 80 to 40 after the installation of machines. NAMA president G. Richard Schreiber said that VMs "are a delivery system pure and simple and not in themselves a nutritional factor."[48]

In the early 1970s, Jean Farmer went to a PTA meeting one night in Bloomington, Indiana where someone complained about junk food in VMs. Farmer thought about it and went home. Putting out garbage at home, the story continued, she found her child's lunch — untouched. Farmer then began a campaign lasting years, in which she wrote letters to editors, educators, dentists, home economists, physicians, and so on. Participation in her child's school's lunch program sagged and was it any wonder, she thought, when, in a typical day, 530 school children bought 500 soft drinks and 300 candy bars from the VMs. However, the school needed money and, noted Farmer, VMs provided an easy way to make money — money that might pay for athletic mats, band uniforms, volley balls, or a host of other needed items. Farmer's agitation finally led the principal to hold a parent poll on the vending issue. When it voted to kick junk food out of VMs, the story made the front page of the Bloomington *Courier Tribune*. Telephone calls and letters of support came pouring into Bloomington from all over America. Indiana's Governor Otis R. Bowen joined the praise, congratulating the PTA for its role in the expulsion of the machines.[49]

Des Moines, Iowa-based Fawn Vendors (an operator) unveiled a new program for locations in 1979. If a business wanted to set up a row of candy and drink machines, it purchased the machines and the merchandise from Fawn, which remained responsible for supplying the merchandise and for servicing the machines. After a time, the machines were paid off with the vending profits and the owner then retained all profits. However, Fawn was still retained as the supplier and servicer. One concern that entered into a cooperative agreement with Fawn was McNeal Memorial Hospital in Berwyn, Illinois. After about a year, the machines had nearly paid for themselves. Another Illinois hospital, St. Mary's in East St. Louis, said its six VMs paid for themselves in seven months. While this type of arrangement did not become widely popular, it did anticipate a future trend in which more and more locations — especially ones with large installations — would take over more of their vending operations themselves, thereby reducing the role of the operators.[50]

Still, the industry did not expand in this period the way most of those involved would have liked. Many moved into other areas of food service. *Business Week* noted in 1964 how many operating companies were moving into areas such as manual food services to complement their VMs, while in that same year *Time* reported that, "Convinced that customers will never go for automatic full-course meals many vendors have recently acquired catering operations, tying in manually served main dishes with vended soup, salad and dessert." One example of the trend, the small operating firm Automatic Merchandising Corporation in Milwaukee, was moving away from VMs exclusively to include mobile catering. Company president Carl Millman said he did not want to increase his vending operation because "the profit margin is not sufficient." Greater margins were said to be available in various catering operations. As a result, some 400 mergers took place in the vending industry in the first half of the 1960s.[51]

According to NAMA in 1968, the "first evolution" in vending was in the decade after World War II when it established itself as a significant retailing channel and a provider of services to such new outlets as factories, offices, and colleges. The "second evolution" occurred in the period 1959 to 1961 and led to consolidations of VM makers and service companies. A "third evolution" then underway showed the majority of companies moving into new areas of operations. One NAMA survey disclosed that 47 percent of the association's members then operated their own food production commissaries and 35 percent of the members then sold food by means other than VMs, mainly through regular cafeterias and lunch counters.[52]

A few years later, in 1973, NAMA explained that over the preceding 10 years several thousand vending concerns had moved into non-vended food services, ranging from mobile catering trucks and office coffee canteens to in-plant cafeterias and snack bars. An estimated 6,500 to 8,000 companies operated five million coin-operated machines with gross annual sales of $6.2 billion in 1970. The industry's non-vended manual food services grossed another $2.3 billion that year. Daniel A. Nimer, vice president of the Canteen Corporation, said "limited growth potential" was the reason his company and others were going into non-vending areas. Every office building or industrial plant, he said, had some sort of vended food operation and the market had become "saturated, static."[53]

A look at statistics early in this period revealed that in 1961 the industry estimated vending sales at $2.74 billion — a little more than one percent of the total US retail sales. Cigarettes accounted for 43 percent of all vending sales that year, soft drinks 18 percent, bulk and packaged confections 14 percent, coffee five percent — in total 80 percent. Industry observer Douglas Dalrymple noted that the 41 percent gross margin of the vending industry made vending a relatively high cost form of retailing. Unless the industry was able to lower that margin to competitive levels, vending was unlikely to become a mass distributor of consumer goods, he thought. Although the consumer might be willing to pay a 40 percent margin on some convenience items, the discount stores and supermarkets, with their 20 percent margins, would probably continue to attract the majority of the consumer's purchases. Dalrymple concluded that vending was unlikely to spark any revolution in retailing and that the vending industry was "apt to continue its specialty role in American retailing."[54]

Sales from VMs reached $4.1 billion in 1966, with some 4.5 million machines on location in the mid 1960s — one for every 43 Americans. Commission rates paid to locations ranged around eight to nine percent.[55]

Industry estimates placed VM annual sales at $9.3 billion in 1975, $9.8 billion in 1976, $10.7 billion in 1977, $11.5 billion in 1978, and $12.8 billion in 1979. Sales of soft drinks in 1979 comprised 35.4 percent of all vending sales, cigarettes 23.5 percent, confections and snacks 12.9 percent, hot beverages 8.3 percent — in total 80.1 percent. Percentage of 1979 VM sales by locations were as follows: 47 percent in factories, 22 percent in public places, seven percent in offices, six percent in colleges and universities, five percent in government offices, four percent in hospitals, three percent in schools, and six percent in all other.[56]

Foreign nations continued to draw comment from American sources for their vending situations. Toward the end of the 1960s, West Germany still had strict closing laws and, with few exceptions, retailers could not open before 7:00 A.M. and had to close at 6:30 P.M. Except for the first Saturday each month and the four before Christmas when businesses remained open until 6:30, Saturday closing time was 2:00 P.M. Shops were closed on Sundays. Elite locations for VMs were after hours in front of supermarkets and at rest stops on the autobahns. Supermarkets often lined their outside walls with VMs offering hundreds of carefully chosen items to the late shopper such as cigarettes, bread, chocolate, and toothpaste. Refrigerated dispensers offered beer and soft drinks, fruits and vegetables, dairy products and meats. Even light bulbs and batteries were available. Some machines held as many as 100 items. All of the 112 federally owned rest stops on West German autobahns had some form of automatic vending machines and 20 of them had "complete automatic restaurants," offering warm and cold meals as well as hot and cold drinks. Sales of goods through VMs in West Germany in 1966 were estimated to be worth $25.5 million. In both supermarket VM areas and autobahn rest stops as well as outside many neighborhood stores, the beer VMs were said to occupy a conspicuous place.[57]

Only 500 British factories had beverage VMs in 1960 while 8,000 had them in 1968. A 1967 survey revealed that in Britain 30 percent of the factories employing 50 or more workers had VMs, compared to 60 percent in the US. Moreover, in America there was one VM for every 20 workers while in Britain the ratio was 1:500.[58]

When beverage industry trade writer Porter Taylor traveled to Russia in 1978, he found soft drink VMs there had no disposable cups. Patrons drank out of reusable glasses. Each VM had a sanitizing system whereby the glass was pressed down on a spot that activated a spray that washed the glass. The most popular beverage with the Russians was reported to be plain carbonated water, which sold for 1.4 cents.[59]

Over in Japan in 1975, the OK supermarket chain opened its 35th outlet in the Tokyo suburb of Kokubunji. What made this outlet unusual was that one-third of its 16,000 square feet was reserved for testing a new computerized selling system developed by the Japanese government at a cost of $1.5 million. Those 67 VMs held 2,469 kinds of goods, dispensing everything from soup to sausages and edible seaweed. Prices were said to be five to eight percent lower than in non-automated stores. Patrons inserted a plastic card in a VM and then pushed a button that dispensed their selection and registered the appropriate information on the card. When the customer was finished shopping, she took her card to a cashier who inserted that into the store's cash computer to get the total bill. OK confidently predicted it would open a fully automatic store within a year and would have 100 such outlets in operation within the next five to seven years. This system was, of course, just a variation of the old Keedoozle experiment and others which took place in America at an earlier time.[60]

Envious American eyes had often been turned to Europe over the seemingly great part VMs played in those countries, especially Germany and the Scandinavian countries. However, that all changed by the 1970s as another country had taken over as the one most in love with VMs. American envy would henceforth turn in this direction. That country was Japan. It is unclear just when Japan passed West Germany in terms of VM penetration, but, in 1977, Japan had 3.2 million VMs, seven times the number it had in 1967. Over that same period, the population grew by only 13 percent. America had one VM for every 53 people while Japan had one for every 36. For 1976, VM sales in Japan totaled $6.4 billion, or $60 per person, while in the US that year sales from the roughly four million machines amounted to $9.8 billion, or $40 per person. The latest vending controversy in Japan concerned the 11,000 machines that sold what were called pornographic magazines—those featuring partly nude women. An outcry came from those who argued that any child with sufficient coins could buy the publications. Nara Prefecture had banned the "porn machines" and the police in Osaka had seized a number of them. One new Nara ordinance prohibited the sale of contraceptives in VMs within 200 yards of a school building. Except in the bar-filled nightlife regions like Tokyo's Ginza or Shinjuku, most stores—especially the thousands of family-run neighborhood shops in Japan—were closed by 7:00 or 8:00 P.M. In Japan at this time the VMs sold a wide array of products including milk, beer, cigarettes, ice, golf balls, fortunes, pantyhose, hamburgers, bags of rice, cans of corn soup, popcorn, whiskey, fishburgers, rice balls, dried fish, noodles, lemon tea, brandy tea, whiskey tea, sake, chocolate milkshakes, fruit juice, and coffee with liquor.[61]

Slugs were still a problem in the industry from time to time. Counterfeit coins were reported to be especially prevalent in 1970, with bulk vendors that dispensed penny and nickel items as favorite targets. According to Ralph Folz, president of the New York Bulk Vendors Association, one percent of the bulk machines' collections were plastic bingo markers in an industry that normally earned a profit of two percent. Blamed for this supposed increase in the use of slugs were a variety of factors including a decline in public morality, an economic slowdown, and increased travel abroad. Bulk VMs were so inexpensive—around $16—that operators were reluctant to spend the estimated $45 it would have cost to install a top-of-the-line slug rejecter. Demand for various foreign coins also rose when people discovered they could substitute for a US coin or token. Favorites of the time for the American quarter were Danish five ores (worth 0.6 cents) and Mexican ten centavos (0.8 cents).[62]

Over a decade later, in 1985, a new Mexican coin the same size and weight as the US quarter (but worth only 0.5 cents) began turning up in coin laundries and other VMs along the Texas-Mexico border. Senator Lloyd M. Bentsen (D — Texas) warned that it was creeping northward and could become a serious problem. He wrote to Secretary of State George P. Shultz, asking him to negotiate with the Mexican government about minting a new coin to replace the one creating the problem.[63]

Scams continued to abound in the industry. In 1979 the consumer magazine *Changing Times* reported on what it found to be common in ads promoting VMs—very high income on a secured investment, and so forth. One ad described was looking for qualified people to service VMs stocked with nationally known brands of chewing gum and mints, with an income potential of $22.50 an hour. Concluded the article: "Authorities in city after city across the country told *Changing Times* of almost countless victims. The Postal Service alone had 3,100 complaints about vending machines and rack sale business gyps last year and made 135 arrests."[64]

Automatic Canteen remained the largest firm in the industry and was acquired by the International Telephone & Telegraph company in 1969. By the late 1970s, it was still moving to increase its in-plant live feeding operations. Vending business then accounted for about 48 percent of Canteen's total revenues. Where Canteen's VMs used to carry private-label candy and beverages, they were then being filled more often with national brand goods. This meant less profit for Canteen since the margin on sales of Hershey chocolate bars was less than that on private brands. However, the company hoped an increased volume would compensate for higher costs.[65]

After a two-year effort and a $25 million investment, some 250,000 VMs stood ready in 1979 to accept the 400,000 new Susan B. Anthony dollar coins that would be poured into the American economy on July 2 that year. It was a calculated risk by the industry that it would be a more popular and more widely used coin than the rarely used Eisenhower dollar coin, which was discontinued at the end of 1978. The cost of machine conversion was estimated to be as low as $25 per unit. It was a cost that could have been higher had it not been for the fact that the VM industry had worked closely with the bureau of the Mint in designing the new coin so that existing coin machines could easily be made to accept it.[66]

VMs were so much a part of life in America by this time that two humorous pieces about them were published in *Reader's Digest* in the

1970s, both condensed from other sources. Both used the same theme of a vending machine running wild, defeating the hapless humans who interacted with it.[67]

The issue of electricity use by VMs surfaced in 1964 when Armand D'Angelo, Commissioner of Water Supply, Gas and Electricity in New York City, in a move to reduce the city's electric bill, set May 1 of that year as the deadline for VM owners to install electricity meters on the machines. New York City was no longer going to supply free electricity to the approximately 850 automatic dispensers located in city buildings. After several conferences with the machine owners, D'Angelo offered them the option of paying the city for the electricity instead of going to the expense of having meters installed for every machine. It was noted that all the VMs in Transit Authority stations were metered. Owners took the option of paying the city and the charge set by D'Angelo for each machine was $1.08 a month for each ampere for which the machine was rated. An average charge, he said, would be between $6 and $8 a month for a unit. Under this new plan, the city would collect about $700,000 a year, with $600,000 going to the Consolidated Edison company and the remaining $100,000 going to the city treasury.[68]

Back in 1973, VM manufacturer Rowe International announced it had devised a computer system to monitor the on-site operation of VMs. Utilizing television-type equipment and a teleprinter, the system enabled one person to keep track of up to 1,000 machines — how much product was in a unit, if change was running low, if the unit was malfunctioning, and so on. Although the first production model of the system was supposedly then being installed, it did not work. However, some 20 years later the concept would return in a more successful version and fuel some big industry hopes.[69]

The period from 1960 to 1985 was, overall, a period in which little happened. VM sales grew, but they remained stuck in the range of one to 1.5 percent of all retail sales. Hopes for automatic stores and automatic restaurants carried over from earlier times were once again dashed. For the 1970s and the first half of the 1980s, the machines only rarely made the news. Stagnation had set in. A narrow range of products — led by cigarettes, colas, candy, and coffee — constituted most of their sales, as had always been true. As cigarette sales declined, those of soft drinks increased. Where VMs did find success was in increasing their presence in certain locations such as plants and offices. But even there the saturation point was being reached. More and more companies turned to some form of live feeding to supplement their VM business. Industry observer Malcolm Morris's statement in 1968 was true for the entire period. He said that, "... despite the crystal ball predictions of some of its proponents, there has been no major evidence nor notable trend indicating that automatic vending will ever be anything other than a supplementary method of distribution." Only products that were small in size and weight, appealed to a mass market, enjoyed a high rate of frequency of purchase, and were truly a convenience item from the viewpoint of the consumer could be sold through VMs, he thought. Morris could not see consumers buying many grocery items from machines because of the many separate transactions involved and the fact that the patron received no bags to carry her purchases in, among other reasons. He saw only a limited role for VMs in the future.[70]

However, the industry itself was not ready to accept such a judgment. It just did not want to see itself as a limited niche form of retailing. With the coming of another highly technical era — the computer age from the mid 1990s onward — the industry would become excited once again.

8

VMs Cut Down on Smoking, Adopt a Healthier Lifestyle, 1986-2001

"Vending machines have become a way of life for just about everybody. What's wrong with also buying videocassettes that way?"
Brandon Chase, 1986

"We are only just beginning to scratch the surface of what advertising potential the machines have. We've already got some 700,000 ministers out there. Why not 700,000 communicators?"
T. Burke McKinney, 1992

"Every 10 years we've had someone come up with a french-fry machine. It disturbs you when they sell a machine with a built-in fire extinguisher."
Bill Buckholz, 1992

"In Kansas City [school districts] were getting 67 cents a kid before, and now they're getting $27."
Dan DeRose, 1999

Optimism for the vending industry was high at the start of this period, although not as effusive as in earlier periods. Reporter Jonathan Hicks said enthusiastically in 1988 that coffee VMs were grinding beans and brewing coffee on the spot. New dispensers were able to change $5 and $10 bills. Prevailing coffee units dispensed freeze-dried or pre-ground coffee into cups six different ways, while the computerized coffee VMs ground the beans in 30 seconds and allowed the brew to be dispensed in any of 56 different ways. Robert Muller, an executive with VM maker Crane Company, predicted clothing, jewelry and other items would be sold in machines. He was quoted as saying: "We have developed the technology for vending machines to accept credit cards which means that a machine could be a substitute for a retail store in some applications."[1]

Four years later, journalist Trish Hall presented a more balanced, but still optimistic, look at vending's near future. Hall reported growing belief in the food industry that the next few years would witness the transformation of vending from "a static, change-resistant business" into one that would provide food anywhere people happened to be situated. The food, she added, would be what many people wanted but often could not get from a machine, things like "fresh pasta cooked on the spot, perfect cappuccino or the finest frozen yogurt." In her mind, signs of change already underway were the coffee VMs that brewed from beans, units that dispensed cappuccino and espresso, and machines that took debit cards rather than cash. However, she did not think it was clear to all operators that their future lay in dispensing meals instead of snacks or candy. "Increasingly, they have been offering entrees, but no matter how fresh or tasty they may be, many customers seem to believe they will not be good." Tim Sanford, executive publisher of *Vending Times*, declared that the VM was the safest way to hold food, "and yet there is that strange public view that things have been in there since the Constitutional Convention." According to David Clayton, vice president of the vending firm Automatic Food Service, "People don't expect to go to a vending machine and buy steak and a baked potato." And, he added, when they bought national brands from VMs, they expected to pay less than if they bought the item in a grocery store.[2]

In *The Futurist* in 1992, Robert Noble, chairman and CEO of the food-consulting firm Noble Communications, said the technology existed to keep entrees frozen until the moment of purchase and then to instantly microwave the customer's selection in the same machine. Noble believed that restaurants crowded at lunch could send diners to their VMs just as banks had shuttled their patrons to teller machines. He also suggested that VMs might someday replace hotel room service — and even the New York City street vendor.[3]

When he was 91 years old and chairman emeritus of Neiman Marcus, legendary retailer Stanley Marcus predicted in 1996 that department store shoppers might find clerks replaced by VMs that dispensed cosmetics, underwear, and stockings by early in the next century. To compete, he explained, a department store would have to reduce costs substantially. That would allow stores to devote a larger portion of their labor costs to products that required fitting or explanation.[4]

One item that did arrive for the vending industry was a more sophisticated technology allowing VMs to communicate with a warehouse computer to report their status. Also arriving were debit cards and the so-called "smart cards." Until around 1990, vending operators would service a route by loading up their trucks, driving to various locations where they would open their dispensers, clean them, fill them, take the money out, and so forth. Electronics began to change this procedure when small handheld computers were introduced around 1992. These allowed operators to check machines without opening them by simply holding the computer up to a scanner on the machine. Back at the truck or in the warehouse, a modem then produced the results. Effective wireless transmission arrived around 1995, using cellular, satellite, or network technology. With wireless technology, the information went directly from the machine to the warehouse without even a visit by the operator. Among other items, the VM could report that it needed change or product, it was jammed, or a forced entry had been attempted. Some of the more high tech coffee units even did their own cleaning and maintenance. If they were not used for a specific period of time, boiling water flowed through the system to clean and sanitize.[5]

Two companies were the main suppliers of wireless technology for VMs in the mid to late 1990s— Real Time Data (RTD) with its Vendlink system and Skywire with Vendview. In 1995, RTD began installing an electronic black box inside VMs. The box recorded all items coming down the coin chute, kept track of coins available for change, detected power outages and unauthorized entries, monitored the cooling system, recorded the time each item was sold, and transmitted all that data via wireless modem to the operator's home office. RTD founder Kit Eldredge envisioned a whole new industry renamed "convenience centers," finely tuned to the needs of customers and backed by sophisticated point-of-purchase data. Yet he acknowledged the difficulties in achieving such a goal in an industry the company described as "extremely primitive," one dominated by ancient equipment and "woefully undercapitalized." Skywire, in contrast, set out to win just one segment of the market— the well-financed beverage machine owners, that is, the soda pop bottlers. Its system initially was only compatible with late model soda machines. It was expensive, costing about $300,000 for the hardware and software for a typical 800-unit operation. RTD set out to be able to retrofit virtually all VMs on site and to be affordable. RTD sold nothing, but rather leased its equipment for $25 per machine per month. However, some machines did not make that much money. Both systems argued that wireless technology would increase revenue by at least 10 percent (no more sold-out machines) and lower labor costs by 30 percent (no more unnecessary service trips). RTD finished 1996 with about 1,500 boxes installed and revenues of less than $50,000. The wireless revolution was slow in taking hold.[6]

One complaint with the new technology was that, while an operator knew what was sold and at what time, he did not know who bought it. Operators awaited the widespread use of debit cards and smart cards in their machines to solve that problem. Cleveland State University introduced a Smart Card on its campus in 1999 and vending sales, said auxiliary services director Kent Dohrman, were expected to increase by 25 to 30 percent. The card held up to $50 and also functioned as an ID card used for everything from retail operations to library book check-outs. Dohrman expected most students to use the cards instead of cash because it was so state of the art, "but faculty and staff may be more reluctant." He concluded that the convenience of having a card with cash on it "and the ease of sliding a card into the machine rather than a rumpled $1 bill will lead to a vending explosion."[7]

Mostly, though, vending continued along much as it had in the past. Its one-time star product, cigarettes, continued its fall from grace, providing operators with less and less revenue. In 1990, US Health Secretary Louis Sullivan urged state governments to enact new laws to discourage the sale of cigarettes to minors. Among the provisions he suggested was a ban on cigarette VMs. According to NAMA, cigarette sales had declined from 45.5 percent of the industry's dollar volume in 1960 to 5.7 percent in 1991.[8]

In 1994, the New Jersey Supreme Court affirmed the right of municipalities to ban cigarette machines as a means of discouraging minors from smoking. Such an ordinance was enacted by the East Brunswick Township in 1990, after an investigation determined that two-thirds of New Jersey high school students who smoked used VMs to obtain cigarettes. VM companies submitted a proposal to modify the machines with remote control devices, but the idea was rejected as too cumbersome.[9]

President Bill Clinton entered the picture in August, 1995, when he announced an initiative to cut sales of cigarettes to youth in half by 2002. To combat smoking among teens, Clinton announced sweeping new regulations on cigarettes and tobacco products—including a proposal to ban all cigarette vendors. His plan to ban cigarette VMs enlarged a debate that had been unfolding in towns and cities across America. Since the late 1980s, over 120 municipalities had banned the dispensers in an effort to discourage smoking by children and teens. An additional 137 communities—including major cities like New York, Chicago and Seattle—had restricted where the VMs could be sited, often limiting them to areas where only adults were allowed. According to US Commerce Department statistics, VMs accounted for just 1.2 percent of all cigarette sales in 1993, whereas in the early 1970s federal data indicated VM sales represented 17.8 percent of all cigarette sales.[10]

The VM industry still argued against Clinton's proposal, claiming it would have little impact on underage smokers. NAMA spokesman Sheldon Silver said a survey commissioned five years earlier by the group found that only nine percent of teens aged 13 to 17 bought cigarettes from VMs; 43 percent said they bought from convenience stores; 29 percent said they made their purchases at gas stations. Those results were at variance with data collected by the Food and Drug Administration (FDA). For example, a 1989 survey of 10th grade students in Minnesota found that 71 percent had purchased tobacco from VMs. In addition, VMs apparently appealed to the youngest smokers. The FDA said another study found that, while only two percent of 17-year-olds used cigarette machines, that number went up to 32 percent for 13-year-olds. FDA official Mitchell Zeller remarked that "A 10- or 11-year-old kid can't pass for 18 even if they have a fake I.D. They are going to do everything they can to avoid a face-to-face transaction and that is the appeal of a machine." Attempting to counter local efforts to curtail machines, vending trade officials argued that so-called "lock-out" devices (a person in the establishment had to I.D. a potential cigarette machine customer and then press a remote button to allow the dispenser to operate) could effectively prevent the sale of cigarettes to underage smokers. A study in Texas found that in Arlington, which had required lock-out devices since 1991, only one of 17 machines inspected had such a mechanism. An underage buyer sent in by a research team was unable to buy cigarettes from that machine, but was able to make purchases at all the other 16 machines.[11]

Predictably, the industry reacted with outrage to the proposed ban. Representing cigarette VM operators in New Jersey, attorney Keith Biebelberg declared "You would be closing down an entire industry, causing massive unemployment. Many of these companies can't stay afloat without the cigarette vending aspect of their business." The industry, he suggested, was "appalled" by Clinton's proposal. Carl Ferraro owned the Dresden restaurant in Los Angeles and earned about $1,000 a year in commission from the machine in his restaurant. He said: "I think President Clinton is stupid. I've been in the business 40 years and I don't need him telling me whether I need a cigarette vending machine.... A ban isn't going to shut me down, but it will be distressful to my business."[12]

A study released in 1995 by the Centers for Disease Control and Prevention and the National Cancer Institute showed that all 50 states banned selling tobacco to minors, with penalties varying greatly. No state had banned the sale of tobacco products through VMs, although 32 had restrictions on youth access to the machines. Twelve states banned VMs outright from areas to which young people had access. In those states, the units were allowed only in bars, liquor stores, and other adults-only establishments.[13]

Clinton would not be successful in getting cigarette VMs banned, but according to a General Services Administration final rule effective January 25, 1996, tobacco VMs were no longer permitted in federal government buildings.[14]

A sting operation took place in Broward County, Florida, in which seven teens, aged seventeen and under, went to bars, restaurants, and hotels in early 1996 to see if they could buy cigarettes from VMs. They succeeded 34 times (33 percent of their attempts), 21 of them in bars. Similar sting projects found teens to be 86 percent successful in Massachusetts and 42 percent successful in Minnesota. While Clinton moved away from requesting a complete ban on cigarette VMs, he did approve US FDA rules that outlawed the machines from grocery stores, restaurants, and other youth haunts, but still allowed them in bars, casinos, and establishments that barred underage patrons. This restriction went into effect in August, 1997.[15]

Another tobacco product, the cigar, was making a comeback of sorts. *Time* magazine did a pre-launch article early in 1997 on a new VM called CigarSir to debut shortly in a couple of posh District of Columbia restaurants. The dispensers, which took up to a $100 bill and credit cards, were also being marketed to golf courses, cruise ships, casinos, and even supermarkets. Cigars contained in the units sold for from $2 to $18 each. Unlike the vending of cigarettes, which the FDA was then in the process of attempting to limit to adults-only places, cigars were exempt from the agency's anti-smoking regulations. Back in the 1920s and 1930s, when cigarette VMs were in their initial phase and in their infancy, cigar VMs were widely available. However, over time they had completely disappeared from the American scene.[16]

On a day in March, 1997, Peter Michaels and Joseph Preston unveiled CigarSir, a refrigerator-size VM, to a large assembly of reporters. That same day, John DePalma, owner of the Fumatore Club, a cigar bar near Chicago, reportedly ordered 80 CigarSirs retailing at $14,500 each. Late one night in the summer of 1996, the partners hit on the idea of a cigar VM when they wanted a cigar, yet tobacco shops were closed. At a VM trade show later that year, the pair found companies willing to make such a machine, but at a cost of $60,000 to $75,000 for a prototype. In the end, they decided to make their own. For $15,000 they bought a refrigerated machine that vended prepackaged ice cream. They hired an engineer and a humidor maker to convert the machine's freezer into a unit that would produce the ideal environment for cigars—70 percent humidity and 70 degrees F—total cost for the prototype, including marketing, was $50,000. Michaels and Preston, though, were not alone in the idea for a cigar VM. In August, 1995, Steven Friedman, founder of the Monroe, Connecticut-based Data Support Associates (designer of humidifier controls), tried unsuccessfully to buy a cigar while playing golf.

Friedman called his chief engineer, Rudy Kraus, and told him to start work on a humidified VM for cigars. Kraus designed the prototype from scratch at a cost of $200,000. Both sides agreed that a well-located cigar VM should be able to sell at least 10 cigars a day, grossing at least $80 a day. Friedman placed his machines on a commission basis, giving restaurants or bars $1 to $3 per cigar sold, out of a full price of $4 to $15. Michaels and Preston sold their machines that accepted credit cards outright for $14,500, or $16,000. Locations then kept all the receipts. At the time of the launch, Michaels and Preston had delivered just three units, while Friedman had placed only one. Both sides were optimistic. Friedman thought his Cigar Vending Corporation had the field locked up until he spotted a pre-launch media article on the partners' units. His reaction: "I punched a hole in the wall of my office."[17]

Friedman's sole unit on site was at the Long Island Brewing Company in Jericho, New York. Microprocessor temperature controls kept the machine interior at precisely 70 degrees F, while an ultrasonic humidifier maintained exactly 70 percent humidity. If you liked what you smoked, an attached phone allowed you to order cigars by the box.[18]

As cigarette machines faded in importance, cola VMs grew. By the end of the 1960s, 12-ounce cans had become the accepted standard size for the vending industry. Over the following two decades, can VMs rapidly replaced returnable bottle vendors across the country. In the early 1990s, cans held a dominating 95 percent of the soda pop vending market. Then bottles—the large plastic ones, or PET bottles—began to re-appear on retail store shelves. Soon thereafter, both Coca-Cola and PepsiCo had launched new 16- and 20-ounce PET bottles. By 1996, PET bottles accounted for an estimated 25 percent share of the packaged VM market versus 70 percent for cans. Vendo company executive Randy Compton remarked: "PET bottles offered several advantages that vending operators never realized with glass. They were lightweight to transport, durable and offered a nice profit margin versus cans." Also helping to fuel the move away from cans was a sharp increase in the price of the aluminum used to make cans in the 1994 to 1995 period.[19]

Around 1996, Coca-Cola was into the second year of its five-year Jump Start program. Much of the program was dedicated to beefing up the company's vending program. New machines were bought and new, individualized graphics, supposedly giving machines an extra edge as a marketing tool, were being put to work. VM manufacturer Royal Vendors was making Troy Aikman- and Emmet Smith- (star players for the Dallas Cowboys professional football team) identified machines for Coca-Cola for use in the Dallas area. According to Ray Kohlepp, vice president of Royal, the Aikman machines had been outselling regular machines by a ratio of three to one. The company also made machines for Universal Studios that featured Bugs Bunny graphics. Beverage companies were also reportedly looking at vending as a test market for new products, as high slotting fees made traditional retail venues prohibitively expensive. Said Vendo's Compton: "the traditional cold drink machine remains the most profitable tool in any bottler's business."[20]

Results from a survey of bottlers conducted by the trade publication *Beverage Industry* indicated that sales per beverage VM ranged between $2,000 and $8,000 annually. Half of the respondents said their machines carried only beverages, while 25 percent said they had dispensers that sold a variety of items such as beverages, snacks, candy and pastries, and other cold foods. Some 58 percent of the respondent companies said that more than half of their units were located in public places, 21 percent said that most machines were in plants or factories, and 13 percent said that more than half of their units were in primary or secondary schools. As of 1996, 50 percent of the respondent firms were using the route accountability software, although 42 percent of the using companies reported that they were somewhat to very unsatisfied with the performance of the software.[21]

As the 21st century neared, the major soft drink companies were reported to be committing enormous financial resources toward vending. According to trade reporter Kent Phillips, "All the major companies have a heavy focus in vending. The two words that best characterize this channel are: 'unknown potential.'" Another reason was profitability. The average vended price in the US was 61 cents per soft drink unit in 1998, or $14.64 in per-case revenue based on a 24-unit case. This would provide an estimated profit of $9.29 per case. A new VM cost a bottler about $2,000. Therefore, a vending location selling five cases a week, or 120 units, would yield almost $50 per week in profits. The machine paid for itself in the first year. Observed Phillips: "The fact is, in vending you almost triple your money." Twenty-ounce PET bottles vended on average at 91 cents, with profits of $14 to $15 per case.[22]

Eileen McMonagle, another trade reporter, observed that, while soft drink sales from vending machines may have made up only 15 percent of sales for some bottlers, they could also represent more than half the company's annual profit. She also noted that the growing popularity of the 20-ounce bottles meant increased revenue and greater margins.[23]

By 1998, the 20-ounce PET bottle, then in mass market distribution for only about three or four years, represented almost 30 percent of soft drink sales in convenience and gas station stores, "with a much smaller but growing percentage represented in the vending market." A number of machines vended the 16- and 20-ounce sizes exclusively, while others could handle 12-ounce cans and the larger bottle sizes simultaneously. Many of the new machines were glass-fronted, allowing for a little showmanship as the customer saw his selection come down. Chuck Currie, an executive at Syracuse University, said he had about 200 12-ounce can machines to cover the 14,000-student campus. Two years earlier in 1996, he began buying glass-front machines, stocking the top two rows with 20-ounce soft drink bottles and the bottom three rows with 16-ounce product, including fruit drinks, juices, water and ready-to-drink teas. In 1998, Syracuse had 45 glass-front machines and 60 to 70 can machines spread out over 57 campus locations. Sales for cold beverages were up 25 percent for Syracuse over those two years. Currie explained that the new machines "merchandise so well. A customer walks up to one of these machines and has 30 different choices of a beverage to buy, instead of the eight or so choices he had previously with the can machines." Per person per year, Americans then consumed more than 54 gallons of soft drinks, 15 gallons of fruit beverages, 12 gallons of bottled water, and two gallons of ready-to-drink teas.[24]

Reasons for the high profitability of soft drinks sold through VMs could be seen in a 1999 study by Mercer Management Consulting. According to the survey, the average price of Coca-Cola per ounce in a US grocery store was two cents, in a vending machine five to seven cents, and in a restaurant 10 cents.[25]

Everything seemed to be sailing along smoothly for the soft drink bottlers in their vending operations. Suddenly, Coca-Cola stumbled. In late 1999 company chairman M. Douglas Ivester revealed that Coca-Cola was testing a VM that could automatically raise prices in hot weather. Ivester explained that a person might want a cold drink more in the heat of summer, "so, it is fair that it should be more expensive. The machine will simply make this process automatic." Wireless technology then in use by many bottlers meant the idea was technically feasible.[26]

Ivester's idea set off a storm of protest. A couple of days after the announcement became public, Coke was forced to "clarify" its position. In a statement on its Web site, Coca-Cola denied that it would introduce VMs that raised the price of its soft drinks in hot weather. During the controversy, arch-rival Pepsi had maintained the high ground by asserting its machines would remain single-priced. Typical of the comments against the idea were those expressed by business reporter Eric Snyder: "Coca-Cola Co. is preparing to take gouging to a new level with a plan to have vending machines charge more for its drinks in hot weather." An estimated 11.9 percent of soft drink sales worldwide in 1998 came from VMs.[27]

Changes also continued in the hot beverage area, especially in the increasingly up-scale coffee vending. It all began in the 1980s with coffee made from beans ground right in the machine. Rowe was one of several VM manufacturers to introduce coffee VMs with bean grinders, at a price of about $4,000 in the late 1980s—around $500 more than conventional coffee vendors.[28]

A decade later, the market was more up-scale as gourmet coffees, cappuccino, and espresso made with soluble, flavored "whipper" mixes were the big growth items in hot beverages. At the University of Illinois at Champaign/Urbana, vending manager Steve Lawson had a total of 500 VMs in 150 buildings for a campus population of 35,000 students and 10,000 faculty and staff. He had about 20 to 30 hot beverage machines, with two offering brewed coffee in the student union building. Most of the other drink machines on campus were contracted to Canteen, "But we found that Canteen machines don't do brewed coffee," said Lawson. To accommodate those new coffees, many hot beverage machines no longer featured tea and soup selections. Some had maintained a decaffeinated or a tea choice, but Lawson reported that they never did well. Tim Dineen, food service assistant manager at the University of California at San Francisco, had one automatic espresso machine that he bought about five years earlier in 1992. It proved so popular that he had just upgraded with a new advanced model. The new unit automatically ground beans and created latte, cappuccino, or espresso. Said Dineen: "This machine has been received fabulously. During the transition period when we were upgrading and we didn't have the machine working for about a day, the crowds went crazy!" On average, the new machine made 400 specialty coffee drinks per day. Charging $1.50 per drink, the $17,000 machine paid for itself in a couple of months.[29]

Even the venerable Canteen company could see the writing on the wall. In 1998, the firm added cappuccino, espresso, French vanilla, and other flavored coffees to its vending offerings. However, Don Lowry, vice president of marketing for the operator Aramark Business Services, warned that VMs simply could not offer the Starbucks experience.[30]

VM makers and operators were said to be in agreement that placing branded and flavored coffees in machines, as well as adding soluble flavored products, helped turn around coffee sales, which had been suffering somewhat in the 1990s. Another added benefit was the ability of operators "to get pricing increases" that were previously harder to put in effect. Operators had often resisted using branded coffees because, with coffee sales flat, they did not believe it would make a difference. Profit margins were also higher using private label product. Dean Winter, Notre Dame University vending manager, had used Maxwell House ground coffee, Sanka bean ground decaffeinated coffee, and water-soluble flavored International Coffee mixes for about four years in eight machines scattered throughout the campus. He said: "Since we started branding our coffees in the vending machines, our sales have improved because our customers tell us that we're using 'quality' coffee in our machines now."[31]

The branding in coffee machines took the form of using brand logos for the buttons used to select products in the hot beverage machines. Other small signs on the dispenser also called attention to the specific products available. In 1997, Nestle USA began offering vending operators the option of selling its products in machines using "billboard" graphics similar in style to those used for several years by soft drink bottlers such as Coke and Pepsi. According to Nestle USA vice president Doug Werts, a "revolution" had taken place as a result of his company's billboard machines, which then numbered 4,000 across the country. At Syracuse (New York) University, eight branded machines were used, selling Nestle coffee at 75 cents per cup and flavored Nestle specialty drinks at $1. Cash operation manager Chuck Currie said that "The new machines have done very well, and I obviously have been able to get a better price with them." He also added that those machines showed sales increases of up to 54 percent when compared to the older coffee machines that were replaced.[32]

Attempts to vend ice cream products continued, but with little success. Business reporter Kathy Blake commented in 1997 that "Successful, widespread ice cream vending is a goal for the future — and maybe it always will be. As it stands now, a huge potential market is certainly recognized." The challenge of getting an ice cream bar from factory to warehouse to VM and into a customer's hands in good condition had not been solved. Jim Ferguson, vice president for VM manufacturer ECC International, said: "Unfortunately, frozen vending's time hasn't come yet. A lot of people talk about it, but not a lot are doing anything about it." Jake Bryan, vending purchaser at the Albany campus of the State University of New York, had 250 VMs in total. Only one was an ice cream machine. "We had old [ice cream] machines that had too many problems, so as they've broken down, we've replaced them with juice machines," said Bryan. At Notre Dame, Dean Winter oversaw 330 machines, only one of which was an ice cream dispenser. "It doesn't do enough business to warrant replacing it with a $7,000 machine," he said. "So when it goes, it goes."[33]

Two years later in the same trade journal, another reporter, Sheldon Silver, also discussed the difficulties in successfully vending ice cream. Makers of the product suggested the temperature of ice cream be kept at between minus 20 degrees F and minus 10 degrees F until delivery to the customer. That was far below the temperature frozen entrees and other frozen items in VMs were usually kept at until purchase. Still, Silver cited supposed technological improvements in dispensers. With no supporting evidence, Silver declared that "ice cream is becoming more popular in vending banks." He predicted that 30,000 of these new machines would be placed on location over the coming five years—an estimated 64,000 of the older ice cream machines were then on site in America.[34]

Popcorn machines were re-invented—again. In the mid 1990s, Protec Manufacturing of Calgary, Alberta, began making a popcorn VM said to produce a bag of cooked popcorn in 60 seconds. Company president Mitch Yurchak said: "Popcorn is one of the highest profit foods available. Basically you start off with a little palm full of seeds and the next thing you know you're getting a buck for that." For some reason, Brazil was said to be buying a lot of Protec's dispensers. Units sold in 1996 numbered 1,400. They have not been heard from recently.[35]

The vending of hot, full meals had long been an industry dream. In 1997, Pinnacle Health System in Harrisburg, Pennsylvania, purchased two Hot Choice VMs—featuring a new technology that heated the product from frozen to serving temperature in two minutes. Hot Choice machines cost $12,000 each and used an advanced system that combined microwave and convection cooking. Provided were seven selections, including pizza, french fries, calzone, cheeseburgers, breakfast pocket sandwiches, and other breakfast items like French toast fingers. The machine's technology first pushed the entire entree out of its wrapper so it was uncovered as it was heating, then pushed it back into the sleeve before it dropped for the customer. Prices ranged from $1.50 to $2. One of the units at Pinnacle, the more successful one, was in an employee lounge on a hospital floor that had no manual food service. It was reportedly doing at least 10 vends per day.[36]

However, the vending of hot meals remained in the experimental, novelty stage. Hot meals remained a goal because each item vended at a high price, thereby producing more profits. Even in 2000, many entrees took over two minutes to prepare, and it was an accepted piece of wisdom in the industry that customers would not wait longer than two minutes for a vended item. Many of the machines available did not even heat the meals internally. Rather, a microwave was provided at the installation. The customer was responsible for moving the item from VM to microwave. Obviously, such installations were limited to captive market locations.[37]

George R. Jensen Jr. ran a company that made coin-less, computerized VMs that dispensed cans of beer and soft drinks and charged the purchases to credit cards. He planned to install the first machines in late 1993 on Florida golf courses, where they had been tested. The machines were equipped with surveillance systems that enabled someone, in the clubhouse, for example, to communicate with customers through a video camera and intercom. Only when the monitor was convinced that a buyer was of appropriate age and sobriety would the machine be activated. Jensen estimated that side-by-side VMs—one selling as many as eight brands of beer, the other eight kinds of soft drinks—could generate annual revenues of more than $20,000, based on prices of $2.50 for a beer and $1 for a soda. Locations were required to have a liquor license and would keep 60 percent of the gross. Dispensers recognized a credit card number for accounting purposes, but did not verify the worthiness of the card—a function that would cost more money. According to Jensen, 28 states had approved the use of coin-less alcohol-serving VMs with an attendant on site. Fourteen of those states, he said, would allow machines that used surveillance for controlled sales. Jensen predicted he would have 2,000 of these beer VMs on site within five years, and that he also might expand into machines that sold other products such as snacks, books, and office supplies. "It's the ultimate in low-overhead merchandising," he said. "If I'm right, there will be millions of machines all over the world. No doubt, they're coming." He was wrong.[38]

Water returned to the list of items available from VMs sometime in the late 1970s. However, it was not until about the mid-1980s that water vending became a viable industry. Concerns about the health effects of contaminants in drinking tap water partly explained the increase in consumer demand for bottled water, vended drinking water, and residential water treatment units. Consumers were also concerned about the aesthetic quality of their water, especially aspects related to taste, odor, and appearance. These factors, in addition to media hype and aggressive marketing, fueled the growth of industries producing alternatives to tap water. According to the Beverage Marketing Corporation, water vending sales in America grew over 60 percent from 1988 to 1990. Vended water also usually cost 50 to 60 percent less than bottled water. The highest demand for vended water reportedly was among Hispanic and Asian populations as well as among the elderly, especially in warmer climates like California, Arizona, and Florida.[39]

In 1957, the National Automatic Merchandising Association (NAMA) established the Automatic Merchandising Health-Industry Council (AMHIC) as an independent advisory group. AMHIC's health members represented professional associations and local, state, and federal regulatory agencies, while its industry members represented VM manufacturers and operators. The Council's original task was to establish a voluntary program for the evaluation of food and beverage VMs as defined by the US Public Health Service Ordinance and Code, The Vending of Food and Beverages.

As a result of its activities, the Council developed the NAMA Standard for the Sanitary Design and Construction of Food and Beverage Vending Machines, which became effective in 1961. Ten subsequent revisions occurred between 1966 and 1990, including the addition of a section on standard water vending machines in 1984. When a VM met the requirements of the standard, a "Letter of Compliance" was issued by an independent public health consultant who conducted the evaluation. Many regulatory agencies relied on the NAMA Evaluation Program as a means of identifying machines that had been manufactured in accordance with nationally accepted public health standards. States such as California, Ohio, and Georgia required that all food and beverage VMs—including water dispensers—carry the NAMA Service Mark, which indicated compliance with the standard. In 1992, there were 22 makers of water VMs participating in the voluntary NAMA certification program.[40]

Founded that same year was Forth Worth, Texas-based Water Point Systems (WP). A year later, the blue chip firm Cadbury Schweppes allowed WP to install its purified water VMs bearing the Canada Dry trademark. Use of that trademark gave WP a major competitive advantage in the rapidly growing market for vending machines that filtered, purified, and disinfected regular city tap water, water many neighborhood residents no longer trusted. Basically, the machines made bottled water right inside the machine, with customers able to fill up their own containers at 25 to 50 cents per gallon. "We identified early on that the customer didn't trust the machine," said WP CEO Mark Hope. They found that while consumers liked the concept of vended water, only about six percent indicated they would ever use a generic machine because they didn't know where the water came from, when the machine was last cleaned, and so forth. But with the Canada Dry name on the dispenser, explained Hope, "we saw the purchase intent go from 6% to 62%. People trust this trademark. It's 105 years old and Canada Dry spends millions of dollars a year advertising it." WP's machines cost around $6,000 to manufacture and install. With estimated monthly revenues of $675 per machine, Hope said operating profits would be $200 a month after amortization, service, and revenue sharing. "Five years ago, people bought bottled water because they didn't like the way their tap water tasted," declared Hope. "Today consumers don't trust their tap water. Many really are afraid of it."[41]

Healthy eating, which became more important in society overall during this period, also received more attention from the vending industry. Nabisco began vending its SnackWell cookies in 1994, a first step in carving out a "wellness" niche in the vending industry. Chuck Klemballa, Nabisco vice president of marketing, said: "There's a real need for a wellness section in vending machines, and we'd like to paint that green with SnackWell's." By this time, industry observers believed that competitors had let the Snack-Well name become synonymous with the fat-free snack category.[42]

Tom Goodwin, owner of an operating company in Aurora, Illinois, agreed that there was a trend toward healthier food in the machines. A few years earlier people wanted such items available, but they were not the most popular items in the machines "because they didn't have as great a taste." Dick Bakala, owner of another operating concern in Aurora, said items such as fat-free pretzels, baked potato chips, and bottled water were all the rage in the trade, whereas five years earlier the healthier items had not sold well. Bakala thought the public was better informed on health issues, creating a demand for nutritious snacks in the machines. He added: "Ten years ago, if you offered a person a bottle of water for sale in a vending machine, he'd probably laugh at you."[43]

Sales of low fat and regular snacks in nine VMs were monitored in 1997 at a university during a four-week baseline, a three-week intervention in which prices of low-fat snacks were reduced 50 percent, and a three-week post-intervention period. The proportion of low-fat snacks purchased (of the total) in those three periods were, respectively, 25.7 percent, 45.8 percent, and 22.8 percent. Total snack purchases did not vary by period. Study authors concluded that reducing relative prices might be effective in promoting lower fat food choices, and that VMs might be a feasible method for implementing such nutrition intervention. Over the entire 10 week study, the average number of snacks sold per machine per week was 142.6 for low-fat (31.6 percent) and 321.0 (68.3 percent) for regular snacks.[44]

In La Crosse, Wisconsin, in 1997 operator Stansfield Vending had initiated the 500 club with a local hospital. A program where each selection was 500 calories or less, the hospital analyzed the sandwiches and Stansfield provided that information at the vending sites. Stansfield manager Steve Bitzer called the 500 club program a "big winner." Healthful foods were also doing well at the University of Pennsylvania at Philadelphia, where vending manager Sandy Bates explained that they had a healthy snack program in place in which the left column of the VM contained the low-fat, low-salt, and low-cholesterol products. "They do really, really well. We've offered them for about two-and-a-half years. People enjoy having that option."[45]

In 1998 Andy Costanzo, vending spokesman for Roger Williams University in Bristol, Rhode Island, said "College students ask for healthy foods, don't buy them when we put them in our vending machines, then complain when they're taken out." At this 2,000-enrollment university with just 30 VMs, SnackWell's, low-fat pretzels, and low-fat chips were offered. University of Notre Dame vending manager Dean Winter remarked: "There's a big wave toward lowfat vended items now and at least 40% of the items we carry on our snack line are low-fat or fat-free.... We tried some lowfat, low-sugar candy items but they didn't sell." The most popular items there were animal crackers followed by low-fat pretzels. "If someone had said eight years ago that bottled water was going to be so popular, we'd have laughed," Jim McKillips, vending coordinator at North Idaho College in Couer d'Alene, Idaho, said. About 25 percent of the items in his snack machines were healthy. Charles Kunkle, general manager of Houser Vending Company in State College, Pennsylvania, said healthy vended food sold best with women. He found such items more popular in business and industrial accounts, where healthy food made up approximately 17 percent of sales, compared to around six percent in colleges. Healthful vended snacks made up about 50 percent of sales near the fitness center at Ohio University in Athens, but just 10 percent in other locations, reported production coordinator Bill Fetty. He added: "We survey students every other year to find out what they want in the machines and the results show that they want 'junk food.'"[46]

As evidence of the popularity of VMs, the magazine *Redbook* let two nutritionists look at the contents of six dispensers and determine which snacks should and should not be chosen — that is, what VM food to choose that would not affect the diet of a person.[47]

A study in 2000 examined the effects of pricing and promotion strategies on purchases of low-fat snacks from VMs. Low-fat snacks were added to 55 machines in a sample of 12 secondary schools and 12 work sites in Minneapolis-St. Paul, Minnesota. Four pricing levels (equal to the other snacks, 10 percent reduction, 25 percent reduction, 50 percent reduction) and three promotional conditions (none, low-fat label, low-fat label plus promotional sign) were used, with sales of low-fat vending snacks measured continuously for the 12-month intervention.

These three price reduction levels were associated with low-fat snack sales increases of, respectively, nine percent, 39 percent, and 93 percent. Promotional signage was only weakly associated with sales increases. As background, this study noted that "the food choices offered in snack vending machines are largely high in fat." One survey of VMs in secondary schools showed that only 27 percent of machines offered a low-fat snack choice such as pretzels, while 60 percent offered candy bars and 57 percent offered chips.[48]

While the vending trade seemed to have almost given up on the idea of a popcorn machine, it turned its attentions to another disaster in the making — a french fry machine. A Salem, New Hampshire firm, Key Packaging

Industries, began to market its new $13,000 french fry unit in 1990. It held 30 to 40 pounds of frozen potatoes and, for a suggested retail price of 75 cents, fried up a four-ounce serving of chips in a little more than 60 seconds. Key felt the best locations would be in convenience stores and cafeterias.[49]

Sales of french fries in America at the start of the 1990s were around $10 billion annually. In 1991, a french fry VM called Prize Frize, being marketed all over the Los Angeles area, was invented by William Bartfield of Palm Springs, California. Each machine, about the same size as a soft drink dispenser, held enough ingredients for some 400 portions. A customer received 33 fries for $1— roughly an ounce more potato than the average serving at McDonald's. During the 72-second wait, flashing lights reassured the customer that his fries were being cooked. Originally invented for the American Navy, the fries were made from pellets of pulverized potato that expanded on contact with water into friable potato dough and then were shaped into fries. It took Bartfield nearly a decade, $8 million of investors' money, and various regulatory approvals to get as far as he had. He hoped to soon be able to launch nationwide, believing there would be enough demand for 30,000 machines— each producing 100 servings a day.[50]

Capturing some of the problems inherent in any french fry VM were the 1992 remarks of Bill Buckholz, president of Goodman Vending Service in Reading, Pennsylvania: "Every 10 years we've had someone come up with a french-fry machine. It disturbs you when they sell a machine with a built-in fire extinguisher."[51]

None of the french fry stories were as bizarre or complicated as the following. Around 1990, Arthur Dalfen, a promoter involved in the penny-stock market all over North America, became involved in a small company listed on the Vancouver Stock Exchange called Harvard Capital (later renamed Harvard International Technologies). In October, 1991, with the stock at 60 cents, Dalfen announced Harvard had acquired the rights to a french fry VM from Sedona Industries of Vancouver. Sedona was one of many casualties in the quest for the perfect french fry machine. Basic problems included keeping the potatoes fresh enough, the oil hot enough and clean enough, avoiding uncontrolled fires, and producing an edible result. Sedona spent $5.5 million developing its version, which reconstituted fries from potato powder and cooked them in hot oil. Nado Electronics, a South Korean manufacturer, had spent another $2 million redesigning the machine and building production facilities. Dalfen needed more than a good machine — he needed credible management — so he hired Edgar Kaiser (heir to Henry Kaiser's Kaiser Steel of Oakland) as Harvard's president and largest single shareholder. As well, he signed on former Canadian Prime

Minister John Turner as chairman of the board. By August of 1993, Kaiser had announced contracts to sell $258 million worth of vending machines and potato powder. Soon the stock price rose, reaching a peak of $28 that year, only to fall off to less than $2 ten months later due to many technical problems and the contracts turning out to be suspect.[52]

Harvard's machine was called the Spud Stop and, while it looked like an average soft drink machine, it was much more complicated. The unit automatically mixed water with dehydrated potato powder, extruded 32 potato strands, dunked them in hot oil, and deposited them in a box— all in 50 seconds. Initial test machines were placed in Vancouver (one) and Philadelphia (four) in the fall of 1992. The one at the University of British Columbia had many problems. Harvard vice president Robert Dunn said: "We found that some university kids would clean out our ketchup supply. So we're looking at some form of rationing." Finally, the unit began to smoke so badly that the UBC fire department was contacted. It was much the same story in Philadelphia. Richard Levin, president of Blue Ribbon Vending, explained that "The machines were unreliable; there was a lot of down time; there were problems with sanitation, the quality of product and safety." Blue Ribbon district manager John Ogara said one of the units caught fire, salt and oil often spilled inside the machine, and servicing was awkward.[53]

Shareholders were not told about any of these problems. Meanwhile, Kaiser installed a Spud Stop in his luxury condo and hosted french fry parties for prospective institutional stock investors. He then announced a string of lucrative contracts, seeming to add up to 16,189 machines and 32.4 million kilograms of potato powder over the following ten years. "You have to say the international market also is going to be huge," said Kaiser. "Our forecast looks like Disney World, it makes so much money." When the business press looked more closely at the contracts, they were seen to be exaggerated—companies that just came into being, firms that had no experience with VMs, and so forth. The market crashed, shareholders sued over concealed facts, and Kaiser resigned from Harvard. By this time, Ogara was working for Canteen. Asked whether that company was experimenting with french fry machines, he said "No, they don't want to be bothered with it at all."[54]

Still working on the idea of a french fry machine was Ore-Ida Foods of Boise, Idaho, a subsidiary of H. J. Heinz. Since Ore-Ida produced about 500 million kilograms of french fries a year, the company was always looking for new ways to sell them. In 1987, it started work on a self-cleaning, hot oil machine, but, said company spokesman Wayne Covington, "We finally concluded that we did not want our name on an oil-cooking machine.

We felt we couldn't adequately protect ourselves against the health and fire hazards." So, starting around 1991, the company spent years working on a convection oven that used hot air to cook the fries. The first machines were slated to be shipped in 1994. Meanwhile, a company called Caltech Investments was working on Freddy's Quick Fries hot oil machines. "Probably one of the most difficult things to overcome was odor. We also had to develop a condiment dispenser that would distribute ketchup, vinegar and salt in an efficient manner," explained Caltech president Roy Allen. "It was easy for salt and vinegar, but ketchup was a real bastard."[55]

Tasty Fries Incorporated (Blue Bell, Pennsylvania) reported in July 1998 that it was close to shipping its first batch of french fry VMs. While the units had been available for several years, only 10 pre-production machines were in use. This system used dehydrated russet potatoes to which water was added in the machine. The fries, which sold for $1, were then cooked in oil and dispensed in a paper cup with ketchup and salt packets attached to the cup's underside. Dispensing time was said to be 90 seconds. A couple of months later, Tasty Fries announced it had signed a letter of intent with an unnamed distributor to install 500 machines in various discount stores around the country. Nothing happened until August of 2000, when the company announced its assembly plant had made the first production models of its french fry VM.[56]

Even a European firm got into the french fry act. German maker Premium Food Systems said its 24-YOU Snacks Around the Clock machines dispensed hot french fries as well as deep-fried snacks such as doughnuts and chicken nuggets. Developed in 1999, the unit was divided into two parts: a freezer on top and a vegetable-oil fryer on the bottom.[57]

Attempts were also made to vend more non-food items, including videotapes. Jeffrey Libman, president of the New Jersey Video Vending Corporation, had visions in 1986 of saving people's time by putting video vending machines in convenience stores, hotels, motels, and so on. At that point, the firm had installed only two, both in New Jersey, though other companies had installed similar machines in Vermont, New Hampshire, New York, California, and Canada. The U.S. Vending Corporation, the machine's distributor, said the first 168-unit machine was installed at a convenience store in Burlington, Vermont, around the start of 1984. Since then, the distributor had sold about 100. To rent a movie from a machine, the patron inserted a credit card, waited 40 seconds while the card was checked, and punched in the code of the selected movie. To return a movie, the customer inserted his credit card and pressed a return button. A drawer opened to receive the video and the machine automatically charged the credit card—$1.99 a day. If a tape was not returned within six days, the customer's account was automatically charged $75. Bernice Bromberg, owner of a nearby video store, said the idea would never catch on because the machine did not have the selection she had.[58]

Brandon Chase's company, Group 1 Entertainment, placed an order at the end of 1986 worth $36 million for 2,000 Movie Machines with Diebold, the nation's largest maker of automated teller machines. Chase remarked: "Vending machines have become a way of life for just about everybody. What's wrong with also buying videocassettes that way?" His units were seven feet tall, weighed 1,250 pounds, and held 374 cassettes. Group 1 predicted it would have 5,400 machines grossing $400 million a year by 1988. Even more fanciful was Chase's expectation that his company would own one-third of the 60,000 video VMs he believed would be in use in America by 1995. Market analysts Paul Kagan Associates were pessimistic about the concept because video stores had such large selections and young people paying cash were a large segment of movie renters.[59]

By the end of 1990, an estimated 1,200 videotape machines had been installed in North America, but, noted business reporter Kathryn Harris, "the reality is that dozens of video vending machines and business plans have failed. And profits still elude survivors who have overcome the technical glitches that plagued earlier efforts." Group 1 quit the market in 1987 after spending more than $5 million. Diebold regained the rights to its machine, but had not found a market for it. One problem was the high cost of these machines, around $18,000 each, and an expenditure just about as high to stock them. One new entrant, the Westport, Connecticut-based Thru-the Wall company, was marketing a unit that fit into a store window, designed to stretch a store's hours and service. Stores leased the machines for $325 to $480 a month and provided their own inventory. Employees of the store could stock the units from inside and the units accepted no cash, credit cards, or returns—they only vended tapes to customers who used membership cards from the store. Payment was made when the tape was returned to the store counter. Although the company started shipping its machines 12 months earlier, only 74 had been installed.[60]

A variation on this theme was provided by a Minneapolis firm's Short Takes VM, which allowed customers to record an instant video greeting in a booth similar to the old photo machine booths. Customers paid $10 for a blank videocassette tape which they inserted in a slot in the machine. A camera in the booth then recorded 10 minutes of whatever message the customer wanted to record. Also included in the fee was a mailing envelope.[61]

Another new product for which vending was attempted was music CDs. Universal City, California-based Vending Intelligence Corporation (VIC) was targeting the older music lovers, fans who stayed away from traditional record stores, by selling a CD VM. The ExpressStop Music Sales Center, capable of stocking 48 different titles and 960 total discs, allowed a 30-second audio sampling of a CD prior to purchase. The transaction could be handled with cash, credit card, or bank ATM card. VIC president Pete Bolger said: "We think the vending machine offers the best chance for delivering product to these [older] people outside the record store environment." The first machine was installed in Los Angeles in November, 1992. By the end of July, 1994, about 80 machines were in operation. Machines cost $15,000 and sold CDs for $13.99 each. VIC owned most of the units and paid a "minimum monthly site fee," sharing profits with the site after certain sales figures were reached. Titles were changed every two weeks— usually four or five titles were replaced.[62]

Another company involved was Miami-based Intune, stating in mid-1998, that it had sold more than $200,000 worth of CDs and $1 million worth of its CD VMs in the previous 18 months. Around the same time, Korea's Hansol Telecom entered the business when it introduced its CD VMs called CDBank. These units allowed customers to select up to five songs, with a total time of seven minutes, for $8.40. Songs could be selected from Hansol's catalog of song titles, ranging from 50s hits to current favorites. One major drawback was that Hansol had only obtained the rights to 1,300 song titles at that time.[63]

The Nashville-based Movie Music company signed a deal in early 2000 with Knoxville-based Regal Cinemas to place CD VMs selling soundtrack and artist releases in more than 400 movie theater lobbies nationwide by the summer of that year. Using a high tech system, sales in the VMs could be tracked in real time by theater chain, by area, by CD title, and so forth. Regal got a percentage of gross sales. Primarily, the units, which could hold up to 24 different titles, were to sell soundtrack titles from current films and popular artists, as determined by Movie Music research. On-screen ads during movie pre-shows and posters on the machines themselves would draw interest to the machines. Starting at the end of 1998, the Movie Music machines underwent more than a year of testing, with units placed in cinemas in Nashville, outside Chicago, and San Diego.[64]

The US Supreme Court ruled in 1995 that a Florida city could enforce regulations for newspaper vending machines on public sidewalks. A ruling was allowed to stand that validated Coral Gables uniformity-of-appearance regulations. The case stemmed from an incident in 1991 when the Spanish-language paper, *Exito*, used VMs violating a Coral Gables requirement that newspaper machines be brown and tan and feature lettering no higher than 1.75 inches. The court turned aside the argument stating that the ordinance violated the right of free speech.[65]

At the end of the 1990s, the mechanical rack remained the newspaper industry vending workhorse, accounting for as much as 90 percent of all newspaper machines on the street. Named the "honor box" because it depended on patron honesty to take only the top paper in a stack, most units sold for $250 to $350. Electronic machines operated with batteries that lasted a year or so. One of their advantages was that they accepted a greater variety of coins, including pennies, than mechanical models. Some models provided information, such as the time they sold out and how many papers were sold in 15-minute segments during a day, and cost $350 and up. Multi-title machines had been sold for 25 years, and could be designed to sell anywhere from six to more than a dozen different papers. Prices for such custom-built models could reach $3,5000 or more. The drive-in rack, a side-opening machine designed to be used by car drivers, was usually placed at a drive-in fast food restaurant, gas station, driveway of an apartment complex, and so on, and cost $325 and over.[66]

At the intersection of Michigan Avenue and Illinois Street near downtown Chicago, one could find 21 newspaper VMs lined up vying for attention. Mayor Richard Daley and the City Council passed a law in 1998 to replace many of those dispensers with new VMs holding multiple titles. Daley said the new machines would make the downtown look more scenic. Critics argued newspapers would be robbed of their First Amendment right to free speech. The law initiated a one-year experiment that replaced 560 VMs along tourist-filled Michigan Avenue and State Street with approximately 60 of the new machines— eight foot by four foot green, iron boxes with pillars on the side featuring two rows of four newspaper boxes. The law awarded the contract to operate the dispensers to Paris-based J. C. Decaux — a company known for its bus shelters and public toilets.[67]

In 1995, Amy Bell, owner of the audio-only store Albert's Audiobooks in Agoura Hills, California, came up with the idea of renting audiobooks through VMs when she discovered some machines that had been used "years ago" to rent videos. Bell bought 10 of them and was looking to install them in office buildings, hospitals, and health clubs. Her first installation was in a downtown Los Angeles office building where customers used their credit card to first rent, and then return, the audiobook —$2.99 for the first day, $1.50 per day thereafter. Each machine could hold between 136 and 184 audiobooks, representing about 100 titles.[68]

Joe Boxer Corporation, a maker of underwear, announced at the end of 1998 that it would begin selling its wares from VMs located at airports, hotels, college dorms, and fitness centers. Customers would swipe their card, make their selection ($14 to $18 a pair), and out would pop a vacuum-packed can of underwear.[69]

Back in the early 1990s, Postal Buddy machines—which printed labels for customers, sold envelopes and stationery, and provided change-of-address material—were installed in 183 postal lobbies. According to postal officials, however, business was well below projections, and the US Postal Service canceled its contract with Postal Buddy as of September, 1993. While revenue projections ranged from $35 to $55 per machine per day, with the USPS receiving a share of any revenue over $42 a day, postal officials said actual sales ranged from $15 to $30 a day.[70]

Based in Des Moines, Vending Consultants devised its own live bait machine in 1996 after discovering that some locations were using modified refrigerated sandwich machines to vend live bait for fishing. The company sold 15 of the new units in 1996, 700 in 1997, and had a total of 2,000 on location near the end of 1998. Machines sold for $3,995 and contained four types of worms and grubs, with the worms reportedly being able to stay alive for as long as 10 days on the mixture of peat moss and powdered newsprint in the cup. A thermostat kept the bait at 40 to 45 degrees in the summer and warmer in winter for ice fishing. A dozen worms were dispensed in each cup. The wholesale cost of worms was around $25 per thousand in the spring and up to $80 or more per thousand in the summer. They could live for many months in the cooler in an operator's shop before being transferred to VMs.[71]

One of the largest operators of worm machines was a Hudson Valley, New York farmer named Daniel Bartholomew. Starting in 1997 with one machine on his front lawn (which generated $900 a month), a year later he had 28 units and expected to have 100 by the year 2000. Bartholomew sited machines at marinas and small convenience stores near boat docks. When asked about his future with worms, he exclaimed, "The sky's the limit."[72]

When it came to location, one element stood out for vending managers in all types of operations: traffic flow. Brad McAllister, assistant director of auxiliary services at Southwest Texas State University in San Marcos, said: "We have the machines placed everywhere. We try to get them into as many high-spots that we can." He had about 160 VMs on campus—100 beverage and 60 snack units serving a 21,000-student population plus faculty and staff. McAllister placed machines strategically in residence halls, at bus stops, in commuter lots, and at all athletic facilities. He added: "We look for certain pathways the students use, and really hit those sites. With newer buildings, we're designing vending areas right into their layouts." Ross Willingham, assistant director of business operations at Oklahoma State University in Stillwater, served 18,000 students and 5,000 faculty and staff with about 300 VMs. "Generally, we look at traffic flow as the biggest factor to try to incorporate into the access to the machine," he explained. "We put them into exits or entrances of buildings so that they're convenient for the customers."[73]

Office and plant locations remained a mainstay for the vending industry, but the area was stagnant. An example of a typical installation could be seen in the Trane Company, maker of heating, ventilating, and air conditioning equipment, of La Crosse, Wisconsin. With 145 VMs and 3,000 employees, nearly 70 percent of all food served to workers came from their VMs. Trane contracted with local operator Stansfield Vending to supply and maintain 17 sandwich machines and another 128 units that offered snacks, sodas, cookies, and pastries. Two cafeterias and a "fine" dining facility (for clients) were also available. Service at the two cafeterias (food there was also supplied by Stansfield) ran from 6:45 A.M. until 1:30 P.M. The most popular sandwiches sold from the dispensers were tuna, egg, and chicken salad.[74]

In a 1997 vending survey the average business and industrial vending installation had a total of 49 machines: cold beverage, 19.9; hot beverage, 5.8; snacks/baked goods, 15.1; cold entrees, 5.9; hot entrees, 1.7; and frozen desserts, 0.7. Vending accounted for 20.4 percent of food service sales at an average business and industrial unit.[75]

Fairs became an increasingly important place to locate machines as fair operators looked for new ways to make money. Two methods used to that end were sponsorship deals—both exclusive and non-exclusive with Coke or Pepsi for live vendors—and putting VMs on the fairgrounds, with the fair receiving a percentage of sales. Live vendors often took issue with fairs having dispensers on the grounds. The Oregon State Fair in Salem had between 50 and 60 Pepsi machines on the grounds. Pepsi set the prices for the beverages, but the fair management tried to keep those prices in line with pricing at the concession stands. "We try to place them so that they are not in sight at all from any food concession," said fair concession manager Wayne Peterson. "And believe me, Pepsi brings out 50 or 60 machines, and they try and put them all over the place." Pepsi also had an exclusive deal with the Dade County Fair & Expo in Miami, which included the placement of a minimum of 60 machines on the fairgrounds. Concession manager Pat Moroney pointed out that the fair worked closely in the placement of the machines: "we are careful to try and put them as far away from our food vendors as possible because they're selling the same product."[76]

VMs located on fairgrounds in the same vicinity as food concessions sometimes created problems other than decreasing the sales made by live vendors. Linda Comer, National Independent Concessionaires Association (NICA) executive director, explained that if patrons lost their money in the machines, "they want the concessionaire to give it back. If the product comes out hot, they want a cup with ice. It's a problem." Concessionaires began seeing more and more VMs, primarily drink machines, sited on fairgrounds from about the mid-1990s onward, at which time machines began to be placed in the same areas as the food concessions.[77]

With mainly a captive population, hospitals were also a favorite location. Some hospitals reduced manual food service in favor of more VMs in order to save money. Increasingly, hospitals and other locations with a large number of dispensers were owning and operating their own machines. In 1995, when the cafeteria was being remodeled, Huguley Memorial Medical Center in Fort Worth, Texas, instituted an increased vending program. Breakfast and dinners were eliminated from the cafeteria, which remained open for lunch from 11 A.M. to 1 P.M. only. Director of support services Mark Penno explained that the hospital bought all new vending machines and built a room for them. Also introduced was the cashless system, with employees using their ID badges to obtain meals from machines or the cafeteria — with payment deducted by payroll. Switching from live food service to VMs was not whole-heartedly accepted: "This is a sensitive issue with employees," said Penno. "We believed that the vending program would also pay for itself." Around $50,000 was spent on the VMs and another $50,000 on the cashless system and other changes. "We paid for both in about one and a half years," Penno declared. "A lot of hospitals just don't realize the opportunities in vending." Huguley started with 18 machines, increased that number to 25, and was thinking of expanding to 30 or 40 units in the near future. Although there was much initial resistance to both changes, employees were said to have adjusted to them within a couple of months. "When we started this, we heard people say 'I don't want to use this cashless system. I don't want to use a vending machine,'" explained Penno. "My advice to others in such a situation is to just do it."[78]

Back in 1986, Russ Couron, food service director at East Pasco Medical Center in Zephyr Hills, Florida, looked at the numbers and found his hospital was receiving about $179 a month in commissions from their outside vending contractor. Yet, a single machine was vending at least 480 cans of pop a day — at 60 cents each — and it was obvious to Couron that someone was making a lot of money from vending, and it was not his hospital. So he invested in his own machines and converted to self-operation. In 1998, the system was further changed to allow debit and payroll-deduction systems. At this 150-bed hospital, vending grossed about $6,000 a month at the end of the 1990s. VMs purchased — at $3,000 to $5,000 each for the 14 units — were paid off in six months.[79]

Schools remained the most controversial location for VMs. Senator Patrick J. Leahy (D — Vermont), chairman of the Senate Agriculture Committee, urged the federal government in 1994 to do more to discourage the consumption of soft drinks from VMs on school property. Leahy wanted to include language in the Better Nutrition & Health For Children Act of 1994 that "clarified" regulations that gave school officials the authority to ban VM sales of soft drinks and snack items, such as candy bars and chips, during school hours. His proposal would have had the USDA send out official reminders to school districts informing them that they had the power to impose such bans and provide them with model language. The National Soft Drink Association (NSDA) was strongly opposed to Leahy's idea, and was backed by the National Association of Secondary School Principals. Instead of rejecting Leahy's proposal, a compromise was reached wherein the USDA's official reminders to schools of model language and their authority to impose bans would be sent only to elementary schools. However, soft drink VMs were not placed in elementary schools. NSDA vice president Drew Davis called it "a mythical solution to a non-existent problem."[80]

Leahy had been trying to circumvent a 1983 federal court decision that okayed a ban on sales of minimally nutritious foods, but limited the time and place of the prohibition to the immediate time and area of meal service. The goal was to bring school lunches into compliance with US dietary guidelines. Testifying at the hearings on behalf of the principals' group was James R. Elliott, principal of Thompson High School in Alabaster, Alabama. He objected to Leahy's proposal because "it encroaches on the local control of our schools." Elliott argued that local school officials were aware of their rights to adopt more stringent policies, but that such a policy should not be mandated by the federal government. Davis argued that there was neither evidence that soft drink consumption in secondary schools was inconsistent with sound nutrition science nor that such sales contributed to lower participation in the school lunch program.[81]

Although the Florida Department of Education rules mandating that secondary schools could not sell "foods with minimal nutritional value" until one hour after the first lunch period had been in place for years, the state Auditor General's office only began enforcing the law in 1996. Most school districts had stopped selling sodas and snacks until after the lunch period, but some were still vending throughout the day. Pinellas County schools stopped selling from VMs in their high schools in 1996, when the law began to be enforced. According to Delores Ford, food service director for Pinellas County public schools, "It did hurt the high schools— they lost an average of $50,000 per school."[82]

The Denver School District in Colorado reached an agreement in 1998 with high school principals that allowed it to sell sodas during the lunch period from dedicated machines located just outside the lunchrooms.

School District food service director Donna Whitrock explained: "In Colorado we have a competitive foods rule that says mechanically vended beverages can be outside the walls of the lunchrooms. We now sell vended sodas during lunch hours from our machines, and we get the profits."[83]

Competitive food rules changed in Florida after Governor Jeb Bush took office at the end of the 1990s. New rules allowed high schools not only to have as many vending machines as they wanted, but also to run them all day if desired.[84]

Self-operation even took hold at some school districts. In 1995, Chesterfield County Public Schools in Virginia began running its own vending program. For fiscal year 1998-1999, revenue reached $1.37 million, with a profit of $524,167. The system had 57 schools (51,000 enrollment) and 66 vending sites containing 132 canned soft drink machines, one bottled soft drink unit, eight juice dispensers, and 108 snack machines. Under self-operation, food and equipment contracts were bid out — machines were stocked, emptied, repaired, and so on, by school district staff. Cypress-Fairbanks Independent School District in Houston, Texas, a 47-school district (61,000 enrollment), started self-operating its vending operation in 1997. It operated 152 beverage machines, 128 snack units, and eight ice cream machines, with profits being split 45 percent to the school district food service department and 55 percent to the individual schools. Profits in 1999 amounted to $375,000.[85]

More common than schools turning to self-operation, however, were schools signing exclusive deals with one of the major soft drink bottlers. Colorado Springs School District #11 (33,500 enrollment) signed such a deal in the late 1990s for its 39 elementary, 10 middle, and five high schools. It was a contract that provided a guaranteed minimum payment of $8.2 million over a 10-year period, with incentives that could increase that amount by up to $3.5 million (based on sales volume). Under the agreement, elementary schools made a guaranteed minimum of $3,000 annually, middle schools received a minimum of $15,000, and high schools got at least $25,000, with the remainder of the $820,000 annual payment going to unfunded educational needs.[86]

In a move that gave it access to more than 300,000 students, Coca-Cola Bottling outbid Pepsi to win an exclusive three-year deal with the Toronto District School Board to sell soft drinks and juice in its schools. Coke paid $5.7 million for those rights. The same company won a similar contract a few months earlier with the Toronto Catholic District School Board, paying an undisclosed amount for exclusive rights to sell soft drinks to that board's 102,000 students. Some 200 Pepsi machines had to be removed from Toronto schools. Pepsi had signed Ontario's first deal between a school board and a soft drink company in 1996, when Pepsi paid $1.14 million for an exclusive three-year deal. Critics opposed corporate control to that extent as well as the replacement of government funding with corporate money. They were also opposed to the spread of sugar- and caffeine-laden products with limited nutritional value to school children. Under the terms of the agreement, soft drinks would not be available to students in grades lower than seven. In elementary schools, VMs would stock bottled water or juices distributed by Coca-Cola.[87]

In 1999, Dan DeRose, based with his company DD Marketing in Pueblo, Colorado, was one of the best known consultants, in a rapidly growing specialty. He worked as a consultant for school districts that were negotiating exclusive contracts for their VMs. Doing the math, he observed that if everyone drank one product a day that meant — in a system with 45,000 students, 180 days of school and a 75 cent charge per can — a gross revenue of $6 million a year. DeRose said he had obtained or was negotiating for exclusive contracts for 63 school systems nationwide. The exclusive contract, a winner-take-all creation of the soft drink companies themselves, eliminated a rivals' products completely from a school or other location. Whoever won the contract would supply not only soft drinks for VMs, but also juices in the school cafeterias as well as water and other drinks for athletic events. In discussing deals he had negotiated, DeRose mentioned deals in Colorado and Kansas— one for $11.1 million, the other for $5.3 million: "In Kansas City they were getting 67 cents a kid before, and now they're getting $27."[88]

Since schools were in need of money for programs, DeRose argued that they were better off signing exclusive deals. He cited his own daughter, Anna, then in first grade in a system where he had negotiated an exclusive deal with Coke. "From now on until she's graduated, all she will drink is Coke.... She doesn't even know how to spell Pepsi." His fee was a percentage of the final contract figure — 25 to 35 percent according to school systems that had hired him. In those contracts, soft drink bottlers also wanted ads in the athletic programs, something on tickets and on the scoreboard, and so on. However, all such requests were subject to negotiation. DeRose argued that he was helping to make schools more realistic for children. "If you have no advertising in schools at all, it doesn't give our young people an accurate picture of our society." Michael Jacobsen, executive director of the Center for Science in the Public Interest, remarked that, "Twenty years ago, teenagers drank twice as much milk as soda pop, and now they drink twice as much soda as milk." Reporter Constance Hays estimated that, as of April, 1998, there were 46 school districts with exclusive deals spread over 16 states, with one school district refusing a solicited deal. As of October, 1998, there were 108 with deals in 23 states, and 10 had refused solicited deals. As of May, 1999, there were a reported 140 school districts in 26 states that had exclusive deals, with 15 school districts refusing solicited deals.[89]

The Center for Science in the Public Interest in Washington, D.C., wanted to ban the sale of soft drinks from VMs in schools, arguing that teens already drank too much pop and that schools should try to undermine that, not promote it. The group also noted that teens consumed up to three times as much sugar as recommended by the federal government, with soft drinks being a prime source and that 25 percent of teens who drank pop got at least 12 percent of their calories per day from that source.[90]

Henrico County (Virginia) School District recorded VM sales of $500,000 in 1999, an increase of $100,000 over the previous year. Beverage sales made up 59 percent of the total, juice 16 percent, and snacks 25 percent. The district had about 200 machines and was planning to install Gatorade and Veryfine machines near the football, soccer, and track fields.[91]

Madison, Wisconsin's school district, after signing an exclusive contract with Coca-Cola in 1997, received a $100,000 signing bonus plus about $500,000 over the life of the three-year contract. The district hoped it could sign an exclusive deal without compromising its educational mission. It sought to maintain its educational honor by accepting far less than the $1.5 million Coke had originally offered. Involved with the higher sum would have been the utilization of Coke T-shirts and Instant Coke awards, software that displayed a Coke logo (while giving information about college scholarships), and a "nutritional curriculum" that featured the Coke product Fruitopia. As the contract neared the end of its duration, teachers and students were upset that, in the absence of competition, the price of a Coke from a school VM had risen from 40 cents to $1. The Center for Commercial Free Public Education, which opposed exclusive school contracts, estimated that, in April of 2000, some 175 school districts across America had exclusive arrangements with either Coke or Pepsi.[92]

Similar trends toward self-operation and exclusive contracts also surfaced on university and college campuses. The University of Minnesota signed an exclusive deal with Coca-Cola in 1996 in which the university was to receive $28 million over 10 years in commissions and other products and services, including an up front commission prepayment of $6 million. When the beverage part of a vending operation was removed, it made it more difficult for a university to self-operate the remaining vending operation since beverage sales typically accounted for 40 to 50 percent of overall sales and were high profit items. The State University of New York at Albany went to a fully self-operated vending service in 1985 and saw an immediate increase in sales.[93]

Vending on campuses could be extremely lucrative. At the University of California at Irvine (18,000 enrollment), 65 snack and candy VMs generated revenue of $6,000 a week in 1998 while beverage machines contributed another $4,200 per week. Food services director Alan Moloney was then involved in a project called "campus mapping" for vending sales. The plan was to design a computer program that would take demographic downloads from the registrar's office for students, together with the demographics on faculty and staff from human resources, and break down the users for each floor of each building. The goal of the program was to use the information quarterly to chart changes in demographics in each area of a building in order to decide what items to stock in the VMs. According to Moloney, a test of this plan on 28 VMs had been "extremely successful" and increased sales in those units by 30 percent.[94]

At Cornell University in Ithaca, New York, vending generated close to $1 million a year at the end of the 1990s, of which 35 to 40 percent was in beverages, 30 percent in snacks, and 10 percent in cold food. UCLA's vending sales totaled $2.7 million in 1999, with $828,000 of that from soft drink sales and $112,000 worth of water sales.[95]

In 1998, the University of Regina, the University of Saskatchewan, the University of Alberta, and McMaster University all signed exclusive deals with Coca-Cola—the University of Manitoba went with Pepsi. Under the 10-year agreement with the University of Regina, Coke was to donate $1 million to the university plus pay an undisclosed percentage of all Coke beverage sales in campus cafeterias, student lounges, and VMs.[96]

Near the end of 1999, Montreal students staged a downtown demonstration protesting against their school (Universite du Quebec) signing an exclusive contract with Coke. So great was the disruption of traffic that police made 70 arrests. Universite du Quebec canceled their Coke contract. Around the same time, at the Universite Laval, students voted 64 percent against the school's plan to give either Pepsi or Coke exclusive rights to place their VMs on campus. Yielding to the students, administrators suspended the plan.[97]

In 1995, the University of British Columbia (UBC) signed a 10-year exclusivity deal with Coca-Cola. Details of the contract were never publicly released. Reporters for the student newspaper soon began filing freedom of information requests to release the contract details. UBC and Coca-Cola fought all such moves and tried to keep the contract sealed. Finally, in the summer of 2001, UBC announced that the details of the Coke deal were being made public—UBC received close to $8.5 million over ten years. In March, 2001, Coca-Cola announced it would no longer encourage the adoption of exclusivity contracts with US schools.[98]

According to the industry, vending dollar volume moved from $2.1 billion in 1987 to more than $36 billion in 1999. However, as always, vending represented a tiny proportion of all retail sales. And, as had also been true from the start, most of the vending income came from the same narrow range of relatively inexpensive products. In 1960, cigarettes generated 44 percent of total income while soft drinks accounted for 16.9 percent. By 1999, cigarettes were down to just three percent but soft drinks accounted for 54 percent of total vending sales. That year cigarettes, soft drinks, coffee, and confections (packaged)—the four Cs—accounted for about 83 percent of income.[99]

In regard to vending in foreign locations, a report in 1998 revealed that Germany had 820,000 cigarette VMs—almost seven times as many as the second place UK (120,000)—and topped the poll in terms of the percentage of cigarettes sold through machines with 32 percent. Last was the UK at five percent. Figures for other European countries were as follows: Spain had 113,000 cigarette VMs (in second place by selling 19 percent of all cigarettes through dispensers); Holland 28,500 (11 percent); Belgium 20,000 (six percent); Switzerland 16,000 (14 percent); and Ireland 10,000 (15 percent).[100]

January, 2002, was the date when the new coin, the euro, was introduced and would replace most national currencies within the EU community. It meant VMs would have to be modified to accept euro coins in all the following countries: Italy, Germany, France, Ireland, the Netherlands, Belgium, Luxembourg, Austria, Finland, Spain, and Portugal. Europe had some 3.8 million VMs in 1999, and several million more coin-operated devices, such as telephones and subway ticket machines. Reportedly, Germany had 2.5 million VMs with food and drink, with a total annual revenue of $2 billion while Italy's 517,000 food and beverage machines had yearly revenues of $1.5 billion. Germany and Italy were Europe's largest vending markets.[101]

In 1991, Danish company Faxe Jyske Breweries installed a coin-operated beer machine in Copenhagen's airport that accepted Danish, Norwegian, Swedish, German, and English coins. It dispensed variable amounts of Faxe beer depending on the amount of money deposited. It could also be modified to accept other currencies or to reflect exchange-rate fluctuations. This machine reportedly met with immediate success.[102]

A decade later, another VM for serving alcohol was launched, this one in Auckland, New Zealand. For two and a half years, Joe Karam had worked on a machine that used smart cards to control access. Five prototypes later, in 2001, he believed he finally had a workable model. Machines were made in Melbourne, Australia, and used European smart card technology. The card contained a chip that could be used to set spending limits and, if required, limit access to non-alcoholic products only. Units could only be placed in premises which had a liquor license. Owners of the locations where the machines were placed were responsible for stocking the units, setting prices, and controlling access. Karam claimed his company had 60 outlets already signed up to take the VMs. One year earlier, the Australian company Lion Nathan had tested beer VMs at a number of outlets in Australia but then abandoned the project. "In terms of the costs and benefits we just decided it wasn't something we saw value in," said company spokesman Graham Seatter.[103]

Back in Europe, an unusual VM called Pizza Magic was introduced in Madrid, Spain, in 1999 by the fast-food company Telepizza. According to a news service report, the VM detected passers-by and called out to them, "Fancy a pizza?" The machine, capable of being programmed in any of 10 languages, defrosted and cooked a small pizza in under two minutes at a cost of $1.80. Over the following three years, Telepizza hoped to distribute 9,000 machines and to vend, in that time, 97 million pizzas.[104]

The British magazine *The Economist* estimated in 2000 that Coca-Cola had thousands of its VMs located in Moscow, despite the many bureaucratic rules that made siting a VM there very difficult.[105]

China's two main cities, Beijing and Shanghai, received condom VMs for the first time in 1999 as part of efforts to reinforce birth control. The country had been intensifying efforts to improve its contraceptive distribution network. A total of 90 condom machines were to be installed in residential areas, college campuses, subway stations, and public toilets in the two cities. A single condom cost 12 cents. According to the official newspaper, *China Daily*, "The entire process takes mere seconds, and is likely not to cause the familiar fear or embarrassment that many youngsters, as well as adults, experience in drug stores."[106]

Australia's telecommunications firm, Telstra, began testing a combined soft drink VM and pay phone in 1999. Customers could pay for their soft drinks (600 ml bottles) and phone calls using either coins or their Telstra Smart Phonecards. Especially targeted by the machine were young people, said Telstra manager Vladas Leonas. "When they hang around and use a payphone, it will be convenient to buy a bottle of Coke."[107]

However, Japan retained its spot as the country where VMs were most pervasive. As early as 1990, many of the soft drink machines in that country were already high tech. New machines with special microchips could play a tune or talk to buyers while reliably dispensing up to 24 varieties of soda, fruit juice, sports drinks, and ready-to-drink canned coffee, and tea— hot in the winter, cold in the summer. Roulette-type games gave lucky buyers free cans, while overhead illuminated cans advertised brand names like Coke, Suntory, or Kirin. An estimated 50 percent of the $24 billion in Japanese soft drink retail sales in 1990 were made through VMs, compared to 10 percent in the US. For canned soft drinks, the machines' share was said to be 70 percent. Business reporter Andrew Tanzer explained that one reason for the difference was that most VMs in Japan were on city sidewalks instead of in offices and factories, as in the US. Vandalism of VMs was also virtually non-existent. This meant that a well-placed machine could move as much product as a medium convenience store — some 10,000 cans a year. It gave the bottlers a strong incentive to spend heavily on high-tech vending. Coca-Cola (Japan) bottlers were investing in 120,000 to 140,000 new VMs a year, at about $4,000 per machine. With about 750,000 VMs, Coca-Cola led the soft drink market with approximately a 30 percent share.[108]

Japan's vending industry had sales of $48 billion a year in 1990. One of the more novel aspects were the 30 Happy Guy machines spread around Tokyo. Lonely males filled out a brief biography of themselves, attached a photo, and paid $40 to have 30 copies ($15 for 10 copies) of their form randomly placed in Happy Guy machines. Women put in $2 to receive a form and the next move was up to them. Profits went to Arche, the advertising agency that came up with the idea. Tokinobu Narita, Arche director, explained: "we think this system is the best for businessmen who have few chances to meet women. After all, now that women are stronger in Japan they prefer to be the ones to take the initiative and call for a date." Narita, who hoped to have 1,000 machines in place by the end of 1992, said his only complaints had been from men who received no calls.[109]

By 1991, Japan led all nations in VMs, having one for every 22 people while the US had one for every 46 and the European Community had one for every 200 people. Japanese VMs were also more productive — sales per machine were almost two-thirds higher than in America — because Japanese machines sold high-value products such as whiskey, as well as the usual gum and soft drinks. Due to the nation's low crime rate and sophisticated electronics, Japan's VMs were much more reliable and much less vandalized. With a declining birth rate, an aging population, and tight controls on immigration creating a shortage of low-wage workers in Japan, many expected a demand for even more, and smarter, machines.[110]

James Sterngold reported in the *New York Times* in 1992 that, besides the usual items, Japanese VMs dispensed jewelry, fresh flowers, frozen beef, rice, whiskey, hamburgers, pornographic magazines, videocassettes, and batteries. At public saunas, VMs sold underwear. Japan had about 5.4 million VMs in 1990, around the same number as in the US, but for half the population. Each of those Japanese units also produced, on average, twice the sales volume as its American counterpart. Sterngold argued that in a country where every social encounter — at work, at home, at the store — was still governed by obligation and ritual, many people preferred to drop a couple hundred yen into a machine than to deal with a person. "In fact, some experts suggest that this is a more important reason for the proliferation of vending machines than their mere convenience: Many Japanese consumers simply feel more comfortable dealing with a machine, contrary to their garrulous reputation." Paul Hasegawa, head of the international division of the large advertising agency I&S remarked that, because of traditional attitudes, it could be psychologically awkward to walk into a store and buy something small, like a pack of cigarettes, and then just leave. "So if you're embarrassed, you buy things you don't really need. You can't just rush off if you're in a hurry. A machine is easier. It may sound odd to you, but that's the way Japanese people think." T. Burke McKinney, director of marketing for Coca-Cola Japan, said "We are only just beginning to scratch the surface of what advertising potential the machines have. We've already got some 700,000 ministores out there. Why not 700,000 communicators?" Japan Vending Machine Manufacturers' Association executive Takashi Kurosaki observed: "We're not worried about bandits here, as I think you are in the United States. The companies have virtually no losses due to vandals or thieves." Japan had about 4.5 million VMs in 1980 and 5.4 million in 1990. Sales, in billions of dollars, were as follows: 1980, 13.5; 1981, 13.7; 1982, 13.4; 1983, 13.9; 1984, 13.4; 1985, 17.9; 1986, 23.6; 1987, 35.9; 1988, 39.4; 1989, 38.7; 1990, 43.3; and 1991, 45.1.[111]

In early September, 1993, three businessmen in Tokyo stocked around 90 VMs in outer Tokyo with used underwear "guaranteed to have been worn by a Japanese schoolgirl." Within a month, around $211,000 worth of used panties had reportedly been sold — each garment sold at 3,000 Yen. After searching through the rule books, police finally charged the three entrepreneurs with violating the Antique Dealings Law, which stipulated that dealers needed a license.[112]

Not everything went smoothly however. In 1998, city officials in the Toyota Aichi Prefecture ordered all 103 VMs removed from municipal buildings. The *Asahi Shimbun* newspaper explained that the ban was ordered "to prompt people to reassess their mass-consumption lifestyles and think more responsibly about the environment."[113]

Japan's 5.4 million VMs used up to 12 kilowatt-hours a day — especially the cold drink dispensers — and accounted for 3.7 percent of the electricity consumed in Japan. The country's two million drink dispensers used 5.7 billion kilowatt-hours annually — the energy cost was $1.1 billion.

Tokyo Electric Power Corporation (TEPCO) developed VMs that achieved energy savings of around 10 to 15 percent through increased insulation and timers. According to TEPCO, if all two million drink VMs adopted the technology, Japan would cut hydro consumption by around 900,000 kilowatt-hours annually. To achieve these savings, Japanese electric companies paid a subsidy to VM makers of about $80 for each installed Eco Vendor, as they were called. As of the end of 1997, there were about 100,000 Eco Vendors in Japan.[114]

Robo Shop Super24, a fully automated 24-hour store, began operating in the Kinshi-cho neighborhood in suburban Tokyo in 1998. Dispensed were some 2,000 food and general merchandise items. The store had a sole employee who stocked the machines and kept track of sales from his office. Customers ordered, paid for, and collected items from separate displays in Robo Shop, which also took credit cards.[115]

At the start of 2001, Japan had 5,537,500 VMs, with most of them expected to soon be converted to the Internet or to wireless networks that channeled inventory and sales data directly into company databases, while news, ads, and streaming video and audio were sent to the machines—or so said a likely exaggerated report. For years, Japan's sake, beer, and whiskey VMs served all comers alike, with those underage expected to honor the rules. The government finally realized this was not enough and, since 2000, machines were required to verify ID before selling alcohol or tobacco. One model was locked up tight unless an age-based ID such as a driver's license was inserted. A closed circuit camera also allowed a sales clerk inside the shop—many beer VMs were located outside mom and pop liquor stores—to hit a button to unlock the machine if the purchaser looked legal. VMs selling sake and beer accounted for 2.4 percent of all VMs in Japan, but took in 10.7 percent of all revenues. Such machines could reportedly pay for themselves in about eight months.[116]

VM bill acceptor mechanisms and dollar coins continued to be problems for the industry. As late as 1992, David Clayton, vice president of the vending firm Automatic Food Service Corporation, said that bill changers failed to work 20 to 30 percent of the time. Back in 1989, the vending industry was vigorously lobbying Congress to pass a measure that called for the minting of a new dollar coin—the Susan B. Anthony coin was still around but languished in obscurity from lack of use. James C. Benfield, the executive director of the Coin Coalition, a group of 18 trade associations pushing for a new dollar coin, said, "It's really vending that's carrying this thing." NAMA president James Rost pointed out that, in the early 1960s, a customer bought a cold drink and a snack with a quarter but, in 1989, the customer needed three quarters for that can of soda and two more for a snack.

Although some vendors had installed devices to accept paper money, their use was not widespread. About 80 percent of the nearly 200,000 VMs made since 1985 included those currency acceptors, "But few of the nearly three million other machines in place have been retrofitted." At this time, few debit cards were in use as they had no universality and could only be used at the site of the issuing institution. Debit cards were then said to be widely in use in Europe and Japan in VMs sited at captive locations.[117]

While bill acceptors were developed in the 1960s, reporter James Ryan stated that it was relatively easy to trick a dollar machine with a black and white photocopy of a bill. Another popular scam involved attaching a string or piece of tape to the back of a bill, enabling a thief to pull it out of the machine once it was recognized. Said Tom Reynolds, president of Cointrol, a major distributor of dollar changers, "Some of these thieves could unload $500 from a changer in a matter of minutes."[118]

All of the lobbying paid off, as the United States Dollar Coin Act of 1997 specified that the new dollar coin be golden in color, have a distinctive edge, and be the same size and weight as the Susan B. Anthony coin. In other words, the new coin had to look and feel different to consumers, but resemble the Anthony dollar closely enough to fool VMs in order to keep retrofitting costs at a minimum for the vending industry. The reason most often given for the failure of the Anthony coin to become popular was that it too closely resembled a quarter. Others believed that a dollar coin would never become popular and widely used unless the dollar bill was also removed from circulation when the new coin was introduced — as happened in Canada and Australia. Sacagawea dollars went into circulation in March 2000. Coins worked a lot better than bills in VMs. "Paper money is fickle," said NAMA vice president Thomas E. McMahon. "Too many times, it's not read properly, which results in a lost sale or at least a frustrated customer." Machines also gave coins as change more easily than bills.[119]

Offering branded products in VMs at the end of the 1990s was considered by some industry analysts as more essential than ever to successful vending. When operators brought in popular brands, they could support them with higher prices. Generally, operators were said to double their costs on items. If an item cost them 75 cents from the wholesaler, then the vending operator priced it at $1.50 in his machines.[120]

Promotional use of VMs had always been limited, at least until the late 1990s. An exception was the branded machines such as those of Coca-Cola and Pepsi-Cola that were very visible billboards — a trend that a few of the snack companies, such as Mars, were beginning to follow. One account argued that the situation was beginning to change in the late 1990s as more and more machines were used to sell machines. Standard electronic VMs could be set for a variety of self-generated promotion — some could display ads, for example. A similar approach combined VMs with other things people wanted to see, such as maps and signposts. An example of that approach was a combination Mars candy bar machine and map/information kiosk in downtown Manchester, England. Another approach was to design units that forced people to notice the machines—"to create a curiosity about it." Included was the lavish use of lights and sounds and, in some cases, visible machinery and moving parts.[121]

Promotions, regarded as essential elements in turning single-item sales into larger, more frequent purchases, were often carried out in partnership with suppliers. At the end of the 1990s, Brian King, a marketing executive with Canteen, created four or five new promotions a year that went out to 90 percent of the firm's clients. These promotions were major events customized in partnership with at least two suppliers. What the promotions tried to do, explained King, was to suggest a combination purchase in one consumer visit by offering "fun activities" and opportunities to win "exciting prizes" with the desired purchase behavior. "But you have to get something in front of consumers that they can understand in two to three seconds. You've got a captive audience, but you still need to capture their interest." Sales increases from these promotions ranged from four percent to, more usually, six to seven percent, and could on occasion exceed 10 percent. In late 2000, King was partnered with Pepsi, Frito-Lay, Hard Rock Café, and American Airlines on a promotion called "Two Ways to Rock Your Snack." A purchase of either Lay's potato chips or regular Pepsi gave buyers a chance to win a coupon that offered a $5 discount on Hard Rock merchandise.[122]

In the Baltimore–Washington D.C. area, vending operator Wood Dining Services had run continuous vending promotions since 1994 at one large account. When a customer got a product with a "Winover" sticker, he called the company's vending office to claim the prize. Over the years prizes had included bicycles, Baltimore Oriole baseball tickets, gas grills, T-shirts, hats, and so on. Participating suppliers, which donated all the prizes, included Frito-Lay, Pepsi, Coca-Cola, Snapple, Nestle, M&M, Mars, and Hershey. Some promotions ran for a week; others ran for a month. Operator Aramark Refreshment Services ran a promotion in 2000 in conjunction with Nabisco— a $5 fold-up Pizza Hut gift certificate was attached to the back of four different products. Prizes from past promotions included a coupon for a free video rental at Blockbuster and a $5 cash card at Kmart. At the U.S. House of Representatives, Beth Stankewich, Guest Services' director of food services, did most of her vending promotions with Coca-

Cola. Sometimes Coke buyers received a coupon for another Coke product right on the bottle or can, or a coupon for a Coke fountain drink or bottled beverage in one of the House's eight food operations.[123]

Canteen Corporation remained the industry leader. As the company grew, Canteen evolved into more than just a vending concern. Cafeteria food service was added and the company branched out into serving the corporate, education, and government institution sectors. Then, in 1994, the firm was purchased by the UK concern Compass Group PLC and absorbed into the North American division of Compass. Its focus was shifted back more to vending, as Canteen generated almost $1 billion in annual revenue and had over 17,000 clients.[124]

As part of its re-focusing efforts, Tony Gagliardi, president of Compass Group USA's Canteen vending division, was prepared to spend some $50 million to improve its equipment, menu selection, and food quality. For example, Canteen was experimenting with machines that sold 16- and 20-ounce bottles of soda, bottles of juice, bottled water, and sports drinks. As recently as 1994, Canteen machines sold only canned sodas. Canteen also planned to introduce more commercial brands to its machines—all in response to some trends in food service that did not favor VMs. Commercial food service operators were making inroads into cafeteria downtime by offering small units that could be operated when the cafeteria was closed. The Port Huron (Michigan) Hospital had recently installed a Subway outlet that was open 24 hours a day. That unit was located in the area that once housed several VMs used by second- and third-shift employees. Especially not pleasing to Gagliardi was the trend wherein some institutions were taking over their vending operations and running them completely themselves. Pride was also involved, as Gagliardi was well aware that vending remained a prime target for jokes about stale food, lost money, and no choices.[125]

Canteen launched its re-focusing effort in late 1998, anchored by its new Market Central "Fresh to You," featuring restaurant brands and proprietary fresh food selections. Included in the program were five new merchandising packages, called "environmental designs," that customized the vending bank to fit the ambience as well as to target consumers in a number of specialized locations—from business and industrial to airports and train stations. Brand partners included Blimpie, Rally's, Hardee's, Newman's Own, and Nathan's.[126]

An unusual VM phenomenon arose in the middle 1980s in some Southern states, where a growing number of residents thought they were onto a good thing; take a used VM, chain it to a tree in your yard and start selling soda. In August, 1986, officials in Little Rock, Arkansas, complaining of a "big boom" in the number of recycled VMs showing up on people's front porches and yards, decided to put a stop to this practice. City resident Ezekiel Kinchen Jr. and several other homeowners were issued citations and were told to remove the machines because they violated zoning ordinances. Kinchen's VM dispensed a cut-rate brand of soda for 25 cents a can, half the price charged by most machines. Atlanta, Georgia, chief zoning inspector Milton Jackson reported that officials in his city received as many as 15 complaints a year about homeowners putting in machines to sell soft drinks or foods from the yard. "We order them to take the machines out," he said. Most of the machines in Little Rock were located in poorer neighborhoods. At a meeting of the City Board of Adjustments, which interpreted zoning regulations, city zoning inspector Kenny Scott complained that some homeowners had put in five to 10 machines. Little Rock Planning Office spokesman Tony Bozynski commented: "By the end of the summer, we were seeing front porches that look like cafeterias."[127]

VMs were increasingly involved in the deaths of patrons. In 1987 in Shieldsville, Minnesota, 15-year-old Christopher Jones was killed when an 800-pound Pepsi VM that he and a companion were apparently rocking back and forth tipped over on him. The friend said the pair had tipped the dispenser on its edge to try and get a soft drink out of the unit. Two years later, in Lawrence, Kansas, a 23-year-old University of Kansas student, rocking a VM that failed to release a can of soda after he had deposited 50 cents, was killed when the machine fell on him.[128]

Kevin Mackle, a 19-year-old student, was found dead in 1998 under an over-turned soft drink VM in his residence at Bishop's University near Montreal. Other students reported that Mackle left a friend's room around 4 A.M. and speculated that he was trying to shake a drink from the machine when it toppled. Bruce Stevenson, public relations director for the university, said most VMs at the institution were bolted to the wall, but the one in Mackle's residence was not because it was in a tight alcove and considered too difficult to move. The machines weighed hundreds of pounds and were considered top heavy. The United States Consumer Product Safety Commission found that, between 1978 and 1995, at least 37 deaths and 113 injuries resulted from falling VMs in the US. Around 1995, seven American manufacturers of soft drink machines started a warning-label campaign to alert customers to the danger. One label read: "Warning! Never rock or tilt. Machine can fall over and cause serious injury or death."[129]

Frauds and scams continued in the industry as they had in past periods. In 1993, the Council of Better Business Bureaus in Arlington, Virginia, received 1,130 complaints about VM operators involving scams against would-be entrepreneurs. Typically, prospects bought several VMs, costing from $65 to $10,000 each, and an inventory of merchandise. In return, they received a promise of help in finding profitable locations and other assistance. Bogus companies usually had prospects talk with "shills" who gave glowing — and usually false — testimony about their own success. Once an investor had paid his money, the operator disappeared. The machines might never arrive or, if they did, no lucrative locations were provided.[130]

Deborah Stewart of Tulatin, Oregon, spent more than $12,000 in 1994 on three popcorn VMs. She said representatives of the company that sold her the Grand popper machines had assured her that she would make her money back in less than a year. Stewart checked the company provided references — with each one giving a tribute. Eighteen months later, two of the units sat gathering dust in her garage while the one she managed to place in a local art school brought in less than $30 a month. In response to a growing number of fraudulent get-rich-quick schemes, the FTC announced legal actions in 1995 against approximately 100 firms nationwide — including the popcorn seller. The actions were part of an initiative called Project Telesweep, in which FTC employees posing as entrepreneurs responded to ads that promised big returns on investments in items such as VMs, pay phones, and amusement games.[131]

Vendo company, conducting a survey of soft drink machine vandalism in the mid-1990s, received responses from 111 bottlers in the US and Canada. The total number of vendors on location for these bottlers was 515,925, with an average of 4,648 vendors per bottler. All firms responding to the survey said they had at least one of their VMs vandalized each month, with an average of 12 times per month. This rate equated to 1.13 percent of their available equipment vandalized monthly, or 13.52 percent annually. Of the bottlers surveyed, 73.9 percent indicated that salting (liquid inserted through either the coin insert or the bill opening) was their most prevalent type of vandalism. Second most common was a break-in through the coin insert assembly. Third was prying the door at the height of the coin insert. Outdoor locations, such as at hotels, motels, and schools, were identified as the most common areas for vandalism. Bottlers who chose to report their VM vandalism costs (45.9 percent of the respondents) indicated vandalism resulted in losses of more than $5,254,000, or $19.33 for every vendor that was on location. Vandals were reported to be successful on 56.75 percent of their attempts — that is, either money or product was stolen during the vandalism.[132]

Traditionally, the first line of defense against vandalism had been evaluating and selecting a suitable spot. "Location abandonment" referred to voluntary action by the bottler of permanently removing a VM from a particular account. "Opportunity abandonment" referred to bottlers not placing a vendor at all. In the survey, bottlers indicated their annual location abandonment was, on average, 43 vendors. Their average annual opportunity abandonment was 484 machines. If vandalism was not an issue, each bottler, on average, could place an additional 527 vendors. Eighty-three of the bottlers felt that vandalism was a serious enough problem for their management to implement a rule regarding abandonment that established specific guidelines for abandoning a location after vandalism occurred.[133]

For the first time, the energy consumption of VMs came under some inspection. A four-day test of a cold beverage VM (about the same size as a 23-cubic foot refrigerator) indicated that it consumed 8.125 kilowatt-hours a day, or 2,966 kilowatt-hours a year — more than twice the energy consumption of a standard refrigerator. About 1,049 of those kilowatt-hours were attributed to the lighting of the unit, the remainder to its cooling. Multiplied by the estimated two million soft drink vendors, some 5.9 billion kilowatt-hours were being consumed each year to provide cold drinks for Americans, more than 22 percent of all the energy used directly by all office machines in the US (26 billion kilowatt-hours annually). Each kilowatt-hour produced 1.54 pounds of CO_2, so generating power just for the lights and ballasts in those soda machines added 3.2 billion pounds of CO_2 to the atmosphere. Reporter Mike Cormier said: "Increasing the efficiency of these vending machines is not a priority for the soda companies. The newest machines are now equipped with two 72-watt fluorescent bulbs, nearly doubling the energy required for lighting."[134]

Another estimate was provided by E-Source, a Boulder based energy consulting group, which estimated refrigerated beverage machines consumed seven to 12 kilowatt-hours per day (costing $200 to $500 a year each). Multiplied by their estimated 2.5 million beverage dispensers in America, the combined annual cost in power bills was between $500 million and $1.25 billion. A typical modern machine equipped with conventional ballasts and fluorescent lights used 180 watts per hour, 24 hours a day. At eight cents per kilowatt-hour, that came to $126 a year. Heat from those lights also increased the refrigeration costs.[135]

As the new century began, the vending industry was in something of a rut. After trying seriously for over 70 years to become a dominant, pervasive method of retailing and distributing products, the industry remained firmly mired in its position as a niche marketing industry dispensing a limited range of mainly low-priced snack items. It had been dominated for decades by one product—cigarettes—and, following that, the industry was, and is, dominated by soft drinks. Dreams of robot stores and more automatic selling in existing retail outlets were rarely heard any more. An exception was Kent Savage, president of Cincinnati-based Vertex Technologies, who saw VMs as miniature retail stores for the sale and distribution of everything from cameras and blue jeans to tools and manufacturing equipment. "The sky's the limit," he enthused, as he looked with envy on Japan. However, the sky was not the limit.[136]

In 2000, business reporter Shelley Wolson observed that even then vending data was, by and large, collected manually — after counting coins and the number and brand of items purchased, drivers turned in vend slips with a list of what had been used, what had been put in, and what was not purchased. Intelligent vending or remote diagnostics were still not often used. Financially well-off soft drink bottlers made the most of such new technologies. Early in 2000, Coca-Cola announced a five-year deal with Marconi Online, in which Coke was expected to invest $100 million in Marconi's online vending technology — already in place in 60,000 Coke machines abroad, mainly Australia and New Zealand. The technology involved various cashless systems, including the use of a cell phone to order a soft drink. A customer used his cell phone to dial a number on the VM, punched in a code to purchase a Coke, with the charge appearing on the customer's next cell phone bill. The technology also involved more communicating: by the VM to the warehouse to advise of its status and needs, and from the warehouse to the VM to, for example, change prices. However, these things were mostly in the future and destined, at least in the short term, to affect only a limited number of vending machines.[137]

Some of these high tech soda machines went a little haywire in Sydney in 1999. Thousands of "smart" VMs installed throughout the city started making crank calls. They were programmed to dial the warehouse whenever they ran out of cold cans of pop. Instead, the machines started dialing the city's emergency numbers — jamming the lines to police, firefighters, hospitals, and ambulance services. An exasperated emergency worker complained that the problem was "getting worse and spreading to other electronic devices."[138]

Vending remains a means of dispensing a small number of inexpensive products to the public under conditions where normal retailing is not feasible. Customers buy these products on impulse and, for the most part, consume them immediately. While these limitations have been inherent in the industry since its earliest days, in the future one should not be surprised if someone invents an equivalent to the shoe shine VM, or the "perfect" popcorn vending machine.

Appendix A

Vended Dollar Volume
(In Thousands of Dollars)

Year	Volume	Year	Volume
1946	600,000	1979	12,803,000
1952	1,400,000	1980	13,864,000
1959	2,377,000	1981	14,582,000
1960	2,586,000	1982	14,373,000
1961	2,739,000	1983	14,860,000
1962	2,956,000	1987	21,075,000
1963	3,222,000	1988	22,662,000
1964	3,494,000	1989	24,480,000
1965	3,800,700	1990	25,879,000
1966	4,165,640	1991	25,999,060
1967	4,500,953	1995	29,514,400
1968	4,956,211	1996	31,408,222
1969	5,665,968	1997	32,886,690
1970	6,223,008	1998	34,838,910
1973	7,847,000	1999	36,600,000

Sources:

Vend 19 (March 15, 1965): 34.
Vend 25 (May, 1971): 32+.
Vending Times Census of the Industry 1984. NY: Vending Times, 1984.
Vending Times Census of the Industry 1992. NY: Vending Times, 1992.
Vending Times Census of the Industry 2000. NY: Vending Times, 2002.

Appendix B

Vending Sales by Location Type
(In Millions of Dollars)

Locations	1964 %	1964 $ vol	1970 %	1970 $ vol	1983 %	1983 $ vol	1991 %	1991 $ vol	1999 %	1999 $ vol
Plants & Factories	32	1,118	35	2,178	36.4	5,410	29.0	7,550	17.1	6,000
Public Locations	38	1,328	26	1,618	20.2	3,002	25.9	6,740	28.5	10,000
Primary & Secondary Schools	n/a	n/a	4	249	4.2	624	2.3	590	2.0	700
Colleges & Universities	11	384	10	622	8.2	1,218	9.2	2,400	11.4	4,000
Offices	4	140	7	435	9.7	1,441	21.8	5,680	24.2	8,500
Hospitals & Nursing Homes	2	70	3.5	218	5.4	802	3.5	900	6.8	2,400
Government & Military	n/a	n/a	2.5	156	6.5	966	3.8	1,000	3.8	1,350
All Other	13	454	12	747	9.4	1,397	4.4	1,139	6.1	2,150

Sources:
  Vend 25 (May, 1971)
  Vending Times Census of the Industry 1984. NY: Vending Times, 1984.
  Vending Times Census of the Industry 1992. NY: Vending Times, 1992
  Vending Times Census of the Industry 2002. NY: Vending Times, 2002.

Appendix C
Vending Sales by Type of Product

1960

Product	Sales Volume, (In 1,000s of $).	% of sales volume	Machines in Operation	% of machines	Sales per week per machine
Packaged Confections	304,647	11.8	585,400	15.6	150 units
Bulk Confections	54,880	2.1	1,120,000	29.8	100 sales
Cigarettes	1,141,920	44.2	793,000	21.1	100 packs
Cigars	8,785	0.3	50,200	1.3	n/a
Soft drinks (cups)	132,338	5.1	122,300	3.3	340 drinks
Soft drinks (bottles)	306,281	11.8	825,000	22.0	135 bottles
Coffee	142,940	5.5	149,800	4.0	300 drinks
Ice Cream	25,555	1.0	36,500	1.0	140 units
Milk	61,630	2.4	52,500	1.4	240 units
Hot Canned Foods	22,121	0.9	22,900	0.6	100 cans
All Others	385,000	14.9	n/a	n/a	n/a
TOTAL	2,586,097		3,757,600		n/a

Source:
Vend 15 (March 15, 1961).

1964

Product	Sales Volume, (In 1,000s of $).	% of sales volume	Machines in Operation	% of machines	Sales per week per machine
Packaged Confections	392,205	11.2	688,110	16.6	127 units
Bulk Confections	64,922	1.9	1,135,000	27.3	100 sales
Cigarettes	1,399,780	40.1	883,700	21.3	100 packs
Cigars	12,348	0.4	59,800	1.4	n/a
Soft drinks (cups)	236,045	6.8	166,900	4.0	320 drinks

Product	Sales Volume, (In 1,000s of $).	% of sales volume	Machines in Operation	% of machines	Sales per week per machine
Soft drinks (bottles)	419,601	12.0	883,000	21.3	132 bottles
Coffee	268,920	7.7	199,200	4.8	300 drinks
Ice Cream	29,694	0.8	42,300	1.0	135 units
Milk	81,900	2.3	63,000	1.5	250 units
Hot Canned Foods	28,564	0.8	31,300	0.8	65
Prepared Foods*	149,700	4.3	67,150**	1.6	n/a
All Others	411,000	11.8	n/a	n/a	n/a
TOTAL	3,494,679		4,152,310		n/a

Source:
Vend 19 (March 15, 1965).
* includes pastry, sandwiches, salads, etc.
** 34,900 pastry machines, 6,250 sandwich machines, and 26,000 "all-purpose" machines.

1970

Product	Sales Volume, (In 1,000s of $).	% of sales volume	Machines in Operation	% of machines	Sales per week per machine
Packaged Confections	671,314	10.8	843,021	16.8	158 units
Bulk Confections	305,416	4.9	1,286,000	25.7	101 sales
Cigarettes	2,116,506	34.0	946,030	18.9	95 packs
Cigars	18,208	0.3	56,900	1.1	38 cigars
Soft drinks (cups)	379,623	6.1	209,783	4.2	325 drinks
Soft drinks (bottles)	697,029	11.2	827,432	16.5	130 bottles
Soft drinks (cans)	420,226	6.8	263,878	5.3	175 cans
Hot Drinks*	451,795	7.3	245,081	4.9	322 drinks
Ice Cream	50,513	0.8	50,226	1.0	145 units
Milk	152,567	2.5	84,606	1.7	249 units
Hot Canned Foods	73,678	1.2	45,607	0.9	90 cans
Pastries	79,679	1.3	78,096	1.6	165
Prepared Foods	223,923	3.6	66,525	1.3	180 foods
All Others	582,531	9.4	n/a	n/a	n/a
TOTAL	6,223,008		5,003,185		n/a

Source:
Vend 25 (May, 1971).
*73% coffee, 22% hot chocolate, 3% soup, 2% tea.

Vending Sales by Type of Product

1983

Product	Sales Volume (In 1,000s of $)	% of sales volume	Machines in Operation	% of machines	Sales per week per machine
Packaged Confections	2,235,000	15.0	850,000	15.1	157 units
Bulk Confections	174,300	1.2	1,400,000	24.9	n/a
Cigarettes	2,926,000	19.7	785,000	14.0	69 packs
Cigars	21,500	0.1	37,000	0.7	43 cigars
Soft drinks (cups)	1,135,000	7.6	217,000	3.9	340 drinks
Soft drinks (bottles)	1,332,000	9.0	813,000	14.4	97 bottles
Soft drinks (cans)	3,500,500	23.6	880,000	15.6	170 cans
Hot Drinks	1,214,000	8.2	264,600	4.7	350 drinks
Ice Cream	70,800	0.5	41,000	0.7	103 units
Milk	343,000	2.3	91,500	1.6	203 units
Hot Canned Foods	144,000	1.0	54,700	1.0	82 cans
Pastries	289,000	1.9	90,500	1.6	139 pastries
Prepared Foods	812,000	5.5	102,850	1.8	188 food items
All Others	664,500	4.5	n/a	n/a	n/a
TOTAL	14,861,600		5,627,150		n/a

Source:
Vending Times Census of the Industry 1984. NY: Vending Times, 1984.

1991

Product	Sales Volume (In 1,000s of $)	% of sales volume	Machines in Operation	% of machines	Sales per week per machine
Packaged Confections	4,561,000	17.5	950,000	15.2	171 units
Bulk Confections	254,579	1.0	1,585,500*	25.4	n/a
Cigarettes	2,882,000	11.1	560,000	9.0	45 packs
Soft drinks (cups)	2,103,000	8.1	221,000	3.5	352 drinks
Soft drinks (bottles)	2,465,000	9.5	786,000	12.6	104 bottles
Soft drinks (cans)	8,107,000	31.2	1,400,000	22.4	192 cans
Hot Drinks	2,085,440	8.0	286,000	4.6	365 drinks
Ice Cream	182,582	0.7	47,500	0.8	112 units
Milk	477,000	1.8	94,500	1.5	194 units
Hot Canned Foods	128,000	0.5	44,000	0.7	80 cans
Pastries	322,450	1.2	78,000	1.2	150 items
Prepared Foods	1,376,000	5.3	118,000	1.9	185 food items
Juice (dedicated)**	361,700	1.4	72,000	1.2	n/a
All Others	692,750	2.7	n/a	n/a	n/a
TOTAL	25,998,501		6,242,500		n/a

Source:
Vending Times Census of the Industry 1992. NY: Vending Times, 1992.
*555,000 bulk capsule VMs (grossing $216 per year each); 13,500 novelty capsule ($430); 256,000 nut/pan candy units ($203); 720,000 ball gum (includes charitable placements—$102); 41,000 all others ($85).
**machines selling only juice. Juices also sometimes available in other types of machines.

1999

Product	Sales Volume, (In 1,000s of $).	% of sales volume	Machines in Operation	% of machines	Sales per week per machine
Packaged Confections	7,200,000	19.7	1,140,000	16.2	182 units
Bulk Confections	347,450	0.9	2,003,000*	28.4	n/a
Cigarettes	1,200,000	3.3	n/a	n/a	n/a
Soft drinks (cups)	2,075,000	5.7	175,000	2.5	340 drinks
Soft drinks (bottles)	1,980,000	5.4	625,000	8.9	92 bottles
Soft drinks (cans)	15,700,000	42.9	2,300,000	32.6	200 cans
Hot Drinks**	2,910,000	8.0	320,000	4.5	380 drinks
Ice Cream	470,000	1.3	75,000	1.1	140 units
Milk	408,000	1.1	84,000	1.2	195 units
Hot Canned Foods	110,600	0.3	28,000	0.4	88 cans
Pastries	210,000	0.6	48,000	0.7	130 items
Prepared Foods	2,520,000	6.9	150,000	2.1	190 food items
Juice (dedicated)	668,600	1.8	103,000	1.5	160 units
All Others	800,450	2.2	n/a	n/a	n/a
TOTAL	36,600,100		7,051,000		n/a

Source:

Vending Times Census of the Industry 2000. NY: Vending Times, 2000.
*660,000 capsule VMs grossing $235 per year each; 18,000 novelty capsule ($425); 380,000 nut/pan candy units ($200); 880,000 ball gum (includes charitable/civic org. placements - $115); 65,000 all others ($120).
** 76% coffee, 11% decaf coffee, 10.5% chocolate, 1% soup, 1% tea.

Notes

Chapter 1

1. G. R. Schreiber. *A Concise History of Vending in the U.S.A.* Chicago: Vend, 1961, p. 9.
2. "Invention in 1889 A.D. vs. invention B.C." *Scientific American* 64 (February 14, 1891): 105; Sidney M. Shalett. "Slot-machine age." *New York Times Magazine*, November 2, 1941, p. 30.
3. Andrew Hecht. "Robots...at your service." *American Mercury* 83 (November, 1956): 52; "Topics." *New York Times*, November 26, 1960, p. 20; "Vended sales of hot foods, non-foods soar." *Advertising Age* 32 (November 13, 1961): 6.
4. G. R. Schreiber, op. cit., p.10.
5. Ibid., pp. 10–12.
6. Nic Costa. *Automatic Pleasures; the History of the Coin Machine.* London: Kevin Francis Publishing, 1988, p. 9.
7. Ibid., p. 9; G. R. Schreiber, op. cit., p. 12.
8. Nic Costa, op. cit., pp. 9, 15; G. R. Schreiber, op. cit., p. 12.
9. G. R. Schreiber, op. cit., pp. 12–13.
10. Ibid., p. 13; "Jobs galore for robot salesmen." *Business Week*, April 16, 1930, p. 28; Charles S. Stein. "The phenomenon of automatic merchandising." *Journal of Retailing* 40 (Spring, 1964): 15.
11. J. H. Hirsch. "How 'automatic' selling began." *Billboard*, June 2, 1934, p. 60.
12. Arch M. Andrews. "Profits from pennies." *Saturday Evening Post* 203 (November 1, 1930): 11.
13. G. R. Schreiber, op. cit., pp. 13–14.
14. Ibid., p. 14.
15. "Nickel-in-the-slot hot water." *Scientific American* 63 (November 15, 1890): 313; "Distribution of hot water at Paris." *Scientific American* 68 (February 25, 1893): 120.
16. "Nickel-in-the-slot gas meter." *Scientific American* 63 (December 6, 1890): 353.
17. G. R. Schreiber, op. cit., p. 14.
18. "Invention in 1889 A.D. vs. invention B.C." *Scientific American* 64 (February 14, 1891): 105.
19. "Automatic distributor of perfumes." *Scientific American* 69 (December 16, 1893): 388.
20. "Automatic distributers of beverages." *Scientific American* 65 (December 26, 1891): 403.

21. "An automatic vending machine." *Scientific American* 74 (February 29, 1896): 133.
22. "Automatic strength tester and vending machine." *Scientific American* 76 (March 20, 1897): 180.
23. Nic Costa, op. cit., p. 17.
24. G. R. Schreiber, op. cit., p. 20.
25. Ibid., pp. 20–22.
26. "Improved vending-machines." *Scientific American* 82 (June 16, 1900): 378.
27. Sheldon Silver. "Big bottle vending." *FoodService Director* 11 (October 15, 1998): 176; G. R. Schreiber, op. cit., p. 26.
28. G. R. Schreiber, op. cit., p. 24; Caitlin Shannon. "Coin-operated restaurant." *Christian Science Monitor*, June 25, 1998, p. 9.
29. G. R. Schreiber, op. cit., p.25.
30. Ibid., p. 26.
31. Ibid.
32. "Subway advertising upheld." *New York Times*, December 11, 1906, p. 7.
33. "Attachment ties up slot-machine money." *New York Times*, March 9, 1909, p. 3.
34. G. R. Schreiber, op. cit., p. 28.
35. "Gasoline slot machine." *Scientific American* 109 (October 18, 1913): 300.
36. J. H. Hirsch, op. cit., pp. 60, 65.
37. Ad. *Variety*, April 10, 1914, pp. 24–25.
38. "Slot-machine trust." *New York Times*, April 2, 1911, sec. 9, p. 12.
39. Ibid.; G. R. Schreiber, op. cit., p. 28; Arch M. Andrews, op. cit., p. 11.
40. Nic Costa, op. cit., p. 19.
41. "Penny-in-the-slot machines." *Times* (London), March 19, 1914, p. 4; "Fined L5 for twopence." *Times* (London), March 19, 1915, p. 10; "2,000 packets of sweetmeats stolen." *Times* (London), August 9, 1915, p. 10.
42. "The working of penny-in-the-slot machines." *Times* (London), April 23, 1914, p. 3.
43. Charles S. Stein, op. cit., p. 17.
44. G. R. Schreiber, op. cit., p. 23.
45. Ibid., p. 24.
46. Nic Costa, op. cit., p. 19.

Chapter 2

1. G. R. Schreiber. *A Concise History of Vending in the U.S.A.* Chicago: Vend, 1961, p. 33.
2. "Devices in use for self-selling." *New York Times*, October 19, 1919, sec. 2, p. 10.
3. Ibid.
4. "Machine as salesman." *Fortune* 35 (March, 1947): 117.
5. Ibid., pp. 117–118.
6. "Vendors pull out all stops." *Business Week*, August 15, 1970, p. 52; G. R. Schreiber, op, cit., pp. 33–34.
7. "Machine sells cigarettes." *New York Times*, April 4, 1928, p. 21; "Installing vending machines." *New York Times*, February 17, 1929, sec. 2, p. 13.
8. "Slot machines amass riches from pennies." *New York Times*, November 13, 1927, sec. 10, p. 2.

Notes—Chapter 2

9. Ibid.
10. Milton Wright. "Robots for salesmen." *Scientific American* 140 (January, 1929): 24–26; G. R. Schreiber, op. cit., pp. 34–35.
11. G. R. Schreiber, op. cit., p. 35.
12. Milton Wright, op. cit.
13. Ibid.
14. "New slot machines to act as humans." *New York Times*, June 7, 1928, p. 32.
15. "Robots to mimic actors." *New York Times*, June 17, 1928, sec. 2, p. 9.
16. "Department store automat to be opened here shortly." *New York Times*, June 10, 1928, sec. 2, p. 20.
17. Milton Wright, op. cit.
18. "Automats apt to help." *New York Times*, July 8, 1928, sec. 2, p. 18.
19. "Looks for big gain in machine vending." *New York Times*, October 14, 1928, sec. 2, p. 20.
20. Ibid.
21. Peter F. O'Shea. "Can selling be done by machinery?" *Magazine of Business*, November 28, 1928, pp. 517–519+.
22. Ibid., pp. 517–518.
23. Ibid., pp. 518–519.
24. Ibid., p. 519.
25. Ibid., pp. 587, 588–590.
26. William A. McGarry. "Robot goes to work." *Saturday Evening Post* 201 (May 11, 1929): 54.
27. Ibid.
28. Ibid.
29. Ibid., p. 56.
30. "More vending machines." *New York Times*, May 26, 1929, sec. 2, p. 8.
31. "But when will robots eat and sleep for us?" *Literary Digest* 102 (September 7, 1929): 53.
32. G. R. Schreiber, op. cit., p. 34.
33. "Jobs galore for robot salesmen." *Business Week*, April 16, 1930, p. 28.
34. "Sales robot makes change; rejects slugs." *Business Week*, October 29, 1930, p. 16.
35. "Now comes the automatic store for apartment house dwellers." *Business Week*, February 25, 1931, p. 9.
36. "A twenty-four hour automatic market." *Scientific American* 144 (May, 1931): 325.
37. Arch M. Andrews. "Profits from pennies." *Saturday Evening Post* 203 (November 1, 1930): 10–11+.
38. Ibid., pp. 11, 88.
39. Ibid., pp. 88–89.
40. Ibid., pp. 89–90.
41. Ibid., p. 90.
42. William A McGarry, op. cit., p. 56.
43. "Low purchasing power shown in decline of sales of candy." *Billboard*, April 8, 1933, p. 56.
44. G. R. Schreiber, op. cit., p. 38.
45. Ibid., p. 37; "German book vendor." *Publishers Weekly* 119 (May 23, 1931): 2511–2512; "Book vendor patented." *Publishers Weekly* 121 (June 4, 1932): 2257.
46. "Drugs from automatic machines." *Times* (London) January 9, 1930, p. 7.
47. "Poisons from automatic machines." *Times* (London), April 22, 1930, p. 14; "Poisons from automatic machines." *Times* (London), June 27, 1930, p. 5.

48. "Corporations." *Time* 67 (June 11, 1956): 91–92, 94; G. R. Schreiber, op. cit., p. 37.
49. G. R. Schreiber, op. cit., p. 37.
50. "Halfpennies for shillings." *Times* (London), December 2, 1924, p. 11.
51. "Temptation of automatic machines." *Times* (London), September 6, 1926, p. 9.
52. "Waifs 'beat' slot machines." *New York Times*, April 30, 1927, p. 5.
53. William A. McGarry, op. cit., p. 54.
54. "News in brief." *Times* (London), May 23, 1929, p. 11.
55. Arch M. Andrews, op. cit., p. 89.
56. "Clink of slugs in slot machines sour music to manufacturers." *Business Week*, April 15, 1931, p. 28.
57. Sandford Brown. "The clink of coins—louder." *Newsweek* 50 (August 5, 1957): 76.
58. "Clink of slugs...," op. cit.
59. "Food device buyers charge swindle." *New York Times*, March 3, 1927, p. 25.
60. "National Chamber of Trade." *Times* (London), October 2, 1928, p. 13.
61. "Automatic machines." *Times* (London), March 14, 1929, p. 12.
62. "Death caused by automatic machine." *Times* (London), July 8, 1925, p. 5.
63. Walter W. Hurd. "Significant trends in the coin-machine business." *Billboard*, July 30, 1932, pp. 76–77.
64. Ibid.; Walter W. Hurd. "Vending machines." *Billboard*, April 2, 1938, p. 76.
65. Walter W. Hurd. "Significant trends...," op. cit.

Chapter 3

1. Silver Sam. "Coin-operated amusement machines." *Billboard*, April 16, 1932, p. 70.
2. "Seeks to enjoin police." *New York Times*, April 23, 1933, p. 5; "Vending machine suit up." *New York Times*, April 27, 1933, p. 8.
3. "Improved racing game has ball gum vendor." *Billboard*, November 4, 1933, p. 59.
4. "List of products." *Billboard*, March 17, 1934, p. 58.
5. "$100,000,000 a year in coin vending machines." *Literary Digest* 116 (October 14, 1932): 32.
6. Walter W. Hurd. "Coin machine progress in 1932." *Billboard*, January 28, 1933, pp. 58–59.
7. "Prospects for vending machines." *Billboard*, February 25, 1933, pp. 62–63.
8. "Clink of slugs in slot machines sour music to manufacturers." *Business Week*, April 15, 1931, p. 28.
9. "Penny cigaret vendor has positive delivery." *Billboard*, December 10, 1932, p. 55.
10. "Improves new machine to vend one cigaret." *Billboard*, January 7, 1933, p. 57.
11. "Penny ciggie vendor about ready for ops." *Billboard*, June 24, 1933, p. 56.
12. "Vends match with cigaret." *Billboard*, July 15, 1933, p. 54.
13. "Penny cigaret vendors called novel devices." *Billboard*, February 8, 1936, p. 73; "Offers penny cig vendor." *Billboard*, May 9, 1936, p. 103.
14. "West Coast cigaret vendors have code." *Billboard*, September 22, 1933, p. 59.
15. Silver Sam. "The first operators' code." *Billboard*, November 4, 1933, pp. 62–63.

Notes—Chapter 3

16. "Stable cigaret prices is help to vendors." *Billboard*, March 24, 1934, p. 62.
17. "Cig vendors go in restaurants." *Billboard*, March 24, 1934, p. 62.
18. "Cig vendors show gains." *Billboard*, May 26, 1934, p. 70; "Beer helps cig vendors." *Billboard*, June 30, 1934, p. 86.
19. "Cigaret vendors share in volume." *Billboard*, January 18, 1936, p. 78; "Cigaret output climbs." *Billboard*, April 4, 1936, p. 70.
20. "Mills heralds new cig. vendor." *Billboard*, April 25, 1936, p. 82.
21. "Commission unit on cig machine." *Billboard*, February 27, 1937, p. 82.
22. "Association bulletin gives tips to operators of cigaret vendors." *Billboard*, May 22, 1937, p. 86.
23. "Bureau hits at promotion." *Billboard*, December 11, 1937, p. 87.
24. "Tobacco Road decides to stop drive against cigaret machines." *Billboard*, February 19, 1938, p. 81.
25. "Lets cigaret sales up to vending machines." *Billboard*, October 29, 1938, p. 69.
26. Jackson Bloom. "Importance of cigaret vendors shown by McGinnis installation." *Billboard*, October 29, 1938, p. 69.
27. "30 per cent by club." *Billboard*, October 15, 1932, p. 56.
28. Silver Sam. "The coin chute." *Billboard*, November 26, 1932, pp. 60–61.
29. "Women's patronage will help scales in summer." *Billboard*, May 22, 1937, p. 86.
30. George Crook. "How business profits from coin machines." *Billboard*, November 13, 1937, p. 76.
31. Silver Sam. "The coin chute." *Billboard*, November 26, 1932, pp. 60–61.
32. George Crook. "The misunderstood vending machine." *Billboard*, May 21, 1938, p. 87.
33. "Vends nuts in sanitary bag." *Billboard*, May 19, 1934, p. 58.
34. "Now you can buy peanuts in a bag." *Billboard*, March 4, 1939, p. 67.
35. Silver Sam. "Coin operated amusement machines." *Billboard*, March 19, 1932, pp. 58, 61; Silver Sam. "Coin operated amusement machines." *Billboard*, April 9, 1932, p. 59.
36. "Play mum on game earnings, urges vending authority." *Billboard*, September 17, 1932, p. 61.
37. "Conditions in candy trade indicate success of vendors." *Billboard*, November 26, 1932, p. 56.
38. "Takes national sales on selective vendor." *Billboard*, October 1, 1932, p. 60.
39. "ARCOR plans to stimulate vending machine business." *Billboard*, November 5, 1932, p. 55.
40. J. W. Coan. "Vending machine future will be hurt by use of small-size bars." *Billboard*, December 11, 1937, p. 87; "U-Select-It shows two new vendors." *Billboard*, December 17, 1938, p. 70.
41. "Pan introduces new vendor candy." *Billboard*, July 29, 1939, p. 82.
42. "Backspin." *Beverage World* 118 (October, 1999): 144.
43. Silver Sam. "Coin-operated amusement machines." *Billboard*, March 19, 1932, p. 58.
44. "Pop dispensers investigated." *Billboard*, September 17, 1932, p. 59.
45. "Beverage vendor shown." *Billboard*, December 3, 1932, p. 83.
46. G. R. Schreiber. *A Concise History of Vending in the U.S.A.* Chicago: Vend, 1961, p. 42; "Widespread use of Coca-Cola vendor." *Billboard*, March 5, 1938, p. 78.
47. G. R. Schreiber, op. cit., p. 41.
48. H. H. Fleer. "A drink dispenser." *Billboard*, February 1, 1936, p. 66.
49. G. R. Schreiber, op. cit., p. 42.

50. Silver Sam. "Coin-operated amusement machines." *Billboard*, April 23, 1932, p. 67.
51. "Popcorn vendor changes." *Billboard*, July 30, 1932, p. 75.
52. "Claims popcorn vendor to open field for large profits." *Billboard*, December 31, 1932, p. 89.
53. "Ranel announces pop-corn vendor." *Billboard*, October 30, 1937, p. 80.
54. "Rowlette recounts Popmatic's history." *Billboard*, March 12, 1938, p. 78.
55. "East watches pop-corn machines." *Billboard*, March 12, 1938, p. 79; Walter Gummersheimer. "Pop-corn merchandising in tune with spirit of fast-moving age." *Billboard*, March 19, 1938, p. 80.
56. "Walgreen orders 300 Airpops-It." *Billboard*, July 23, 1938, p. 78.
57. H. F. Reves. "Vending machines in Detroit." *Billboard*, December 25, 1937, p. 71; "Sell 'em sandwiches." *Billboard*, September 3, 1932, p. 62.
58. Silver Sam. "Coin operated amusement machines." *Billboard*, April 23, 1932, p. 68.
59. "Test orange juice vendors." *Billboard*, November 4, 1939, p. 64.
60. "Juice vendor seen greatly under-rated." *Billboard*, May 17, 1947, p. 106.
61. Silver Sam. "Coin operated amusement machines." *Billboard*, April 30, 1932, p. 74; "Considers apple vendors." *Billboard*, September 17, 1932, p. 59.
62. "Error causes tangle on vending machines." *New York Times*, February 1, 1935, p. 28.
63. Silver Sam. "Coin operated amusement machines." *Billboard*, April 16, 1932, p. 70.
64. "Takes national sales on selective vendor." *Billboard*, October 1, 1932, p. 60.
65. "Ice cream vendor making start for next summer trade." *Billboard*, January 21, 1933, p. 57.
66. "Ice cream vendor succeeds on test." *Billboard*, February 13, 1937, p. 72.
67. "Louisville has new milk vendors." *Billboard*, January 8, 1938, p. 70.
68. H. F. Reves. "Vending machines in Detroit." *Billboard*, December 25, 1937, pp. 70–71.
69. "Newsweek comment on book vendors." *Billboard*, December 23, 1939, p. 64.
70. H. F. Reves, op. cit.; "Washing machine field overcrowded." *Billboard*, March 12, 1938, p. 78.
71. G. R. Schreiber, op. cit., p. 43.
72. "Razor blades in limelight." *Billboard*, September 3, 1932, p. 62; "ARCOR plans to stimulate vending machine business." *Billboard*, November 5, 1932, p. 55.
73. "Aspirin to the front." *Billboard*, November 26, 1932, p. 63; H. F. Reves, op. cit.
74. "Detroit bars certain types of vendors." *Billboard*, April 21, 1934, p. 60.
75. "Perfume vendor is launched in East." *Billboard*, April 9, 1938, p. 151.
76. "New hand soap vendor ready." *Billboard*, March 7, 1936, p. 79.
77. Albert A. Silberman. "Future of parking meters seems definitely assured." *Billboard*, August 1, 1936, p. 73.
78. "Firm to operate service machines." *Billboard*, February 8, 1936, p. 73.
79. H. F. Reves, op. cit.; "Lighter fluid vendor ready." *Billboard*, August 4, 1934, p. 62.
80. G. R. Schreiber, op. cit., p. 41.
81. "Introduce foot massage machine." *Billboard*, March 4, 1939, p. 67.
82. George Crook. "How business profits from coin machines." *Billboard*, November 13, 1937, p. 76.
83. "Astrology has popular appeal." *Billboard*, August 10, 1935, p. 73.

Notes—Chapter 3

84. "Firm to operate service machines." *Billboard*, February 8, 1936, p. 73; "Op succeeds with fortune machines." *Billboard*, May 1, 1937, p. 84.
85. "Astrologist lauds talkie horoscope." *Billboard*, January 22, 1938, p.90.
86. Silver Sam. "Coin operated amusement machines." *Billboard*, March 19, 1932, pp. 58, 61; Silver Sam. "Coin operated amusement machines." *Billboard*, May 28, 1932, p. 71.
87. "Interested in prospects for sanitary coin devices." *Billboard*, July 30, 1932, p. 74.
88. "To offer an extensive line of medical and sanitary products." *Billboard*, August 20, 1932, p. 64.
89. "Rapid growth in use of vending machines to modernize restroom." *Billboard*, December 17, 1932, p. 57.
90. "Talk soap vendors in new move to modernize rooms." *Billboard*, April 1, 1933, p. 61.
91. Silver Sam. "The coin chute." *Billboard*, May 6, 1933, p. 62.
92. "Lotion vendors are new field." *Billboard*, November 4, 1933, p. 59.
93. "Restroom shows automatic trend." *Billboard*, November 23, 1935, p. 66.
94. "World's Fair restrooms are using coin machines." *Billboard*, April 8, 1933, p. 56.
95. "Coin machines prominent at Chicago World's Fair." *Billboard*, June 3, 1933, pp. 57–58.
96. "Restroom fee is protested." *Billboard*, June 3, 1933, p. 58.
97. "World's Fair has big week." *Billboard*, June 10, 1933, p. 80.
98. "World's Fair gives test for variety of machines." *Billboard*, September 22, 1934, p. 60.
99. "Chewing gum, candy and weighing machines." *New York Times*, July 11, 1932, p. 12.
100. Silver Sam. "What type machines are best if theater concessions are available." *Billboard*, July 7, 1934, p. 67.
101. William Gersh. "Automatic merchandising in theaters." *Billboard*, October 6, 1934, pp. 66–67.
102. Ibid.
103. Ibid.
104. Silver Sam. "Coin operated amusement machines." *Billboard*, April 23, 1932, pp. 66–67.
105. "Druggists' meet will emphasize drug stores as locations." *Billboard*, September 17, 1932, p. 62.
106. "First reports show automatic store to be successful venture." *Billboard*, January 14, 1933, p. 56.
107. Charles R. Goeldner. "Automatic selling—will it work?" *Journal of Retailing* 38 (Summer, 1962): 41–46.
108. "Mobile vending unit is success." *Billboard*, October 23, 1937, p. 78.
109. "Canteen Co. ideas and service promote wide vending sales." *Billboard*, July 16, 1938, p. 74.
110. "Expanding candy markets." *Billboard*, April 15, 1939, p. 78.
111. "Coin machines at the fair." *Billboard*, May 13, 1939, p. 72.
112. Ibid.
113. "Coin machines gross $305,598 in 108 days at N.Y. World's Fair." *Billboard*, September 16, 1939, p. 67.
114. "Vendors win approval." *Billboard*, January 21, 1933, p. 57.
115. "Petite vendors prove useful for coverage." *Billboard*, June 30, 1934, p. 86.

116. W. E. Bolen. "How to operate general route of bulk product vending machines." *Billboard*, March 24, 1934, pp. 62, 64.
117. H. R. Reves. "The locations speak." *Billboard*, December 29, 1934, p. 290.
118. Ibid.
119. Ibid.
120. C. S. Spooner. "Managing a merchandising route." *Billboard*, September 7, 1935, pp. 66–7.
121. Ibid.
122. Ibid.
123. H. F. Reves. "Making money with vending machines." *Billboard*, June 26, 1937, p. 140.
124. George Crook. "How business profits from coin machines." *Billboard*, November 13, 1937, p. 76.
125. J. H. Hirsch. "How 'automatic' selling began." *Billboard*, June 2, 1934, pp. 60, 65.
126. "New York merchandiser mad." *Billboard*, April 11, 1936, p. 136.
127. Silver Sam. "Those slower nickels." *Billboard*, August 15, 1936, p. 66; "Robbins gives reasons for using the vendors." *Billboard*, January 30, 1937, p. 65.
128. David S. Bond. "Merchandise machine progress." *Billboard*, January 18, 1936, p. 80.
129. George Crook, op. cit.; H. F. Reves. "Vending machines in Detroit." *Billboard*, December 25, 1937, pp. 70–71.
130. Walter W. Hurd. "Analysis of machine trends as indicated at the December show." *Billboard*, December 24, 1938, p. 67.
131. "Expanding candy markets." *Billboard*, April 15, 1939, p. 78.
132. "Facts and figures necessary to operate bulk vending machines." *Billboard*, September 28, 1935, p. 66; "Vendor profits are discussed." *Billboard*, December 14, 1935, p. 74.
133. "Money in merchandisers, Robbins firm announces." *Billboard*, May 2, 1936, p. 78; Dave Robbins. "Penny mdsr. profits." *Billboard*, September 4, 1937, p. 82.
134. "Vending machine firms unite in plea against Massachusetts." *Billboard*, February 19, 1938, p. 80.
135. "Conditions in candy trade indicate success of vendors." *Billboard*, November 26, 1932, p. 56.
136. "Michigan group offers strong appeal to operators in state." *Billboard*, February 25, 1933, pp. 64–65.
137. "Standard of commission." *Billboard*, July 14, 1934, p. 58.
138. "Vigorous debate on rates and merchandising ethics." *Billboard*, October 27, 1934, p. 62.
139. "Cig operators set commission." *Billboard*, February 13, 1937, p. 72.
140. "Proper commission important to ops." *Billboard*, January 22, 1938, p. 91.
141. "Among boosters of vendor page." *Billboard*, June 2, 1934, p. 60.
142. Silver Sam. "Public relations policies for coin machine operators." *Billboard*, May 23, 1936, p. 68.
143. "Boost salted nut sales by 'heat-fag' campaign." *Billboard*, July 9, 1938, p. 72.
144. "Conditions in candy trade indicate success of vendors." *Billboard*, November 26, 1932, p. 56.
145. Bill Gersh. "New trend to merchandisers." *Billboard*, October 2, 1937, p. 81.
146. "More generous slot machines." *Times* (London), December 11, 1933, p. 13.
147. Walter W. Hurd. "Vending machines." *Billboard*, April 2, 1938, p. 76.
148. G. R. Schreiber, op. cit., p. 43.

Notes—Chapter 3

149. H. F. Reves. "Vending machines in Detroit." *Billboard*, December 25, 1937, pp. 70–71.

150. Henry N. Wertheimer. "Cigaret operators should seek full return on machine costs." *Billboard*, November 27, 1937, pp. 144–145.

151. George W. Mehrtens. "Commerce report shows increase in exports of coin machines in '34." *Billboard*, March 16, 1935, p. 68.

152. "Slot machines sell abroad." *New York Times*, April 26, 1938, p. 28.

153. "Newspapers in slot machines." *Times* (London), June 27, 1933, p. 14.

154. William Rabkin. "The European market." *Billboard*, July 27, 1935, pp. 82–83.

155. William Rabkin. "Market prospects in Holland." *Billboard*, August 3, 1935, p. 63.

156. "Netherlands has vendors." *Billboard*, September 30, 1939, p. 78.

157. Jack Capaldi. "Coin machines in Europe." *Billboard*, October 14, 1933, pp. 60–61; "Coin Men of Paris in Chi." *Billboard*, February 10, 1934, p. 62.

158. Hans Ullendorff. "Coin machines in Europe." *Billboard*, March 5, 1938, pp. 80–81.

159. Dave Robbins. "European observations." *Billboard*, September 30, 1939, p. 77.

160. "Automatic sales hurt in Reich." *New York Times*, November 14, 1939, p. 39.

161. Lee S. Jones. "Pres Jones of CMMAA." *Billboard*, April 2, 1932, p. 59; "The coin chute." *Billboard*, July 30, 1932, p. 74; "Result record brings operators flocking to Chicago association." *Billboard*, October 29, 1932, p. 54; "Detroit pin-game operators join merchandising association." *Billboard*, December 24, 1932, p. 57.

162. "Michigan group offers strong appeal to operators in state." *Billboard*, February 25, 1933, pp. 64–65.

163. G. R. Schreiber, op. cit., p. 43.

164. Silver Sam. "Coin operated amusement machines." *Billboard*, April 23, 1932, p. 70.

165. "San Francisco operators fighting proposed tax." *Billboard*, July 30, 1932, p. 74; "Coin men continue fight for reasonable license." *Billboard*, February 4, 1933, p. 63.

166. "Ordinance is amended." *Billboard*, December 31, 1932, p. 89; "New license ordinance to recognize machine types." *Billboard*, January 20, 1934, p. 58.

167. "Await court verdict on Flint vending license." *Billboard*, April 4, 1936, p. 70.

168. "Play mum on game earnings, urges vending authority." *Billboard*, September 17, 1932, p. 61; J. H. Hirsch. "Nat'l Automatic Merchandising Assn." *Billboard*, June 30, 1934, p. 86.

169. "Thefts from automatic machines." *Times* (London), October 12, 1931, p. 7; "French coins in slot machines." *Times* (London), July 12, 1932, p. 11; "News in brief." *Times* (London), August 16, 1932, p. 7.

170. Silver Sam. "Coin operated amusement machines." *Billboard*, June 11, 1932, p. 102; "Heavy penalty on slugs." *Billboard*, September 24, 1932, p. 67.

171. Silver Sam. "Coin operated amusement machines." *Billboard*, March 19, 1932, p. 61; "Operator wins in case." *Billboard*, December 31, 1932, p. 89.

172. "Ice 'slugs' and others forbidden in Rhode Island." *Billboard*, April 23, 1932, p. 70.

173. "Corporations." *Time* 67 (June 11, 1956): 94.

174. "Sues on slug claims." *Billboard*, December 31, 1932, p. 89.

175. "Slugs a pinball menace." *Billboard*, June 29, 1935, p. 106.

176. "Mills heralds new cig. vendor." *Billboard*, April 25, 1936, p. 82.

177. Silver Sam. "Coin operated amusement machines." *Billboard*, April 23, 1932, p. 67.

178. Walter W. Hurd. "Unemployment." *Billboard*, September 11, 1937, p. 74; Walter W. Hurd. "Vending machines." *Billboard*, April 2, 1938, p. 76.
179. George Crook. "The misunderstood vending machine." *Billboard*, May 21, 1938, p. 87.

Chapter 4

1. H. F. Reves. "A new era for coin machines." *Billboard*, January 20, 1940, p. 66h.
2. H. F. Reves. "Vending machines to the fore." *Billboard*, July 27, 1940, pp. 80–81.
3. Walter W. Hurd. "The 1940 show." *Billboard*, January 27, 1940, pp. 64–65, 69.
4. "Tribute to coin machines in magazine published by Eagles." *Billboard*, January 20, 1940, p. 68.
5. Ibid.
6. David C. Teague. "Vending machines." *Billboard*, February 24, 1940, pp. 66–67.
7. Sidney M. Shalett. "Slot-machine age." *New York Times*, November 2, 1941, p. 30.
8. G. R. Schreiber. *A Concise History of Vending in the U.S.A.* Chicago: Vend, 1961, p. 44.
9. "Jennings has new drink vendor." *Billboard*, February 17, 1940, p. 62.
10. Walter W. Hurd. "Beverage vendors." *Billboard*, June 8, 1940, p. 64; Walter W. Hurd. "Beverage machine progress." *Billboard*, June 8, 1940, pp. 70–71.
11. Ibid.
12. Herb Jones. "Where to place cold vendors." *Billboard*, June 8, 1940, p. 69.
13. "500 drink vendors in Baltimore area." *Billboard*, April 12, 1941, p. 144.
14. "Milk vendors survey." *Billboard*, January 18, 1941, pp. 110–111.
15. "N.Y. World's Fair will have coin machine quota." *Billboard*, May 18, 1940, p. 66.
16. Leon Silver. "Penny vendors on the West Coast." *Billboard*, February 28, 1942, p. 69.
17. G. R. Schreiber, op. cit., p. 44.
18. "Vending machine statistics." *Billboard*, January 31, 1942, p. 93; Haviland F. Reves. "Basic machines in field of vending." *Billboard*, February 23, 1946, p. 138.
19. "Too busy to talk." *Business Week*, March 13, 1943, pp. 72, 74.
20. "Record mint production due to slot machines." *New York Times*, July 9, 1940, p. 15.
21. Arthur Krock. "In the nation." *New York Times*, June 16, 1942, p. 22.
22. Walter W. Hurd. "Taxing vendors." *Billboard*, January 30, 1943, p. 56.
23. "Sterling future for coin op machines." *Advertising Age* 70 (May 31, 1999): 75; "Plans peak output in vending machine." *New York Times*, October 6, 1945, p. 20.
24. David C. Teague, op. cit.
25. "The 1941 war on slugs." *Billboard*, February 21, 1942, pp. 72–74.
26. Arthur E. Nack. "Federal men stop slugs." *Billboard*, July 19, 1941, p. 78.
27. "Slugs in slots going to defense." *New York Times*, June 7, 1941, p. 8; "Gets new trial." *New York Times*, December 31, 1942, p. 17.
28. "Signs bill against slug making." *New York Times*, April 4, 1944, p. 23.

Chapter 5

1. "Nickel paradise." *Business Week*, November 17, 1945, pp. 88–90.
2. "New vendors widen field." *Billboard*, February 23, 1946, pp. 133, 139.
3. Walter W. Hurd. "Ultra self-service." *Billboard*, June 8, 1946, p. 100.
4. "Coin machine sales $500,000,000 yearly." *New York Times*, April 10, 1947, p. 43.
5. "3 billion sales due by vending machines." *New York Times*, October 18, 1946, p. 35.
6. "Vending picks up." *Business Week*, November 16, 1946, pp. 57–60.
7. "Machine as salesman." *Fortune* 35 (March, 1947): 118–119.
8. Ibid., pp. 119–121.
9. "Direct-to-location sales rise." *Billboard*, April 2, 1949, pp. 113, 128.
10. G. R. Schreiber. *A Concise History of Vending in the U.S.A.* Chicago: Vend, 1961, p. 45.
11. "Candy vending sales gain." *Billboard*, January 12, 1946, pp. 82, 86.
12. "Study of vending needed." *Billboard*, January 26, 1946, p. 90.
13. "Vending machine in rising demand." *New York Times*, November 8, 1948, p. 33.
14. "Retail trade." *Time* 48 (December 16, 1946): 92.
15. Don Wharton. "They hit the coffee jackpot." *Reader's Digest* 52 (April, 1948): 127–128; "Machine to serve hot coffee." *New York Times*, September 25, 1947, p. 50.
16. "Coin milk vendors planned in homes." *New York Times*, December 31, 1949, p. 17.
17. Ross L. Holman. "A meal or a shine by robot vendors." *Science Digest* 19 (June, 1946): 25.
18. "Sparkling water given try in vendor at Philly plant." *Billboard*, February 2, 1946, p. 94.
19. "Chi's first launderette gets enthusiastic play." *Billboard*, March 16, 1946, p. 103.
20. "And now a book vendor." *New York Times*, December 20, 1946, p. 21.
21. "Subway to vend shoe shines." *New York Times*, January 30, 1949, p. 27.
22. "To cook hot dogs with radio waves." *New York Times*, December 24, 1945, p. 12.
23. "Speedy weeny, electron-cooked hot dog vendor." *Billboard*, March 9, 1946, p. 97.
24. "Edwards urges wholesale tobacco group to realize importance of cig vendor." *Billboard*, June 26, 1946, p. 91.
25. Fred W. Amann. "Lunch pails get coin slots." *Billboard*, February 1, 1947, pp. 134, 136.
26. "Popcorn comeback credited to interest shown by vendor ops." *Billboard*, March 22, 1947, p. 98.
27. "Vendor machines boon to airfields." *New York Times*, March 30, 1949, p. 37.
28. Charles G. Bennett. "Coins in slot hit jackpot for city." *New York Times*, April 9, 1949, p. 19.
29. Charles G. Bennett. "Transit concessions yield $3,932,333 in 11 months." *New York Times*, July 24, 1949, pp. 1, 56.
30. "Concessions pay $4,298,561 to city." *New York Times*, November 27, 1949, p. 75.
31. "You now can dial a railroad ticket." *New York Times*, September 1, 1949, p. 44; "Long Island ends trial of ticket vending device." *New York Times*, September 23, 1949, p. 29.

32. "Vending picks up." *Business Week*, November 16, 1946, pp. 57, 60; "Retail trade." *Time* 48 (December 16, 1946): 92.
33. Haviland F. Reves. "The vendor comes of age." *Billboard*, February 1, 1947, pp. 130–131.
34. "Machine as salesman." *Fortune* 35 (March, 1947): 152, 154.
35. "Jackpot for coin vendors." *Business Week*, December 20, 1947, pp. 50–52.
36. Paul Cohen. "Robot salesmen save money." *Science Digest* 26 (July, 1949): 37–40.
37. "Coin machine reports." *Billboard*, May 18, 1946, p. 109; "Coin machine exports." *Billboard*, April 2, 1949, p. 141.
38. "Retail trade." *Time* 48 (December 16, 1946): 94.
39. "Machine as salesman." *Fortune* 35 (March, 1947): 116.
40. "Coin trouble." *Business Week*, February 15, 1946, p. 76.
41. "Paper cup machine catches girl's hand." *New York Times*, July 23, 1947, p. 25.
42. "46 slot cents retrieved." *New York Times*, April 8, 1949, p. 27.
43. "Jackpot for coin vendors." *Business Week*, December 20, 1947, p. 52.
44. "Wider use seen for coin machine." *New York Times*, January 8, 1948, p. 42.
45. Tom Bernard. "Small change is big business." *American Magazine* 146 (September, 1948): 46–47+.
46. "New vistas opened for coin machine." *New York Times*, June 4, 1949, p. 24.

Chapter 6

1. Joseph Nolan. "Voice of the vendor." *New York Times*, October 17, 1954, p. 20.
2. "The coffee break." *Time* 67 (February 27, 1956): 90.
3. "From soup to nuts—literally." *Business Week*, December 15, 1956, p. 68.
4. James J. Nagle. "Vending devices slake U.S. thirst." *New York Times*, June 21, 1959, sec. 3, pp. 1, 11.
5. "Boeing boosts candy vendors." *Billboard*, March 29, 1952, p. 78.
6. John Sharnik. "Coin-in-the-slot." *New York Times Magazine*, December 3, 1950, p. 58.
7. "Even the milkman is automatic now." *New York Times*, February 6, 1953, p. 21.
8. William M. Freeman. "16,000 vending machines help Daisy get rid of her surplus milk." *New York Times*, July 9, 1955, pp. 18, 21.
9. Andrew Hecht. "Robots...at your service." *American Mercury* 83 (November, 1956): 56.
10. Sandford Brown. "The clink of coins—louder." *Newsweek* 50 (August 5, 1957): 76; "Milk slot machines off streets." *New York Times*, September 30, 1954, p. 10.
11. Joseph Nolan. "Voice of the vendor." *New York Times*, October 17, 1954, p. 20; "Automatic cows." *Business Week*, May 15, 1954, pp. 126–127.
12. "Dewey aids milk drive." *New York Times*, June 10, 1954, p. 39.
13. "Random notes from Washington." *New York Times*, January 17, 1955, p. 16.
14. John Sharnik. "Coin-in-the-slot." *New York Times Magazine*, December 3, 1950, p. 60.
15. "Frozen juice makers move vendor programs in high gear." *Billboard*, September 29, 1951, pp. 88, 91.
16. "Avon introduces new book vending machine." *Publishers Weekly* 158 (August 5, 1950): 574–575.
17. Is Horowitz. "Vendors move mags, books." *Billboard*, September 8, 1951, p. 87; "Coincidence? Or safety first?" *Business Week*, May 17, 1952, p. 42.

Notes—Chapter 6

18. Is Horowitz, op. cit., pp. 1, 74, 87.
19. "Coincidence? Or safety first?" *Business Week*, May 17, 1952, p. 42.
20. "Coin-operated circulation studied." *Billboard*, February 26, 1955, pp. 87, 97.
21. "News in brief." *Billboard*, September 9, 1957, p. 96.
22. "The machine age in vending." *Monetary Times* 121 (October, 1953): 27.
23. "Hair oil op grows, adds lotion units." *Billboard*, September 29, 1951, p. 88.
24. "British hair oil vendor is offered here." *Billboard*, March 29, 1952, p. 81.
25. Risdon Tillery. "Insert coin here." *Reader's Digest* 61 (September, 1952): 92; "Coin-slot drinks barred in Jersey." *New York Times*, July 11, 1954, p. 56.
26. Sam Abbott. "Hunts, lands spots, builds ops' routes." *Billboard*, September 16, 1957, pp. 90–91.
27. "Survey reveals 32 per cent of theaters using vendors." *Billboard*, February 25, 1950, p. 100.
28. Is Horowitz. "Subway vending tops 3 million." *Billboard*, February 17, 1951, pp. 1, 76, 79.
29. Meyer Berger. "About New York." *New York Times*, August 7, 1953, p. 21.
30. "Vendors greet Chicagoans at 12 new subway stations." *Billboard*, March 3, 1951, pp. 64, 66.
31. "Chi transit vendor volume off in '53." *Billboard*, March 27, 1954, pp. 78, 86.
32. "News notes from the field of travel." *New York Times*, September 23, 1951, sec. 2, p. 19.
33. "Tryout." *The New Yorker* 27 (November 10, 1951): 29–30; Sandford Brown. "The clink of coins—louder." *Newsweek* 50 (August 5, 1957): 77.
34. "Springfield bus vendors gain favor." *Billboard*, March 27, 1954, pp. 78, 86; "Gumming up the bus." *Business Week*, May 22, 1954, p. 132.
35. "Growth of plant vending since World War II peak." *Billboard*, May 12, 1951, p. 71.
36. Cedric Larson. "Our growing robot army." *American Mercury* 78 (April, 1954): 115.
37. "Food sales machines move in." *Business Week*, November 13, 1954, pp. 126–128.
38. "Industry turning to robots for food." *New York Times*, January 3, 1956, p. 118.
39. Aaron Sternfield. "In-office vending." *Billboard*, July 4, 1953, pp. 89–90.
40. "11 ops, 500 vendors in store center." *Billboard*, March 19, 1955, p. 78.
41. "Dentist takes schools to task." *New York Times*, June 2, 1956, p. 10.
42. "Coin-vending machines may even change diaper." *New York Times*, September 28, 1950, p. 37.
43. "Automatic window vending units spur candy sales." *New York Times*, August 18, 1956, p. 21.
44. "Penn. store installs store-front vendor." *Billboard*, September 16, 1957, p. 90.
45. "Forgetful shopper gets a second chance in Jersey." *New York Times*, October 25, 1956, pp. 47, 51.
46. Aaron Sternfield. "Major grocery chains plan full-scale vending ventures." *Billboard*, November 10, 1956, pp. 159, 165, 167.
47. "How will vending boom affect selling?" *Printers' Ink* 269 (October 30, 1959): 68.
48. "Dinner ex machina." *Economist* 182 (January 5, 1957): 32–33.
49. "Can robots sell?" *Business Week*, May 13, 1950, p. 83.
50. "Filene's new self-service set-up sells goods by vending machine." *New York Times*, May 16, 1950, p. 39.
51. "Robot selling gets its first big test." *Business Week*, May 27, 1950, pp. 70–71, 73.

Notes — Chapter 6

52. "Where vending machines fall short." *Billboard*, February 21, 1953, p. 154.
53. "New advances seen in vending machines." *New York Times*, November 15, 1951, p. 47; Risdon Tillery. "Insert coin here." *Reader's Digest* 61 (September, 1952): 91.
54. "Selling by machine." *New York Times*, March 8, 1953, sec. 3, p. 10.
55. "Bow Lunch-O-Mat new flexible unit." *Billboard*, June 14, 1952, p. 112.
56. Risdon Tillery. "Insert coin here." *Reader's Digest* 61 (September, 1952): 91–92; "Best year in history for vending machines." *New York Times*, January 2, 1953, p. 22.
57. Cedric Larson. "Our growing robot army." *American Mercury* 78 (April, 1954): 113–115.
58. "Vending machines learning to talk." *New York Times*, January 3, 1955, p. 101; Andrew Hecht. "Robots...at your service." *American Mercury* 83 (November, 1956): 51–57; Sandford Brown. "The clink of coins—louder." *Newsweek* 50 (August 5, 1957): 75–77.
59. "Dollar-in-the-slot?" *Printers' Ink* 261 (November 22, 1957): 37–39; Norris Willatt. "Robot salesmen." *Barron's* 38 (August 4, 1958): 11, 13.
60. "First vending machine census." *Billboard*, January 28, 1950, pp. 87, 92.
61. "Vendors gross record $1.5 billion in 1953." *Billboard*, January 30, 1954, pp. 71, 80.
62. "Department store doldrums." *Business Week*, October 23, 1954, p. 53.
63. "Vending machine 'hot' as seller." *New York Times*, January 6, 1958, p. 72.
64. Norris Willatt. "Robot salesmen." *Barron's* 38 (August 4, 1958): 11.
65. J. E. McMahon. "Jingle of coins in pockets gains." *New York Times*, September 27, 1959, sec. 3, p. 14; "Coin-operated machines grow." *Business Week*, June 6, 1959, p. 53; "New ways to sell." *Times* (London), July 6, 1959, p. 7.
66. "Total exports for 1950." *Billboard*, July 28, 1951, p. 84; "How exports have grown." *Billboard*, June 7, 1952, pp. 75, 84; "Vendor exports." *Billboard*, May 30, 1953, p. 85.
67. "Postwar vendor operation in France hits comeback trail." *Billboard*, February 18, 1950, pp. 105, 109.
68. Risdon Tillery, op. cit., p. 92; Andrew Hecht, op. cit., p. 57.
69. Peter Newman. "The five-cent piece is coming back." *Financial Post*, January 23, 1954, pp. 19–20.
70. "Sees $10 billion vend sales by '67." *Billboard*, February 16, 1957, p. 80; Andrew Hecht, op. cit., p. 55.
71. "Automatic Canteen in F.T.C. order." *New York Times*, June 21, 1950, p. 46.
72. "Automatic Canteen is ordered by F.T.C. to sell subsidiaries." *New York Times*, July 3, 1958, p. 33.
73. "City aide gets 30 days for use of slugs in stamp vending machines in Times Sq." *New York Times*, April 20, 1950, p. 58.
74. "Slug problem grows in Pitts plant stops." *Billboard*, May 30, 1953, p. 78.
75. "N.Y. subways move against slug passers." *Billboard*, January 21, 1956, p. 82.
76. John Sharnik, op. cit., p. 58; Andrew Hecht, op. cit., p. 56.
77. "Blue sky promoters under business bureau, ad fire." *Billboard*, July 19, 1952, pp. 78–79.
78. "Vending machines." *New York Times*, November 1, 1953, sec. 3, p. 8.
79. "How to get stuck with gumballs." *Business Week*, October 27, 1956, pp. 59–60.
80. "Sugar-coated Soviet line at 1c sours police fast." *New York Times*, January 13, 1952, p. 9.
81. "Anger costs him plenty." *Billboard*, May 30, 1953, p. 78.
82. "Device that gives coins for $1 bill is displayed." *New York Times*, November 26, 1957, p. 14.

83. Norris Willatt. "Robot salesmen." *Barron's* 38 (August 4, 1958): 11, 13.
84. E. B. Weiss. "Vending machines to get into higher price lines." *Advertising Age* 29 (December 29, 1958): 32.
85. "How will vending boom affect selling?" *Printers' Ink* 269 (October 30, 1959): 65, 68.

Chapter 7

1. E. B. Weiss. "The vending machine era new begins." *Advertising Age* 31 (June 13, 1960): 96; "Vending hits the jackpot." *Iron Age* 187 (June 29, 1961): 40–41; "Checkout counter 'archaic': Weiss to vending men." *Advertising Age* 34 (September 16, 1963): 1.
2. "The automatic salesmen." *Time* 75 (May 16, 1960): 93–94.
3. "From peanuts to panties." *Sales Management* 84 (June 3, 1960): 38–40.
4. W. J. Manning Jr. "Automatic selling." *The Management Review* 49 (October, 1960): 14–22.
5. "Automatic millionaires." *Time* 78 (November 10, 1961): 88, 90.
6. "Vended sales of hot foods, non-foods soar." *Advertising Age* 32 (November 13, 1961): 6, 161.
7. "Vending group acts." *New York Times*, January 18, 1964, p. 9.
8. "Hospitals act to curb cigarette sales, smoking." *New York Times*, February 9, 1964, p. 47.
9. Philip M. Boffey. "A.M.A. votes to seek total ban on advertising tobacco products." *New York Times*, December 11, 1985, pp. A1, A32.
10. "A video pause that refreshes." *Newsweek* 100 (November 22, 1982): 106.
11. "Zap! Smok! Crunch!" *Forbes* 131 (January 3, 1983): 188.
12. "Reddi-Wip testing peanut butter vending machines." *Advertising Age* 36 (February 8, 1965): 2.
13. "Drycleaning due for do-it yourself boom?" *Chemical Week* 86 (March 19, 1960): 105–106.
14. "Automatic cleaners pass dry run." *Business Week*, August 27, 1960, pp. 53–54.
15. "Paperback vending machine demonstrated in New York." *Publishers Weekly* 181 (June 18, 1962): 38–39.
16. "Paperback vending machine." *Library Journal* 87 (December 1, 1962): 4414–4415.
17. Cornelius Brodersen. "The East." *National Petroleum News* 53 (October, 1961): 19, 21.
18. "Jersey court bars coin machine sales of contraceptives." *New York Times*, May 7, 1963, p. 45.
19. "Vending service for readers." *Library Journal* 89 (October 1, 1964): 3723.
20. "Creeping technology." *Time* 97 (April 5, 1971): 63.
21. Shawn G. Kennedy. "Town seeks to keep 'air' free." *New York Times*, July 12, 1978, p. B2.
22. "In Des Moines: worms for sale." *Time* 126 (October 21, 1985): 16, 20.
23. Rick Lanning. "Tike Miller's can-eating 'goat' pays for its supper and may gnaw on litterbugs." *People* 9 (March 13, 1978): 52.
24. "Reverse vending machines swallow aluminum cans." *The Futurist* 18 (February, 1984): 73.
25. "Penny gumball in trouble." *New York Times*, January 5, 1975, p. 43.
26. "Big vendor at Macy's tells good money from bad." *New York Times*, June 14, 1960, pp. 49, 54; Michael Benson. "Macy's vending machine stirs interest in retail automation." *New York Times*, June 20, 1960, p. 43.

27. "Automatic vending goes national." *Printers' Ink* 272 (September 2, 1960): 18–22.

28. "Department stores test robot salesmen." *Business Week*, January 7, 1961, pp. 86–88.

29. Alan R. Andreasen. "New developments in automatic vending." *Journal of Retailing* 37 (Winter 1961–1962): 21.

30. Ibid., p. 22.

31. Richard R. Krepela. "How is Rich's doing?" *Vend* 17 (April 15, 1961): 40–43.

32. Alan R. Andreasen, op. cit., p. 17.

33. "Vendo tests first coin-operated grocery-snack shop drive-in in K.C." *Advertising Age* 31 (December 19, 1960): 4; "Vending machine drive-in forecasts new food retailing technique." *Progressive Grocer* 40 (June, 1961): 58–61.

34. "Vended sales of hot foods, non-foods soar." *Advertising Age* 32 (November 13, 1961): 6, 161.

35. Alan R. Andreasen. "Automated grocery shopping." *Journal of Marketing* 26 (October, 1962): 64–66.

36. Ibid.

37. "Restaurants: vended food." *National Petroleum News* 56 (February, 1964): 74–77; "Sohio-Stouffer: end of an experiment." *National Petroleum News* 55 (November, 1963): 82.

38. "Can stations sell groceries?" *National Petroleum News* 55 (July, 1963): 91.

39. Susan Marsh. "Fill 'er up" now means car and customers, too." *New York Times*, January 4, 1970, sec. 10, p. 19.

40. David A. Loehwing. "Versatile vendors." *Barron's* 40 (April 11, 1960): 5–6.

41. J. Russell Boner. "Robot restaurants: plant meals from soup to nuts." *Management Review* 49 (May, 1960): 66–68.

42. "The automatic salesman." *Time* 75 (May 16, 1960): 93–94.

43. "Vendors pull out all stops." *Business Week*, August 15, 1970, p. 54.

44. David A. Loehwing. "Versatile vendors." *Barron's* 40 (April 11, 1960): 5–6.

45. "Retailing." *Time* 84 (October 23, 1964): 102.

46. "Vending flunks the entrance exam." *Business Week*, February 10, 1968, pp. 91–92, 94.

47. Thomas W. Ennis. "Operations cover most aspects of food purveying." *New York Times*, July 26, 1971, p. 36.

48. "School vending machines assailed for junk food." *New York Times*, April 18, 1973, p. 12.

49. Sue Cross. "Fighting the yum-yum machines." *The PTA Magazine*, April, 1974, pp. 18–19.

50. "Splitting the take from the vending area." *Management Review* 70 (June, 1981): 40.

51. "Vendors outgrow machines." *Business Week*, October 10, 1964, pp. 138, 140; "Retailing." *Time* 84 (October 23, 1964): 100; "'67 vending sales will exceed $4.5 billion: McGuire." *Advertising Age* 38 (November 13, 1967): 42.

52. "'Third evolution' seen in vending machines." *New York Times*, September 22, 1968, sec. 3, p. 17.

53. Thomas W. Ennis. "Operations cover most aspects of food purveying." *New York Times*, July 26, 1971, pp. 35–36.

54. Douglas Dalrymple. "Will automatic vending topple retail precedents?" *Journal of Retailing* 39 (Spring, 1963): 27–31.

55. "'67 vending sales will exceed $4.5 billion: McGuire." *Advertising Age* 38 (November 13, 1967): 42; "Retailing." *Time* 84 (October 23, 1964): 100; G. R. Schreiber. "What's the trend in operating profits." *Vend* 17 (October 15, 1961): 27–29.

56. "Vending unit sales slide with economy." *New York Times*, August 18, 1980, p. D4.
57. "German coin machines: big job after hours." *New York Times*, May 27, 1967, pp. 36, 41.
58. "Vending machines in Britain." *Foreign Trade* 131 (June 7, 1969): 29–30.
59. Porter V. Taylor. "Vending in Russia." *Beverage World* 97 (November, 1978): 170.
60. "Now: 'unmanned' supermarkets." *U.S. News & World Report* 79 (November 3, 1975): 90; "Click, click, click." *Newsweek* 85 (June 30, 1975): 57–58.
61. Andrew H. Malcolm. "In Japan, you can buy almost anything from a vending machine." *New York Times*, October 25, 1977, p. 2.
62. "Slugs pose mounting problem." *New York Times*, January 2, 1971, p. 19.
63. "Pesos confuse coin machines." *New York Times*, March 18, 1985, p. 16.
64. "Vending machine and rack sale schemes." *Changing Times* 33 (August, 1979): 45–47.
65. "Canteen's profitable new menu." *Business Week*, August 15, 1977, p. 134.
66. "Machines ready for dollar coin." *New York Times*, May 12, 1979, pp. 27, 30.
67. Charles McDowell Jr. "Better living with machinery." *Reader's Digest* 97 (August, 1970): 113–114; Skip Rozen. "Duel with a devil." *Reader's Digest* 109 (November, 1976): 15–16.
68. Charles G. Bennett. "Vending machine owners to pay city for the electricity they use." *New York Times*, May 12, 1964, p. 41.
69. "A computer for coin devices." *New York Times*, October 28, 1973, p. 91.
70. Malcolm L. Morris. "Growth parameters for automatic vending." *Journal of Retailing* 44 (Fall, 1968): 31–45.

Chapter 8

1. Jonathan P. Hicks. "New vending machines to elevate snacking." *New York Times*, October 5, 1988, p. D9.
2. Trish Hall. "Vending machines, the next generation in dining." *New York Times*, September 9, 1992, p. C1.
3. "Vending machines to compete with restaurants." *The Futurist* 26 (September-October, 1992): 8.
4. "Machines in store?" *Montreal Gazette*, October 29, 1996, p. C5.
5. Christina N. Oldham. "Office snackers still craving the not-so-fat-free food fare." *Business Press* 10 (May 2, 1997): 18+.
6. David Whitford. "Entrepreneur aims to make change in vending machines." *Inc* 9 (February, 1997): 17.
7. "Vending jumps 25% at Cleveland St." *FoodService Director* 12 (February 15, 1999): 1.
8. "Kicking butts off campus." *Time* 135 (June 4, 1990): 71; Trish Hall, op. cit.
9. "Smoking regs." *ABA Journal* 80 (June, 1994): 67.
10. "Public health reaches out to reduce tobacco use among teens." *Nation's Health* 25 (December, 1995): 7; Ed Carson. "Teen angst." *Reason* 27 (December, 1995): 18; Barry Meier. "Cigarette vending machine debate is broadened." *New York Times*, August 15, 1995, p. D4.
11. Barry Meier, op. cit.
12. "Northern business interview." *Northern New Jersey Business* 3 (September 6, 1995): 19; Don Nichols. "Cigarette machine profits could go up in smoke." *Restaurant Business* 94 (October 10, 1995): 17+.

13. "Tobacco control laws vary nationwide." H&HN: Hospitals & Health Networks 69 (November 20, 1995): 17.
14. "Tobacco vending machines." FDA Consumer 30 (April, 1996): 27.
15. Keith Key. "Cigarette machines continue to be easy access in Florida." Health Letter of the CDC, December 13, 1996, p. 5.
16. Charlotte Faltermayer and Janice M. Horowitz. "Holy smokes." Time 149 (January 20, 1997): 18.
17. Daniel Roth. "Press B-1 for Macanudo." Forbes 159 (May 19, 1997): 74+.
18. Jim Wilson and Fred Chesbro. "Vending humidors debut." Popular Mechanics 174 (May, 1997): 37.
19. Eric Sfiligoj. "Good news comes in threes." Beverage World 115 (February, 1996): 58, 60, 62.
20. Joan Holleran. "Vending dynamics." Beverage Industry 87 (May, 1996): 40+.
21. "Beverage industry's 1996 vending survey." Beverage Industry 87 (August, 1996): 54.
22. Kent Phillips. "Statistical insights." Beverage World 117 (February, 1998): 126.
23. Eileen McMonagle. "Issues and trends in soft drink vending." Beverage Industry 89 (August, 1998): 45.
24. Sheldon Silver. "Big bottle vending." FoodService Director 11 (October 15, 1998): 176.
25. John MacIntyre. "Figuratively speaking." Across the Board 36 (April, 1999): 13.
26. Joseph P. Griffith. "The shape of things to come." Westchester County Business Journal 38 (December 6, 1999): 13.
27. Rance Crain. "Is thirst for alpha status behind Coke's high-tech talk?" Advertising Age 48 (November 22, 1999): 26; "Coca-Cola looks to variable-price vending machines." Consumer's Research Magazine 82 (December, 1999): 41; Eric Snyder. "Spanked by the invisible hand." Inside Tucson Business 9 (November 1, 1999): 4; Kathleen Schmidt. "News roundup." Marketing News 33 (November 22, 1999): 3.
28. Jack Steinberg. "What's new in vending machines." New York Times, October 8, 1989, sec. 3, p. 17.
29. Shelley Wolson. "Specialty drinks set the pace: hot beverages." FoodService Director 10 (October 15, 1997): 196.
30. Ted Knutson. "Vending machine operators try upscale for change." Grand Rapids Business Journal 16 (November 9, 1998): B3.
31. Sheldon Silver. "Helps turn sales around: branded coffee." FoodService Director 12 (October 15, 1999): 156.
32. Ibid.
33. Kathy Blake. "Ice cream vending." FoodService Director 10 (May 15, 1997): 206.
34. Sheldon Silver. "New machines, specialty items promote: ice cream vending." FoodService Director 12 (May 15, 1999): 178.
35. "Seed capitalist." Canadian Business 70 (June, 1997): 228.
36. "Hospital installs hot-food vending." FoodService Director 10 (May 15, 1997): 1+.
37. "A close look at today's technology: do frozen entrees make the cut?" FoodService Director 11 (June 15, 1998): 176.
38. Michael Janofsky. "A bartender with buttons serves brews to go." New York Times, July 8, 1993, p. D1.
39. David Z. McSwane and William A. Oleckno. "Drinking water quality concern and water vending machines." Journal of Environmental Health 56 (June, 1994): 7+.
40. Ibid.
41. Fred Scaglione. "Water Point Systems: water, water everywhere." Equities 42 (July, 1994): 27+.

42. Betsy Spethmann. "Nabisco's SnackWell's vending." *Brandweek* 35 (November 14, 1994): 4.
43. "Consumers demanding healthier food from vending machines." *Marketing News* 30 (September 23, 1996): 39.
44. Simone A. French and Robert W. Jeffery. "A pricing strategy to promote low-fat snack choices through vending machines." *American Journal of Public Health* 87 (May, 1997): 849+.
45. Marian Bond. "At Trance Co. in La Crosse: 70% of meals are vended." *FoodService Director* 10 (September 15, 1997): 66; Shelley Wolson. "In college vending: 'special contracts' shift operating, sales balance." *FoodService Director* 10 (September 15, 1992): 212.
46. Amanda Chater. "Finding today's balance for 'healthier' business." *FoodService Director* 11 (August 15, 1998): 170.
47. Stephanie Young. "Healthy eating in a hurry." *Redbook* 194 (March, 2000): 48+.
48. Simone A. French, Robert W. Jeffery and Mary Story. "Pricing and promotion effects on low-fat vending snack purchases: the chips study." *American Journal of Public Health* 91 (January, 2001): 112+.
49. "TGIF: thank God, it's fried." *Business NH Magazine* 7 (February, 1990): 11.
50. "Let them eat pellets." *Economist* 319 (May 4, 1991): 74.
51. Trish Hall. "Vending machines, the next generation in dining." *New York Times*, September 9, 1992, p. C6.
52. David Baines. "The frying game." *Canadian Business* 67 (September, 1994): 32+.
53. Ibid.
54. Ibid.
55. Ibid.
56. "Equipment briefs." *Nation's Restaurant News* 32 (July 20, 1998): 22; "Equipment briefs." *Nation's Restaurant News* 32 (October 12, 1998): 18; "Faster than McDonald's." *Hudson Valley Business Journal* 11 (August, 2000): 27.
57. "A low- frying machine." *Maclean's* 48 (November 29, 1999): 14.
58. William R. Greer. "Videotape vending machines: for viewers in the fast lane." *New York Times*, June 12, 1986, pp. C1, C6.
59. "In goes your credit card; out comes Amadeus." *Business Week*, November 10, 1986, p. 127.
60. Kathryn Harris. "Wanted: instant gratification." *Forbes* 146 (December 24, 1990): 116, 118.
61. "Lights! Action! Roll 'em!" *Time* 133 (June 19, 1989): 49.
62. Jim Bessman. "CD vending machines go to market." *Billboard*, July 9, 1994, p. 62+.
63. "Cd-lodeon?" *Marketing News* 32 (April 27, 1998): 2; "Sponsored phone cards, CD vending machines, a punk compilation." *Billboard*, August 7, 1999, p. APQ-4.
64. Jill Pesselnick. "Movie Music to place CD machines in lobbies." *Billboard*, February 19, 2000, p. 10+.
65. "Supreme Court OKs rack regulation." *Editor & Publisher* 128 (November 18, 1995): 44.
66. Joe Nicholson. "Current and future models." *Editor & Publisher* 131 (March 28, 1998): 47.
67. Jon Marshall. "City beautification plan irks Chicago papers." *Christian Science Monitor*, April 22, 1938, p. 3.
68. Trudi Miller Rosenblum. "Vending machines offer audiobooks." *Billboard*, October 7, 1995, p. 85.

69. David Clark Scott. "Skivvies on parade." *Christian Science Monitor*, October 31, 1998, p. 54+.
70. Elaine Satoro. "USPS shuts down Postal Buddies." *Direct Marketing* 56 (November, 1993): 15.
71. Andrew C. Revkin. "The coins go in, and the worms come out." *New York Times*, October 4, 1998, pp. 1, 46.
72. "Worms, vending machines and vermiculture." *In Business* 20 (September/October, 1998): 12.
73. Shelley Wolson. "Location, location, location." *FoodService Director* 10 (November 15, 1997): 180.
74. Marian Bond. "At Trane Co. in La Crosse: 70% of meals are vended." *FoodService Director* 10 (September 15, 1997): 66.
75. Bob Krummert. "In b&i, lunch is the hour of power." *ID: The Voice of Foodservice Distribution* 33 (September, 1997): 35+.
76. Athena Schaffer. "Fairs hope beverage vending machines, sponsorship deals will bolster profits." *Amusement Business* 112 (May 22, 2000): 35.
77. Pam Sherborne. "Vending machines pose competitive threat." *Amusement Business* 112 (March 12, 2000): 29.
78. Marian Bond. "Vending is top generator of revenues at TX hospital." *FoodService Director* 11 (February 15, 1998): 56.
79. Sue Grossbauer. "At East Pasco Med. Ctr.: how self-op vending is linked to software." *FoodService director* 12 (April 15, 1999): 170.
80. Bob Gatty. "NSDA goes to the principal's office." *Beverage Industry* 85 (July, 1994): 24+.
81. Ibid.
82. "Seminole schools appeal to state." *FoodService Director* 11 (April 15, 1998): 8.
83. "Soda sales OK in Denver schools." *FoodService Director* 11 (October 15, 1998): 1.
84. "And who spends revenues: Florida schools address vending machine rules." *FoodService Director* 12 (November 15, 1999): 5.
85. Amanda Chater. "For all non-commercial operators: the benefits of centralized vending." *FoodService Director* 13 (May 15, 2000): 158.
86. Leslie Vallie. "Soda contracts dispense liquid revenue for schools." *Government Procurement* 7 (August, 1999): 16+.
87. Louise Brown. "Coke is it in schools." *Toronto Star*, November 26, 1999, p. B10.
88. Constance L. Hays. "Today's lesson: soda rights." *New York Times*, May 21, 1999, pp. C1, C9.
89. Ibid.
90. Ken Schroeder. "Make the fizz fizzle." *Education Digest* 64 (February, 1999): 77.
91. "In schools: product mix keeps students coming back." *FoodService Director* 13 (October 15, 2000): 66.
92. Constance L. Hays. "School district rethinks its soda-pop strategy." *New York Times*, April 9, 2000, p. B11.
93. Shelley Wolson. "In college vending: 'special contracts' shift operating sales balance." *FoodService Director* 10 (September 15, 1997): 212.
94. "Computer maps campus eating trends: Ucal/Irvine customizes vending to match customers." *FoodService Director* 12 (August 15, 1999): 40.
95. "In colleges: machines help deliver product to fit lifestyle." *FoodService Director* 13 (October 15, 2000): 64+.

Notes—Chapter 8

96. "Campus goes Pepsi-free in exchange for $1 million." *Montreal Gazette*, May 2, 1998, p. A18.
97. "Cola wars." *Montreal Gazette*, December 9, 1999, p. B2.
98. Nicholas Bradley. "The truth about Coca-Colanisation." *The Ubyssey Magazine*, September 7, 2001, pp. 6–7.
99. See Appendix.
100. "UK bottom in machine sales." *Tobacco Europe*, March/April, 1998, p. 2.
101. John Tagliabue. "Vending machines face an upheaval of change." *New York Times*, February 16, 1999, p. C4.
102. "Now you can fly on pocket change." *Newsweek* 118 (October 7, 1991): 48.
103. Karyn Scherer. "Alcohol vending machines put to test." *New Zealand Herald*, February 1, 2001.
104. Paul King. "Side dishes." *Nation's Restaurant News* 33 (April 12, 1999): 26.
105. "A Coke and a frown." *Economist* 357 (October 7, 2000): 73.
106. "China's two main cities to get condom machines." *Aids Weekly Plus*, August 23, 1999, p. 11.
107. David Greenfield. "Carbonated data." *Data Communications* 28 (May 21, 1999): 18.
108. Andrew Tanzer. "War of the sales robots." *Forbes* 147 (January 7, 1991): 294+.
109. Emily Thornton. "Japan's new cupid: vending machines." *Fortune* 125 (April 6, 1992): 13.
110. "Push-button lover." *Economist* 321 (November 16, 1991): 88.
111. James Sterngold. "Why the Japanese adore vending machines." *New York Times*, January 5, 1992, pp. 1, 12.
112. "Unacceptable lace of capitalism." *Economist* 329 (October 9, 1993): 76.
113. "De-vend the earth." *Earth Island Journal* 13 (Spring, 1998): 3.
114. Myron Beard. "Vending machine as energy hog." *Electric Perspectives* 23 (March/April, 1998): 10+.
115. Len Lewis. "Robo retailing." *Progressive Grocer* 77 (April, 1998): 9.
116. Daniel Scuka. "Veni, vedi, vended." *J@pan Inc* 3 (January, 2001): 30+.
117. Trish Hall. "Vending machines, the next generation in dining." *New York Times*, September 9, 1992, p. C6; Jack Steinberg. "What's new in vending machines." *New York Times*, October 8, 1989, sec. 3, p. 17.
118. James Ryan. "In vending machines, brains that tell good money from bad." *New York Times*, April 8, 1999, p. G13.
119. Corinna Wu. "The buck starts here." *Science News* 157 (April 1, 2000): 216.
120. Shelley Wolson. "Brands lift prices, profits." *FoodService Director* 10 (December 15, 1997): 164.
121. "Today's models: a new breed of 'self promoters.'" *FoodService Director* 10 (July 15, 1997): Sup., p. 2S+.
122. Shelley Wolson. "Promotional techniques: pushing bigger buys." *FoodService Director* 13 (November 15, 2000): 150.
123. Ibid.
124. Paul King. "Canteen vending bets that everything old will be new." *Nation's Restaurant News* 32 (August 17, 1998): 18.
125. Paul King. "Compass Group's Gagliardi plans vending overhaul." *Nation's Restaurant News* 31 (November 24, 1997): 19.
126. "Canteen redefines vending biz." *FoodService Director* 11 (October 15, 1998): 20.
127. William E. Schmidt. "Little Rock fights dream of a soda machine in every yard." *New York Times*, September 4, 1986, p. 12.

128. "Soda machine kills youth." *New York Times*, September 15, 1987, p. 16; "Vending machine kills youth." *New York Times*, May 9, 1989, p. A20.

129. "Student dies under soft-drink machine." *Montreal Gazette*, December 14, 1998, p. A3.

130. Timothy L. O'Brien. "Vending scams are on the rise, officials warn." *Wall Street Journal*, July 1, 1994, East. Ed., pp. B1–B2.

131. "No experience necessary—but send money." *U.S. News & World Report* 119 (July 31, 1995): 13.

132. Jane Offen. "Every bottler experiences vandalism, supplier survey finds." *Beverage Industry*, 1994/95 Special Issue Annual, p. 52+.

133. Ibid.

134. Mike Cormier and Steve Cook. "Soda shocker." *Earth Island Journal* 9 (Summer, 1994): 18.

135. "Reviewing the soda machine." *In Business* 18 (May/June, 1996): 9.

136. Thomas Love. "Pushing the envelope with vending machines." *Nation's Business* 86 (October, 1998): 10.

137. Shelley Wolson. "Remote technology gaining acceptance: 'smart machines.'" *FoodService Director* 13 (August 15, 2000): 136.

138. "Code red: Coke bust goin' down." *Earth Island Journal* 14 (Winter 1999/2000): 17.

Bibliography

Abbott, Sam. "Hunts, lands spots, builds ops' routes." *Billboard*, September 16, 1957, pp. 90–1.
Amann, Fred W. "Lunch pails get coin slots." *Billboard*, February 1, 1947, pp. 134, 136.
"Among boosters of vendor page." *Billboard*, June 2, 1934, p. 60.
"And now a book machine." *New York Times*, December 20, 1946, p. 21.
"And who spends revenues: Florida schools address vending machine rules." *Food-Service Director* 12 (November 15, 1999): 5.
Andreasen, Alan R. "Automated grocery shopping." *Journal of Retailing* 26 (October, 1962): 64–66.
_____. "New developments in automatic vending." *Journal of Retailing* 37 (Winter, 1961–1962): 17–23.
Andrews, Arch M. "Profits from pennies." *Saturday Evening Post* 203 (November 1, 1930): 10–11+.
"Anger costs him plenty." *Billboard*, May 30, 1953, p. 78.
"ARCOR plans to stimulate vending machine business." *Billboard*, November 5, 1932, p. 55.
"Aspirin to the front." *Billboard*, November 26, 1932, p. 63.
"Association bulletin gives tips to operators of cigaret vendors." *Billboard*, May 22, 1937, p. 86.
"Astrologist lauds talkie horoscope." *Billboard*, January 22, 1938, p. 90.
"Astrology has popular appeal." *Billboard*, August 10, 1935, p. 73.
"Attachment ties up slot-machine money." *New York Times*, March 9, 1909, p. 3.
"Automatic Canteen in F.T.C. order." *New York Times*, June 21, 1950, p. 46.
"Automatic Canteen is ordered by F.T.C. to sell subsidiaries." *New York Times*, July 3, 1958, p. 33.
"Automatic cleaners pass dry run." *Business Week*, August 27, 1960, pp. 53–54.
"Automatic cows." *Business Week*, May 15, 1954, pp. 126–127.
"Automatic distributor of perfumes." *Scientific American* 69 (December 16, 1893): 388.
"Automatic distributors of beverages." *Scientific American* 65 (December 26, 1891): 403.
"Automatic machines." *Times* (London), March 14, 1929, p. 12.
"Automatic millionaires." *Time* 78 (November 10, 1961): 88, 90.
"Automatic sales hurt in Reich." *New York Times*, November 14, 1939, p. 39.
"The automatic salesmen." *Time* 75 (May 16, 1960): 93–94.
"Automatic strength tester and vending machine." *Scientific American* 76 (March 20, 1897): 180.
"Automatic vending goes national." *Printers' Ink* 272 (September 2, 1960): 18–22.

"An automatic vending machine." *Scientific American* 74 (February 29, 1896): 133.
"Automatic window vending units spur candy sales." *New York Times*, August 18, 1956, p. 21.
"Automats apt to help." *New York Times*, July 8, 1928, sec. 2, p. 18.
"Avon introduces new book vending machine." *Publishers Weekly* 158 (August 5, 1950): 574–5.
"Await court verdict on Flint vending license." *Billboard*, April 4, 1936, p. 70.
"Backspin." *Beverage World* 118 (October, 1999): 144.
Baines, David. "The frying game." *Canadian Business* 67 (September, 1994): 32+.
Beard, Myron. "Vending machine as energy hog." *Electric Perspectives* 23 (March/April, 1998): 10+.
"Beer helps cig vendors." *Billboard*, June 30, 1934, p. 86.
Bennett, Charles G. "Coins in slot hit jackpot for city." *New York Times*, April 9, 1949, p. 19.
_____. "Transit concessions yield $3,932,333 in 11 months." *New York Times*, July 24, 1949, pp. 1, 56.
_____. "Vending machine owners to pay city for the electricity they use." *New York Times*, May 12, 1964, p. 41.
Benson, Michael. "Macy's vending machine stirs interest in retail automation." *New York Times*, June 20, 1960, p. 43.
Berger, Meyer. "About New York." *New York Times*, August 7, 1953, p. 21.
Bernard, Tom. "Small change is big business." *American Magazine* 146 (September, 1948): 46–47+.
Bessman, Jim. "CD vending machines go to market." *Billboard*, July 9, 1994, 62+.
"Best year in history for vending machines." *New York Times*, January 2, 1953, p. 22.
"Beverage industry's 1996 vending survey." *Beverage Industry* 87 (August, 1996): 54.
"Beverage vendor shown." *Billboard*, December 3, 1932, p. 83.
"Big vendor at Macy's tells good money from bad." *New York Times*, June 14, 1960, pp. 49, 54.
Blake, Kathy. "Ice cream vending." *FoodService Director* 10 (May 15, 1997): 206.
Bloom, Jackson. "Importance of cigaret vendors shown by McGinnis installations." *Billboard*, October 29, 1938, p. 69.
"Blue sky promoters under business bureau, ad fire." *Billboard*, July 19, 1952, pp. 78–79.
"Boeing boosts candy vendors." *Billboard*, March 29, 1952, p. 78.
Boffey, Philip M. "A.M.A. votes to seek total ban on advertising tobacco products." *New York Times*, December 11, 1985, pp. A1, A32.
Bolen, W. E. "How to operate general route of bulk product vending machines." *Billboard*, March 24, 1934, pp. 62, 64.
Bond, David. "Merchandise machine progress." *Billboard*, January 18, 1936, p. 80.
Bond, Marian. "At the Trane Co. in La Crosse: 70% of meals are vended." *FoodService Director* 10 (September 15, 1997): 66.
_____. "Vending is top generator of revenues at TX hospital." *FoodService Director* 11 (February 15, 1998): 56.
Boner, J. Russel. "Robot restaurants: plant meals from soup to nuts." *Management Review* 49 (May, 1960): 66–68.
"Book vendor patented." *Publishers Weekly* 121 (June 4, 1932): 2257.
"Boost salted nut sales by 'heat-fag' campaign." *Billboard*, July 9, 1938, p. 72.
"Bow Lunch-O-Mat new flexible unit." *Billboard*, June 14, 1952, p. 112.
Bradley, Nicholas. "The truth about Coca-Colanisation." *The Ubyssey Magazine*, September 7, 2001, pp. 6–7.
"British hair oil vendor is offered here." *Billboard*, March 29, 1952, p. 81.

Brodersen, Cornelius. "The East." *National Petroleum News* 53 (October, 1961): 19, 21.
Brown, Louise. "Coke is it in schools." *Toronto Star*, November 26, 1999, p. B10.
Brown, Sandford. "The clink of coins—louder." *Newsweek* 50 (August 5, 1957): 75–77.
"Bureau hits at promotion." *Billboard*, December 11, 1937, p. 87.
"But when will robots eat and sleep for us?" *Literary Digest* 102 (September 7, 1929): 53.
"Campus goes Pepsi-free in exchange for $1 million." *Montreal Gazette*, May 2, 1998, p. A18.
"Can robots sell." *Business Week*, May 13, 1950, p. 83.
"Can stations sell groceries?" *National Petroleum News* 55 (July, 1963): 91.
"Candy vending sales gain." *Billboard*, January 12, 1946, pp. 82, 86.
"Canteen Co. ideas and service promote wide vending sales." *Billboard*, July 16, 1938, p. 74.
"Canteen redefines vending biz." *FoodService Director* 11 (October 15, 1998): 20.
"Canteen's profitable new menu." *Business Week*, August 15, 1977, p. 134.
Capaldi, Jack. "Coin machines in Europe." *Billboard*, October 14, 1933, pp. 60–61.
Carson, Ed. "Teen angst." *Reason* 27 (December, 1995): 18.
"Cd-lodeon?" *Marketing News* 32 (April 27, 1998): 2.
Chater, Amanda. "Finding today's balance for 'healthier' business." *FoodService Director* 11 (August 15, 1998): 170.
_____. "For all non-commercial operators: the benefits of centralized vending." *FoodService Director* 13 (May 15, 2000): 158.
"Checkout counter 'archaic': Weiss to vending men." *Advertising Age* 34 (September 16, 1963): 1, 121.
"Chewing gum, candy and weighing machines." *New York Times*, July 11, 1932, p. 12.
"Chi transit vendor volume off in '53." *Billboard*, March 27, 1954, pp. 78, 86.
"China's two main cities to get condom machines." *Aids Weekly Plus*, August 23, 1999, p. 11.
"Chi's first launderette gets enthusiastic play." *Billboard*, March 16, 1946, p. 103.
"Cig operators set commission." *Billboard*, February 13, 1937, p. 72.
"Cig. vendors go in restaurants." *Billboard*, March 24, 1934, p. 62.
"Cig vendors show gains." *Billboard*, May 26, 1934, p. 70.
"Cigaret output climbs." *Billboard*, April 4, 1936, p. 70.
"Cigaret vendors share in volume." *Billboard*, January 18, 1936, p. 78.
"City aide gets 30 days for use of drugs in stamp vending machines in Times Sq." *New York Times*, April 20, 1950, p. 58.
"Claims popcorn vendor to open new field for large profits." *Billboard*, December 31, 1932, p. 89.
"Click, click, click." *Newsweek* 85 (June 30, 1975): 57–58.
"Clink of slugs in slot machines sour music to manufacturers." *Business Week*, April 15, 1931, p. 28.
"A close look at today's technology: do frozen entrees make the cut?" *FoodService Director* 11 (June 15, 1998): 176.
Coan, J. W. "Vending machine future will be hurt by use of small-size bars." *Billboard*, December 11, 1937, p. 87.
"Coca-cola looks to variable-price vending machines." *Consumers' Research Magazine* 82 (December, 1999): 41.
"Code red: Coke bust goin' down." *Earth Island Journal* 14 (Winter 1999/2000): 17.
"The coffee break." *Time* 67 (February 27, 1956): 90.
Cohen, Paul. "Robot salesmen save money." *Science Digest* 26 (July, 1949): 37–40.
"The coin chute." *Billboard*, July 30, 1932, p. 74.
"Coin machine exports." *Billboard*, April 2, 1949, p. 141.

"Coin machine reports." *Billboard*, May 18, 1946, p. 109.
"Coin machine sales $500,000,000 yearly." *New York Times*, April 10, 1947, p. 43.
"Coin machines at the fair." *Billboard*, May 13, 1939, p. 72.
"Coin machines gross $305,598 in 108 days at N. Y. World's Fair." *Billboard*, September 16, 1939, p. 67.
"Coin machines prominent at Chicago World's Fair." *Billboard*, June 3, 1933, pp. 57–58.
"Coin men continue fight for reasonable license." *Billboard*, February 4, 1933, p. 63.
"Coin men of Paris in Chi." *Billboard*, February 10, 1934, p. 62.
"Coin milk vendors planned in homes." *New York Times*, December 31, 1949, p. 17.
"Coin-operated circulation studied." *Billboard*, February 26, 1955, pp. 87, 97.
"Coin-operated machines grow." *Business Week*, June 6, 1959, p. 53.
"Coin-slot drinks barred in Jersey." *New York Times*, July 11, 1954, p. 56.
"Coin trouble." *Business Week*, February 15, 1947, p. 76.
"Coin-vending machines may even change diaper." *New York Times*, September 28, 1950, p. 37.
"Coincidence? Or safety first?" *Business Week*, May 17, 1952, p. 42.
"A Coke and a frown." *Economist* 357 (October 7, 2000): 73.
"Cola wars." *Montreal Gazette*, December 9, 1999, p. B2.
"Commission unit on cig machines." *Billboard*, February 27, 1937, p. 82.
"A computer for coin devices." *New York Times*, October 28, 1973, p. 91.
"Computer maps campus eating trends: UCal/Irvine customizes vending to match customers." *FoodService Director* 12 (August 15, 1999): 40.
"Concessions pay $4,298,561 to city." *New York Times*, November 27, 1949, p. 75.
"Conditions in candy trade indicate success of vendors." *Billboard*, November 26, 1932, p. 56.
"Considers apple vendors." *Billboard*, September 17, 1932, p. 59.
"Consumers demanding healthier food from vending machines." *Marketing News* 30 (September 23, 1996): 39.
Cormier, Mike and Steve Cook. "Soda shocker." *Earth Island News* 9 (Summer, 1994): 18.
"Corporations." *Time* 67 (June 11, 1956): 91–92, 94.
Costa, Nic. *Automatic Pleasures: The History of the Coin Machine.* London: Kevin Frances Publishing, 1988.
Crain, Rance. "Is thirst for Alpha status behind Coke's high-tech talk?" *Advertising Age* 48 (November 22, 1999): 26.
"Creeping technology." *Time* 97 (April 5, 1971): 63.
Crook, George. "How business profits from coin machines." *Billboard*, November 13, 1937, p. 76.
_____. "The misunderstood vending machine." *Billboard*, May 21, 1938, p. 87.
Cross, Sue. "Fighting the yum-yum machines." *The PTA Magazine*, April, 1974, pp 18–19.
Dalrymple, Douglas J. "Will automatic vending topple retail precedents?" *Journal of Retailing* 39 (Spring, 1963): 27–31.
"Death caused by automatic machine." *Times* (London), July 8, 1925, p. 5.
"Dentist takes schools to task." *New York Times*, June 2, 1956, p. 10.
"Department store automat to be opened here shortly." *New York Times*, June 10, 1928, sec. 2, p. 20.
"Department store doldrums." *Business Week*, October 23, 1954, p. 53.
"Department stores test robot salesmen." *Business Week*, January 7, 1961, pp. 86–88.
"Detroit bans certain types of vendors." *Billboard*, April 21, 1934, p. 60.

"Detroit pin-game operators join merchandising association." *Billboard*, December 24, 1932, p. 57.
"De-vend the earth." *Earth Island Journal* 13 (Spring, 1998): 3.
"Device that gives coins for $1 bill is displayed." *New York Times*, Nov. 26, 1957, p. 14.
"Devices in use for self-selling." *New York Times*, October 19, 1919, pt. 2, p. 10.
"Dewey aids milk drive." *New York Times*, June 10, 1954, p. 39.
"Dinner ex machina." *Economist* 182 (January 5, 1957): 32–33.
"Direct-to-location sales rise." *Billboard*, April 2, 1949, pp. 113, 128.
"Distribution of hot water at Paris." *Scientific American* 68 (February 25, 1893): 120.
"Dollar-in-the-slot?" *Printers' Ink* 261 (November 22, 1957): 37–39.
"Druggists' meet will emphasize drug stores as locations." *Billboard*, September 17, 1932, p. 62.
"Drugs from automatic machines." *Times* (London), January 9, 1930, p. 7.
"Drycleaning due for do-it-yourself boom?" *Chemical Week* 86 (March 19, 1960): 105–106, 108.
"East watches pop-corn machines." *Billboard*, March 12, 1938, p. 79.
"Edwards urges wholesale tobacco group to realize importance of cig vendor." *Billboard*, January 26, 1946, p. 91.
"11 ops, 500 vendors in store center." *Billboard*, March 19, 1955, p. 78.
Ennis, Thomas W. "Operations cover most aspects of food purveying." *New York Times*, July 26, 1971, pp. 35–36.
"Equipment briefs." *Nation's Restaurant News* 32 (July 20, 1998): 22.
"Equipment briefs." *Nation's Restaurant News* 32 (October 12, 1998): 18.
"Error causes tangle on vending machines." *New York Times*, February 1, 1935, p. 28.
"Even the milkman is automatic now." *New York Times*, February 6, 1953, p. 21.
"Expanding candy markets." *Billboard*, April 15, 1939, p. 78.
"Facts and figures necessary to operate bulk vending machines." *Billboard*, September 28, 1935, p. 66.
Faltmayer, Charlotte and Janice M. Horowitz. "Holy smokes." *Time* 149 (January 20, 1997): 18.
"Faster than McDonald's." *Hudson Valley Business Journal* 11 (August 14, 2000): 27.
"Filene's new self-service set-up sells goods by vending machine." *New York Times*, May 16, 1950, p. 39.
"Fined L5 for twopence." *Times* (London), March 19, 1915, p. 10.
"Firm to operate service machines." *Billboard*, February 8, 1936, p. 73.
"First reports show automatic store to be successful venture." *Billboard*, January 14, 1933, p. 56.
"First vending industry census." *Billboard*, January 28, 1950, pp. 87, 92.
"500 drink vendors in Baltimore area." *Billboard*, April 12, 1941, p. 144.
Fleer, H. H. "A drink dispenser." *Billboard*, February 1, 1936, p. 66.
"Food device buyers charge swindle." *New York Times*, March 3, 1927, p. 25.
"Food sales machines move in." *Business Week*, November 13, 1954, pp. 126–128, 130.
"Forgetful shopper gets a second chance in Jersey." *New York Times*, October 25, 1956, pp. 47, 51.
"46 slot cents retrieved." *New York Times*, April 8, 1949, p. 27.
Freeman, William M. "16,000 vending machines help Daisy get rid of her surplus milk." *New York Times*, July 9, 1955, pp. 18, 21.
"French coins in slot machines." *Times* (London), July 12, 1932, p. 11.
French, Simone A. and Robert W. Jeffery. "A pricing strategy to promote low-fat snack choices through vending machines." *American Journal of Public Health* 87 (May, 1997): 849+.

French, Simone A., Robert W. Jeffery, and Mary Story. "Pricing and promotion effects on low-fat vending snack purchases: the chips study." *American Journal of Public Health* 91 (January, 2000): 112+.
"From nuts to soup — literally." *Business Week*, December 15, 1956, pp. 68, 70.
"From peanuts to panties." *Sales Management* 84 (June 3, 1960): 38–40, 42.
"Frozen juice makers move vendor programs in high gear." *Billboard*, September 29, 1951, pp. 88, 91.
"Gasoline slot machine." *Scientific American* 109 (October 18, 1913): 300.
Gatty, Bob. "NSDA goes to the principal's office." *Beverage Industry* 85 (July, 1994): 24+.
George, C. S. "Future in merchandising." *Billboard*, March 20, 1937, p. 81.
"German book vendor." *Publishers Weekly* 119 (May 23, 1931): 2511–2512.
"German coin machines: big job after hours." *New York Times*, May 27, 1967, pp. 36, 41.
Gersh, Bill. "New trend to merchandisers." *Billboard*, October 2, 1937, p. 81.
Gersh, William, "Automatic merchandising in theaters." *Billboard*, October 6, 1934, pp. 66–67.
"Gets new trial." *New York Times*, December 31, 1942, p. 17.
Goeldner, Charles R. "Automatic selling — will it work?" *Journal of Retailing* 38 (Summer, 1962): 41–46+.
Greenfield, David. "Carbonated data." *Data Communications* 28 (May 21, 1999): 18.
Greer, William R. "Videotape vending machines: for viewers in the fast lane." *New York Times*, June 12, 1986, pp. C1, C6.
Greiner, W. R. "Merchandise for bulk vendors." *Billboard*, January 29, 1938, pp. 79–80.
Griffith, Joseph P. "The shape of things to come." *Westchester County Business Journal* 38 (December 6, 1999): 13.
Grossbauer, Sue. "At East Pasco Med. Ctr.: How self-op vending is linked to software." *FoodService Director* 12 (April 15, 1999): 170.
"Growth of plant vending since World War II peak." *Billboard*, May 12, 1951, p. 71.
Gummersheimer, Walter. "Pop-corn merchandising in tune with spirit of fast-moving age." *Billboard*, March 19, 1938, p. 80.
"Gumming up the bus." *Business Week*, May 22, 1954, p. 132.
"Hair oil op grows, adds location units." *Billboard*, September 29, 1951, p. 88.
"Halfpennies for shillings." *Times* (London), December 2, 1924, p. 11.
Hall, Trish. "Vending machines, the next generation in dining." *New York Times*, September 9, 1992, pp. C1, C6.
Harris, Kathryn. "Wanted: instant gratification." *Forbes* 146 (December 24, 1990): 116, 118.
Hays, Constance L. "School district rethinks its soda-pop strategy." *New York Times*, April 9, 2000, p. B11.
_____. "Today's lesson: soda rights." *New York Times*, May 21, 1999, pp. C1, C9.
"Heavy penalty on slugs." *Billboard*, September 24, 1932, p. 67.
Hecht, Andrew. "Robots...at your service." *American Mercury* 83 (November, 1956): 51–57.
Hicks, Jonathan P. "New vending machines to elevate snacking." *New York Times*, October 5, 1988, p. D9.
Hirsch, J. H. "How 'automatic' selling began." *Billboard*, June 2, 1934, pp. 60, 65.
_____. "Nat'l Automatic Merchandising Assn." *Billboard*, June 30, 1934, p. 86.
Holleran, John. "Vending dynamics." *Beverage Industry*." 87 (May, 1996): 40+.
Holman, Ross L. "A meal or a shine by robot vendors." *Science Digest* 19 (June, 1946): 24–26.
Horowitz, Is. "Subway vending tops 3 million." *Billboard*, February 17, 1951, pp. 1, 76, 79.

___. "Vendors move mags, books." *Billboard*, September 8, 1951, pp. 1, 74, 87.
"Hospital installs hot-food vending." *FoodService Director* 10 (May 15, 1997): 1.
"Hospitals act to curb cigarette sales, smoking." *New York Times*, February 9, 1964, p. 47.
"How to get stuck with gumballs." *Business Week*, October 27, 1956, pp. 59–60.
"How will vending boom affect selling?" *Printers' Ink* 269 (October 30, 1959): 65, 68.
Hurd, Walter W. "Analysis of machine trends as indicated at the December show." *Billboard*, December 24, 1938, p. 67.
___. "Beverage machine progress." *Billboard*, June 8, 1940, pp. 70–71.
___. "Beverage vendors." *Billboard*, June 8, 1940, p. 64.
___. "Beverage vendors." *Billboard*, June 8, 1940, p. 64.
___. "Coin machine progress in 1932." *Billboard*, January 28, 1933, pp. 58–59.
___. "Significant trends in the coin-machine business." *Billboard*, July 30, 1932, pp. 76–79.
___. "Taxing vendors." *Billboard*, January 30, 1943, p. 56.
___. "The 1940 show." *Billboard*, January 27, 1940, pp. 64–65, 69.
___. "Ultra self-service." *Billboard*, June 8, 1946, p. 100.
___. "Unemployment." *Billboard*, September 11, 1937, p. 74.
___. "Vending machines." *Billboard*, April 2, 1938, p. 76.
"Ice cream vendor making start for next summer trade." *Billboard*, January 21, 1933, p. 57.
"Ice cream vendor succeeds on test." *Billboard*, February 13, 1937, p. 72.
"Ice 'slugs' and others forbidden in Rhode Island." *Billboard*, April 23, 1932, p. 70.
"Improved racing game has ball gum vendor." *Billboard*, November 4, 1933, p. 59.
"Improved vending-machines." *Scientific American* 82 (June 16, 1900): 378.
"Improves new machine to vend one cigaret." *Billboard*, January 7, 1933, p. 57.
"In colleges: machines help deliver product to fit lifestyles." *FoodService Director* 13 (October 15, 2000): 64+.
"In Des Moines: worms for sales." *Time* 126 (October 21, 1985): 16, 20.
"In goes your credit card, out comes Amadeus." *Business Week*, November 10, 1986, p. 127.
"In schools: product mix keeps students coming back." *FoodService Director* 13 (October 15, 2000): 66+.
"Industry turning to robots for food." *New York Times*, January 3, 1956, p. 118.
"Installing vending machines." *New York Times*, February 17, 1929, sec. 2, p. 13.
"Interested in prospects for sanitary coin devices." *Billboard*, July 30, 1932, p. 74.
"Introduce foot massage machine." *Billboard*, March 4, 1939, p. 67.
"Invention in 1889 A. D. vs. invention B. C." *Scientific American* 64 (February 14, 1891): 105.
"Jackpot for coin vendors." *Business Week*, December 20, 1947, pp. 50–52.
Janofsky, Michael. "A bartender with buttons serves brew to go." *New York Times*, July 8, 1993, p. D1.
"Jennings has new drink vendor." *Billboard*, February 17, 1940, p. 62.
"Jersey court bars coin machine sales of contraceptives." *New York Times*, May 7, 1963, p. 45.
"Jobs galore for robot salesmen." *Business Week*, April 16, 1930, p. 28.
Jones, Herb. "Where to place cold vendors." *Billboard*, June 8, 1940, p. 69.
Jones, Lee S. "Pres Jones of CMMAA." *Billboard*, April 2, 1932, p. 59.
"Juice vendor seen greatly under-rated." *Billboard*, May 17, 1947, p. 106.
Kennedy, Shawn G. "Town seeks to keep 'air' free." *New York Times*, July 12, 1978, p. B2.
Key, Keith. "Cigarette machines continue to be easy access in Florida." *Health Letter of the CDC*, December 13, 1996, p. 5.

"Kicking butts off campus." *Time* 135 (June 4, 1990): 71.
King, Paul. "Canteen vending bets that everything old will be new." *Nation's Restaurant News* 32 (August 17, 1998): 18.
_____. "Compass Group's Gagliardi plans vending overhaul." *Nation's Restaurant News* 31 (November 24, 1997): 19.
_____. "Side dishes." *Nation's Restaurant News* 33 (April 12, 1999): 26.
Knutson, Ted. "Vending machine operators try upscale for change." *Grand Rapids Business Journal* 16 (November 9, 1998): B3.
Krepela, Richard R. "How is Rich's doing?" *Vend* 17 (April 15, 1961): 40–43.
Krock, Arthur. "In the nation." *New York Times*, June 16, 1942, p. 22.
Krummert, Bob. "In b&i, lunch is the hour of power. *ID: The Voice of Foodservice Distribution* 33 (September, 1997): 35+.
Lanning, Rich. "Tike Miller's can-eating 'goat' pays for its supper and may gnaw on litterbugs." *People* 9 (March 13, 1978): 52.
Larson, Cedric. "Our growing robot army." *American Mercury* 78 (April, 1954): 113–115.
"Let them eat pellets." *Economist* 319 (May 4, 1991): 74.
"Lets cigaret sales up to vending machines." *Billboard*, October 29, 1938, p. 69.
Lewis, Len. "Robo retailing." *Progressive Grocer* 77 (April, 1998): 9.
"Lighter fluid vendor ready." *Billboard*, August 4, 1934, p. 62.
"Lights! Action! Roll 'Em!" *Time* 133 (June 19, 1989): 49.
"List of products." *Billboard*, March 17, 1934, p. 58.
Loehwing, David A. "Versatile vendors." *Barron's* 40 (April 11, 1960): 5–6.
"Long Island ends trial of ticket vending device." *New York Times*, September 23, 1949, p. 29.
"Looks for big gain in machine vending." *New York Times*, October 14, 1928, sec. 2, p. 20.
"Lotion vendors are new field." *Billboard*, November 4, 1933, p. 59.
"Louisville has new milk vendors." *Billboard*, January 8, 1938, p. 70.
Love, Thomas. "Pushing the envelope with vending machines." *Nation's Business* 86 (October, 1998): 10.
"A low-frying machine." *Maclean's* 48 (November 29, 1999): 14.
"Low purchasing power shown in decline of sales of candy." *Billboard*, April 8, 1933, p. 56.
"The machine age in vending." *Monetary Times* 121 (October, 1953): 22–27, 94–95.
"Machine as salesman." *Fortune* 35 (March, 1947): 116–121, 152, 154.
"Machine sells cigarettes." *New York Times*, April 4, 1928, p. 21.
"Machine to serve hot coffee shown." *New York Times*, September 25, 1947, p. 50.
"Machines in store?" *Montreal Gazette*, October 29, 1996, p. C5.
"Machines ready for dollar coin." *New York Times*, May 12, 1979, pp. 27, 30.
MacIntyre, John. "Figuratively speaking." *Across the Board* 36 (April, 1999): 13.
Malcolm, Andrew H. "In Japan, you can buy almost anything from a vending machine." *New York Times*, October 25, 1977, p. 2.
Manning, W. J. Jr. "Automatic selling." *Management Review* 49 (October, 1960): 14–22.
Marsh, Susan. "'Fill 'er up' now means car and customers, too." *New York Times*, January 4, 1970, sec. 10, p. 19.
Marshall, Jon. "City beautification plan irks Chicago papers." *Christian Science Monitor*, April 22, 1998, p. 3.
McDowell, Charles Jr. "Better living with machinery." *Reader's Digest* 97 (August, 1970): 113–114.
McGarry, William A. "Robot goes to work." *Saturday Evening Post* 201 (May 11, 1929): 54, 56.

McMahon, J. E. "Jingle of coins in pockets gains." *New York Times*, September 27, 1959, sec. 3, p. 14.
McMonagle, Eileen. "Issues and trends in soft drink vending." *Beverage Industry* 89 (August, 1998): 45.
McSwane, David Z. and William A. Oleckno. "Drinking water quality concerns and water vending machines." *Journal of Environmental Health* 56 (June, 1994): 71.
Mehrtens, George W. "Commerce report shows increase in exports of coin machines in '34." *Billboard*, March 16, 1935, p. 68.
Meier, Barry. "Cigarette vending machines debate is broadened." *New York Times*, August 15, 1995, p. D4.
"Michigan group offers strong appeal to operators in state." *Billboard*, February 25, 1933, pp. 64–65.
"Milk heralds new cig. vendor." *Billboard*, April 25, 1936, p. 82.
"Milk slot machines off streets." *New York Times*, September 30, 1954, p. 10.
"Milk vendors survey." *Billboard*, January 18, 1941, pp. 110–111.
"Mobile vending unit is success." *Billboard*, October 23, 1937, p. 78.
"Money in merchandisers, Robbins firm announces." *Billboard*, May 2, 1936, p. 78.
"More generous slot machines." *Times* (London), December 11, 1933, p. 13.
"More vending machines." *New York Times*, May 26, 1929, sec. 2, p. 8.
Morris, Malcolm L. "Growth parameters for automatic vending." *Journal of Retailing* 44 (Fall, 1968): 31–45.
Nack, Arthur E. "Federal men stop slugs." *Billboard*, July 19, 1941, p. 78.
Nagle, James. "Vending devices slake U.S. thirst." *New York Times*, June 21, 1959, sec. 3, pp. 1, 11.
"National Chamber of Trade." *Times* (London), October 2, 1928, p. 13.
"Netherlands has vendors." *Billboard*, September 30, 1939, p. 78.
"New advances seen in vending machines." *New York Times*, November 15, 1951, p. 47.
"New hand soap vendor ready." *Billboard*, March 7, 1936, p. 79.
"New license ordinance to recognize machine types." *Billboard*, January 20, 1934, p. 58.
"New slot machines to act as humans." *New York Times*, June 7, 1928, p. 32.
"New vendors widen field." *Billboard*, February 23, 1946, pp. 133, 139.
"New vistas opened for coin machine." *New York Times*, June 4, 1949, p. 24.
"New ways to sell." *Times* (London), July 6, 1959, p. 7.
"New York merchandiser mad." *Billboard*, April 11, 1936, p. 136.
Newman, Peter. "The five-cent piece is coming back." *Financial Post*, January 23, 1954, pp. 19–20.
"News in brief." *Billboard*, September 9, 1957, p. 96.
"News in brief." *Times* (London), May 23, 1929, p. 11.
"News in brief." *Times* (London), August 16, 1932, p. 7.
"News notes from the field of travel." *New York Times*, September 23, 1951, sec. 2, p. 19.
"Newspapers in slot machines." *Times* (London), June 27, 1933, p. 14.
"*Newsweek* comment on book vendors." *Billboard*, December 23, 1939, p. 64.
Nichols, Don. "Cigarette machine profits could go up in smoke." *Restaurant Business* 94 (October 10, 1995): 17+.
Nicholson, Joe. "Current and future models." *Editor & Publisher* 131 (March 28, 1998): 47.
"Nickel-in-the-slot gas meter." *Scientific American* 63 (December 6, 1890): 353.
"Nickel-in-the-slot hot water." *Scientific American* 63 (November 15, 1890): 313.
"Nickel paradise." *Business Week*, November 17, 1945, pp. 88–90.
"The 1941 war on slugs." *Billboard*, February 21, 1942, pp. 72–74.

"No experience necessary—but send money." *U.S. News & World Report* 119 (July 31, 1995): 13.

Nolan, Joseph. "Voice of the vendor." *New York Times*, October 17, 1954, p. 20.

"Northern business interview." *Northern New Jersey Business* 3 (September 6, 1995): 19.

"Now comes the automatic store for apartment house dwellers." *Business Week*, February 25, 1931, p. 9.

"Now: 'unmanned' supermarkets." *U.S. News & World Report* 79 (November 3, 1975): 90.

"Now you can buy peanuts in a bag." *Billboard*, March 4, 1939, p. 67.

"Now you can fly on pocket change." *Newsweek* 118 (October 7, 1991): 48.

"N. Y. subways move against slug passers." *Billboard*, January 21, 1956, p. 82.

"N. Y. World's Fair will have coin machine quota." *Billboard*, May 18, 1940, p. 66.

O'Brien, Timothy L. "Vending scams are on the rise, officials warn." *Wall Street Journal*, July 1, 1994, east. ed., pp. B1–B2.

Offen, Janet. "Every bottler experiences vandalism, supplier survey finds." *Beverage Industry* 1994/95 Special Issue Annual, p. 52+.

"Offers penny cig vendor." *Billboard*, May 9, 1946, p. 103.

Oldham, Christina N. "Office snackers still craving the not-so-fat-free food fare." *Business Press* 10 (May 2, 1997): 18+.

"$100,000,000 a year in coin vending machines." *Literary Digest* 116 (October 14, 1933): 32.

"Op succeeds with fortune machines." *Billboard*, May 1, 1937, p. 84.

"Operator wins in case." *Billboard*, December 31, 1932, p. 89.

"Ordinance is amended." *Billboard*, December 31, 1932, p. 89.

O'Shea, Peter. "Can selling be done by machinery?" *Magazine of Business*, November, 1928, pp. 517–519+.

"Pan introduces new vendor candy." *Billboard*, July 29, 1939, p. 82.

"Paper cup machine catches girl's hand." *New York Times*, July 23, 1947, p. 25.

"Paperback vending machine." *Library Journal* 87 (December 1, 1962): 4414–4415.

"Paperback vending machine demonstrated in New York." *Publishers Weekly* 181 (June 18, 1962): 38–39.

"Penn. store installs store-front vendor." *Billboard*, September 16, 1957, p. 90.

"Penny cigaret vendor has positive delivery." *Billboard*, December 10, 1932, p. 55.

"Penny cigaret vendors called novel devices." *Billboard*, February 8, 1936, p. 73.

"Penny ciggie vendor about ready for ops." *Billboard*, June 24, 1933, p. 56.

"Penny gumball in trouble." *New York Times*, January 5, 1975, p. 43.

"Penny-in-she-slot machines." *Times* (London), March 19, 1914, p. 4.

"Perfume vendor is launched in East." *Billboard*, April 9, 1938, p. 151.

"Pesos confuse coin machines." *New York Times*, March 18, 1985, p. 16.

Pesselnick, Jill. "Movie Music to place CD machine in lobbies." *Billboard*, February 19, 2000, p. 10+.

"Petite vendors prove useful for coverage." *Billboard*, June 30, 1934, p. 86.

Philips, Kent. "Statistical insights." *Beverage World* 117 (February, 1998): 126.

"Plans peak output in vending machine." *New York Times*, October 6, 1945, p. 20.

"Play mum on game earnings, urges vending authority." *Billboard*, September 17, 1932, p. 61.

"Poisons from automatic machines." *Times* (London), April 22, 1930, p. 14.

"Poisons from automatic machines." *Times* (London), June 27, 1930, p. 5.

"Pop dispensers investigated." *Billboard*, September 17, 1932, p. 59.

"Popcorn comeback credited to interest shown by vendor ops." *Billboard*, March 22, 1947, p. 98.

"Popcorn vendor changes." *Billboard*, July 30, 1932, p. 75.
"Postwar vendor operation in France hits comeback trail." *Billboard*, February 18, 1950, pp. 105, 109.
"Proper commission important to ops." *Billboard*, January 22, 1938, p. 91.
"Prospects for vending machines." *Billboard*, February 25, 1933, pp. 62–63.
"Public health reaches out to reduce tobacco use among teens." *Nation's Health* 25 (December, 1995): 7.
"Push-button lover." *Economist* 321 (November 16, 1991): 88.
Rabkin, William. "The European market." *Billboard*, July 27, 1935, pp. 82–83.
_____. "Market prospects in Holland." *Billboard*, August 3, 1935, p. 63.
"Random notes from Washington." *New York Times*, January 17, 1955, p. 16.
"Ranel announces pop-corn vendor." *Billboard*, October 30, 1937, p. 80.
"Rapid growth in use of vending machines to modernize restroom." *Billboard*, December 17, 1932, p. 57.
"Razor blades in limelight." *Billboard*, September 3, 1932, p. 62.
"Record mint production due to slot machines." *New York Times*, July 9, 1940, p. 15.
"Reddi-Wip testing peanut butter vending machines." *Advertising Age* 36 (February 8, 1965): 2.
"Restaurants: vended food." *National Petroleum News* 56 (February, 1964): 74–77.
"Restroom fee is protested." *Billboard*, June 3, 1933, p. 58.
"Restroom shows automatic trend." *Billboard*, November 23, 1935, p. 66.
"Result record brings operators flocking to Chicago association." *Billboard*, October 29, 1932, p. 54.
"Retail trade." *Time* 48 (December 16, 1946): 92, 94.
"Retailing." *Time* 84 (October 23, 1964): 100, 102.
"Reverse vending machines swallow aluminum cans." *The Futurist* 18 (February, 1984): 73.
Reves, H. F. "The locations speak." *Billboard*, December 29, 1934, p. 290.
_____. "Making money with vending machines." *Billboard*, June 26, 1937, p. 140.
_____. "A new era for coin machines." *Billboard*, January 20, 1940, p. 66h.
_____. "Vending machines in Detroit." *Billboard*, December 25, 1937, pp. 70–71.
_____. "Vending machines to the fore." *Billboard*, July 27, 1940, pp. 80–81.
Reves, Haviland F. "Basic machines in field of vending." *Billboard*, February 23, 1946, p. 138.
_____. "The vendor comes of age." *Billboard*, February 1, 1947, pp. 130–131.
"Reviewing the soda machine." *In Business* 18 (May/June, 1996): 9.
Revkin, Andrew C. "The coin go in, and the worms come out." *New York Times*, October 4, 1998, pp. 1, 46.
Robbins, Dave. "European observations." *Billboard*, September 30, 1939, p. 77.
_____. "Penny mdsr. profits." *Billboard*, September 4, 1937, p. 82.
"Robbins gives reasons for using the vendors." *Billboard*, January 30, 1937, p. 65.
"Robot selling gets its first big test." *Business Week*, May 27, 1950, pp. 70–71, 73.
"Robots to mimic actors." *New York Times*, June 12, 1928, sec. 2, p. 9.
Rosenblum, Trudi Miller. "Vending machines offer audiobooks." *Billboard*, October 7, 1995, p. 85.
Roth, Daniel. "Press B-1 for Macanudo." *Forbes* 159 (May 9, 1997): 74+.
"Rowlette recounts Popmatic's history." *Billboard*, March 12, 1938, p. 78.
Rozen, Skip. "Duel with a devil." *Reader's Digest* 109 (November, 1976): 15–16.
Ryan, James. "In vending machines, brains that tell good money from bad." *New York Times*, April 8, 1999, p. G13.
"Sales robot makes change; rejects slugs." *Business Week*, October 29, 1930, p. 16.

"San Francisco operators fighting proposed tax." *Billboard*, July 30, 1932, p. 74.
Satoro, Elaine. "USPS shuts down Postal Buddies." *Direct Marketing* 56 (November, 1993): 15.
Scaglione, Fred. "Water Point Systems: water, water everywhere." *Equities* 42 (July, 1994): 27+.
Schaffer, Athena. "Fairs hope beverage vending machines, sponsorship deals will bolster profits." *Amusement Business* 112 (May 22, 2000): 35.
Scherer, Karyn. "Alcohol vending machines put to test." *New Zealand Herald*, February 1, 2001.
Schmidt, Kathleen. "News roundup." *Marekting News* 33 (November 22, 1999): 3.
Schmidt, William E. "Little Rock fights dream of a soda machine in every yard." *New York Times*, September 4, 1986, p. 12.
"School vending machines assailed for 'junk food.'" *New York Times*, April 18, 1973, p. 12.
Schreiber, G. R. *A Concise History of Vending in the U.S.A.* Chicago: Vend, 1961.
_____. "What's the trend in operating profits." *Vend* 17 (October 15, 1961): 27–29.
Schroeder, Ken. "Make the fizz fizzle." *Education Digest* 64 (February 1999): 77.
Scott, David Clark." Skivvies on parade." *Christian Science Monitor*, October 31, 1998, p. 54+.
Scuka, Daniel. "Veni, vedi, vended..." *Jap@n Inc* 3 (January, 2001): 30+.
"Seed capitalist." *Canadian Business* 70 (June, 1997): 228.
"Seeks to enjoin police." *New York Times*, April 23, 1933, p. 5.
"Sees $10 billion vend sales by '67." *Billboard*, February 16, 1957, p. 80.
"Sell 'em sandwiches." *Billboard*, September 3, 1932, p. 62.
"Selling by machine." *New York Times*, March 8, 1953, sec. 3, p. 10.
"Seminole schools appeal to state." *FoodService Director* 11 (April 15, 1998): 8.
Sfiligoj, Eric. "Good news comes in threes." *Beverage World* 115 (February, 1996): 58, 60, 62.
Shalett, Sidney M. "Slot-machine age." *New York Times Magazine*, November 2, 1941, p. 30.
Shannon, Caitlin. "Coin-operated restaurants." *Christian Science Monitor*, June 25, 1998, p. 9.
Sharnik, John. "Coin-in-the-slot." *New York Times Magazine*, December 3, 1950, pp. 58, 60.
Sherborne, Pam. "Vending machines pose competitive threat." *Amusement Business* 112 (March 13, 2000): 29.
"Signs bill against slug making." *New York Times*, April 4, 1944, p. 23.
Silberman, Albert A. "Future of parking meters seems definitely assured." *Billboard*, August 1, 1936, p. 73.
Silver, Leon. "Penny vendors on the West Coast." *Billboard*, February 28, 1942, p. 69.
Silver Sam. "The coin chute." *Billboard*, November 26, 1932, pp. 60–61.
_____. "The coin chute." *Billboard*, May 6, 1933, p. 62.
_____. "Coin operated amusement machines." *Billboard*, March 19, 1932, pp. 58, 61.
_____. "Coin operated amusement machines." *Billboard*, April 9, 1932, p. 59.
_____. "Coin operated amusement machines." *Billboard*, April 16, 1932, p. 70.
_____. "Coin operated amusement machines." *Billboard*, April 23, 1932, pp. 66–68, 70.
_____. "Coin operated amusement machines." *Billboard*, April 30, 1932, p. 74.
_____. "Coin operated amusement machines." *Billboard*, May 28, 1932, p. 71.
_____. "Coin operated amusement machines." *Billboard*, June 11, 1932, p. 102.
_____. "The first operators' code." *Billboard*, November 4, 1933, pp. 62–63.
_____. "Public relations policies for coin machine operators." *Billboard*, May 23, 1936, p. 68.

_____. "Those slower nickels." *Billboard*, August 15, 1936, p. 66.
_____. "What type machines are best if theater concessions are available." *Billboard*, July 7, 1934, p. 67.
Silver, Sheldon. "Big bottle vending." *FoodService Director* 11 (October 15, 1998): 176.
_____. "Helps turn sales around: branded coffee." *FoodService Director* 12 (October 15, 1999): 156.
_____. "New machines, specialty items promote: ice cream vending." *FoodService Director* 12 (May 15, 1999): 178.
"'67 vending sales will exceed $4.5 billion: McGuire." *Advertising Age* 38 (November 13, 1967): 42.
"Slot-machine trust." *New York Times*, April 2, 1911, pt. 9, p. 12.
"Slot machines amass riches from pennies." *New York Times*, November 13, 1927, pt. 10. p. 2.
"Slot machines sell abroad." *New York Times*, April 26, 1938, p. 28.
"Slug problem grows in Pitts plant stop." *Billboard*, May 30, 1953, p. 78.
"Slugs a pinball menace." *Billboard*, June 29, 1935, p. 106.
"Slugs in slots going to defense." *New York Times*, June 7, 1941, p. 8.
"Slugs pose mounting problem." *New York Times*, January 2, 1971, p. 19.
"Smoking regs." *ABA Journal* 80 (June, 1994): 67.
Snyder, Eric. "Spanked by the invisible hand." *Inside Tucson Business* 9 (November 1, 1999): 4.
"Soda machine kills youth." *New York Times*, September 15, 1987, p. 16.
"Soda sales OK in Denver schools." *FoodService Director* 11 (October 15, 1998): 1.
"Sohio-Stouffer: end of an experiment." *National Petroleum News* 55 (November, 1963): 82.
"Sparkling water given try in vendor at Philly plant." *Billboard*, February 2, 1946, p. 94.
"Speedy Weeny, electron-cooked hot dog vendor." *Billboard*, March 9, 1946, p. 97.
Spethmann, Betsy. "Nabisco's SnackWell's go vending." *Brandweek* 35 (November 14, 1994): 4.
"Splitting the take from the vending area." *Management Review* 70 (June, 1981): 40.
"Sponsored phone cards, CD vending machines, a punk compilation." *Billboard*, August 7, 1999, p. APQ-4.
Spooner, C. S. "Managing a merchandising route." *Billboard*, September 7, 1935, pp. 66–67.
"Springfield bus vendors gain favor." *Billboard*, March 27, 1954, pp. 78, 86.
"Stable cigaret prices in help to vendors." *Billboard*, March 24, 1934, p. 62.
"Standards of commission." *Billboard*, July 14, 1934, p. 58.
Stein, Charles S. "The phenomenon of automatic merchandising." *Journal of Retailing* 40 (Spring, 1964): 15–19+.
Steinberg, Jack. "What's new in vending machines." *New York Times*, October 8, 1989, sec. 3, p. 17.
"Sterling future for coin-op machines." *Advertising Age* 70 (May 31, 1999): 75.
Sternfield, Aaron. "In-office vending." *Billboard*, July 4, 1953, pp. 89–90.
_____. "Major grocery chains plan full-scale vending ventures." *Billboard*, November 10, 1956, pp. 159, 165, 167.
Sterngold, James. "Why the Japanese adore vending machines." *New York Times*, January 5, 1992, pp. 1, 12.
"Student dies under soft-drink machine." *Montreal Gazette*, December 14, 1998, p. A3.
"Study of vending needed." *Billboard*, January 26, 1946, p. 90.
"Subway advertising upheld." *New York Times*, December 11, 1906, p. 7.
"Subway to vend shoe shines." *New York Times*, January 30, 1949, p. 27.

"Sues on slug claims." *Billboard*, December 31, 1932, p. 89.
"Sugar-coated Soviet line at 1c sours police fast." *New York Times*, January 13, 1952, p. 9.
"Supreme Court OKs rack regulation." *Editor & Publisher* 128 (November 18, 1995): 44.
"Survey reveals 32 per cent of theaters using vendors." *Billboard*, February 25, 1950, p. 100.
Tagliabue, John. "Vending machines face an upheaval of change." *New York Times*, February 16, 1999, p. C4.
"Takes national sales on selective vendor." *Billboard*, October 1, 1932, p. 60.
"Talk soap vendors in new move to modernize rooms." *Billboard*, April 1, 1933, p. 61.
Tanzer, Andrew. "War of the sales robots." *Forbes* 147 (January 7, 1991): 294+.
Taylor, Porter V. "Vending in Russia." *Beverage World* 97 (November, 1978): 170.
Teague, David C. "Vending machines." *Billboard*, February 24, 1940, pp. 66–67.
"Temptation of automatic machines." *Times* (London), September 6, 1926, p. 9.
"Test orange juice vendors." *Billboard*, November 4, 1939, p. 64.
"TGIF: Thank God, it's fried." *Business NH Magazine* 7 (February, 19990): 11.
"Thefts from automatic machines." *Times* (London), October 12, 1931, p. 7.
"'Third evolution' seen in vending machines." *New York Times*, September 22, 1968, sec. 3, p. 17.
"30 per cent by club." *Billboard*, October 15, 1932, p. 56.
Thornton, Emily. "Japan's new cupid: vending machines." *Fortune* 125 (April 6, 1992): 13.
"3,500,000,000 pennies a year dropped in vending machines." *New York Times*, January 18, 1928, p. 1.
"3 billion sales due by vending machine." *New York Times*, October 18, 1946, p. 35.
Tillery, Risdon. "Insert coin here." *Reader's Digest* 61 (September, 1952): 91–92.
"To cook hot dogs with radio waves." *New York Times*, December 24, 1945, p. 12.
"To offer an extensive line of medical and sanitary products." *Billboard*, August 20, 1932, p. 64.
"To test stamp machines." *New York Times*, March 13, 1908, p. 4.
"Tobacco control laws vary nationwide." *H&HN: Hospitals & Health Networks* 69 (November 20, 1995): 17.
"Tobacco Record decides to stop drive against cigaret machines." *Billboard*, February 19, 1938, p. 81.
"Tobacco vending machines." *FDA Consumer* 30 (April, 1996): 27.
"Today's models: a new breed of 'self promoters.'" *FoodService Director* 10 (July 15, 1997): Sup. 2S+.
"Too busy to talk." *Business Week*, March 13, 1943, pp. 72, 74.
"Topics." *New York Times*, November 26, 1960, p. 20.
"Tribute to coin machines in magazine published by Eagles." *Billboard*, January 20, 1940, p. 68.
"Tryout." *The New Yorker* 27 (November 10, 1951): 29–30.
"A twenty-four hour automatic market." *Scientific American* 144 (May, 1931): 325.
"2,000 packets of sweetmeats stolen." *Times* (London), August 9, 1915, p. 10.
"UK bottom in machine sales." *Tobacco Europe*, March/April, 1998, p. 2.
Ullendorff, Hans. "Coin machines in Europe." *Billboard*, March 5, 1938, pp. 80–81.
"Unacceptable lace of capitalism." *Economist* 329 (October 9, 1993): 76.
"U-Select-It shows two new vendors." *Billboard*, December 17, 1938, p. 70.
Vallie, Leslie. "Soda contracts dispense liquid revenue for schools." *Government Procurement* 7 (August, 1999): 16+.
"Vended sales of hot foods, non-foods soar." *Advertising Age* 32 (November 13, 1961): 6, 161.

"Vendor profits are discussed." *Billboard*, December 14, 1935, p. 74.
"Vendors greet Chicagoans at 12 new subway stations." *Billboard*, March 3, 1951, pp. 64, 66.
"Vendors gross record $1.5 billion in 1953." *Billboard*, January 30, 1954, pp. 71, 80.
"Vendors win approval." *Billboard*, January 21, 1933, p. 57.
"Vending flunks the entrance exam." *Business Week*, February 10, 1968, pp. 91–92, 94.
"Vending group acts." *New York Times*, January 18, 1964, p. 9.
"Vending hits the jackpot." *Iron Age* 187 (June 29, 1961): 40–41.
"Vending jumps 25% at Cleveland St." *FoodService Director* 12 (February 15, 1999): 1.
"Vending machine and rack sale schemes." *Changing Times* 33 (August, 1979): 45–47.
"Vending machine drive-in forecasts new food retailing technique." *Progressive Grocer* 40 (June, 1961): 58–61, 145.
"Vending machine firms unite in plea against Massachusetts law." *Billboard*, February 19, 1938, p. 80.
"Vending machine 'hot' as seller." *New York Times*, January 6, 1958, p. 72.
"Vending machine in rising demand." *New York Times*, November 8, 1948, p. 33.
"Vending machine kills youth." *New York Times*, May 9, 1989, p. A20.
"Vending machine statistics." *Billboard*, January 31, 1942, p. 93.
"Vending machine suit up." *New York Times*, April 27, 1933, p. 8.
"Vending machines." *New York Times*, November 1, 1953, sec. 3, p. 8.
"Vending machines in Britain." *Foreign Trade* 131 (June 7, 1969): 29–30.
"Vending machines learning to talk." *New York Times*, January 3, 1955, p. 101.
"Vending machines to compete with restaurants." *The Futurist* 26 (September-October, 1992): 8.
"Vending picks up." *Business Week*, November 16, 1946, pp. 57, 60.
"Vending service for readers." *Library Journal* 89 (October 1, 1964): 3723.
"Vending unit sales slide with economy." *New York Times*, August 18, 1980, p. D4.
"Vendo tests first coin-operated grocery-snack shop drive-in in K. C." *Advertising Age* 31 (December 19, 1960): 4.
"Vendor machines boon to airfields." *New York Times*, March 30, 1949, p. 37.
"Vendors outgrow machines." *Business Week*, October 10, 1964, pp. 136. 138, 140.
"Vendors pull out all stops." *Business Week*, August 15, 1970, pp. 52, 54.
"Vends match with cigaret." *Billboard*, July 15, 1933, p. 54.
"Vends nuts in sanitary bag." *Billboard*, May 19, 1934, p. 58.
"A video pause that refreshes." *Newsweek* 100 (November 22, 1982): 106.
"Vigorous debate on rates and merchandising ethics." *Billboard*, October 27, 1934, p. 62.
"Waifs 'beat' slot machines." *New York Times*, April 30, 1927, p. 5.
"Walgreen orders 300 Airpops-It." *Billboard*, July 23, 1938, p. 78.
"Washing machine field overcrowded." *Billboard*, March 12, 1938, p. 78.
Weiss, E. B. "The vending machine era now begins." *Advertising Age* 31 (June 13, 1960): 96.
_____. "Vending machines to get into higher price lines." *Advertising Age* 29 (December 29, 1958): 32.
Wertheimer, Henry N. "Cigaret operators should seek full return on machine costs." *Billboard*, November 27, 1937, pp. 144–145.
"West Coast cigaret vendors have code." *Billboard*, September 22, 1933, p. 59.
Wharton, Don. "They hit the coffee jackpot." *Reader's Digest* 52 (April, 1948): 127–128.
"Where vending machines fall short." *Billboard*, February 21, 1953, p. 154.
Whitford, David. "Entrepreneur aims to make change in vending machines." *Inc* 19 (February, 1997): 17.
"Wider use seen for coin machine." *New York Times*, January 8, 1948, p. 42.

"Widespread use of Coca-Cola vendor." *Billboard*, March 5, 1938, p. 78.

Willatt, Norris. "Robot salesmen." *Barron's* 38 (August 4, 1958): 11, 13.

Wilson, Jim and Fred Chesbro. "Vending humidors debut." *Popular Mechanics* 174 (May, 1997): 37.

Wolson, Shelley. "Brands lift prices, profits." *FoodService Director* 10 (December 15, 1997): 164.

_____. "In college vending: 'Special contracts' shift operating, sales balance." *FoodService Director* 10 (September 15, 1997): 212.

_____. "Location, location, location." *FoodService Director* 10 (November 15, 1997): 180.

_____. "Promotional techniques: pushing bigger buys." *FoodService Director* 13 (November 15, 2000): 150.

_____. "Remote technology gaining acceptance: 'smart machines.'" *FoodService Director* 13 (August 15, 2000): 136.

Wolson, Shelley. "Specialty drinks set the pace: hot beverages." *FoodService Director* 10 (October 15, 1997): 196.

"Women's patronage will help scales in summer." *Billboard*, May 22, 1937, p. 86.

"The working of penny-in-the-slot machines." *Times* (London), April 23, 1914, p. 3.

"World's Fair gives test for variety of machines." *Billboard*, September 22, 1934, p. 60.

"World's Fair has big week." *Billboard*, June 10, 1933, p. 80.

"World's Fair restrooms are using coin machines." *Billboard*, April 8, 1933, p. 56.

"Worms, vending machines and vermiculture." *In Business* 20 (September/October, 1998): 12.

Wright, Milton. "Robots for salesmen." *Scientific American* 140 (January, 1929): 24–26.

Wu, Corinna. "The buck starts here." *Science News* 157 (April 1, 2000): 216.

"You now can dial a railroad ticket." *New York Times*, September 1, 1949, p. 44.

Young, Stephanie. "Healthy eating in a hurry." *Redbook* 194 (March, 2000): 48+.

"Zap! Smok! Crunch!" *Forbes* 131 (January 3, 1983): 188.

Index

Adams, Thomas 7
advertising, national 30
advertising on 97–98, 197–198, 201
Aikman, Troy 197–198
air, for tires 175
airports 132, 159
alcoholic beverages 10, 202–203, 221–222
Alexander, Harry 49, 50
Allen, Roy 209
American Chicle 18, 133, 150–151
American Medical Association 171
American Scale Manufacturing Company 147
American Tobacco 51
amusement games 45, 80, 81, 95
Andrews, Arch 7–8, 37–39
anti-trust violations 164–165
apartment buildings 35–36, 84, 128, 143
apples 68–69
Arens, Egmont 140
Arnett, Leslie 63–64
aspirin 72
Atlanta, Georgia 229
audiobooks 212
Austin, J. H. 89
Austin, Minnesota 143
Automatic Merchandisers Association 43
automats 13
Autosales Gum and Chocolate Company 17–18
Avon Publishing 145
Aylsworth, George A. 70

Babson, Roger 33
bait, live (fishing) 175, 213
Bakala, Dick 205
Baker, C. E. 152
Baltimore 112

bans 56–57, 194–195
Barreras, Frank F. 149–150
Barrymore, John 84
bars 123
Bartfield, William 207
Bartholomew, Daniel 213
Bates, Sandy 205
Beal, Louis 90
beer 10
beer gardens 55
Belgium 101–102
Bell, Amy 212
Bell, Stoughton 94–95
Bello, Abraham 55
Benfield, James C. 225
Benson, Ezra 144
Berger, Meyer 150–151
Bernard, Tom 139–140
Better Business Bureau (New York City) 166
Biebelberg, Keith 195
Biertuempfel, F. Edward 144
bill changer 167–168, 225
Bitzer, Steve 205
Blake, Kathy 201
Blandford, Francis 42
blood pressure tester 79
Bloom, Jackson 57–58
Bloomington, Indiana 183–184
Boeing company 142
Bolen, W. E. 89
Bolger, Pete 211
Bond, David 93
books 5, 11, 39–40, 71, 129–130, 145–146, 173
Bowen, Oti R. 184
Bowling, Otto S. 43
Bowman, W. W. 64

277

Bozynski, Tony 229
brand names 98
branded coffee 200–201
branded merchandise 188, 226
Brinkmann, Charles 152
Bromberg, Bernice 210
Brooks Contracting 79
Brown, Sandford 43, 161
Bryan, Jake 201
Brylcream 149
Buckholz, Bill 207
bulk units 50, 59–60, 89, 93–94
bulk units, sanitary 60
Burge, Frank 182
Burke, William 145
bus terminal 158
buses, city 22, 152
Bush, Jeb 217
Business Week 35–37, 119–120, 142, 182

California Cigaret Vending Operators' Association 54
Callahan, Miles 102
Canada 163
Canada Dry 204
candy 8, 16, 38, 60–62, 86–87, 125–126, 142; popular types 62; sales 125–126; undersized 62
Canteen (company) 41, 60–61, 86, 97–98, 126, 164–165, 180, 188, 200, 228
Capaldi, Jack 101
carbonation 64
Carlile, Richard 5
cashews 59
cashless systems 215
CDs (music) 210–211
cell phone, to use VM 232
Center for Commercial Free Public Education 219
Center for Science in the Public Interest 219
Centers for Disease Control 195
chain stores 27
change, attached 32, 110
change-making abilities 32, 135, 136, 138
Chase, Brandon 210
Chicago Better Business Bureau 56–57
Chicago City Council 212
Chicago Fair 1933–1934, 79–81
Chicago Transit Authority 151
China 4, 222
cigarette machines, talking 24, 27
cigarettes 23–24, 27, 53–58, 122–125, 141–142, 171–172, 194–196, 221; single item units 50–53

cigars 11, 196–197
City Milk Company 127–128, 143
Clayton, David 192, 225
Clegg, R. I. 20
clerks: female 81, 82; retail 28–29, 30–31, 45, 98
Clinton, Bill 194–196
Coan, J. W. 61–62
Coca-Cola 62, 111, 126, 172, 197–199, 217–220
coffee 127–128, 142, 200–201
coffee breaks 142
Cohen, Paul 136
coins: composition 114–115; dollar 188, 225–226; foreign 42, 104, 188; not returned 138, 151; testing of 116
Colen, Louis A. 73–74, 75
Colonial Oil 180
Colorado Springs School District #11 217
Comer, Linda 214–215
commissions 54, 84, 88, 89, 95–97, 123, 150–151
Communist propaganda 167
Compton, Randy 197–198
computerization 192–194
Consolidated Automatic Merchandising Corporation (CAMCO) 25–28, 46
contracts, exclusive 217–220
Cook, Victor 104
Coral Gables, Florida 211
Cornell University 220
Costa, Nic 20
Costanzo, Andy 205
counterfeiting 116–117
Couron, Russ 215
Covington, Wayne 208–209
credit cards 197, 209–210
Crook, George 93, 107
Crowell-Collier Publishing 147
Ctesibius (Tesibius) 3–4
Cummings, Nathan 122
Cunningham Drug Store 35
Currie, Chuck 199
Curtis Publishing 146–147
Curtiss, Robert S. 132

Daley, Richard 212
Dalfen, Arthur 207–208
Dalrymple, Douglas 185
D'Amato, Alfonse 175
D'Angelo, Antoinette 138
D'Angelo, Armand 189
Davis, Drew 216
Davis, Morris 54–55

Davis, William Howe 149
death and injury from 44–45, 229
debit cards 194
De Frece, Walter 44
Delamat 36–37
demographics 220
Denham, Simeon 5
density of 91–92
department stores 24, 29, 34, 59, 157–158, 176–178
Derlot, Francois 104
DeRose, Dan 218
Detroit Retail Druggists' Association 72
De Vere Novelty Company 117
Dewey, Charles S. 115
Dewey, Thomas 144
Diamond, Maurice 146
Diebold company 210
Dineen, Tim 200
Distribution of goods 33–34
distrust of, public 33
divorce papers 11
Dixie Cup Company 12–13
Dr. Pepper (soft drink) 112
Dohrman, Kent 194
Douglas, A. S. 66
Doyle, John 90
drug stores 83
drugs 40
dry cleaning 172–173
Dutton, William 11

The Economist 156–157
Edwards, J. 131
Egypt, ancient 3
Eldredge, Kit 193
electric VMs 125
electricity, usage of 189, 224–225, 231
Elliott, James R. 216
employees, effects on 28–29
Europe 11, 100–102, 110, 163–164, 221
Everitt, Percival 6
exports of 99, 137, 163
Faber, E. H. 78
fairs 214–215
Farmer, Jean 183–184
Federal Trade Commission (FTC) 164–165, 230
Ferguson, Jim 201
Ferraro, Carl 195
Fetty, Bill 206
Filene's (dept. store) 158–159
fire hazards 67, 207–209
Flint, Charles R. 18

Flint, Michigan 104
Florida Citrus Exchange 68
food: healthy 204–206; heated 130–131, 170–171
Food and Drug Administration (FDA) 195
foot massager 74
Ford, Delores 216
fortune cards 25
fortune telling 75
France 8–9, 100, 101, 163
Franco-Swiss Chocolate Company 14
frauds 43–44, 166–167, 188, 229–230
Free Library of Philadelphia 175
French fries 206–209
Friedman, Steven 196–197
Fruen, W. H. 6

Gagliardi, Tony 228
gambling machines 20, 135
gasoline 9, 16; pumps 173–174; stations 170, 173–174, 180
General Electric 74, 130, 181
General Metal Products 53
Germany 164, 186
Gersh, William 82
Glover, Samuel 104
Goldman, Hymen 23
Goldsmith, Charles W. 11
Goodwin, Tom 205
Gottfried, John 137
Granat, A. 26–27, 31
Grand Union supermarkets 155–156
Greene, Robert 23, 123, 135, 155, 161
gum: ball 166–167, 176; chewing 7, 19, 38, 90, 151, 152
Gummersheimer, Walter 66

Haines, Frederick 41
hair oil 149
Haldeman–Julius, E. 71
Hall, Trish 192
Hammond, Stephen 44–45
handkerchiefs 34
Hansol Telecom 211
Hardart, Paul 13
Harvard International Technologies 207–208
Hasegawa, Paul 224
Hays, Constance 218
health concerns 154, 171–172, 183–184, 194–195, 216–217
Hecht, Andrew 4, 143
Hedstrom, Lars 72
Helms Vending Machine company 52–53

Hempstead, Long Island 175
Herman, N. H. 101
Hero (Heron) 3–4
Hershey chocolate 39, 61, 188
Hicks, Jonathan 191
Hill, Lister 117
Hirsch, J. H. 16, 92
Hoffman, Lawrence 147–148
homeowners, siting of VMs in yards 228–229
honor boxes 4–5
Hope, Mark 204
Horn, Joseph 13
horoscopes 75
hospitals 171, 215
hot dogs 130–131
hotels 90
hours, retail 44
J. L. Hudson (dept. store) 157–158
Hull, H. H. 67
Humphrey, William 154
Humphreys, John R. 143
Hurd, Walter 45–46, 49–50, 93, 106–107, 111, 115–116, 121

ice blocks 39
ice cream 69–70, 201–202
industrial plants 73, 85–87, 113, 131, 152–154, 181–182, 214
insurance, travel 109
Interborough Rapid Transit 15
Iron Age 169

J. P. Manning Company 124
Jackson, Milton 229
Jackson, Robert H. 17
Jacobsen, Michael 218
Japan 186–187, 222–225
Jensen, George R. 202–203
Joe Boxer Corporation 212
Johnson, Charles O. 84
joke dispenser 175
Jones, Christopher 229
Jones, Glyn 40
Jones, Herb 112
juice: canned 68; fruit 67–68, 144–145; orange, fresh 128
jukeboxes 48

Kaiser, Edgar 207–208
Kansas City, Missouri 103, 179
Karam, Joe 221–222
Keedoozle 85
Kinchen, Ezekiel Jr. 229

King, Brian 227
Klein, Joseph 105
Klembala, Chuck 204–205
Knight, Ed 105
Kohlepp, Ray 197–198
Kraus, Rudy 197
Kresberg, Sam 126–127
Krock, Arthur 115
Krouse, Morton 138
Kunkle, Charles 206
Kurosaki, Takashi 224

labor shortages 22
Land O'Lakes Creamery 143
Larson, Cedric 153, 160
Laundromats 72, 129
Lawson, Steve 200
Leahy, Patrick J. 215–216
legislation 117, 211–212
legitimizing effect 92–93
Leonas, Vladas 222
Leoni, P. 10
Leverone, Nathaniel 41, 60–61, 81, 86, 95, 104, 181
Levin, Richard 208
Libman, Jeffrey 209
Life (magazine) 146–147
lighter fluid 15, 74
lipstick 76
Little Rock, Arkansas 228–229
live feeding (of employees) 181, 184–185
locations 50, 89–91, 97, 105, 112, 121, 149–150; chain 25; for cigarettes 55; high-class 57–58; owning VMs 215, 217; selection 213–214, 230–231; weigh scales 59
locator (occupation) 149–150
Loehwing, David 181
Loft Candy Shop 155
Logan International Airport 159
Lombardi, Anthony 117
London (UK) 99–100
lotion, hand 79
low fat products 205–206
Lowry, Don 200
Luden, Emil 15
Lunch-O-Mat Corporation 159–160
Lyday, L. S. 58–59
Lynde, Frederick C. 6

machine age 28
Macke, Gordon 23
Mackle, Kevin 229
Macy's 176–177

Index

magazines 29–30, 39–40, 70–71, 146–147
Manning, W. J. 170
Marcus, Stanley 192
market for, limited 98, 107, 159, 185, 190, 231
Martin, F. R. 105
Martin, James E. 12
Martin, Josephine 183
matches 55
matchmaking unit 164
McAllister, Brad 213
McClintic, Glenn 175
McGarry, William 32–34
McGinnis of Sheepshead Bay 57–58
McKillips, Jim 206
McKinney, T. Burke 224
McMonagle, Eileen 198
meals: complete 181; hot 162, 202
mechanization 33–34
media attention 24–39, 97, 109, 160–161, 188–189
medical items 77
Medical Products Sales Company 77
Melikian, Cy 127
mergers 17–18, 25–26, 33
Michaels, Peter 196–197
Midol tablets 77
milk 70, 112–113, 127–128, 142–144; surplus 144
Miller, Tike 176
Millman, Carl 184
Mills, Bert E. 14, 127
Mills Novelty company 48
Milo, John 11
minors, access by 56–57, 171–172, 195–196
Minute Maid 14–145
mirrors 12
Moloney, Alan 220
Montgomery Ward 177
Moroney, Pat 214
Morris, Malcolm 189–190
Morton Salt 97
Moscow 42
Movie Music 211
Muller, Robert 191
multi-product units 11, 22–23, 35–36, 159–160
Mutual Life Insurance 142

napkins, sanitary 15
Narita, Tokinobu 223
National Automatic Merchandising Association (NAMA) 95–96, 103, 135, 171, 184–185, 203–204
National Chamber of Trade 44
National Dairy Council 112–113
National Dairy Milk Producers Federation 144
National School Lunch Act 182–183
National Slug Rejectors 137
National Soft Drink Association 216
Nelson, James 166–167
Nestle USA 201
Netherlands 100–101
New York City World's Fair 1939–1940, 87–88, 113
New York Telephone Co. 181
newspapers 29–30, 71, 147, 211–212
Nobler, Robert 192

ocean liners 39
offices 154, 181–182, 214
Ogara, John 208
Ogren, Carroll 171
Olympic Games, Winter, 1960, 170
opera glasses 16
operating firms 14, 22
opposition to 143–144, 182–184, 214–215, 216–217, 220
optimism, for industry 108–109, 139–140, 169–170, 191–192
Oregon State Fair 214
Ore-Ida Foods 208–209
organization, of industry 102–103
Oriental Refining 173
O'Shea, Peter 30–32
oxygen dispensers 149

packaging, standardized 30, 171
Paper Cup and Container Institute 152, 154
Paramount Theater (Times Square) 82
Paris 8–9
parking meters 73
Parry, L. Moreton 40
patents 5–6
peanut butter 172
peanuts 12, 38, 59; stale 91
Pemberton-Billings, Noel 39
pencils 4, 99
Penno, Mark 215
Pennsylvania Railroad 151–152
penny machines 19, 176
Pepsi-Cola 129, 170, 199, 217–218
perfume 10, 72–73, 147–148
Peterson, Wayne 214
Pharmaceutical Society of Great Britain 40
Phillips, Kent 198

photographs 8
Pierson, Elmer F. 170
pinball 47–48, 92, 106
Pinkerton Detective Agency 75
pistachios 59
pizza 222
Plagge, Gretchen 183
Pocket Books 129–130
popcorn 64–67, 131–132, 202
pornographic magazines 187
postage metering units 109–110
postage stamps 5–6, 11, 14, 25–26, 32
Postal Buddy 213
predictions 34, 45–46, 108, 119–121, 139–140, 160–161, 169–170, 178, 192
Preston, Joseph 196–197
prevalence of 9–10, 109
price increases, due to weather 199
pricing experiments 206
pricing, of product 94
Printers' Ink 161
products available 20, 32–33, 49, 110, 136, 139; Europe 100–101
profitability 48, 94–95, 120, 124
promotions 61, 97–98, 226–228
prophylactics 72, 77, 174, 222
public acceptance of 93
public relations 97
Pulver Company 11–12

Quick (magazine) 146

Rabkin, William 100
rail stations, city 83
railroads 133–134, 151–152; stations 7, 8
Railway Express Agency 78
razor blades 72
Reader's Digest 146
Real Time Data company 193
receipts: cigarettes 55; industry 29, 49, 88, 121
recycling 176
Redbook 206
Reddi-Wip 172
refrigeration 37, 69–70, 111, 201–202
Reiss, Lawrence Mrs. 159–160
restaurants 55
retailers, opposition to 44–45, 115–116, 143
reverse machines 176
Reves, H. F. 70–71, 89–90, 108
Reynolds, Tom 226
Rich's (dept. store) 177–178
Robbins, Dave 93, 101–102
robots 30, 32

Rock-ola company 75
Roosevelt, Franklin D. 117
Root, William D. 64–65
Ross, Nellie 114
Rost, James 225
Roth, C. A 51–52
route servicing 192–193, 232
Rowe, William H. 23
Rowe Manufacturing 122–123, 141–142
Rowlette, V. H. 66
Rubenstein, Charles 165
Rudd, Lloyd 127
Russell, Charles H. 6
Russia 186, 222

Sack, A. J. 25–26
St. Louis 154
sales, direct to locations 98–99, 124–125
sales tax 104
salesmanship 28, 31
San Francisco 103
sandwiches 67
Sanford, Tim 192
Sanitary Automatic Candy Company 83
sanitation concerns 12
Saunders, Clarence 85
Savage, Kent 231
Schermack, Joseph J. 25–26
Schnapp, Solomon 165
school lunch programs 216–217
schools 154, 182–184, 215–220
Schosberg, Max 82
Schrafft's restaurants 142
Schreiber, G. R. 18, 98, 110
Schulman, I. W. 77
Schuster, Frederick L. 178
science, belief in 28
scientific management 30
Scott, Kenny 229
Sears Roebuck 77
Seedman, George 117
selective units 41, 61, 93
self service 121
Sen-Sen Chiclet Company 18
Serva, Gene 176
service stations 89
Shalett, Sidney 4, 110
Sharnik, John 142, 144, 166
Shell Oil 180
shoe shine 74–75, 130
Shoemaker, C. A. 55
shopping 98, 190
shopping centers 154
Sideman, Abner 146

Index

Silberman, Albert 73
Silver, Leon 113
Silver, Sheldon 194–195, 201–202
slot machine (derogatory term) 20, 152
slot machines 47–48
slug proof 105
slugs 4, 7, 12, 18–19, 41–43, 82, 91, 104–106, 116–117, 137, 165–166, 187–188; ice 105; laws 43
smart cards 194
snack bars 170
SnackWell 204–205
snuff 4
Snyder, Eric 199
soap 73, 78
Sodamats 35
soft drinks 14, 62–64, 111–112, 126–127, 142, 172, 197–199; consumption of 218
Spooner, C. S. 90–91
Springfield, Ohio 152
Standard of Ohio 180
Stankewich, Beth 227–228
stationery 11, 174–175; postal 213
statistics, industry 92, 114, 134–136, 161–163, 185, 221
Stember, Jack 90
Sternfield, Aaron 154
Sterngold, James 223–224
Stevens, John S. 68
Stevenson, Bruce 229
Stewart, Deborah 230
Stollwerck Brothers 15
store fronts 155
stores, automatic 21, 28–29, 84–85, 139, 179–180, 225
subscriptions, magazine 147
subway systems 14–15, 38, 132–133, 150–151
Suffridge, James A. 178
Sugar, Leon 104
Sullivan, Louis 194
supermarkets 155–156, 179–180
Sutcliffe Oil Company 173–174
Sweetmeat Automatic Delivery Company 7
Syracuse university 199

talking machines 9, 27, 141–142, 172
Tanzer, Andrew 223
taverns, beer 89
taxes and licensing 103–104, 115–116
taxis 9
Teague, David 110
temples, Egyptian 4

Terry, Luther 171
Texaco 180
theaters 16, 37–38, 60, 81–83, 90, 150; seats 16–17
thefts from 18–19, 41–42, 104–105, 117, 165
Theismeyer, Lincoln 178
tickets: pari-mutual 134; theater 134; travel 11, 133–134
Tillery, Risdon 160
Time (magazine) 147, 170
Times (London) 98
tissue unit 80
tobacco 4–5
Tobacco Road 57
toilet seat covers 37–38, 78
toilets, pay 15, 76, 90
Tokyo Electric Power Corp. 225
toothbrushes 76
Toronto District School Board 217–218
towels, paper 15
Turner, John 207–208
typewriters 73–74

underwear 212, 224
unemployment, caused by 31, 34, 106–107
Union, New Jersey 143–144
United Cigar Stores 24
United Kingdom 163, 186
United States Consumer Product Safety Commission 229
United States Mint 114–115
United States Post Office 13–14
United States Senate Select Committee on Nutrition and Human Needs 183
United States Supreme Court 211
Universal Match 176–177
Universal Studios 198
Universite du Quebec 220
Universite Laval 220
universities 219–220
University of British Columbia 220
usage of 136

vacuum cleaner 74
vandalism 6, 137, 166, 167, 230
Vending Machine Manufacturers' Association of America 43
Vendo Corp. 63, 170, 179
video games 172
video greeting recordings 210
videotapes 209–210
Von Myer, George 13–14

wages, retail 22
Wagstaff, Robert 179
washing machines 39, 72
washrooms, public 76–81, 88
water 8–9, 12, 129, 144, 203–204
Water Point Systems 204
Watkinson, Harry 40
Webb, G. Creighton 44
weigh scales 6, 7–8, 24–25, 37–38, 58–59, 82, 147; household 147; talking 9, 34
Weiss, E. B. 168, 169–170
Welch Grape Juice 144–145
Wertheimer, Henry 99
Werts, Doug 201
Wetsman, Frank A. 90
wheat cakes 35
Whirlpool company 173
Whitrock, Donna 217

Wieder, Leon 28–29
Wienel, Denis Philip 42
Willatt, Norris 161, 167
Williams, John 11
Willingham, Ross 213
wine 10
Winter, Dean 200–201, 206
wireless technology 193–194, 232
Wolff, Ronald 171
Wolson, Shelley 232
Wood Dining Services 227
World War II 102, 113, 116
Wright, Milton 26

Youngman, Henny 175

Zeller, Mitchell 195
Ziegler, M. T. 39

www.ingramcontent.com/pod-product-compliance
Ingram Content Group UK Ltd.
Pitfield, Milton Keynes, MK11 3LW, UK
UKHW041929140426
5217IPUK00014B/376